The Arts and the Teaching of History

Penney Clark · Alan Sears

The Arts and the Teaching of History

Historical F(r)ictions

palgrave
macmillan

Penney Clark
Department of Curriculum &
Pedagogy
University of British Columbia
Vancouver, BC, Canada

Alan Sears
University of New Brunswick
Fredericton, NB, Canada

ISBN 978-3-030-51512-6 ISBN 978-3-030-51513-3 (eBook)
https://doi.org/10.1007/978-3-030-51513-3

This Palgrave Macmillan imprint is published by the registered company Springer Nature Switzerland AG
The registered company address is: Gewerbestrasse 11, 6330 Cham, Switzerland

To Peter Seixas, for many years an inspiring mentor, colleague, and friend

Acknowledgements

As always, with a project as lengthy as this one, we owe a debt of gratitude to many individuals and institutions. We have had much support throughout this journey.

We are grateful for the institutional support we received from the Faculty of Education, University of New Brunswick and the Department of Curriculum & Pedagogy and Faculty of Education, University of British Columbia. Without it, this project would never have come to fruition.

The members of the Executive Board of *The History Education Network/Histoire et éducation en réseau* (THEN/HiER) were very supportive of this project and generously shared their insights over several years as we developed our ideas. They were a joy to work with over the tenure of THEN/HiER (2008–2016) because they were committed to students, to the betterment of history education in Canada, and to the mobilization of research in order to improve practice at every level including K–12 and both, undergraduate, and teacher education courses. Board members who contributed to the conceptualization of this book were: Margaret Conrad, University of New Brunswick; Catherine Duquette, l'Université du Quebec a Chicoutimi; Anne-Marie Goodfellow, Manager, THEN/HiER; Viviane Gosselin, Museum of Vancouver; Jan Haskings-Winner, Ontario History and Social Sciences Teachers' Association; Kevin Kee, Brock University; Jocelyn Létourneau, l'Université Laval;

Stéphane Lévesque, University of Ottawa; Heather McGregor, University of British Columbia; Ruth Sandwell, Ontario Institute for Studies in Education/University of Toronto; Peter Seixas, University of British Columbia; and Amy von Heyking, University of Lethbridge. We are particularly grateful to Dr. Margaret Conrad for suggesting our book title. THEN/HiER was funded by a Social Sciences and Humanities Research Council of Canada Strategic Knowledge Clusters Grant (Penney Clark, Director).

This is the sixth book in the THEN/HiER series of scholarly books. Other books in this series are *New Possibilities for the Past: Shaping History Education in Canada*, edited by Penney Clark (UBC Press, 2011), *Pastplay*, edited by Kevin Kee (University of Michigan Press, 2014), *Becoming a History Teacher: Sustaining Practices in Historical Thinking and Knowing*, edited by Ruth Sandwell and Amy von Heyking (University of Toronto Press, 2014), *New Directions in Assessing Historical Thinking*, edited by Kadriye Ercikan and Peter Seixas (Routledge, 2015), and *Museums and the Past: Constructing Historical Consciousness*, edited by Viviane Gosselin and Phaedra Livingstone (UBC Press, 2016).

We are thankful to Jack Jedwab, President and CEO of the Association for Canadian Studies, for allowing us to reuse whatever we wished from our article "Historical Frictions: History, Art and Pedagogy," published in *Canadian Issues/Thèmes canadiens* (Fall, 2014). We also appreciate the opportunity he provided for us to workshop our ideas at the 2014 *[Re]Making Confederation: [Re]Imagining Canada* Conference in Charlottetown, Prince Edward Island. Jack's enormous contributions to history education in Canada often go unacknowledged.

We wish to acknowledge the willingness of Taylor & Francis to allow us to use a portion of our article, "Fiction, History and Pedagogy: A Double-Edged Sword," *Journal of Curriculum Studies* (2017) in this publication. We are particularly grateful to the two anonymous reviewers and to Associate Editor Abby Reisman. Dr. Reisman's meticulous comments pushed us to think about our work in new ways.

The Social Sciences and Humanities Research Council of Canada-funded Partnership Grant, *Thinking Historically for Canada's Future*, provided funds to defray publication costs. This project, under the leadership of Carla Peck at the University of Alberta, is carrying on the knowledge mobilization work of THEN/HiER, as well as charting its own path towards innovative research in history education. We are pleased to have this volume acknowledged as a contribution to that work.

Jason Ellis, Associate Professor, Department of Educational Studies, University of British Columbia, is always so generous with his suggestions. In this instance, we thank him for bringing the Arthur Lismer mural at Humberside Collegiate in Toronto to our attention. We also wish to thank social studies educator Craig Harding for suggesting that we look at Thomas Piketty's *Capital in the Twenty-First Century*, a source that proved to be useful to our discussion of the work of Jane Austen.

We appreciate the support of Carey Watt, Department Head, Department of History, St. Thomas University, who agreed to arrange to record a presentation, "Making (Up) History" by author Linden MacIntyre, so that an interested party on the west coast could have access to it.

Artist Kent Monkman generously permitted us to use images of his paintings, *The Daddies* and *The Scream* at no charge. We are humbled by the opportunity he has provided us to share the pedagogical implications of these groundbreaking pieces of art.

We have presented parts of this work at various conferences, national and international, and in courses and more informal seminars in our respective faculties and we deeply appreciate the thoughtful feedback from colleagues and students.

We are grateful for the patient and cheerful support from Editorial Assistant Linda Braus at Palgrave MacMillan. Freelance indexer Dania Sheldon did wonderful work on the index and Kristina Paul was very helpful in locating images.

We thank the Department of Social and Educational Studies, University of British Columbia, under the leadership of Jane Gaskell, who took a leap of faith about thirty years ago on behalf of two graduate students, offering them an unprecedented level of support.

To Ian, Emily and Rob who sustain Penney and give her the courage to embark on new ventures, such as this. To Jane Ann, Matt, Jenny, and Rebekah who do the same for Alan. To our grandchildren, Hudson Finley and Everett Hugh, Cara Jane and Kallie Rebekah who bring us joy simply by being who they are.

Contents

List of Figures

CHAPTER 1

The Place of the Arts in Teaching History

In the mid-eighteenth century Aminata Diallo, a West African girl of about 11, was kidnapped from her family. After enduring days of forced march to the coast and months of a horrific voyage on a slave ship she arrived in the British colony of South Carolina where she was sold into slavery. Years of misery followed, including forced labour on a plantation, rape, and permanent separation from her husband and child. Eventually, Aminata managed to escape slavery and make her way to the British colony of Nova Scotia as part of the Loyalist migration of the mid-1780s and from there she joined the migration of former slaves to Sierra Leone.[1]

Just thirty years before Aminata arrived in Nova Scotia, Evangeline Bellefontaine, a young Acadian woman, was forcefully deported from the colony along with other French-speaking inhabitants of her village of Grand-Pré and other Acadian settlements across the region. A popular monument at the Grand-Pré National Historic Site evocatively portrays the stricken young woman whose father died of distress on the eve of the deportation and whose fiancé, Gabriel Lajeunesse, was sent out on a different ship (see Fig. 1.1). Evangeline spent most of the rest of her life searching the vast Acadian diaspora for Gabriel, only finding him years later close to death in a poorhouse in Philadelphia. A second monument in St. Martinsville, Louisiana, one of the stops in her quest, also commemorates her faithfulness and persistence.

On the other side of the world in 1765, just about midway between the expulsion of the Acadians from Nova Scotia and the arrival of Aminata

P. Clark and A. Sears, *The Arts and the Teaching of History*,
https://doi.org/10.1007/978-3-030-51513-3_1

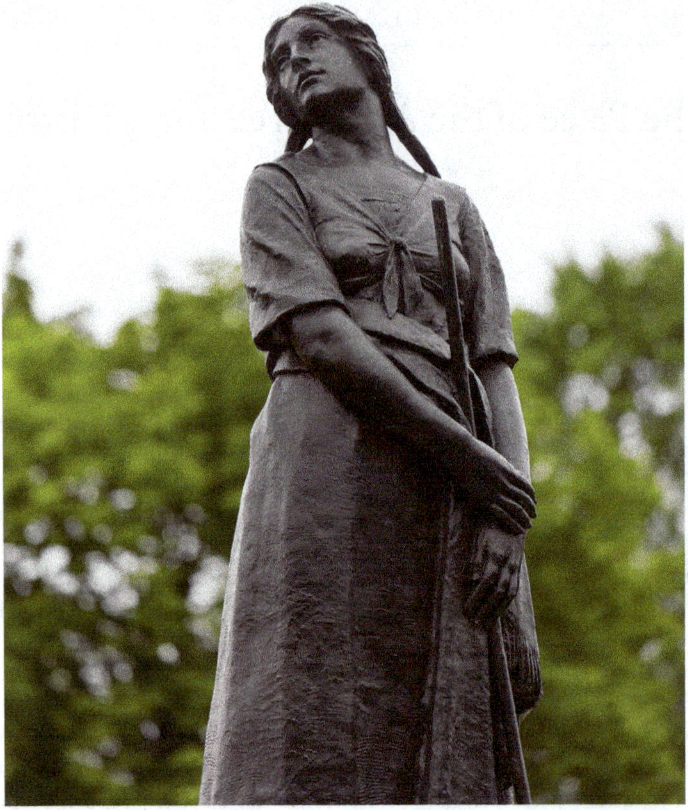

Fig. 1.1 Statue of Evangeline at Grand-Pré (*Source* Rob Crandall/Alamy Stock Photo)

Diallo in that colony, representatives of the British East India Company received the Diwani, later to be called the Treaty of Allahabad, from Shah Alam the Mughal Emperor over much of the territory of modern India, Pakistan, and Bangladesh. In effect, the Emperor was giving the company effective economic control, including the power to levy taxes, over most of what is today northeast India and Bangladesh. The event is commemorated in a painting by Benjamin West which shows the Emperor on a

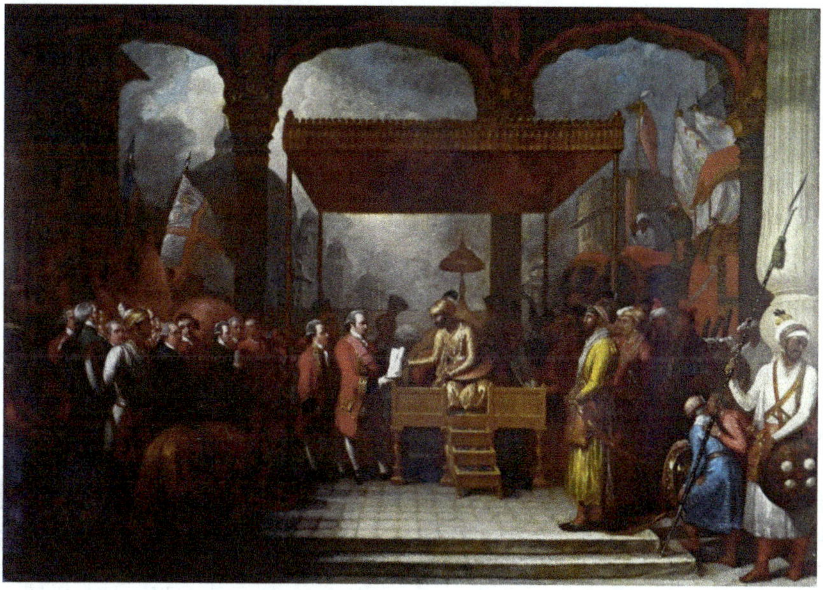

Fig. 1.2 *Shah Alam conveying the Diwani*, painting by Benjamin West (*Source* The picture art collection/Alamy stock photo)

raised throne, in a grand palace, dressed in a robe and turban of gold brocade handing the document down to the British representative Lord Clive who is standing on the ground beside the raised dais (see Fig. 1.2). The scene shows the two men flanked by grandees from both sides turned out in their best finery.[2] The impression given is of the granting of the treaty as an act of benevolence by a great Emperor to British supplicants.

Aminata Diallo, Evangeline Bellefontaine, and Shah Alam are compelling historical characters and as history teachers and educators of history teachers we see all kinds of ways to use their stories with students. The first two are quite ordinary folk, not the "great men" who so often dominate the textbooks. Our students can relate to them. Further, a substantial part of their story takes place when they are young, and this also provides a potential connection with students. The third, while an important national leader, comes from a part of the world and an historical context often ignored or downplayed in history classes in the West. While they are not the type of people who often appear in history curricula, their lives touch on great historical events and themes: slavery, the Loyalist migration to Canada, forced migration/ethnic cleansing, and the processes of intercultural contact and colonization. Finally, their stories deal with aspects of history and particular populations that are often left out of school history courses. They open up important parts of the history of African Canadians, Acadian refugees, and the diverse peoples of the Indian subcontinent.

While these historical stories are gripping and have great potential to interest students in key events and processes in world history, what we know about them is shaped more by artistic imagination than historical investigation. Both Aminata Diallo and Evangeline Bellefontaine are fictional characters, products of the imaginations of the Canadian novelist Lawrence Hill, the American poet Henry Wadsworth Longfellow, and the sculptors who created the statues of Evangeline at Grand-Pré and St. Martinsville.[3]

While Shah Alam and Lord Clive were historical personages and the Diwani was actually given by the former to the latter in 1785, Benjamin West's iconic painting of the event that still hangs for public view in the museum at Powis Castle and Garden in Wales, significantly distorts the event in order to present a more positive narrative of Mughal–British relations. As historian William Dalrymple points out,

> The painting of Clive and Shah Alam at Powis is subtly deceptive: the painter, Benjamin West had never been to India…In reality there was no grand public ceremony. The transfer took place privately, inside Clive's tent, which had just been erected on the parade ground of the newly seized Mughal fort at Allahabad. As for Shah Alam's silken throne, it was in fact Clive's armchair, which for the occasion had been hoisted on to his dining-room table and covered with a chintz bedspread.[4]

While these narratives are not often the stuff of textbooks or academic history articles, they are powerful accounts that capture public attention and help shape people's, including the students in our history classes, views about the past. Hill's novel was a bestseller in several countries and the Canadian Broadcasting Corporation (CBC) and the American Black Entertainment Television (BET) collaborated in producing a six-episode television mini-series of the novel. Longfellow's poem became his most influential publication and the historic monuments of Evangeline are visited by tens of thousands every year. The one at Grand-Pré is part of a UNESCO World Heritage Site commemorating Acadian history. It is no exaggeration to say that Evangeline is the central symbol of the horrors of what Acadians call Le Grand Dérangement (The Great Upheaval). Finally, West's painting distorted history in order to appeal to Victorian sensibilities. "[Victorians] liked to think of the empire as a *mission civilisatrice*: a benign transfer of knowledge, railways and the arts of civilization from West to East, and there was a calculated and deliberate amnesia about the corporate looting that opened British rule in India."[5]

There is significant evidence to show that artistic representations of the past are both popular and influential in shaping people's sense of history and collective memory. We see this in, for example, the increased popularity of visits to museums and historic sites, historical documentaries by Ken Burns in the United States and Mark Starowicz in Canada,[6] non-fiction books on historical topics, historical Hollywood films, historical novels, and historical graphic novels. We note that Charles Frazier's immensely popular American civil war novel *Cold Mountain* sold 1.5 million copies in the first nine months after its 1997 publication.[7] The controversies in nations around the world over public commemorations and representations of historic figures and past events in historical monuments also attest to a vibrant interest in history.

Historian David Harlan has acknowledged the abundance and popularity of historical forms beyond the academic:

> We assume that our primary responsibility is to convey this professionally certified knowledge to our undergraduates, and the techniques for producing it to our graduate students. In other words, we teach them how to read and write academic history. But a new history is being produced, outside the academy, by novelists, memoirists, autobiographers and filmmakers. If we intend to meet the challenge of this new history, if we want our students to develop historical imaginations that are morally sustaining and politically relevant, we must teach them to be thoughtful, reflective and resourceful readers of all the forms in which their society represents the past to itself. Academic history is one of those forms, of course, but it is only one, and it is neither the most interesting nor the most important.[8]

This is a thoughtful remark for an academic historian to make and one to take seriously. As authors, we presume that the prime audience for this book will be academic and public historians, history educators who prepare teachers, and practicing history and social studies teachers, and it is important for all these groups to acknowledge that artistic representations from the past, such as historical fiction, historical visual art, and commemorative art, surround students in their daily lives and to recognize the place of artistic representations as a source of history. It is useful to consider the possibilities for introducing these art forms into history courses and a significant pedagogical mistake to allow them to remain unexamined either as historical sources or historical accounts.

Historians as Artists and Artists as Historians

It is almost a tautology to state that artists are producers of creative products. Historians, on the other hand, are not typically viewed in this way. The uninitiated may assume that historians simply make forays into dusty archives where they gather old records of various kinds and subsequently use what they have collected to construct a historical narrative—one that was, presumably, just waiting for the opportunity to reveal itself. Canadian literary critic, Renée Hulan, contends that a historian may also be an artist. We agree with Hulan. In fact, we see the historian as no less an artist than is a novelist. As historian Hayden White so aptly put it: "Novelists might be dealing only with imaginary events whereas historians are dealing with real ones, but the process of fusing events, whether imaginary or real, into a comprehensible totality capable of serving as the object of a representation, is a poetic process."[9]

We are also aligned with historian Barbara Tuchman, who sees the historian as "a creative writer on the same level as the poet or novelist."[10] Tuchman goes on to explain her position. She says: "As I see it, there are three parts to the creative process: first, the extra vision with which the artist perceives a truth and conveys it by suggestion. Second, medium of expression: language for writers…Third, design or structure."[11] By "extra vision," she means the sympathy and imagination that she maintains is necessary in order to fully understand the evidence and convey its meaning: "Without sympathy and imagination the historian can copy figures from a tax roll forever […] but he [*sic*] will never know or be able to portray the people who paid the taxes."[12] With regard to language, she says "it takes hard work, a good ear, and continued practice, as much as it takes Heifetz to play the violin."[13] As for structure, her choice of form was narrative:

> Narrative history is neither as simple nor as straightforward as it might seem. It requires arrangement, composition, planning just like a painting—Rembrandt's "Night Watch," for example. He did not fit in all those

> figures with certain ones in the foreground and others in back and the light falling on them just so, without much trial and error and innumerable preliminary sketches. It is the same as writing. Although the finished result may look to the reader natural and inevitable, as if the author had only to follow the sequence of events, it is not that easy.[14]

The historian has to "exercis[e] the artists' privilege of selection"[15] by asking thoughtful questions of sources in order to make meaning from the disparate and sometimes conflicting pieces of information she is able to collect. Hayden White endorses this point when he refers to "the unprocessed historical record [where] the facts exist as a congeries of contiguously related fragments"[16] until the historian shapes them into a meaningful narrative.

Tuchman points out that there are other challenges for historians: "how to explain background and yet keep the story moving, how to create suspense and sustain interest in a narrative of which the outcome (like who won the war) is, to put it mildly, known. If anyone thinks this does not take creative writing, I can only say, try it."[17] Renée Hulan captures this idea exquisitely when she states, "historical writing that renders an aesthetic experience of the past" is "the dialectical relation of material evidence and imagination."[18]

Now, we will turn to the idea of the artist as historian. As Hulan puts it, with reference to novelists, "a novelist is a historian, the preserver, the keeper, and expounder of human experience."[19] We make a distinction between period novels, which are written in the time period of the novel itself and historical novels, which are about an earlier period. Period novelists are, in a sense, inadvertent historians, if there is such a thing, in that they are not writing in the role of historians. Their novels are not works of history, but rather, can serve as primary source documents for future historians. They are sources of information about what life was like where and when the events of the novel occur. Historical novelists, on the other hand, can be considered to be historians, although this depends on the extent to which they adhere to primary sources and consult secondary sources in constructing their accounts, that is, their novels. There is a huge variation in terms of historical novelists' sense of responsibility to adhere to the historical evidence. These ideas are discussed in Chapter 3.

The concept of artist as historian is not as applicable to commemorative art or to historical paintings as it is to historical novels. In the case of commemorative art, there is an "artist for hire" element, since it is art that is typically commissioned by individuals or government bodies that want to represent an event or people from the past in a particular way. It is also less straightforward in the case of historical paintings, since they are typically more like period novels, in that they are painted in a particular time and depict that time and can be used later as primary sources in order to learn about that time.

Visual art is a primary source of information about the past, and it is particularly useful when written sources do not exist. We explore the potential of certain visual art, in particular the *Bayeux Tapestry*, *The Death of General Wolfe*, and the *First German Attack at Ypres* as both primary sources and primary accounts. These examples of visual art are primary sources that can be used to gather evidence about the events they depict, but they are also constructed accounts that are designed to convey particular messages.

Visual art can also provide a revisionist history by presenting counter narratives to existing constructed accounts. We see this in the work of Canadian Indigenous artist, Kent Monkman who has transformed the famous painting, *The Fathers of Confederation* by Robert Harris into *The Daddies*, a startling critique of the values embodied in the original painting. Visual art is discussed in Chapter 4 of this volume.

The Power of Art

The arts can engage students in a range of ways. Cultural scholar Ann Rigney contends that fiction (defined by her as "a general umbrella term to designate cultural practices that are governed by the principle of 'poetic licence'"[20]) "is a stepping-stone medium for encouraging people to look beyond their present social frame of reference."[21] History educators Evelyn B. Freeman and Linda Levstik point out that fiction, for example, "presents history in a subjective form that is closer [than didactic historical accounts] to the way in which young children explain themselves and understand the world.... They will also discover the consequences of human failure in relationships, both personal and historical."[22] Freeman and Levstik further explain that historical fiction supports a range of common social studies knowledge and skill goals. Student interest in compelling fictional historical characters stands in stark contrast to research findings about the teaching of history in schools, which is often described as dull, boring, and disconnected from students' lives and interests.[23]

Historian John Demos uses the novel *Cold Mountain* by Charles Frazier as an example of the power of a novel to bring history to life. He says, "to follow Frazier's central character on his journey home from Civil War soldiering is to know the life of that time and place in a wholly immediate way."[24] Frazier provides details about the devastation of war, including the general disorientation, the destruction of homes and livelihoods, the subsistence level to which the rural poor were reduced, and the prevailing racism. Tuchman highlights the importance of such corroborative details and their role in "keeping one grounded in historical reality."[25]

We suggest that there are ways to engage the power of fictional accounts to enliven and enrich the more formal study of history in schools and universities. History education scholar Peter Seixas makes the same point. Seixas uses Canadian novelist Lawrence Hill's *The Book of Negroes*[26] as an example of a useful source for wrestling with the implications of ethical questions in history and the present. He acknowledges the power of the novel in encouraging readers to "imagine themselves into the consciousness of [Hill's] protagonist,"[27] but describes that power as "a double-edged sword."[28] The narrative force that draws the reader in and connects him or her to the experience of the characters also mitigates against alternative readings of the situation and "can trump our attempts to historicize and take into account the foreignness of the people of the past."[29]

While double-edged swords are dangerous because they can cut both ways and wound the bearer rather than the enemy, they were developed because, used skilfully, they are a more powerful weapon than a blade with a single edge. We contend that in the hands of an effective teacher the double-edged sword of fiction can be a powerful tool in the teaching of history.

As Canadian literature scholar Herb Wyile has put it: "*Both* history and literature, then, make meaning of the past, and any attempt to see the one as 'science' and the other as 'entertainment' is reductive to say the least – especially when it comes to a genre like historical fiction."[30]

The Value of History Education

Canadian historian and history educator Ken Osborne has offered three arguments that can be made to students about the importance of history education. The first is that history is "gripping, as it deals with what has actually happened and how we find out about it."[31] He suggests that the best way to approach history in a way that will arouse students' interest is to present problems that they can explore. The focus is on human agency as students consider the problems which people in the past confronted, the limited information with which they had to work, and the values and expectations of the social, economic, and political contexts in which they operated.

Osborne's second argument is that history provides a "form of intellectual self-defense."[32] He offers seven ways in which this argument could be developed:

> First, history armours us against all those people who claim to know it and are only too anxious to tell us what it proves. Second, it releases us from the grip of the past which so easily holds us captive and shapes our lives. Third, it teaches us how to be constructively sceptical (but not cynical or blindly rejectionist) when faced with appeals and arguments. Fourth, it protects us from being misled by the taken-for-granted conventional wisdom of our own times. Fifth, by showing us a wide variety of alternative belief systems, social practices, cultural norms, and the like, it enlarges our awareness of alternatives and choices. Sixth, it helps us understand and take part in the debates that are going on around us about the future of Canada and of the world more generally, debates that are going to affect us whether we like it or not. And, finally, it makes us less short-sighted and narrow-minded than we would otherwise be by helping us situate the present in the context of the transition from past to future so that we are not governed solely by the short-term imperatives of the here and now.[33]

Osborne's third argument is that history "enlarges our experience by showing us a wide range of human institutions and behaviour, thereby freeing us from the constraints of the present."[34] Eminent British historian of education, Richard Aldrich would agree. He has pointed out that history affords:

> an acquaintance with a much greater range of human experience than would be possible simply by reference to the contemporary world; an enlarged understanding of that experience which may promote a richer

> understanding of one's own potential and possibilities; opportunities for creating interpretations of human experience which may be of interest in themselves and which, though not directly transferable from one situation to another, may promote the capacity better to interpret other situations – both historical and contemporary; a more sophisticated awareness of the nature of knowledge and of truth.[35]

The Place of Historical Mindedness

Ken Osborne has proposed a conception of history education that he calls historical mindedness. He describes this as a broad understanding of the past that "is a way of looking, not so much at history, but at the world at large, that derives from a familiarity with the past and with trying to understand and interpret it."[36]

We think of this as adding a fourth approach to history education. The first approach that has dominated history classrooms is a focus on *what* historians know (the names, dates, narratives, and counter narratives of the discipline of history—often referred to as content). This has often had a nation-building focus. Every nation has its own narratives. In the case of Canada, this has involved presenting students with a chronological framework of important events around a theme of overcoming adversity and making progress towards nationhood and greater autonomy from Great Britain, an approach that is characterized by textbook titles such as *Challenge & Survival* or *Bold Ventures*. This approach has always had an important place in the teaching of Canadian history and is certainly an important aspect of history education in the history of other nations as well. Aspects of it have persisted regardless of other influences.

The second approach has to do with developing facility with *how* historians know (the processes and procedures of doing history—often referred to as historical thinking). Historical thinking is found in most Canadian provincial/territorial curricula and authorized resources. This approach, as it is currently interpreted in Canada, has been conceptualized and guided by the work of Peter Seixas of the Centre for the Study of Historical Consciousness at the University of British Columbia. He first articulated a framework of six second-order or procedural concepts in his article, "Conceptualizing the Growth of Historical Understanding," published in *The Handbook of Education and Human Development* in 1996.[37] The historical thinking framework has evolved over the years to its present iteration of six concepts:

- The problem of *historical significance*: From the entire human past, what is worth learning about?
- The problem of *evidence*: How do we know what we know, how can we use the traces, the leftovers, of the past to support claims about what happened?
- The problem of *continuity and change*: How are historical changes interwoven with continuities?
- The problems of *cause and consequence*: What are the layers of cause that led, over time, to any particular event? What are the consequences that rippled out afterwards?
- The problem of *historical perspective-taking*. What was it like to live in times so different from our own; can we truly understand?
- The *ethical dimension*. How can we in the present, judge actors in different circumstances in the past; when and how do crimes and sacrifices of the past bear consequences today; and what obligations do we have today in relation to those consequences?[38]

The underlying ideas are that (1) history and the past are not the same because history is a subset of everything that happened in the past and (2) history is composed of accounts developed from interpretations by historians based on the myriad of primary sources that are remnants of the past. It is important to note that this focus on the processes of doing history does not imply an emphasis on skills rather than content. As Seixas and Tom Morton make clear, "the six historical thinking concepts make no sense at all without the material, the topics, the substance, or what is often referred to as the 'content' of history."[39]

These first two approaches have dominated history education in school, and in the literature are often presented as unfolding chronologically with the former representing a tradition bound archaic approach to teaching history that is gradually being superseded by the later more progressive and constructivist approach. Ironically, this is indicative of a naïve progress-oriented understanding of history that researchers argue is often characteristic of how young children think about the past. As Osborne and others have shown conclusively, these approaches have co-existed for more than 100 years, and are not always as simplistic or antithetical as popularly presented.[40] Over time, one or the other crescendos and for a period becomes the dominant approach in the field, but not so much that the other is entirely silenced.[41]

We propose there is a third, related approach critically important to how people engage with the past that is often absent from academic history education, and it involves wrestling with the relationship between individual and collective memory, and personal and communal ways of engaging with and understanding the past, particularly in terms of how it shapes the present and the future—often called historical consciousness. As Seixas points out, attention to historical consciousness has been largely missing in history education in the United Kingdom, North America, and other regions influenced by British and American approaches.[42] We argue the arts provide a dynamic vehicle for attending to it in school history.

Osborne suggests that historical mindedness has elements of all three of the other approaches. He writes that historical mindedness,

> combines historical thinking with historical knowledge (yes, even dates and events), together with the ability to take the long view, to locate the present in the context of a transition from past to future, and, not least, to appreciate what G.M. Trevelyan described as the 'poetry of history,' a recognition that the people of the past were once as real as we are, with their own hopes and dreams, frustrations and ambitions, loves and hates.[43]

In the case of the facts-based nation-building narrative, he points out that learning narratives of Canada's trajectory does not presuppose "a return to the exclusionary nation-building narrative of a generation ago, with all its claims of definitiveness and authority."[44] Students do not need a compendium of handy facts about Canadian history, but they do need some idea of important themes that will help them to better understand the dilemmas that arise in the present. Historical mindedness includes facility with all three approaches, including the ability to reflectively assess the impact they have on shaping human understanding of, and engagement with, the past, present, and future.

The Place for a Sense of Wonder

Historical thinking has been criticized for being too academic and sterile. As one scholar put it, "It is as if the historical procedures identified as relevant for student study have been extracted in labs from historians who lack hopes, fantasies, or racialized, gendered, classed, and desiring bodies and who also lack political intelligence."[45] British Columbia teacher Patrick Clarke has referred to it as a "very safe, rationalistic pedagogy that leaches out almost all of the romance in history." He points to the danger of "unremitting pondering" that avoids what he calls the "romantic mythology" that can lead to citizens who are passionately engaged with the task of bettering the societies in which they find themselves.[46]

Historian Gerald Friesen would agree. He highlights the importance of inspiring a sense of wonder in students, something that he sees as lacking in historical thinking approaches. Friesen suggests that "Using primary sources, discussing historical context and historical significance, identifying decisive moments of change, debating evidence, uncovering uncertainty about meaning, considering morality and ethical choices will all endure. But so, too, will the teacher's obligation to inspire a sense of wonder."[47] He contends that teachers must fire students' imaginations and "kindle an infectious delight."[48] He quotes from historian G.M. Trevelyan: "The poetry of history lies in the quasi-miraculous fact that once on this earth, once on this familiar spot of ground, walked other men and women, as actual as we are today, thinking their own thoughts, swayed by their own passions but now all gone one generation vanishing into another, gone as utterly as we ourselves shall shortly be gone, like ghosts at cockcrow."[49] He wants students to wonder about the lives of people in the past and to use their imaginations, grounded in knowledge about the historical contexts in which these people lived, to develop a rich understanding of the challenges they faced, and the possibilities and limitations of their lives.

We believe engaging with the arts in history classes provides the opportunity to bring together all of these approaches to history education in ways that will stimulate students' interest in history, help them to see the connections between history and contemporary concerns and broaden their understandings of, and empathy with, historical agents' circumstances, including motives, desires, ambitions, limitations, and opportunities, and ultimately, spark a sense of wonder about the possibilities inherent in studying history.

The Value of the Arts in History Education

It is our hope that the arts discussed in this book—fiction, visual art, and commemorative art—will deepen students' historical understandings by revealing perspectives, motives, and consequences beyond those they have directly experienced, thereby giving rise to insights that broaden their understanding of the possibilities for historical figures in the particular eras in which they lived.

We also offer three more specific reasons for teaching history in a way that includes the arts. The first and most evident reason to include the arts in teaching history is that the arts are powerfully engaging. They draw students in and add another dimension to their learning. The arts, and historical fiction, in particular, allow students to connect with people from the past in ways that are not available in the historical accounts they read in textbooks and other sources because they provide a window into people's motivations; fears; affections; social connections; economic, social, and political aspirations; and other personal aspects of their lives that students would not be privy to by simply consulting the historical record. Reading historical fictional accounts will increase students' interest in historical nonfiction accounts. Readers see historical fictional characters as real. It is difficult to imagine how a teenager who has read *Rilla of Ingleside* by L. M. Montgomery, could not find an historical account of the Canadian home front during the First World War compelling, for example. Or, students could gain deep insights about the possibilities for women in provincial life in England in the first half of the nineteenth century by reading about protagonist Dorothea Brooke in *Middlemarch* by George Eliot (Mary Anne Evans) that would scaffold, and increase their interest in, the information they encounter in nonfiction accounts. We discuss this point in greater depth in Chapter 3.

Second, the arts help students learn to interrogate all representations for their implicit meanings. For example, a painting, or any other form of art, is a product of deliberate decisions by the artist. Students can ask who (which individuals or what type of person) was the artist trying to please and why. The arts present opportunities to closely examine how personal, social, religious, economic, and political motivations affect artistic representations. For example, students could ask why the artist Benjamin West chose not to include the people who actually did witness British General James Wolfe's death in his painting *The Death of General Wolfe* and, instead, depict people who were not present. They could ask what was the purpose of the Christian iconography in the painting: why are the people arranged like a Pieta? With some help from their teacher, students can come to understand how this painting represents the founding myth of English Canada, the victory of the British Empire over the claims of the French in British North America, and how this determined the choices the artist made. These ideas are discussed in Chapter 4.

Third, students can develop an understanding of how the arts can shape collective memory and historical consciousness. All art can do this, but commemorative art, with its "uplifting and sacred stor[ies]," is particularly powerful in this regard. As historians Ian McKay and Jamie Swift note about what they call "Vimyism" with reference to the Vimy Canadian National Memorial in France, "Vimyism thus offers Canadians an uplifting and sacred story of their origins—something to believe in."[50] It is important that students are aware of how commemorative art shapes collective memory and historical consciousness so that they are able to engage it as a historical source and subject it to critical interrogation. This is discussed in Chapter 5.

Navigating This Volume

In Chapter 2 we address five scholarly conversations about history, history education, and the relationship between history education and the arts. We will return to these conversations in various ways in the chapters that follow. The first conversation is about the nature of history and historical truth and the role of interpretation in history. We explore the question: Is history a science or an art? Historian Peter Novick has described the boundary between history and fiction as "fuzzier than as traditionally represented:"[51]

> What we are doing is exploring and thinking about the past with as much energy and intelligencc as we can muster and then making up interesting, provocative, and even edifying stories about it as contributions to collective self-understanding(s). We would make no greater (but also no lesser) truth claims than poets or painters: no greater (but also no lesser) claim for support from society for this endeavor.[52]

The second scholarly conversation is about connections between history and the arts. This conversation considers the value of fictional representations of various kinds for promoting engagement with the past—for acquainting us with the "allure"[53] of the past, as Ann Rigney puts it. It looks at how history and the arts can be connected in order to create new and richer narrations that broaden and deepen our understandings of the past. These help us to better understand the present and, in turn, the future. The rise of cultural history is an aspect of this conversation. Cultural historians acknowledge the significant place of fictional representations in our contemporary world and suggest that they warrant recognition as sources for engagement with, and understanding of, the past.

The third scholarly conversation is about collective memory and historical consciousness. History educator Peter Seixas says that collective memory "retains the immediacy of individual memory, but it also depends on what French historian Pierre Nora has called 'lieux de memoire,' or sites of memory. Our common, collective or public memory is built and maintained through a range of structures, symbols, and practices: statues, commemorations, place names … films."[54] Anna Clark and Carla Peck define historical consciousness as "the ways people orient themselves in time and how they are bound by the historical and cultural contexts which shape their sense of temporality and collective memory."[55]

The fourth scholarly conversation explores the question: What place do Indigenous perspectives have in history education? This question is topical in nations with Indigenous populations. We focus on the Canadian context for two reasons. We are most familiar with Canada and the question is more central here than in some other countries, for example, the United States, where it appears to be less apparent, at least to date. We review the positions of several Canadian scholars, Indigenous and non-Indigenous, who have different views on this question and consider possibilities for a way forward.

The final scholarly conversation is about history education. One of the key themes addressed in this conversation deals with the ways individuals and collectives construct narratives about their place in the world and the sources on which they draw in doing so. A central finding of a large body of research in this area is that individuals and groups understand themselves and their place in the world temporally; they have a well-developed sense of historical consciousness that includes a deeply rooted sense of place as well as understandings of their past which shape their views of the present and future.[56] Whether or not we accept the arts as potential sources for historical investigation or as accounts of the past worth considering in history class, teachers are left with a dilemma: for the broader public, including many of our students, the arts, particularly in the form of books and films are a common source for the collective stories learners bring with them to class. The cognitive frames of students have been and continue to be shaped by the arts and a plethora of evidence demonstrates that failure to engage with this kind of prior knowledge renders teaching largely ineffectual.[57]

Anita Clair Fellman has pointed out that "If [children] believe a story, find it credible as a narrative, then they also read it as telling what really happened in a larger sense."[58] Part of this conversation is about the implications of constructivism for teaching and learning history, a discussion that is rooted in the "cognitive revolution."[59] A central tenet of that revolution is that "prior knowledge matters"[60] to teaching and learning: learners come to any learning situation with a set of cognitive structures that alter and shape new information in powerful ways.

In Chapter 3 we consider the use of fiction in the history classroom. As mentioned earlier, we distinguish between two kinds of historical fiction: period novels, which are novels written in a particular time about that time and historical novels, which are written about an earlier time. Each of these must be approached differently if we are to use them effectively as windows into the past. We examine period novels for their usefulness as primary sources, for what they can reveal about the time period and place. For example, a historian could read *Grapes of Wrath* by John Steinbeck in order to learn about the economic effects of the Great Depression and the creation of the Dust Bowl on sharecroppers in Oklahoma. *The House of Mirth* and other books by Edith Wharton are sources of information about the intersection of class and gender among the *riche*, the *nouveau riche,* and those living in genteel poverty in old New York. We pay particular attention to several novels by Jane Austen, *Rilla of Ingleside* by L. M. Montgomery, and *The Great Gatsby* by F. Scott Fitzgerald. Historical novels are considered in terms of the way in which authors use or don't use primary sources in their creation. What is interesting here is the question, to what extent is the author of a historical novel responsible for adhering to the extant historical evidence? Authors respond to this question in a range of ways, which will be discussed in the chapter.

Chapter 4 considers the purpose and place of visual art in the history classroom. This chapter examines historical visual art both as a primary source and as a constructed account. For example, in *Vermeer's Hat* historian Timothy Brook points out that seventeenth-century Dutch painter Johannes Vermeer's painting *Officer and Laughing Girl* is "an almost generic account of the new rules governing how young men and women in polite Dutch society courted in the late 1650s."[61] Then Brook takes the reader beyond what is easily evident in the painting to its connections to Canada and the fur trade (which had begun because of the European demand for beaver hats), and the dream of finding a route to China; the officer's fur hat being a by-product of that search.

A painting or sculpture can convey a particularly vivid sense of a historical period, just as a novel can. However, as with all sources, there are limitations to the use of images and students must be made aware of those limitations. For example, visual representations are not simply traces of the past to be accepted as evidence but are constructed accounts that reflect the perspective and purposes of the artist and his or her sponsors. This means that artistic products can be "fiction" in the same way that a novel is fiction. Historical reality may have been altered in order to please a wealthy patron or potential purchaser. Historical details may have been altered or omitted because they were not aesthetically pleasing to the artist or were not relevant to the particular narrative the artist was intending to communicate.

We look at three examples of art often found in history textbooks: the Bayeux Tapestry, Benjamin West's *The Death of General Wolfe*, and Canadian War Artist William Roberts' *The First German Gas Attack at Ypres*. All of these raise questions about the value and limitations of visual art both as primary source and as account.

Chapter 5 is about public commemorative art and the importance of helping students ask questions both about the ideas and values it is designed to disseminate and about who made it, for what purposes, and in what contexts. We argue that commemorative art provides an excellent vehicle for history education for a number of reasons. First, commemorative art is ubiquitous and therefore accessible to students and teachers. Commemoration is a key part of public history in every society and fundamental to understanding those societies both historically and in the present.[62] Second, it is iconic and a key purpose of history education is to challenge and investigate icons.[63] Third, it is multilayered and complex. As war historian Tim Cook points out, with reference to the Canadian National Vimy Memorial, "Vimy, like all legends, is a layered skein of stories, myths, wishful thinking, and conflicting narratives."[64] It provides us with a window into examining how history works in the construction of personal and collective identity. Finally, it is contested and thereby provides opportunities for students to examine controversial historical perspectives.

Chapter 6 examines the implications of the foregoing discussions for the teaching and learning of history. Teachers of history should not ignore the relationship between history and art, but should instead find creative ways to engage students in considering its complexities. The chapter explores four implications of current history education research: developing students' understandings of how art shapes personal and collective historical narratives and how those operate to construct the social world; enhancing students' abilities to work with a range of historical sources; engaging students with the ethical dimension of the past; and fostering historical perspective taking.[65]

In Chapter 7, the concluding chapter, we discuss the ubiquitous nature of artistic representations from the past in the form of historical fiction, visual art, and commemorative art. Students need to encounter artistic representations in their classrooms under the guidance of a teacher in order to consider them, not only as primary historical sources, but also as constructed accounts. The study of history offers the potential to develop the knowledge, skills, and sensibilities that assist in understanding ourselves and others in more nuanced ways. The two central missions of history education are to contribute to our growth as human beings and citizens and to use that understanding as a platform for fruitful and vigorous civic engagement. Engaging the arts in history class fosters: more complex understandings of history and the nature of truth; cross-curricular/disciplinary connections; consideration of the relationship between history, historical consciousness and collective memory; the introduction of Indigenous perspectives; and the development of critical thinking.

Literary scholar Renée Hulan suggests that "the writing and reading of historical fiction has been and continues to be one of the ways Canadians collectively imagine the past and thus remember, commemorate, and re-evaluate history."[66] The identical argument could be made for any other historical art forms, including the others we discuss in this volume, namely, historical paintings and commemoration art.

Notes

1. This story was used in Penney Clark and Alan Sears, "Historical Frictions: History, Art and Pedagogy," *Canadian Issues/Thèmes canadiens* (Fall 2014): 18–23. Used with permission.
2. National Trust, "Shah 'Alam (Mughal Emperor 1759–1806) Conveying the Grant of the Diwani to Lord Clive, August 1765" (National

Trust Collections, n.d). http://www.nationaltrustcollections.org.uk/object/1181123.

3. Lawrence Hill, *The Book of Negroes* (Toronto: HarperCollins, 2007). In the U.S., Australia, and New Zealand this book is published with the title, *Someone Knows My Name*. Henry Wadsworth Longfellow, "Evangeline: A Tale of Acadie." NS Legislature, n.d. https://nslegislature.ca/sites/default/files/pdfs/about/evangeline/Evangeline.pdf.
4. William Dalrymple, *The Anarchy: The Relentless Rise of the East India Company*. Kindle (New York & London: Bloomsbury Publishing, 2019), Loc 298. In Chapter 4 we deal with another of West's painting, *The Death of General Wolfe,* that is similarly deceptive.
5. Dalrymple, *The Anarchy* Loc. 244.
6. Ken Burns has produced many documentaries including *The Civil War* (1990), *The Dust Bowl* (2012) and *The Vietnam War* (2017); Mark Starowicz was producer of *Canada: A People's Histor*y (2000), a series that dealt with the history of Canada from 15,000 BCE to 1990 and is still used widely in Canadian classrooms.
7. Bruce Cook, "Peeps Into The Past," *Washington Post*, 18 July 1999, p. X4, quoted in David Harlan, "Historical Fiction and Academic History," in *Manifestos for History*, ed. Keith Jenkins, Sue Morgan, and Alun Munslow (London and New York: Routledge, 2007), 123.
8. David Harlan, "Historical Fiction and Academic History," in *Manifestos for History*, ed. Keith Jenkins, Sue Morgan, and Alun Munslow (London and New York: Routledge, 2007), 121.
9. Hayden White, "The Fictions of Factual Representation," in *The Literature of Fact: Selected Papers from the English Institute*, ed. Angus Fletcher (Harvard University, English Institute, 1976), 28.
10. Barbara W. Tuchman, "The Historian as Artist," in *Practicing History: Selected Essays* (New York: Random House, 2014), 49.
11. Tuchman, "The Historian as Artist," 52.
12. Tuchman, 50–51. We acknowledge the inappropriate use of "he" as a universal pronoun, but will not comment again.
13. Tuchman, 52.
14. Tuchman, 52.
15. Tuchman, 51.
16. White, "The Fictions of Factual Representation," 28.
17. Tuchman, "The Historian as Artist," 53.
18. Renée Hulan, *Canadian Historical Writing: Reading the Remains* (New York: Palgrave Macmillan, 2014), xvii.
19. Hulan, *Canadian Historical Writing,* 6.
20. Ann Rigney, "Fiction as a Mediator in National Remembrance," in *Narrating the Nation: Representations in History, Media and the Arts*, ed. Stefan Berger, Linas Eriksonas, and Andrew Mycock (New York, NY: Berghahn, 2008), 82.

21. Rigney, "Fiction as a Mediator," 92.
22. Evelyn B. Freeman and Linda Levstik, "Recreating the Past: Historical Fiction in the Social Studies Curriculum," *The Elementary School Journal* 88, no. 4 (March, 1988): 329–37; L.S. Levstik, "A Child's Approach to History," *The Social Studies* 74, no. 6 (1983): 232–36.
23. Anna Clark, "Teaching the Nation's Story: Comparing Public Debates and Classroom Perspectives on History Education in Australia and Canada," *Journal of Curriculum Studies* 4, no. 6 (2009), 745–62, https://doi.org/10.1080/00220270903139635; A.B. Hodgetts, *What Culture? What Heritage? A Study of Civic Education in Canada* (Toronto: Ontario Institute for Studies in Education, 1968).
24. John Demos, "In Search of Reasons for Historians to Read Novels," *The American Historical Review* 103 (December 1998): 1529.
25. Barbara W. Tuchman, "History by the Ounce," in *Practicing History: Selected Essays* (New York: Random House, 2014), 36.
26. Hill, *The Book of Negroes*.
27. Peter Seixas, "Looking for History," in *Joined-up History: New Directions in History Education and Research*, ed. Arthur Chapman and Arie Wilschut (Charlotte, NC: Information Age, 2015), 271.
28. Seixas, "Looking for History," 272.
29. Seixas, 272.
30. Herb Wyile, *Speculative Fictions: Contemporary Canadian Novelists and the Writing of History* (Montreal, QC & Kingston, ON: McGill-Queen's University Press, 2002), 21.
31. Ken Osborne, "Why We Need to Teach and Study History," in *To the Past: History Education Public Memory, & Citizenship in Canada*," ed. Ruth Sandwell (Toronto, ON: University of Toronto Press, 2006), 126.
32. Osborne, "Why We Need to Teach and Study History," 127.
33. Osborne, 127.
34. Osborne, 128.
35. Richard Aldrich, "Introduction," in *Lessons from History of Education: The Selected Works of Richard Aldrich* (London and New York: Routledge, 2006), 2.
36. Ken Osborne, "*Knowing, Teaching, and Learning History*, ed. by Peter N. Stearns, Peter Seixas, Sam Wineburg, and: *Ľhistoire à Ľécole: Matière à Penser* by Robert Martineau (Review)," *Canadian Historical Review* 82, no. 3 (September 2001): 553.
37. Peter Seixas, "Conceptualizing the Growth of Historical Understanding," in *The Handbook of Education and Human Development: New Models of Learning, Teaching and Schooling*, ed. David R. Olson and Nancy Torrance, 765–83 (Cambridge MA: Blackwell, 1996).
38. Peter Seixas, "A Modest Proposal for Change in Canadian History Education," *Teaching History* 137 (2009), 26–30. For more detailed

explanations of the concepts see Peter Seixas and Tom Morton, *The Big Six Historical Thinking Concepts* (Toronto, ON: Nelson Education Ltd., 2013).
39. Seixas and Morton, *The Big Six*, 4.
40. Ken Osborne, "'Our History Syllabus Has Us Gasping': History in Canadian Schools—Past, Present and Future," *Canadian Historical Review* 81, no. 3 (2000): 404–35; Ken Osborne, "Teaching Canadian History: A Century of Debate," in *New Possibilities for the Past: Shaping History Education in Canada*, ed. Penney Clark, 55–96 (Vancouver: UBC Press, 2011); Keith Barton and Linda Levstik, *Teaching History for the Common Good* (Mahwah, NJ: Lawrence Erlbaum Associates, 2004).
41. For a fuller discussion of this see Carla L. Peck and Alan Sears, "Canada," in *Education, Globalization and The Nation*, ed. King Man Chong, Ian Davies, Terrie Epstein, Carla L. Peck, Andrew Peterson, Alistair Ross, Maria Auxiliadora Schmidt, Alan Sears, and Debbie Sonu, 59–80 (Hampshire, UK: Palgrave Macmillan, 2016).
42. Peter Seixas, "Translation and Its Discontents: Key Concepts in English and German History Education," *Journal of Curriculum Studies* 48, no. 4 (2016): 427–39. https://doi.org/10.1080/00220272.2015.1101618.
43. Ken Osborne, "A History Teacher Looks Back," *The Canadian Historical Review* 93, no. 1 (2012): 137.
44. Osborne, "Why We Need to Teach and Study History," 121.
45. Kent den Heyer, "History Education as a Disciplined 'Ethics of Truths'," in *New Possibilities for the Past: Shaping History Education in Canada*, ed. Penney Clark (Vancouver, BC: UBC Press, 2011), 157.
46. Patrick Clarke, *History, Memory, Heritage, Myth: What Should We Teach in School?* Response to Presentation by Dr. Peter Seixas, UBC Faculty of Education Public Lecture Series, Vancouver, BC, 26 January, 2000.
47. Gerald Friesen, "The Shape of Historical Thinking in a Canadian History Survey Course in University," in *New Possibilities for the Past: Shaping History Education in Canada*, ed. Penney Clark (Vancouver, BC: UBC Press, 2011), 222.
48. Friesen "The Shape of Historical Thinking," 211.
49. G.M. Trevelyan, "Autobiography of an Historian," in *An Autobiography and Other Essays* (London: Longmans, Green 1949), quoted in Friesen, "The Shape of Historical Thinking," 215.
50. Ian McKay and Jamie Swift, *The Vimy Trap or, How We Learned to Stop Worrying and Love the Great War* (Toronto, ON: Between the Lines Press, 2016), 257. The Canadian National Vimy Memorial commemorates the Canadians who died at the Battle of Vimy Ridge between April 9–12, 1917, as well as all Canadians who gave up their lives in World War One.
51. Peter Novick, "(The Death of) the Ethics of Historical Practice (and Why I Am Not in Mourning)," ANNALS, AAPSS 560 (November 1998), 37.

52. Novick, 39.
53. Rigney, "Fiction as a Mediator in National Remembrance," 80.
54. Seixas, "What is Historical Consciousness?" 13.
55. Anna Clark and Carla L. Peck, "Introduction: Historical Consciousness, Theory and Practice," in *Contemplating Historical Consciousness: Notes from the Field*, ed. Anna Clark and Carla L. Peck (New York and Oxford: Berghahn Books, 2019), 2.
56. Alan McCully and F. Waldron. "A Question of Identity? Purpose, Policy and Practice in the Teaching of History in Northern Ireland and the Republic of Ireland," in *Identity, Trauma, Sensitive and Controversial Issues in the Teaching of History*, ed. Hilary Cooper and Jon Nichol (Newcastle upon Tyne: Cambridge Scholars Publishing, 2015), 2–24.
57. Alan Sears, "Children's Understandings of Democratic Participation: Lessons for Civic Education," *Civic Education and Youth Political Participation*, ed. Murray Print and Henry Milner, 143–58 (Rotterdam/Boston/Taipei: Sense, 2009); Alan Sears, "Historical Thinking and Citizenship Education: It is Time to End the War," in *New Possibilities for the Past: Shaping History Education in Canada*, ed. Penney Clark, 344–64 (Vancouver, BC: UBC Press, 2011).
58. Anita Clair Fellman, *Little House Long Shadow: Laura Ingalls Wilder's Impact on American Culture* (Columbia: University of Missouri, 2008); quoted in Susan R. Fisher, *Boys and Girls in No Man's Land: English-Canadian Children and the First World War* (Toronto, ON: University of Toronto Press, 2011), 217.
59. Howard Gardner, *The Development and Education of the Mind: The Selected Works of Howard Gardner* (London: Routledge, 2006), 74.
60. Sears, "Children's Understandings of Democratic Participation," 145.
61. Timothy Brook, *Vermeer's Hat: The Seventeenth Century and the Dawn of the Global World* (Toronto, ON: Viking, 2008), 27.
62. Barton and Levstik, *Teaching History for the Common Good*, 2004; Karel Van Nieuwenhuyse and Kaat Wils, "Remembrance Education Between History Teaching and Citizenship Education," *Citizenship Teaching and Learning* 7, no. 2, (2005), 157–71; Karen Stanworth, *Visibly Canadian: Imagining Collective Identities in the Canadas, 1820–1910* (Montreal & Kingston: McGill-Queen's University Press, 2014).
63. Margaret MacMillan, *The Uses and Abuses of History* (Toronto: Viking, 2008); Edda Sant, Neus González-Monfort, Antoni Santesteban Fernández, Jorn Pages Blanch, and Montserrat Oller Freixa, "How do Catalan Students Narrate the History of Catalonia When They Finish Primary Education?" *McGill Journal of Education* 50, no. 2/3 (2015): 341–362.
64. Tim Cook, *Vimy: The Battle and the Legend* (Toronto: Allen Lane, 2017), 6.

65. Seixas and Morton, *The Big Six.*
66. Hulan, "The Past is an Imagined Country," 591.

Bibliography

Aldrich, Richard. "Introduction." In *Lessons from History of Education: The Selected Works of Richard Aldrich*, 1–14. London and New York: Routledge, 2006.

Barton, Keith and Linda Levstik. *Teaching History for the Common Good.* Mahwah, NJ: Lawrence Erlbaum Associates, 2004.

Brook, Timothy. *Vermeer's Hat: The Seventeenth Century and the Dawn of the Global World.* Toronto: Viking Canada, 2008.

Clark, Anna. "Teaching the Nation's Story: Comparing Public Debates and Classroom Perspectives on History Education in Australia and Canada." *Journal of Curriculum Studies* 4, no. 6 (2009): 745–62.

Clark, Anna and Carla L. Peck. "Introduction: Historical Consciousness Theory and Practice." In *Contemplating Historical Consciousness: Notes from the Field*, edited by Anna Clark and Carla L. Peck, 1–15. New York and Oxford: Berghahn Books, 2019.

Clarke, Patrick. *History, Memory, Heritage, Myth: What Should We Teach in School?* Response to Presentation by Dr. Peter Seixas, UBC Faculty of Education Public Lecture Series, Vancouver, BC, January 26, 2000.

Cook, Bruce. "Peeps Into the Past." *Washington Post*, 18 July, 1999, X4.

Cook, Tim. *Vimy: The Battle and the Legend.* Toronto: Allen Lane, 2017.

Dalrymple, William. *The Anarchy: The Relentless Rise of the East India Company.* Kindle. New York and London: Bloomsbury Publishing, 2019.

Demos, John. "In Search of Reasons for Historians to Read Novels." *The American Historical Review* 103, no. 5 (December 1998): 1526–1529.

den Heyer, Kent. "History Education as a Disciplined 'Ethics of Truths'." In *New Possibilities for the Past: Shaping History Education in Canada*, edited by Penney Clark, 154–72. Vancouver, BC: UBC Press, 2011.

Eliot, George. *Middlemarch.* Oxford: Oxford University Press, 1871/2008.

Fellman, Anita Clair. *Little House, Long Shadow: Laura Ingalls Wilder's Impact on American Culture.* Columbia, MO: University of Missouri Press, 2008.

Fisher, Susan R. *Boys and Girls in No Man's Land: English-Canadian Children and the First World War.* Toronto, ON: University of Toronto Press, 2011.

Frazier, Charles. *Cold Mountain.* Toronto: Vintage Canada, 1998.

Freeman, Evelyn and Linda Levstik. "Recreating the Past: Historical Fiction in the Social Studies Curriculum." *The Elementary School Journal* 88, no. 4 (March 1988): 329–37. https://doi.org/10.1080/00220270903139635.

Friesen, Gerald. "The Shape of Historical Thinking in a Canadian History Survey Course in University." In *New Possibilities for the Past: Shaping History Education in Canada*, edited by Penney Clark, 210–23. Vancouver, BC: UBC Press, 2011.

Gardner, Howard. *The Development and Education of the Mind: The Selected Works of Howard Gardner*. London: Routledge, 2006.

Harlan, David. "Historical Fiction and the Future of Academic History." In *Manifestos for History*, edited by Keith Jenkins, Sue Morgan and Alun Munslow, 108–30. London and New York: Routledge, 2007.

Hill, Lawrence. *The Book of Negroes*. Toronto, ON: HarperCollins, 2007.

Hodgetts, A.B. *What Culture? What Heritage? A Study of Civic Education in Canada*. Toronto, ON: Ontario Institute for Studies in Education, 1968.

Hulan, Renée. "The Past is an Imagined Country: Reading Canadian Historical Fiction Written in English." In *Settling and Unsettling Memories: Essays in Canadian Public History*, edited by Nicole Neatby and Peter Hodgins, 591–614. Toronto, ON: University of Toronto Press, 2012.

Hulan, Renée. *Canadian Historical Writing: Reading the Remains*. New York: Palgrave Macmillan, 2014.

Jordanova, Ludmilla. "Approaching Visual Materials." In *Research Methods for History*, edited by S. Gunn and I. Faire, 30–47. Edinburgh, SCT: University of Edinburgh, 2011.

Levstik, L.S. "A Child's Approach to History." *The Social Studies* 74, no. 6 (1983): 232–36.

Longfellow, Henry Wadswoth. "Evangeline: A Tale of Acadie." Nova Scotia Legislature, n.d.

MacMillan, Margaret. *The Uses and Abuses of History*. Toronto, ON: Viking, 2008.

McCully, Alan and F. Waldron. "A Question of Identity? Purpose, Policy and Practice in the Teaching of History in Northern Ireland and the Republic of Ireland." In *Identity Trauma, Sensitive and Controversial Issues in the Teaching of History*, edited by Hilary Cooper and Jon Nichol, 2–24. Newcastle upon Tyne: Cambridge Scholars Publishing, 2015.

McKay, Ian and Jamie Swift. *The Vimy Trap or, How We Learned to Stop Worrying and Love the Great War*. Toronto, ON: Between the lines Press, 2016.

Montgomery, L.M. *Rilla of Ingleside*. Toronto, ON: Seal Books, 1920/1996.

Novick, Peter. "(The Death of) the Ethics of Historical Practice (and Why I Am Not in Mourning)." ANNALS, AAPSS560 (November 1998): 28–42.

Osborne, Ken. "'Our History Syllabus Has Us Gasping': History in Canadian Schools—Past Present and Future." *Canadian Historical Review* 81, no. 3 (2000): 404–35.

Osborne, Ken. "*Knowing, Teaching and Learning History*, ed. by Peter N. Stearns, Peter Seixas, and Sam Wineburg and *Lhistoire à Lécole: Matière à*

Penser by Robert Martineau (Review)." *Canadian Historical Review* 82, no. 3 (September 2001): 548–54.

Osborne, Ken. "Why We Need to Teach and Study History." In *To the Past: History Education, Public Memory, & Citizenship in Canada*, edited by Ruth Sandwell, 103–31. Toronto, ON: University of Toronto Press, 2006.

Osborne, Ken. "Teaching Canadian History: A Century of Debate." In *New Possibilities for the Past: Shaping History Education in Canada*, edited by Penney Clark, 55–96. Vancouver, BC: UBC Press, 2011.

Osborne, Ken. "A History Teacher Looks Back." *The Canadian Historical Review* 93, no. 1 (2012): 108–37.

Peck, Carla L. and Alan Sears. "Canada." In *Education, Globalization and the Nation*, edited by King Man Chong, Ian Davies, Terrie Epstein, Carla L. Peck, Andrew Peterson, Alistair Ross, Maria Auxiliadora Schmidt, Alan Sears, and Debbie Sonu, 59–80. Hampshire UK: Palgrave Macmillan, 2016.

Rigney, Ann. "Fiction as a Mediator in National Remembrance." In *Narrating the Nation: Representations in History, Media and the Arts*, edited by Stefan Berger, Linas Eriksonas, and Andrew Mycock, 79–96. New York: Berghahn, 2008.

Sant, Edda, Neus González-Monfort, Antoni Santesteban Fernández, Jorn Pages Blanch, and Montserrat Oller Freixa. "How do Catalan Students Narrate the History of Catalonia When They Finish Primary Education?" *McGill Journal of Education* 50, no. 2/3 (2015), 341–62.

Sears, Alan. "Children's Understandings of Democratic Participation: Lessons for Civic Education." In *Civic Education and Youth Political Participation*, edited by Murray Print and Henry Milner, 143–58. Rotterdam/Boston/Taipei: Sense, 2009.

Sears, Alan. "Historical Thinking and Citizenship Education: It is Time to End the War." In *New Possibilities for the Past: Shaping History Education in Canada*, edited by Penney Clark, 344–64. Vancouver, BC: UBC Press, 2011.

Seixas, Peter. "Conceptualizing the Growth of Historical Understanding." In *The Handbook of Education and Human Development: New Models of Learning, Teaching and Schooling*, edited by David R. Olson and Nancy Torrance, 765–83. Cambridge, MA: Blackwell, 1996.

Seixas, Peter. "What is Historical Consciousness? In *To the Past: History Education, Public Memory, & Citizenship in Canada*, edited by Ruth Sandwell, 11–22. Toronto, ON: University of Toronto Press, 2006.

Seixas, Peter. "A Modest Proposal for Change in Canadian History Education." *Teaching History* 137 (2009): 26–30.

Seixas, Peter. "Looking for History." In *Joined-up History: New Directions in History Education and Research*, edited by Arthur Chapman and Arie Wilschut, 255–76. Charlotte, NC: Information Age, 2015.

Seixas, Peter. "Translation and Its Discontents: Key Concepts in English and German History Education." *Journal of Curriculum Studies* 48, no. 4 (2016): 427–39. https://doi.org/10.1080/00220272.2015.1101618.

Seixas, Peter and Tom Morton. *The Big Six Historical Thinking Concepts*. Toronto, ON: Nelson Education Ltd., 2013.

Stanworth, Karen. *Visibly Canadian: Imagining Collective Identities in the Canadas, 1820–1910*. Montreal, QC & Kingston, ON: McGill-Queen's University Press, 2014.

Trevelyan, G.M. "Autobiography of an Historian." In *An Autobiography and Other Essays*, 1–51. London: Longmans, Green, 1949.

Tuchman, Barbara W. "History by the Ounce." In *Practicing History: Selected Essays*, 35–47. New York: Random House, 2014.

Tuchman, Barbara W. "The Historian as Artist." In *Practicing History: Selected Essays*, 48–54. New York: Random House, 2014.

Van Nieuwenhuyse, Karel and Kaat Wils. "Remembrance Education Between History Teaching and Citizenship Education." *Citizenship Teaching and Learning* 7, no. 2 (2005): 157–71.

White, Hayden. "The Fictions of Factual Representation." In *The Literature of Fact: Selected Papers from the English Institute*, edited by Angus Fletcher, 21–44. Harvard University, English Institute, 1976.

Wyile, Herb. *Speculative Fictions: Contemporary Canadian Novelists and the Writing of History*. Montreal, QC & Kingston, ON: McGill-Queen's University Press, 2002.

CHAPTER 2

Five Scholarly Conversations Related to History, History Education, and the Arts

In this chapter we situate our work within a complex set of five interrelated scholarly conversations around the nature of history and historical truths, history and the arts, collective memory and historical consciousness, Indigenous perspectives in history education, and implications for history education. At times these conversations are so intertwined it is difficult to extricate one from another, but we will make these somewhat artificial separations in order to establish a broader context for our work and point to the issues inherent within it.

Nature of History and Historical Truths

The ancient Greek historian Thucydides pointed out that earlier historians framed their histories as moral or heroic tales. He denigrated these historians as "Prose chroniclers who are less interested in telling the truth than in catching the attention of the public whose authorities cannot be checked and whose subject matter, owing to the passage of time, is mostly lost in the unreliable streams of mythology."[1] Unlike these "prose chroniclers" Thucydides aimed to write "true" histories based on evidence.

Questions about the purposes and nature of history and historical truths have continued to intrigue and concern historians. Two centuries after Thucydides, the Roman historian Polybius felt the necessity to speak

P. Clark and A. Sears, *The Arts and the Teaching of History*,
https://doi.org/10.1007/978-3-030-51513-3_2

out on behalf of objectivity and use of evidence. "It is not a historian's business to represent speeches which might have been delivered. ... It is his task first and foremost to record with fidelity what actually happened."[2] Polybius also noted "If history is deprived of the truth, we are left with nothing but an idle, unprofitable tale."[3] However, as John Burrow reminds us, several of the Roman historians who followed Polybius were more concerned with conveying moral lessons than with creating evidence-based historical accounts.[4]

There are echoes of these ancient debates in more contemporary writing about the nature of history. In his 1988 volume, *That Noble Dream: The "Objectivity Question" and the American Historical Profession*, American historian Peter Novick traces changes in historiography and the philosophy of history in the United States over 100 years (from the 1880s to the 1980s). He describes historical objectivity as "a commitment to the reality of the past, and to truth as correspondence to that reality; a sharp separation between knower and known ... and, above all, between history and fiction. Historical facts are seen as prior to and independent of interpretation. ... Truth is one, not perspectival."[5] Until the 1960s, he found an overwhelming consensus around the idea of history as a scientific endeavour focused on producing objective and disinterested accounts of the past, with signs of "historical relativism" along the way, but never to the point where it became the dominant perspective. In the 1960s, there was an upheaval that hit history harder than any other discipline. "In no other field was there such a widespread sense of disarray; in no other discipline did so many leading figures express dismay and discouragement at the current state of their realm."[6] He adds that "the evolution of historians' attitudes on the objectivity question has always been closely tied to changing social, political, cultural, and professional contexts."[7] However, as historian Sarah Maza points out, "The conflicts of the 1960s, in sum, productively destabilized the discipline by introducing sharply differing perspectives, but stopped short of mounting a philosophical challenge to the truth-claims of historical narratives."[8]

In 1998, a decade after his influential publication, Novick participated in a colloquium titled "The Future of Fact," where he explicitly articulated his own place in the debate about the possibility of objectivity in history and the relationship of historical and literary accounts. He described the border between history and fiction as "fuzzier than as traditionally represented"[9] and declared that "We (historians) would make no greater (but also no lesser) truth claims than poets or painters:

no greater (but also no lesser) claims for support from society for this endeavour."[10] At the same colloquium, philosopher Judith Lichtenberg offered a stirring rebuke to what she saw as Novick's dangerous conflating of history and fiction. She accused him of "run[ning] amok,"[11] arguing it is neither necessary nor sensible to respond to the questions raised by critical theorists by jettisoning history's traditional commitment to truth and the establishment of the validity of facts. She contended that "interpretations are ... fact laden: the uncovering of new facts renders some interpretations more plausible and others less."[12] She added: "Falliblism - the recognition that we can be wrong, the humility to suspect we might be - does not mean there is nothing to be known or understood. Quite the contrary, it reflects a deep respect for the factuality of the world and the difficulty of penetrating it."[13] She concluded by saying, "Honesty—fidelity to truth—might be the best policy for a novelist. For a historian, nothing else will do."[14]

Historian Richard Evans, who steers a course somewhere between Novick and Lichtenberg, asks, "If history is not a science, then are historians any different in essence from novelists or poets?"[15] He concludes that history is a blend of science, craft, and art. It is a "science in the weak sense of the German term *Wissenschaft*, an organized body of knowledge acquired through research carried out according to generally agreed methods, presented in published reports, and subject to peer review."[16] It is a craft "because its practitioners learn on the job how to handle their materials and wield the tools of their trade."[17] Finally, it is art "in the sense that in skilful hands it can be presented in a literary form and language that achieves comparability with other literary works of art."[18] Historians Joyce Appleby, Lynn Hunt, and Margaret Jacob would agree. They say the "science" comes in the assiduous attention to what archival records can reveal in the context of what is already known. The "art" lies in "the imaginative casting of narrative and interpretation."[19]

The intellectual historian and theorist Hayden White, in his foundational 1966 article "The Burden of History," made the point that "both science and art have transcended the older, stable conceptions of the world which required that they render a literal copy of a presumably static reality. And both have discovered the essentially provisional character of the metaphorical constructions which they use to comprehend a dynamic universe."[20] Interestingly, he uses a novel, George Eliot's nineteenth-century *Middlemarch*, to make his point.[21] In the novel, Dorothea Brooke abandons the scholar, Casaubon, for Ladislaw, the artist. White interprets Eliot's point to be, "artistic insight and historical learning are opposed, and the qualities of the response to life which they respectively evoke are mutually exclusive."[22]

White contended that "a specifically *historical* inquiry is born less of the necessity to establish *that* certain events occurred than of the desire to determine what certain events might mean for a given group, society, or culture's conception of its present tasks and future prospects."[23] He argued that historical narratives are "a work of construction rather than of discovery."[24] The historian shapes the narrative by deciding where to begin, which events are significant enough to include in the middle and where to end. He implied that it is foolish for some historians to "feign to aspire to the status of sciences without any hope of achieving the kind of procedures developed in the physical sciences for the resolution of conflicting interpretations of their specific objects of study."[25]

White's position was enormously controversial, at least initially. As Peter Novick points out, White was not saying that history is the same thing as fiction, but rather, that "the conventional distinction between the two realms underestimated the constraints on the writer of fiction and overestimated those on the historian."[26] He found the similarities between the two both more interesting and more significant than the differences.

We agree with these historians and emphasize one point in particular. Historians are artists because "when it comes to creating a coherent account out of … evidentiary fragments, the historical method consists only of appealing to the muse."[27] Historians are accountable to their evidence, but they are on their own in creating narratives from that evidence. Evans contends that one of the benefits of postmodern questioning of the foundations of history as a discipline is that "History is becoming a more theoretically and epistemologically self-conscious discipline, and that's all to the good."[28] In this book we hope to make a small contribution to that self-consciousness as it relates to history education.

However, we cannot ignore the crucial point that historians can never recreate the past as it was because the past is over. As historian Barbara Tuchman has put it: "we who write about the past were not there. We can never be certain that we have recaptured it as it really was. [She adds] But the least we can do is to stay within the evidence."[29] Historian John Lewis Gaddis, too, reminds us that the past is "inaccessible to us … We can only represent it."[30] In fact, historians can never capture the past as it really was, no matter how hard they might try, and contemporary historians recognize this reality. The narratives created by historians as history, are only partial and "imagined." There are several reasons for this. First, the archival record is, and always will be, incomplete. Regardless of how many documents, artefacts or oral histories are added to archival collections, they can never collectively encompass everything that has happened. As Jonathan Nield put it in 1902, "it is impossible for us to breathe the atmosphere of a bygone time, since all those thousand-and-one details which went to the building up of both individual and general experience, can never be reproduced."[31] Second, although always and forever incomplete, at the same time the archival remains are too vast for any historian to encounter all that may be relevant to a particular historical investigation. There will always be more to seek out. Therefore, at some point the historian has to acknowledge that the time has come to cease the search and begin to create the narrative. Some other historian may one day take up the task, using some of the same and some other historical remains to create a new narrative. History is not static, but rather, it is fluid because it is constantly being constructed and re-constructed. Every historian has to accept and work within this reality. Finally, the historian is restricted by the narrative form through which history is conveyed. As Australian scholar of literary and narrative journalism and novelist Christopher Kremmer has put it, "history is not imaginary, but it is imagined. Real things really happened, but the ways in which we represent them – literally, re-present them – in narrative form, using a combination of facts and our historical imaginations, can only ever achieve a partial, incomplete and distorted version of the past."[32]

Historians Appleby, Hunt, and Jacob add another layer to the conversation: "The records are left by people who lived in the past, but—and this is the tricky part—the records are extant in the present. The past, insofar as it exists at all, exists in the present; the historian too is stuck in time present, trying to make meaningful and accurate statements about time past. Any account of historical objectivity must provide for this crucial temporal dimension."[33]

A further crucial point is that history is about interpretation. Perhaps the most compelling description of the degree to which the construction of an historical narrative is interpretive can be found in historian William Cronon's iconic comparison of a number of historical narratives about the Dust Bowl. He highlights *The Dust Bowl* by Paul Bonnifield and *Dust Bowl* by Donald Worster, both published in 1979. Bonnifield paints a picture of people who continued producing during the Depression years and, by doing so, contributed to the well-being of the nation-at-large. He says, "Because those determined people did not flee the stricken area during a crisis, the nation today enjoys a better standard of living."[34] Bonnifield contends that New Deal planners characterized residents of the Plains as defeated people in an attempt to encourage them to leave the land and thus solve the problem of reducing the national overproduction of wheat. He saw "their chief problem [as] less a hostile nature than a hostile government."[35] According to Worster, on the other hand, "The Dust Bowl … was the inevitable outcome of a culture that deliberately, self-consciously, set itself [the] task of dominating and exploiting the land for all it was worth."[36] For Bonnifield, the focus is on the valiant struggle of the victims to maintain their livelihoods and their families' well-being in the face of a devastating natural disaster. For Worster, the situation was cultural, the failure of human beings to cope with the vicissitudes of nature. As Cronon points out, "it is not merely their *conclusions* that differ. Although both narrate the same broad series of events, with an essentially similar cast of characters, they tell two entirely different *stories*."[37]

Cronon asks how these narratives, and the others he discusses, can be so different when they rely on the same evidence. He concludes that moral purposes, ideological perspectives, and even political ends shape the narratives historians tell. With reference to these examples, Bonnifield looks at events through a focus on the negative aspects of the New Deal. Worster's lens is one of the effects of capitalist expansion, which he viewed as leading to exploitation of the land, which in turn, led to the crisis of the Dust Bowl.

Cronon makes the sweeping statement, "I would assert the virtues of narrative as our best and most compelling tool for searching out meaning in a conflicted and contradictory world."[38] However, he reminds his readers that historical narrative possibilities are not endless. There are boundaries and protocols. First, narratives must not conflict with known facts. "Good history does not knowingly lie." Second, historians do their work within a community of historians and, hence, all historical accounts are open for critique from other historians. He says, this criticism "keep[s] us honest by forcing us to confront contradictory evidence and counternarratives." We would add that the value of the peer-review process should not be underestimated in terms of the possibilities it presents to improve scholarship. Also, there is an expectation that a historian will be familiar with the range of interpretations in the secondary literature. Third, the absence of censorship is an important precondition for scholarship.

Finally, we make the point that the range of topics for historical investigation has expanded. Until the 1960s, political history took precedence. As historian Sarah Maza points out, this prioritization of political history was based on particular assumptions: "that the state and government are the most important arenas of human activity, that political leaders more than anyone drive historical change, and that 'politics' is an activity that happens in the public sphere."[39] Women, children, the working class, and even the environment are a few of the areas of interest that have come to the fore over the past half century.

History and the Arts

The second conversation is around the relationship between history and the arts. This conversation is key to this book. Subsequent chapters will return to it in more depth, with discussion of fiction (Chapter 3), visual art (Chapter 4), and commemorative art (Chapter 5).

Christopher Kremmer argues that, "[Both] our histories – fictional and non-fictional – are hybrid creations comprising evidence, speculation and invention."[40] History and art are alike in that both tell stories about the past. They are different in that historical accounts are limited by the availability of sources and what the sources have to say, while in the case of works of art, the point "is the creation of an artwork, in this case, an artwork inspired by history."[41]

Like Richard Evans, historian John Lewis Gaddis sees history, science, and art as having much in common. "They all depend on metaphor or on the recognition of patterns, on the realization that something is 'like' something else."[42] Literary historian Jerome de Groot reminds us that "both novelist and historian are using trope, metaphor, prose, narrative style, to interpret and render a version of something which is innately other and unknown."[43] However, as Gaddis points out, there are crucial differences in their approaches and in what they can produce. An historical narrative can be shaped by the historian's imagination, but it cannot originate there. It exists separately from the interpretation. "Imagination in history, then, as in science must be tethered to and disciplined by sources; that's what distinguishes it from the arts and all other methods of representing reality."[44]

The historian does not have total control over her subject matter because she must be guided by her sources and what she finds in them. A historical novelist has more control. Jerome de Groot refers to "the kinds of historical lacunae which allow authors [of fiction] creative wriggle room. … it is here, in the gaps of history, in the spaces between knowledges, in the lacking texts, within the misunderstood codes, that historical novelists work, and it is the very insubstantiality of the past that allows them to introduce their version of events."[45] However, even the historical novelist must be attentive to authenticity. Events must "ring true" to what could plausibly have occurred at that time and that place. They cannot contradict available evidence if they wish readers to take them seriously. This is applicable to filmic versions of fiction as well. Recently, critic Katherine Ashenburg commented in the *Globe & Mail* that there were a number of annoying anachronisms in the 2019 film version of the nineteenth-century novel *Little Women*. For example, tomboy Jo March sometimes sat with her knees wide apart or with her ankle crossed over the other knee when the family was entertaining visitors. While this may be an effective way of conveying Jo's individualism to a twenty-first-century audience, it is simply not an action that a well brought-up young woman would have taken at the time without enduring censure. Furthermore, it is not something that Louisa May Alcott described in her period novel. Ashenburg comments, "Do we really want to be deprived of seeing in a film the way people moved, talked, thought and lived 150 years ago?"[46]

The rise of cultural history, which has taken place over the past 40 years or so, is an aspect of the conversation related to history and the arts that is relevant here. Cultural history includes an interest in the popular culture of "ordinary" people. Edward Thompson's *Making of the English Working Class* was one of the first and the most influential of the early studies in this area.[47] Thompson examined the role of a wide range of aspects of popular culture in working-class formation, including food, fairs, dialect poetry, Methodist hymns, and the initiation rituals of artisans. According to cultural historian Peter Burke, cultural history has "extend[ed] the territory of the historian as well as making history more accessible to a wide public."[48] In *Eyewitnessing: The Use of Images as Historical Evidence*, Burke makes many points about using historical films that are made in Chapter 3 of this volume with regard to novels. For example, he talks about the opportunity to observe "the material culture of the upper classes in the nineteenth century,"[49] as depicted in Martin Scorsese's *The Age of Innocence* (an Edith Wharton novel) and the provincial gentry in the BBC's *Pride and Prejudice* (a Jane Austen novel).

Historian David Harlan acknowledges the claims to legitimacy of what he calls popular history. He points in particular to the popularity of novels, contending that people are drawn to them because they have something to offer that academic histories lack, namely the voices of individuals from the past. "Novels are aesthetic objects. … the meaning of a novel lies in the experience of *reading* it, the experience of hearing the voice of another resonate deeply within us (rather than in whatever 'facts' we may carry around from our reading)."[50] Harlan emphasizes this point with a quote from Hayden White: "Those aspects of the past that can be studied scientifically do not yield the kinds of information or knowledge that drive us to the study of the past in the first place."[51] In other words, works of art about the past offer an aesthetic dimension that gives us the feel of the past, a sense of what it might have been like to reside there. These aspects draw us into studying the past. Harlan also points to the moral dimension of learning history:

> If our students are to become thoughtful and resourceful readers of the past in a culture as dispersed and eclectic as this one, they will have to become adept at finding their way between competing but equally valid truth claims made in distinct and often divergent modes of historical representation. They will have to become *bricoleurs*, sophisticated multimedia rag-pickers, quick, shrewd and witty readers of *all* the forms in which their culture represents the past, shuttling back and forth, to and fro, cutting and pasting, weaving and reweaving interpretive webs of their own devising. For only thus can they hope to develop a historical imagination that is morally coherent and politically effective.[52]

Cultural scholar and professor of comparative literature Ann Rigney cautions that "historical fiction fails to do many things, and … not every work in the genre attains the same level of complexity, nuance, and insight into historical experience."[53] Yet, she argues that while academic history "wins on authority, [fiction] may win on allure."[54] Novels, films, and plays are "generally more popular and thus arguably more influential."[55] She uses Alison Landsberg's colourful term "prosthetic memory,"[56] a concept that refers to the power of literature to help the reader or listener experience events vicariously. "As a medium of prosthetic memory, storytelling helps mediate across temporal and cultural boundaries by presenting individual experience to third parties in a vivid and highly imaginable way."[57] Cultural historians acknowledge the significant place of fictional artistic representations of various kinds in our contemporary world and suggest that they warrant recognition as sources for engagement with, and understanding of, the past.

Collective Memory and Historical Consciousness

In November of 2019, Japanese-Canadian Lorene Oikawa presented the document, "Recommendations for Redressing Historical Wrongs Against Japanese Canadians in B.C." to the government of the province of British Columbia, Canada. At the time, she commented, "It's about history, but it's also about now. And it's about our future." She added, "And it's about all of us."[58] We begin with Oikawa's comment because it neatly captures the essence of both collective memory and historical consciousness, the two concepts that form the basis of this scholarly conversation, and it demonstrates the timeliness of discussion of these concepts in a period when attention to the redressing of historical wrongs is on the minds of Canadians and other peoples around the world.

Historian Wulf Kansteiner makes the important point that, "collective memory is not history, though it is sometimes made from similar material."[59] Collective memory is about how people encounter the past in the context of the social, cultural, ethnic, national, and other groups, including the family, in which they conduct their daily lives, although formal history education, in practice, also can serve as a conduit for collective memory. Sociologist Barry Schwartz notes that "[c]ollective memory works by subsuming individual experiences under cultural schemes that make them comprehensible and therefore meaningful."[60] Collective memory, or "public memory"[61] as it is sometimes called, is about "the creation of a usable past."[62] As history education scholar Peter Seixas has put it, "Public memory brings the past into present consciousness and allows it to be mobilized for decisions about the future."[63]

In the case of history education, the usable past has, in practice, been about the nurturing of a cohesive sense of national identity. In fact, until the 1970s, this was the central purpose of history education in schools in Canada and remains a central purpose in many parts of the world.[64] Collective memory is also important in the broader civic life. Political leaders place great importance on citizens' collective memory because it is central to their sense of national identity.[65] As sociocultural anthropologist James Wertsch emphasizes, collective memory is not about accuracy, as is the case with individual memory. It is more about belief. He quotes John Bodnar's definition of collective (public) memory:

> Public memory is a body of beliefs and ideas about the past that help a public or society understand both its past, present, and by implication, its future. It is fashioned ideally in a public sphere in which various parts of the social structure exchange views. The major focus of this communicative and cognitive process is not the past, however, but serious matters in the present such as the nature of power and the question of loyalty to both official and vernacular cultures.[66]

Elsewhere, Wertsch makes a distinction between knowledge and belief based on his fascinating study in Estonia. He found that Estonians were knowledgeable concerning the official historical narrative provided by the Soviet Union of the events in 1940 that had resulted in Estonia's becoming part of the Soviet Union, but they did not believe it. As Wertsch puts it, "appropriation did not follow mastery."[67] This study indicates how powerful collective memory can be. They also knew at least one unofficial version learned from unofficial sources such as family, friends, and underground literature. The official version was highly visible and present at commemorative events and in school textbooks. Because the unofficial versions were banned, they were available only on private occasions. However, it was the unofficial versions that people believed.

We note that collective forgetting may be as central to national identity as collective remembering. Historian Sarah Maza notes two key examples of this. She cites David Blight's *Race and Reunion* in which he makes the important point that North and South were able to carry on together after the American Civil War because they both chose to "forget" slavery, which was the impetus for the conflict, and the outcome of Black emancipation. Her other example is the postwar effort by the government of Charles de Gaulle to promote the false view that the majority of French people supported the Resistance and not the collaborationist Vichy government during the Second World War.[68]

Communication scholar Marita Sturken argues that, "We must rethink cultures' valorization of memory as the equivalent of experience. If memory is redefined as a social and individual practice that integrates elements of remembrance, fantasy, and invention, then it can shift from the problematic role of standing for the truth to a new role as an active, engaging practice of creating meaning."[69] Many scholars have made a point of distinguishing between history and collective memory. Peter Seixas notes that, "'History' invokes notions of objectivity and science. 'Memory' invokes notions of subjectivity and feeling. 'History' has a method. 'Memory' if it is there at all, is immediately so."[70] Drawing from French historian Pierre Nora,[71] he adds: "memory is deeply felt, it affirms community ties, collective identities, and common foes; and it thrives on preservation and enhancement. History is analytic, and intellectual … and thrives on evidence-based critique and revision."[72] Peter Novick contends that history can confront complexity and multiple perspectives, while memory sees things from one perspective and cannot incorporate ambiguity. He says: "Typically a collective memory … is understood to express some eternal or essential truth about the group – usually tragic. A memory, once established, comes to define that eternal truth, and, along with it, an eternal identity, for the members of the group."[73] Collective memory promotes the cohesiveness of the group and can be self-serving. History differentiates the past from the present, but collective memory is more about linking them. Collective memory is generally considered to be about continuity, while history is about change.[74] We recognize that historical accounts change, for example, when new evidence is brought to light, when historians with new theoretical perspectives bring them to bear on existing evidence, or when new analytical tools are used. History organizes events into periods according to changing conditions or particular events that are considered to be turning points. James Wertsch makes the point, however, that memory may not be as unchanging as it seems. He says that "[d]espite its claims for stability and constancy … it is likely to undergo change."[75] Its changes are in response to evolving concepts of what makes the past usable in the present.[76]

Kansteiner points out that "collective memories exist on the level of families, professions, political generations, ethnic and regional groups, social classes, and nations. … Collective memory works by subsuming individual experiences under cultural schemes that make them comprehensible and therefore meaningful."[77] Collective memory makes use of symbolic devices such as monuments, statues, paintings, place names, plaques, commemorative ceremonies, and school textbooks to keep memory alive. French historian Pierre Nora calls these symbols *lieux de memoire*, or sites of memory. He claims that "memory attaches itself to sites, whereas history attaches itself to events."[78] Citizens often place great importance on such symbols, which is why they are so frequently at the centre of controversy, particularly recently, as both scholars and the public at large in Canada and in other countries around the world question who is remembered in these tangible ways, for what reasons, and to what extent these reasons are sustainable.[79]

In 2016, in the German blog, *Public History Weekly*, Peter Seixas asked:

> What is the role of state-based history education in open democratic societies, in respect to the memories that arise from the collective phenomena of war, oppression, displacement, injustice, trauma, nation building, or, indeed, everyday life? On what grounds do the interventions of school history rest? Why not simply accept "spontaneous" community memory, family myth, commercially produced narratives (e.g. Hollywood cinema) or other state-sponsored memories (e.g., national commemorations) that contribute to people's understandings of the past?[80]

Seixas proposed a history/memory matrix in the form of a circle with three sections (see Fig. 2.1). The top (blue) section is disciplinary history, which involves "the interpretation and reading of primary sources and the construction and critique of historical accounts." Seixas mentions the British Schools History Project, launched in 1972, and the current Stanford University project, "Reading like a Historian," as examples. The bottom (red) section is called "Memory & Life Practice." "Origins, triumphs over adversity, the defeat of enemies from within and without, and the core beliefs, values and character traits that made triumph possible are all embedded in such a narrative." Across the middle of the circle is a purple bar, which serves as a "bridge between historical practices and memorial beliefs, where skilled teachers have considerable autonomy to address the memorial cultures of the students in their classes and where community memories—perhaps even divided memories—are subjected to and enlarged by critical, historical scrutiny feeding back into public memory."[81] He notes that while this is an ideal conception of school history, there are several current European projects that exemplify this approach, including the German FUER-model, which will be discussed later in this chapter. This proposal and the many thoughtful responses on the *Public History Weekly* blog have helped to clarify the distinction between history and collective memory and what each has to offer history education.

History educator Stéphane Lévesque has offered a critique of the Seixas matrix in an initial response in *Public History Weekly*, "Going beyond 'Narratives' vs. 'Competencies': A model of history education," and with

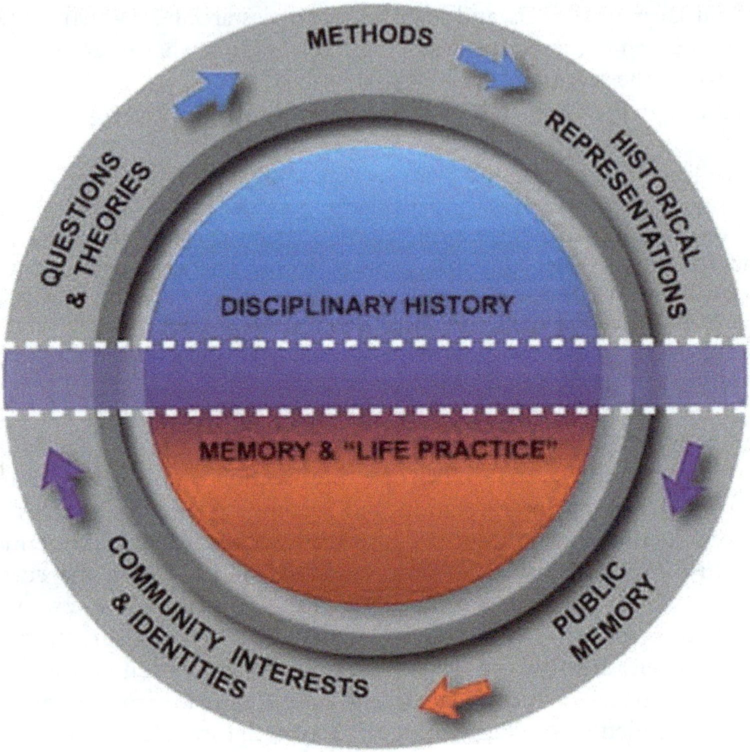

Fig. 2.1 A history/memory matrix for history education. Peter Seixas (*Source Public History Weekly*)

co-author Jean-Philippe Croteau, in their book *Beyond History for Historical Consciousness.* Lévesque and Croteau take issue with the assumption behind Seixas' matrix that scholarly knowledge developed through the scientific, evidence-based history method, directly informs daily life and public memory. They do not see how history education can bridge the two zones of historical scholarship and life practice because, in their view, history education, as it is practiced, is a part of the public culture of history and has a greater connection to life practices than to disciplinary history. They propose an alternative matrix that recognizes that disciplinary history and public memory often overlap and co-exist in people's daily lives and that historical practices take place in the context of historical culture (see Fig. 2.2).[82] The blue zone on top is Disciplinary history. They make the point that "historians generate interpretations within a community of specialists, thus producing a vast 'theoretical surplus' beyond people's needs for life orientation and identity-building. This surplus is not reinvested in public memory and most often remains dormant or even ignored by society at large."[83] The bottom, red zone, is Culture and Life practice. It "reaffirm[s] connections with the past and shape[s] people's sense of belonging and community-building."[84] History education is the middle, purple zone. It should not be exclusively "a practice of public memory or a set of scholastic competencies

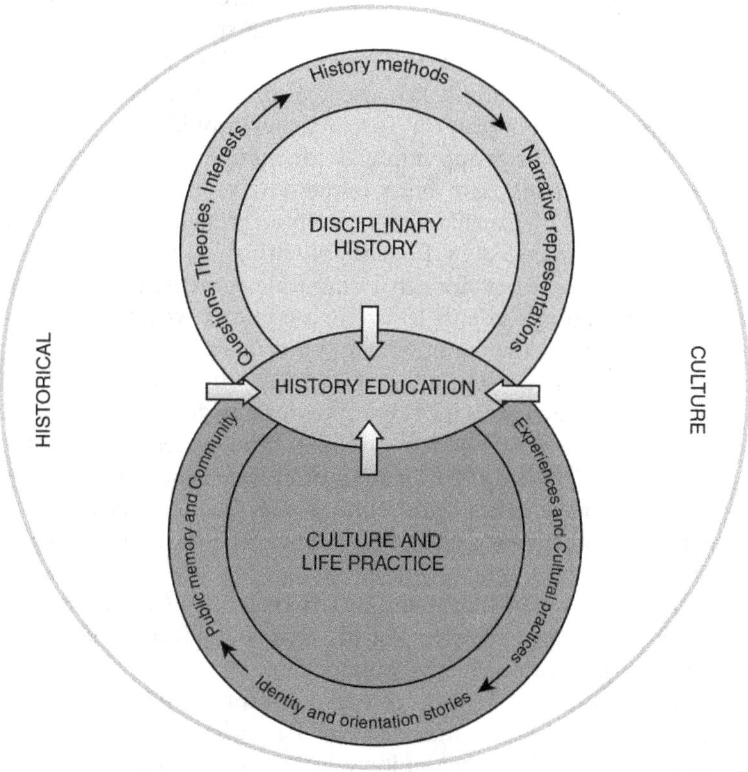

Fig. 2.2 Historical cultural matrix. Stéphane Lévesque (*Source Beyond History for Historical Consciousness*)

of historical thinking but … the effective result of the interplay among historical culture, public memory, practical life, schooling and the practice of history."[85] Finally, they denote a white zone which surrounds the other zones. It represents "the totality of discourses whereby a societal community understands itself and its future by interpreting and narrating the past."[86]

They make three suggestions for history education in order to "mobilize young people's historical representations for the purpose of life orientation:" (1) Educators should adopt a constructivist view of learning and build on students' "own ideas of the collective past." (2) Educators should teach that historical narratives are constructed. "If we want students to think historically and to develop more critical approaches to the collective past, educators should explain the structure, the grammar, the mode of expression, and the purpose of historical narratives in society." (3) Educators should not use narratives of collective memory to promote national identification. Instead, they should make it clear that individual members of a group might hold multiple viewpoints and that viewpoints of Canadians have been influenced by histories beyond the national framework of Canada. For example, French Canadian history has been heavily influenced by French and British as well as Indigenous historical experiences. They note that "multiple contextualization is a key principle for educating students to live in a complex world."[87]

Seixas responded to the commentary in *Public History Weekly*, offering the view that what distinguishes disciplinary history from identity-building memory practices is its "Open, critical, evidence-based approach to investigating the past" which provides "the generative benefit for history education."[88] As for the location of history education at the intersection of disciplinary history and cultural life practice, Seixas acknowledges that although history education should be located there, it is not often found there.

This conversation, and the many others on the *Public History Weekly* blog, are examples, in themselves, of the scholarly critique that serves to distinguish history from collective memory.

Historical consciousness is a central concept in history education. However, as Maria Grever and Robbert-Jan Adriaansen point out, its meaning is "vague and rather enigmatic."[89] In *Contemplating Historical Consciousness*, history education scholars Anna Clark and Carla Peck define the concept as "the ways people orient themselves in time and how they are bound by the historical and cultural contexts which shape their sense of temporality and collective memory."[90] John Lewis Gaddis defines it as the process of "interpret[ing] the past for the purposes of the present with a view to managing the future, but to do so without suspending the capacity to assess the particular circumstances in which one might have to act, or the relevance of past actions to them."[91] Gaddis adds that historical consciousness prepares one for operating in the future "by expanding experience, so that you can increase your skills, your stamina—and, if all goes well, your wisdom."[92] History educator Paul Zanazanian says historical consciousness "constitutes an entryway into how individuals perceive, explain, and give meaning to (past) events and life experiences, as well as into how they understand their situatedness, belonging, and intentionality for living their lives."[93] Taken together, these explanations provide a comprehensive definition of historical consciousness. All of these separate definitions highlight the temporal dimension: Clark and Peck acknowledge the notion of the influence of cultural and historical contexts, and the role of collective memory, Gaddis is oriented towards the future, and Zanazanian emphasizes the past and present.

German philosopher Jörn Rüsen whose work is foundational, has posited a typology that involves a hierarchy of four types of historical consciousness. Each level exhibits a particular stance towards the past which points to a moral orientation in the present. The *traditional* type, which is where collective memory is situated, depends on the permanence of values and moral obligations in people's lives and history serves to remind us of these values. This type does not acknowledge significant change over time. The *exemplary* type depends on the application of principles to specific and concrete situations. Seixas notes that "the celebratory history of heroes to inspire strong character in the present"[94] would be an example of this type. The *critical* type depends on historical reasoning to develop a new interpretation. This type relies on the use of evidence in order to narrate counter narratives that "render problematic present value systems."[95] An example here would be Indigenous histories that present an opposing view of colonial history or feminist histories that give women a prominent place. The *genetic* type temporalizes morality, acknowledging the ongoing legacy of the past while recognizing that present circumstances may have changed significantly. It acknowledges a "pluralism of viewpoints and the acceptance of the concrete 'otherness' of the other and mutual acknowledgement of that 'otherness' as the dominant notion of moral valuation."[96] A. J. P. Taylor's controversial *Origins of the Second World War* may be considered an example of work at this level in that it offers a fresh look at the factors that led to the Second

World War, pointing out that Hitler was aided by circumstances to which other nations contributed.[97]

Because Rüsen does not define the relationship between historical consciousness and the disciplinary practices of historians, it has been challenging to operationalize his typology. Seixas and others have called for further work to be done to define what student advancement in historical consciousness would look like for the purposes of teaching and student assessment.[98] Progress has been made on several fronts. Quebec scholar Catherine Duquette has developed a four-tier (primary, intermediate, composite, and narrative) developmental theoretical model of historical consciousness[99] in which the tiers are placed along a continuum from nonreflective to reflective historical consciousness, or as Seixas puts it, "from uncritical to critical approaches."[100] "To be reflective, historical consciousness must base its understanding of the past on the interpretations emanating from the process of historical thinking."[101] Students at the primary level were unable to provide a precise response to the contemporary problem posed. They did not refer to the past in their answers. At the intermediate level students brought up causes related to their own lives and again, did not refer to the past. At the composite level students brought up causes from both the past and the present, but did not necessarily link them. At the narrative level students used the past to explain the present. They combined past events to construct a cohesive narrative. These students came closest to displaying a form of reflective historical consciousness. Duquette's work implies that there is a progression with regard to mastery of the second-order concepts of use of evidence, understanding historical significance, and so on, and that the mastery of particular concepts is dependent on the mastery of other concepts. Her work also implies that the level of historical consciousness exhibited by students is an indicator of their ability to think historically because her study revealed development in historical consciousness after teaching in historical thinking occurred.

Scholars in Germany are looking for ways to operationalize historical consciousness in the form of competencies, which do not involve specific content knowledge, but, rather, the ability to deal with new issues. One of these efforts is the HITCH (Historical Thinking Competencies in History) project. Andreas Körber and his colleagues developed the FUER-model, which, according to Körber, is the only model "to be based on a specific theory of historical thinking" and "to introduce both a differentiation of dimensions of historical competence *and* a concept for distinguishing *levels*."[102] The model defines four dimensions of historical competencies, the first three of which are based on Rüsen's model. Competence in questioning is the ability to construct historical questions and to identify and assess the questions behind historical narratives. Methodological competence involves constructing historical statements from information and assessing those statements. Orientation competence involves connecting information and insights about the past to one's own life. "The fourth dimension (subject matter competences) includes first order concepts such as 'imperialism,' 'enlightenment,' or 'autocracy,' as well as all of the second-order concepts identified by British and Canadian researchers, such as 'use of evidence,' 'accounts,' and 'historical significance.' It also includes "procedural concepts, such as knowledge (theoretical and/or experience-based) of how to get access to archival sources, how to order information chronologically, and how to analyze and interpret a document."[103] This model indicates a development "from a tabula rasa-like state of ignorance and indifference towards the past ... through a second state of uncritical appropriation of the past, to a third state of knowledge-based understanding of the past, to a final stage of full historical consciousness that equals a critical understanding of one's own historicity."[104]

So far, international research on competencies in historical consciousness has examined a number of aspects of historical learning: (1) relationship between past and present in chronological and societal context; (2) influence of progress, presentism, and moral judgements on students' historical ideas; (3) analysis of evidence-based narratives; and (4) production of historical narratives for identity and cultural life orientation.[105]

Seixas, too, has attempted to operationalize historical consciousness. He has identified the components of historical consciousness as the understandings that comprise the central goals of history education, which include the following:

1. an understanding of the present in terms of developments and crisis points in the past;
2. an awareness of the vast differences between ways of life and ways of thinking in the present and those in the past, the profound challenges posed by transcendence of those differences, and the historical mutability of "human nature'; and
3. an understanding of the interplay between intentional human agency and the unintended consequences of human action, as well as the

constraints imposed on human actors by structures inherited from the past.

They also include modes of investigating the past:

4. understanding history as an interpretive discipline that requires criteria for inclusion and omission;
5. the ethical dimension: that crimes from the past notwithstanding their historical distance, may impose demands for action in the present; and
6. a critical stance toward tradition and myth, enabled by the analysis of traces for primary sources from the past.[106]

One of the key themes addressed in this conversation deals with the ways individuals and collectives construct narratives about their place in the world, and the sources on which they draw in doing so. A central finding of a large body of research in this area is that individuals and groups understand themselves and their place in the world temporally: they have a well-developed sense of historical consciousness that includes a deeply rooted sense of place as well as understandings of their past which shape their views of the present and future.[107] Researchers in places as diverse as Canada, Ireland, the United States, Spain, Argentina, and Germany have documented widely shared collective understandings of the past drawn from family stories, public history, literature, and sometimes even school history.[108] These accounts often bear little resemblance to academic history, but nevertheless, are powerful forces in shaping the ways in which individuals and groups engage with learning and life.

Collective memory and historical consciousness are essential ingredients of history education and all three are connected to the representations of the arts that will be explored in this volume. We will return to these concepts in the chapters to come.

Indigenous Perspectives in History Education

This scholarly conversation has become increasingly prominent of late. It is centred around the question: How might Indigenous[109] worldviews and Western disciplinary perspectives co-exist in scholarly discourse and in school curriculum in a spirit of reconciliation? Around the world, nation-states and multilateral institutions of governance are increasingly recognizing how colonialism and state educational systems have been used to subjugate Indigenous Peoples and undermine their traditional ways of knowing and engaging with the world. Efforts are in place in many countries to use the education system to address this history of assimilation in ways that will promote reconciliation and foster deeper understandings of Indigenous ways of knowing.

Writing about the history of citizenship education in Australia, for example, Andrew Peterson acknowledges that "the need for recognition of, and reconciliation with, Indigenous Peoples – Aboriginals and Torres Strait Islanders – remains the most central and compelling issue facing Australia today."[110] In Brazil, Maria Auxiliadora Schmidt argues that a key policy direction for education there is to construct a curriculum, particularly a history curriculum, that acknowledges the colonial history of the country and provides space for both Indigenous and Afro-Caribbean histories and perspectives.[111]

Articles 15 and 31 of The United Nations Declaration on the Rights of Indigenous Peoples affirm their right to have their histories and worldviews reflected in education systems both for their own benefit but also for that of the wider society:

> *Article 15*: Indigenous Peoples have the right to the dignity and diversity of their cultures, traditions, histories and aspirations which shall be appropriately reflected in education and public information.
>
> *Article 31*: Indigenous Peoples have the right to maintain, control, protect and develop their cultural heritage, traditional knowledge and traditional cultural expressions ...[112]

Space does not permit a detailed examination of how this conversation is playing out around the world so we will focus on what is happening in Canada, the jurisdiction we know best. We will present some of the issues that are being raised and the answers that are offered, but we note that Canadian scholars have only recently embarked on this journey and any "answers" are provisional.

We write this piece in the wake of the 2015 recommendations of the Truth and Reconciliation Commission of Canada.[113] The Commission defined reconciliation as "an ongoing process of establishing and maintaining respectful relationships,"[114] a definition that is both straightforward and clear and the one that we will use herein. The report noted that "reconciliation is not an Aboriginal problem; it is a Canadian one. Virtually all aspects of Canadian society may need to be reconsidered."[115]

The Truth and Reconciliation Commission findings ushered in what is likely to become a sea change in attitudes towards Indigenous Peoples on the part of non-Indigenous Peoples as they come to a better understanding of the effects of the residential school system, a catastrophic legacy that has been insufficiently acknowledged in Canadian history. Until recently, many Canadians have been unaware of the detrimental effects of the system (and even the system itself), not only on the actual survivors of the experience, but on subsequent generations.

The commission placed much of the responsibility for improving the lives of Indigenous Peoples in Canada squarely on education. Justice Murray Sinclair, Commission Chair, commented, "Education is what got us into this mess … but education is the key to reconciliation."[116] Of the report's 94 calls to action, 13 pertain directly to education. The Commission's calls to action related to curriculum are wide-ranging and significant, encompassing Kindergarten to Grade 12 curriculum policy, content, and learning resources; the teaching of Indigenous spiritual beliefs; curriculum in publicly funded denominational schools; and teacher education. The calls that are most relevant to this discussion are as follows:

(62) We call upon the federal, provincial, and territorial governments, in consultation and collaboration with Survivors, Aboriginal peoples, and educators, to:

i. Make age-appropriate curriculum on residential schools, Treaties, and Aboriginal peoples' historical and contemporary contributions to Canada a mandatory education requirement for Kindergarten to Grade Twelve students.
ii. Provide the necessary funding to post-secondary institutions to educate teachers on how to integrate Indigenous knowledge and teaching methods into classrooms.
iii. Provide the necessary funding to Aboriginal schools to utilize Indigenous knowledge and teaching methods in classrooms.
iv. Establish senior-level positions in government at the assistant deputy minister level or higher dedicated to Aboriginal content in education.

(63) We call upon the Council of Ministers of Education, Canada to maintain an annual commitment to Aboriginal education issues, including:

i. Developing and implementing Kindergarten to Grade Twelve curriculum and learning resources on Aboriginal peoples in Canadian history, and the history and legacy of residential schools.
ii. Sharing information and best practices on teaching curriculum related to residential schools and Aboriginal history.
iii. Building student capacity for intercultural understanding, empathy, and mutual respect.
iv. Identifying teacher-training needs relating to the above.

(64) We call upon all levels of government that provide public funds to denominational schools to require such schools to provide an education on comparative religious studies, which must include a segment on Aboriginal spiritual beliefs and practices developed in collaboration with Aboriginal Elders.[117]

According to Justice Murray Sinclair, five years after publication of the Commission report, the above recommendations have not yet been adequately addressed.[118] However, although provincial and territorial governments have a long way to go to comply with the Commission's calls to action, there have been efforts made to the same ends both prior to and following the Commission report.[119] Provincial and territorial ministries of education have begun to integrate Indigenous knowledges into their curricular mandates.[120] Alberta's current social studies curriculum (2005), incorporates Aboriginal perspectives throughout.[121] One of the outcomes in the grade 11 Alberta social studies curriculum calls for students to "analyze nationalism as an identity, internalized feeling and/or collective consciousness shared by a people, [including] First Nations and Métis nationalism [and] Inuit perspectives."[122] In 2018, Ontario revised its social studies, history and geography, and Canadian and World Studies curricula (Grades 1–9) to incorporate Indigenous content, including information about residential schools. The province released a revised First Nations, Métis, and Inuit Studies curriculum for Grades 9–12 in 2019. These courses "provide opportunities for students to learn about First Nations, Métis and Inuit perspectives, cultures, contributions and histories in areas such as art, literature, law, humanities, politics and history."[123] Teachers in British Columbia are expected to integrate First Peoples' Principles of Learning across all curricular areas.[124]

As discussed in Chapter 1, Canadian history education has traditionally been based on a nation-building framework. Canadian historian and history education scholar Ken Osborne describes the purpose of Canadian history courses in English-speaking Canada until the 1970s, as being "to instill in students a historically rooted sense of Canadian identity and a reasoned pride in the Canadian past. Above all, it was a story of progress … geographic, economic, political, international, or any other."[125] Penney Clark concludes an analysis of representations of Indigenous people in Canadian history textbooks over time by arguing, "The narrative … is overwhelmingly one of progress—progress in taming the wilderness and the people who lived in it at the time of European arrival; progress in establishing orderly (European) systems of law and government; progress in building efficient networks of transportation, communication and trade."[126] It has been challenging for Indigenous people to find a place in this narrative. Mi'kmaq scholar Marie Battiste has called for educators to "help students understand the Eurocentric assumptions of superiority within the context of history and to recognize the continued dominance of these assumptions in all forms of contemporary knowledge."[127]

As discussed earlier, over the past twenty years a new approach to history education has come to the fore. This historical thinking approach involves teaching students that history is a construction based on historians' interpretations of the evidence they use. There are a number of specific frameworks for historical thinking, but common to them all is an emphasis on developing student competencies with the key disciplinary processes of historical work—students are expected not only to know the content of history, but to understand the processes used by historians to construct that content.[128] The model of historical thinking that is most influential in driving policy and curricular reform in public schooling across Canada is that developed by Peter Seixas.[129] Seixas sets out a framework of six historical thinking concepts that are designed to "help students think about how historians transform the past into history and to begin constructing history themselves" (see Chapter 1).[130] This framework, in whole or in part, has been incorporated into provincially mandated curricula and authorized textbooks across Canada.[131]

There has been vigorous scholarly debate in Canada about how to acknowledge Indigenous Peoples and their histories in Canadian history courses. This debate is by no means close to being settled. A central question concerns whether disciplinary approaches to teaching history, such as those embodied in historical thinking frameworks, are in and of themselves colonialist in that they are grounded in a Eurocentric epistemology. Indigenous scholars and others make the argument that it takes much more than a change of topics to Indigenize the curriculum; change must also include a reframing of the nature of knowledge itself. Battiste puts it this way: "Since the 1970s provincial education authorities have taken great strides to include multiculturalism, heritage and treaty rights, and human rights in research, policy reform and inclusive educational practices. But education has not yet transformed the social constructions of Eurocentrism."[132]

Indigenous scholar Michael Marker opens this conversation by describing four themes of Indigenous historical consciousness.[133] They are the circular nature of time as opposed to a more linear concept, relationships with landscapes and non-humans, an emphasis on the local, and Indigenous narratives and perspectives on the histories of colonization.[134] We will briefly discuss each of these in turn.

As Marker correctly states, and as mentioned earlier, "History curricula for schools in Canada have emphasized notions of progress that tend to relegate First Nations to a primitive past on a timeline leading to a more progressive present era."[135] From an Indigenous perspective, history is "rather a spiralling of events and themes that appear and reappear within circles of seasons and that are identified in oral traditions."[136] It is important that Western notions of progress be deconstructed in history classrooms and examined for the assumptions behind them, to determine who is included and excluded, and how to overcome omissions.

Second, Marker argues that when Canadian history textbooks discuss plants and animals, it is within an economic framework in which they are viewed as resources to be exploited by humans. He notes that the Indigenous perspective is very different in that it has a metaphysical dimension which many who work in the Western disciplinary tradition cannot accept. He points out that acceptance would take a "major revision of some taken-for-granted assumptions regarding evidence about the past."[137] It would indeed call for a major revision of ideas about plants and animals, but one could argue that historians' understandings of evidence and its uses are not taken for granted assumptions, but rather, they undergo ongoing examination. The realm of the metaphysical exists in a place that is about as far from the location of Western science as it would be possible to travel. As Seixas says, with regard to history, "animals are not invested with the historical agency that can only be a consequence of intentional action: they cannot occupy the moral ground that is the province of human beings."[138] This is an area where there is a huge difference in perspective and it needs to be carefully, cautiously, and respectfully probed.

The third theme discussed by Marker involves the central place of local histories from an Indigenous perspective. Seixas questions the purpose of considering local histories if we do not look for greater significance beyond their local limits. He notes that, "Students will grapple with multiple narratives, and if there is not one grand narrative that they memorize uncritically, they should still understand the necessity of the quest for larger stories in order to make sense of their lives, and the importance of the search for good ones."[139] Elsewhere, he points out that an emphasis on the local negates the "need to contextualize the specific and local in a larger narrative."[140] One of the criteria stipulated by historians to determine the historical significance of a particular event, individual or development is degree of impact. Disciplinary history probes the deeper meanings that go beyond isolated local events, not only asking if the event or people made a difference at the time, but also what were the long-term effects. According to Seixas, "even the intensely local microhistories of Laurel Thatcher Ulrich, Natalie Zemon Davis, and Carlo Ginzburg elevate their formerly unknown protagonists to a level of historical significance by embedding their stories in larger historical developments, such as evolving medical practice, gender relations and religious beliefs."[141] The idea that the local is of prime importance is in direct contrast to the concept of historical significance. Clearly, this requires "ongoing dialogue."[142]

Marker's fourth theme explores the challenges of "reconcil[ing] a history curriculum that seeks to inculcate national identity and citizenship with indigenous desires to assert sovereignty and reclaim pre-contact understandings of time and space." He suggests that an approach that is more decolonizing would be to consider "a history of their own 'borderless' territory from the perspective of their own traditional way of seeing space [rather than] a telling of how nation-states fought with each other over how to divide Coast Salish land."[143] This option seems quite feasible within a traditional Eurocentric history course, which would continue to include histories of the political entity of Canada.

Independent scholar, Samantha Cutrara contends that historical thinking, as conceptualized by Peter Seixas, is so grounded in Eurocentric knowledge constructions that it is entirely unable to respond to the TRC's Calls to Action.[144] Cutrara sees no opportunity for a historical thinking approach and Indigenous ways of knowing to come together to enrich history education. She states that, "historical thinking as conceptualized by Peter Seixas, imposes a settler grammar over the study of the past in such ways that widens the gulf between Aboriginal and Euro-Canadian knowledge systems, lessening the space available to develop the respect, openness for truth, and room for relationality needed to develop relationships of reconciliation."[145] Seixas, too, argues that historical thinking and Indigenous Knowledges represent two very different paradigms, with significant differences in worldviews, and in particular, understandings about what is knowledge. He points out that a central tenet of historical thinking is the use of evidence to support conclusions. Indigenous knowledges, on the other hand, are based on oral tradition and belief. However, Seixas offers a more hopeful approach. While he recognizes that there are "contradictions and problems," he suggests that they be addressed by means of "ongoing dialogue with Aboriginal scholars,"[146] implicitly acknowledging that we are at the beginning of a lengthy process.

In "One Classroom, Two Teachers?" curriculum theorist Heather McGregor helpfully addresses these same issues. While McGregor acknowledges the tensions between Indigenous and Eurocentric approaches to history, she also sees possibilities for encompassing them both in a history classroom; albeit with more questions than answers at this early stage. McGregor cautions that educators must "resist representing historical thinking itself as a fixed universal or uncontested system for constructing knowledge." She reminds her readers that "historical thinking comes from a particular group of people, in particular places, with culturally situated understandings of the past, of the flow of time and of meanings derived from human experience." She suggests that educators start with "the history of the land where their schools are situated, and the community or Nation with whom they are in relation. Echoing Marker, she suggests they might also move towards a view of Indigenous experience that exceeds the borders and boundaries imposed through colonization such as those of nation states." She calls for "a think-tank and network … focused on the alignment between history and Indigeneity." Finally, she asks six helpful questions that such communities of practice might address:

- What is the role of identity in the production of, and responses to, histories? (of the historian/person sharing the story, and their right to share it at the correct time, of the people in the story in question, of the listener-learner)?
- What unique insights into the past can be accessed through memory and oral history, and how do they relate to other types of primary sources?
- How do histories differently represent responsibility and agency in the past, and produce responsibility/agency in the present?
- How does understanding the intended use/purpose of histories become relevant to understanding their construction (political, social, antiracist etc.)?
- Under what conditions is it useful to acknowledge that we are uncertain about the past and its meaning and what implications does *not knowing* have?
- How does acknowledging the historicity or situatedness of any given system within which histories are constructed help us navigate between more than one system?[147]

Like Heather McGregor and others, history educator James Miles sees more questions than answers at this stage. He contributes to the discussion by pointing to the historical thinking framework to assist teachers in teaching for reconciliation, stating that "the historical thinking concepts provide an important entry point and model for engaging with historical injustice." He goes on to say, "By opening up history to be understood as a human constructed narrative, not a set list of facts, historical thinking provides an essential starting place for challenging existing narratives that may exclude, erase, or silence Indigenous voices." Miles urges greater awareness of the conceptual challenges to which history educators must be attentive. He posits three major tensions related to conceptions of narrativity, temporality, and identity. His first has been discussed here already—that Canadian historical narratives tend to be taught as a nation-building story. He asks, "How should Canadian historical narratives and their representations in curricula and texts, be revised or rethought with reconciliation in mind?" Second, he points to the practice of situating injustice solely in the distant past. He asks, "How can teachers avoid allocating the abuses of settler colonialism to the dustbins of history?"[148] Third, he suggests that teachers and students must, as Roger Simon has put it, develop "a renewed historical consciousness."[149] Here he asks, "How might teachers and students ethically reflect on their individual and collective identities and how they are implicated in the colonial project?"[150]

History educators Lindsay Gibson and Roland Case, argue that "the significant and important changes that history educators must undertake to address the TRC's Calls to Action can be implemented without radical epistemological restructuring of the discipline of history, as some would suggest."[151] They offer three pragmatic recommendations for teaching history in a way that acknowledges Indigenous perspectives, but does not involve radical restructuring. The first recommendation involves strengthening the representations and centrality of Indigenous Peoples in Canadian history courses.[152] They suggest that this can be achieved by these approaches:

- "Introduce significant Indigenous events, developments, and people." The authors mention, as examples, "the history of treaties and landmark court cases, and official non-compliance with their terms" ... [as well as] "the contributions of notable Indigenous leaders ... the developing circumstances and fortunes of Indigenous Peoples interrelated with the evolving profiles of pioneers, settlers, labourers, entrepreneurs, and other groups."
- "Problematize ideology-laded terms." The authors mention "the colonial connotations that seemingly neutral terms often perpetuate." One such example is "references to traditional Aboriginal people's homeland as a wilderness."
- "Present nuanced portrayals of Indigenous people." Provide examples of Indigenous "successes, resilience and sophistication."
- "Embed multiple interpretations, including Indigenous perspectives." This might involve exploring ways to connect teachers with members of local Indigenous communities.
- "Frame inclusive narratives." This involves incorporating Indigenous perspectives, avoiding such narratives as "the march of civilization," the "settlement of the West," and "the conquering of a foreign and hostile land."

- "Showcase Indigenous sources of historical evidence." Historians have increasingly accepted oral histories as legitimate sources of evidence, as has the Supreme Court of Canada.[153]

The second recommendation offered by Gibson and Case is to use an historical thinking approach rather than teaching history as an established body of conclusions. (This involves taking a very different position than Cutrara, who posits that there is no possibility of reconciling a historical thinking approach with the incorporation of Indigenous perspectives in the curriculum.) They suggest that "interpreting historical evidence, challenging problematic assumptions, and identifying the perspectives inherent in the historical narratives they encounter [is] especially important for overcoming the discriminatory views about Indigenous Peoples that students have encountered in school, society, and the media."[154] They caution that teacher professional development is essential to implementing this approach effectively.

The third recommendation offered by Gibson and Case is to "acknowledge the limits of what disciplinary history courses can offer in terms of understanding Indigenous knowledge and worldviews, and recognize the need for a broader, integrated course on Indigenous ways of knowing."[155] Again, they suggest that this approach allows for an integrating of Indigenous perspectives without requiring a complete restructuring of the history curriculum. They also issue a caution that Cutrara's approach implies that students should be encouraged to question the historical conclusions emerging from non-Indigenous people, but to accept without question the historical conclusions emerging from Indigenous knowledge holders.

> Non-Indigenous people can appreciate that Elders and traditional stories have authority within Indigenous communities, but it is a separate matter to require that non-Indigenous people adopt these stories as historical facts. In other words, treating Indigenous and Euro-Canadian knowledge systems with equal respect should be taken to mean that Indigenous worldviews deserve equal respect among other worldviews, but it cannot require that all communities adopt Indigenous worldviews as their own. …. while Elders have much to contribute to our scientific and historical understanding, they are not indisputable authorities in these areas. As such, their

> historical claims are appropriately subject to scrutiny. In the spirit of reconciliation, this seems the fairest method for adjudicating among competing claims.[156]

Gibson and Case identify many stakeholders who must play a part in implementing policies and curricula and in developing appropriate learning resources for reconciliation: "provincial and territorial ministries of education; First Nations, Metis, and Inuit Elders, knowledge holders, and educators; teacher education programs; school boards; teachers' unions; and K-12 schools."[157] It will take a concerted and respectful effort over time on the part of all of these stakeholders to achieve reconciliation in the context of K-12 history teachers, history curriculum, history resources, and classroom instruction. However, the scholarly conversations that are taking place are even more essential at this time because it is by this means that scholars will begin to see ways through the thorny thickets of divergent views. They will begin to sort out the underlying issues and determine to what degree they can be reconciled, or if not reconciled, then how they can respectfully co-exist.

Indigenous activists, scholars, and artists have challenged traditional artistic manifestations of both history and collective memory. For the purposes of this book, we are particularly concerned with the work of the latter which takes at least two forms. The first has been critical engagement with art works and installations including monuments, murals, and paintings that offer uncritical colonial perspectives on the past. This has resulted in calls to historicize, modify, or remove particular works of art. The second form of this work has been to offer creative works that explicitly "[reverse] the colonial gaze" to present Indigenous perspectives on the past and the present.[158] Several of the chapters of this book examine both of these approaches.

Implications for History Education

The fifth scholarly conversation important to our work is in history education. Peter Seixas clearly expresses the importance of history education:

> The challenge for history education is to devise ways to introduce young people to these same historical tools, processes, and ways of thinking [used by historians], not to make them mini-historians, or to give them an early start on academic careers; rather, to help them make sense of who they are,

> where they stand, and what they can do – as individuals, as members of multiple, intersecting groups, and as citizens with roles and responsibilities in relation to nations and states in a complex, conflict-ridden, and rapidly changing world.[159]

There have been a number of critiques of the historical thinking model. According to Seixas, the model "has been accused of being atheoretical, of omitting attention to the interpretive nature of history, of paying insufficient attention to the dynamic interrelationship of past, present, and future captured by the concept of historical consciousness and of drawing insufficient connection among six 'independent' historical thinking concepts."[160] He addresses this in a recent article, "A Model of Historical Thinking," in which he describes the concepts as problems grounded in the fundamental relationship between past and present and points to the ways they are interrelated. As he points out:

> While they look like concepts, the reason they are so generative is that they function, rather, as problems, tensions, or difficulties that demand comprehension, negotiation and, ultimately, an accommodation that is never a complete solution. History takes shape from efforts to work with these problems. Students' abilities to think historically can be defined in terms of their competence in negotiating productive solutions to them.[161]

Ken Osborne has remarked that new work related to the teaching and learning of history "is remarkably a-historical."[162] One explanation that he offers for this situation is that it may be due to the fact that psychologists have been influential in its development. Osborne also notes that the findings may not be as new as its proponents think they are "and there is a long tradition of work in the teaching of history that has for too long remained unknown, leaving each generation of history teachers to reinvent their work anew."[163]

Whether or not we accept fiction as a potential source for historical investigation, or as narratives about the past worth considering in history class, teachers are left with a dilemma: fictional accounts in the form of novels, the historical paintings often found in textbooks, and the commemorative art in the form of monuments and statues that learners see around them every day, are a common source for the collective stories they bring with them to class. The cognitive frames of students have been and continue to be shaped by such fictional accounts of history and a plethora of evidence demonstrates that failure to engage this kind of prior knowledge renders teaching largely ineffectual.[164]

History educators argue that a central purpose of school history is to engage prior knowledge in order to help students acquire more complex and reflective understandings of the past, how it has shaped the present, and might influence the future. Historian Stefan Berger, for example, argues that shared national histories "need to become more self reflective, laying open their own perspectivity and relativity, allowing for a plurality of national perspectives."[165] Similarly, Keith Barton argues that school history should help students understand the contingent nature of their understandings of the past and engage in more reflective and complex identity construction. It is important, then, for teachers to spend some time assessing the personal and shared histories of their students and finding ways to include those as important sources for critically investigating the past.[166]

Part of the conversation about history education involves the implications of constructivism for teaching and learning history, a discussion that is rooted in the "cognitive revolution"[167] of the twentieth century. A central tenet of that revolution is that "prior knowledge matters"[168] to teaching and learning: learners come to any learning situation with a set of cognitive structures that filter and shape new information in powerful ways and these must be understood and engaged for significant cognitive change to occur.[169]

Barton and Levstik provide a clear example from their research of how pre-existing frameworks shape new knowledge. A large body of work in this field demonstrates that American students have a conception of the history of the United States framed by the twin themes of freedom and progress.[170] This view allows for slight deviations from the nation's commitment to freedom or minor setbacks on the road to progress in the American story, but the overall direction of national history is towards greater freedom as well as social and economic progress. Barton and Levstik exposed students to historical sources that countered these ideas and found that "so powerful was the narrative of progress that it led students to distort the historical evidence to fit their preconceptions."[171]

The constructivist premise flowing from this body of research is that understanding students' prior knowledge is an important component of history teaching, as that knowledge has to be confronted and disrupted before new learning can take place. Consequently, scholars from around the world have engaged in numerous studies to map how students understand history. One of the key findings across many studies is that groups of people often have collective understandings of the history of their nation or particular ethno-cultural group. These understandings differ widely across contexts and are often very different from those of academic historians. A recent study of the historical understanding of students in the Catalan region of Spain demonstrates some of this variance.

> In contrast with students elsewhere, Catalan students seem to narrate a decline history. Whereas American[172] and English students[173] narrate a progressive history and German[174] and Northern Irish students[175] narrate an ambivalent history, Catalan students narrate an ambivalent history that … ends with a traumatic event or dramatic climax.[176]

The study *Canadians and their Pasts*,[177] as well as other work,[178] make it clear that these historical frames are shaped by many factors including museums, films, national ceremonies, ethno-cultural festivals, family stories, and literature. A key part of our argument for using historical fiction, historical paintings, and commemorative art in the teaching of history is that it is important for teachers and students to understand its role, whether historically accurate or not, in shaping how people think about the past.

Student assessment is an important part of teaching and learning, but it is only recently that it has begun to receive sufficient attention in scholarly conversations concerning history education. The US National Research Council (NRC) Committee on the Foundations of Assessment has established three components that should form the basis for all assessments: "a model of cognition and learning; assumptions about tasks that are 'most likely to elicit demonstrations' of that cognition; and assumptions about how to interpret the evidence drawn from those demonstrations."[179] To this list, Seixas adds assumptions about educational goals, the ends towards which progress is measured.

Seixas reviews key findings of assessment theorists and researchers, relating them to his own work on perspective taking. The first key finding is that factual material is important. The more that students know, the more competent they will be in confronting the evaluative tasks set out for them. The second key finding is that assessment should contribute to student learning. Third, experiences with historical thinking concepts should build on one another, so that students become increasingly comfortable with more complex aspects of the concepts. Fourth, the process of assessing student work increases teachers' own understandings of historical thinking concepts.[180] We continue this discussion of history education research in Chapter 6 of this volume.

Conclusion

These scholarly conversations are an attempt to capture the essence of five central areas of deliberation inherent in history education at this time. As space is a consideration, this discussion is of necessity truncated. However, brief as the treatment of these conversations is, it brings up a number of questions for consideration. These are only a few:

- Are historians artists? Are artists historians? If so, how?
- Can fiction serve as an authentic and useful source for the purpose of creating historical narratives? If so, how?
- What is the level of responsibility of a historical fiction author to limit the narrative to available evidence?
- Should works of commemorative art be kept in public spaces even when they no longer reflect prevailing views? How might their messages be examined and contextualized?
- How can teachers help students to view historical paintings as constructed accounts created for a range of purposes?
- Why is it important to engage with the collective memories students bring to their history courses?
- How might scholars address the gap between history and collective memory/historical consciousness? How might history educators?
- Are disciplinary approaches to history teaching and learning adequate to address Indigenous Knowledges in ways that are fair, respectful, and productive?
- Should Indigenous Knowledges be open to scholarly critique?

There are many more.

Notes

1. Thucydides, *History of the Peloponnesian War*, trans. R. Warner, intro., and notes M.I. Finley (Penguin, 1972), quoted in John Burrow, *A History of Histories: Epics, Chronicles, Romances & Inquiries from Herodotus and Thucydides to the Twentieth-Century* (London: Penguin 2009), 33.
2. Polybius, *The Rise of the Roman Empire*, trans. I. Scott-Kilvert, selected and intro. F. Walbank (London: Penguin, 1979), quoted in Burrow, *A History of Histories*, 68.
3. Polybius, quoted in Burrow, 73.
4. Some of the material in this chapter first appeared in Penney Clark and Alan Sears, "Fiction, History and Pedagogy: A Double-Edged Sword," *Journal of Curriculum Studies* 49, no. 5 (2017): 620–39, http://doi.org/19.1080/00220272.2016.1238108, https://www.tandfonline.com/toc/tcus20/49/5?nav=tocList. It is used here with permission.
5. Peter Novick, *That Noble Dream: The "Objectivity Question" and the American Historical Profession* (Cambridge: Cambridge University Press, 1988), 1–2.
6. Novick, *That Noble Dream*, 578.
7. Novick, 628.
8. Sarah Maza, *Thinking About History* (Chicago: The University of Chicago Press, 2017), 203–4.
9. Peter Novick, "(The Death of) The Ethics of Historical Practice (and Why I Am Not in Mourning)," *The Annals of the American Academy of Political and Social Science* 560 (November 1998): 37.
10. Novick, "(The Death of) the Ethics of Historical Practice)," 39.
11. Judith Lichtenberg, "The Will to Truth: A Reply to Novick," *The Annals of the American Academy of Political and Social Science* 560 (November 1998): 45.
12. Lichtenberg, "The Will to Truth," 48.
13. Lichtenberg, 52.
14. Lichtenberg, 52.
15. Richard Evans, *In Defence of History* (London: Granta, 2000), 62.
16. Evans, *In Defence of History*, 73.
17. Evans, 74.
18. Evans, 74.
19. Joyce Appleby, Lynn Hunt, and Margaret Jacob, *Telling the Truth About History* (New York and London: W. W. Norton, 1994), 249.
20. Hayden V. White, "The Burden of History," *History and Theory* 5, no. 2 (1966): 134.
21. George Eliot, *Middlemarch* (Oxford: Oxford University Press, 1871/2008).

22. White, "The Burden of History," 116.
23. Hayden White, "Historical Pluralism," *Critical Inquiry* 12, no. 3 (Spring 1986): 487.
24. White, "Historical Pluralism," 487.
25. White, 484.
26. Novick, *That Noble Dream*, 600.
27. Ellen Somekawa and Elizabeth A. Smith, "Theorizing the Writing of History or, 'I Can't Think Why It Should Be so Dull for a Great Deal of It Must Be Invention,'" *Journal of Social History* 22, no. 1 (Fall 1988): 149–61, quoted in Evans, 64.
28. Evans, 257.
29. Barbara Tuchman, *Practicing History: Selected Essays* (New York: Random House, 1981), 19.
30. John Lewis Gaddis, *The Landscape of History: How Historians Map the Past* (Oxford, UK: Oxford University Press, 2002), 3.
31. Jonathan Nield, *Guide to the Best Historical Novels and Tales*, Project Gutenberg e-book, www.gutenbeg.org/etext/1359, quoted in Jerome de Groot, *The Historical Novel* (London and New York: Routledge, 2010), 5.
32. Christopher Kremmer, "From Dialectics to Dialogue: Bakhtin, White and the 'Moorings' of Fiction and History," *TEXT* 28 (April 2015): 2.
33. Appleby, Hunt, and Jacob, *Telling the Truth About History*, 253.
34. Paul Bonnifield, *The Dust Bowl: Men, Dirt, and Depression* (Albuquerque: University of New Mexico Press, 1979), 202, quoted in William Cronon, "A Place for Stories: Nature, History, and Narrative," *The Journal of American History* 78, no. 4 (March 1992): 1348.
35. Cronon, "A Place for Stories," 1363.
36. Donald Worster, *Dust Bowl: The Southern Plains in the 1930s* (New York, 1979), 4, quoted in Cronon, "A Place for Stories," 1348.
37. Cronon, "A Place for Stories," 1348.
38. Cronon, "A Place for Stories," 1373, 1373, 1374.
39. Maza, *Thinking About History*, 13.
40. Kremmer, "From Dialectics to Dialogue," 2.
41. Kremmer, 7.
42. Gaddis, *The Landscape of History*, 2.
43. de Groot, *The Historical Novel*, 113.
44. Gaddis, *The Landscape of History*, 43.
45. de Groot, *The Historical Novel*, 182.
46. Katherine Ashenburg, "March, to a Different Tune: The Many Modernizations of Alcott's Little Women," *Globe & Mail*, February 8, 2020, R3.
47. Edward Thompson, *Making of the English Working Class* (New York: Vintage Books, 1963).

48. Peter Burke, *What Is Cultural History?*, Second edition (Malden, MA: Polity, 2008), 128.
49. Peter Burke, *Eyewitnessing: The Uses of Images as Historical Evidence* (Ithaca, NY: Cornell University Press, 2001), 161.
50. David Harlan, "Historical Fiction and the Future of Academic History," in *Manifestos for History*, ed. Keith Jenkins, Sue Morgan, and Alun Munslow (London: Routledge, 2007), 118.
51. Hayden White, "The Public Relevance of Historical Studies: A Reply to Dirk Moses," *History and Theory* 44, no. 3 (October 2005): 333, quoted in Harlan, "Historical Fiction and the Future of Academic History," 115.
52. Harlan, 122–23.
53. Ann Rigney, "Fiction as a Mediator in National Remembrance," in *Narrating the Nation: Representations in History; Media and the Arts*, ed. Stefan Berger, Linas Eriksonas, and Andrew Mycock (New York: Berghahn, 2008), 93.
54. Rigney, "Fiction as a Mediator in National Remembrance," 80.
55. Rigney, 80.
56. Alison Landsberg, *Prosthetic Memory: The Transformation of American Remembrance in the Age of Mass Culture* (New York: Columbia University Press, 2004), quoted in Rigney, "Fiction as a Mediator in National Remembrance," 87.
57. Rigney, "Fiction as a Mediator in National Remembrance," 87.
58. Dan Fumano, "Report on Historical Wrongs 'About Now and Future,'" *Vancouver Sun*, December 30, 2019, A1.
59. Wulf Kansteiner, "Finding Meaning in Memory: A Methodological Critique of Collective Memory Studies," *History and Theory* 41, no. 2 (May 2002): 181. See also Patrick Hutton, *History as an Art of Memory* (Hanover, NH: University Press of New England, 1993), 180.
60. Barry Schwartz, *Abraham Lincoln and the Forge of National Memory* (Chicago: University of Chicago Press, 2000), xi, quoted in Kansteiner, "Finding Meaning in Memory," 189.
61. John Bodnar, *Remaking America: Public Memory, Commemoration, and Patriotism in the Twentieth Century* (Princeton: Princeton University Press, 1992), 15, quoted in James V. Wertsch, *Voices of Collective Remembering* (Cambridge: Cambridge University Press, 2002), 24. When quoting, we will use the term employed by the author being quoted. Otherwise, we will use the term "collective memory."
62. Wertsch, *Voices of Collective Remembering*, 70.
63. Peter Seixas, "What Is Historical Consciousness?" in *To the Past: History Education, Public Memory, & Citizenship in Canada*, ed. Ruth Sandwell (Toronto: University of Toronto Press, 2006), 12.

64. Ken Osborne, "Teaching Canadian History: A Century of Debate," in *New Possibilities for the Past Shaping History Education in Canada*, ed. Penney Clark (Vancouver, BC: UBC Press, 2011), 56. Teaching history in K-12 classrooms has been at the intersection of collective memory and individual memory because much of it has involved memorization of information in the hope that knowing about their country would encourage students to develop an emotional connection to it. It was thought that nurturing individual memory would, in turn, nurture development of collective memory. Alan Sears illustrates the tension between this nationalistic approach to fostering collective memory and more disciplinary approaches to history education in a number of jurisdictions around the world in "Trends and Issues in History Education in International Contexts," *Debates in History Teaching*, ed. Ian Davies, Second edition, 42–52 (London and New York: Routledge, 2017).
65. Canada has several national organizations that target schools and the public at large in an effort to promote a stronger sense of national identity. The main goal of the non-profit organization Historica Canada, for example, is "enhancing awareness of Canadian history and citizenship" (Historica Canada, retrieved December 16, 2018 at https://www.historicacanada.ca/about). This organization provides learning tools for teachers; as well as other resources for teachers and for members of the public; including the *Heritage Minutes*, online vignettes related to topics about Canadian history; and *The Canadian Encyclopedia*, a free online reference book.
66. Bodnar, *Remaking America*, 15, quoted in Wertsch, *Voices of Collective Remembering*, 33.
67. James Wertsch, "Is It Possible to Teach Beliefs, as Well as Knowledge About History?" in *Knowing, Teaching & Learning History: National and International Perspectives*, ed. Peter N. Stearns, Peter Seixas, and Sam Wineburg (New York: New York University Press, 2000), 48.
68. Maza, *Thinking About History*, 55–56.
69. Marita Sturken, *Tangled Memories: The Vietnam War, the AIDS Epidemic, and the Politics of Remembering* (Berkeley: University of California Press, 1997), 259.
70. Seixas, "What Is Historical Consciousness?" 11.
71. Pierra Nora, *Realms of Memory: Rethinking the French Past*, trans. Arthur Goldhammer (New York: Columbia University Press, 1996).
72. Peter Seixas, "A History/Memory Matrix for History Education," *Public History Weekly—The International Blogjournal* 4, no. 6 (2016), https://doi.org/10.1515/phw-2016-5370.

73. Peter Novick, *The Holocaust in American Life* (Boston: Houghton Mifflin Company, 1999), 4.
74. Maurice Halbwachs, *The Collective Memory*, trans. Francis J. Didder Jr. and Vida Yazdi Ditter (New York: Harper & Row, 1980).
75. Wertsch, *Voices of Collective Remembering*, 46.
76. Wertsch, 43–45.
77. Kansteiner, "Finding Meaning in Memory," 188–89.
78. Pierre Nora, "Between Memory and History: Les Lieux de memoire," *Representations* 26 (Spring 1989): 22.
79. "Controversial Cornwallis Statue Removed from Halifax Park," CBC News, January 31, 2018, https://www.cbc.ca/news/canada/nova-scotia/cornwallis-statue-removal-1.4511858; "John A. Macdonald statue removed from Victoria City Hall," CBC News August 11, 2018, https://www.cbc.ca/news/canada/british-columbia/john-a-macdonald-statue-victoria-city-hall-lisa-helps-1.4782065.
80. Seixas, "A History/Memory Matrix for History Education" 1.
81. Seixas, 4.
82. Stéphane Lévesque and Jean-Philippe Croteau, *Beyond History for Historical Consciousness: Students, Narrative, and Memory* (Toronto: University of Toronto Press, 2020), 16–18.
83. Lévesque and Croteau, *Beyond History for Historical Consciousness*, 15–16. The references to the colours of the various components of the matrix are taken from Stéphane Lévesque, "Going Beyond 'Narratives' vs. 'Competencies': A model of history education," *Public History Weekly* 4 (2016): 12, https://doi.org/10.1515/phw-2016-5918. *Beyond History for Historical Consciousness* does not mention colours because the model is black and white.
84. Lévesque and Croteau, 16–17.
85. Lévesque and Croteau, 20.
86. Lévesque and Croteau, 17–18.
87. Lévesque and Croteau, 161–65.
88. Seixas, "Author's Reply, A History/Memory Matrix for History Education," 2016.
89. Maria Grever and Robbert-Jan Adriaansen, "Historical Consciousness: The Enigma of Different Paradigms," *Journal of Curriculum Studies* 51, no. 6 (2019): 815.
90. Anna Clark and Carla L. Peck, "Introduction: Historical Consciousness, Theory and Practice," in *Contemplating Historical Consciousness: Notes from the Field*, ed. Anna Clark and Carla L. Peck (New York and Oxford: Berghahn Books, 2019): 2.
91. Gaddis, *The Landscape of* History, 10.
92. Gaddis, 11.

93. Paul Zanazanian, "History Teaching and Narrative Tools: Towards Integrating English-Speaking Youth into Quebec's Social Fabric," *Minorités linguistiqes et Société/Linguistic Minorities and Society* 7 (2016): 9–10, https://doi.org/10.7202/1036417ar.
94. Peter Seixas, "Historiographies and Historical Consciousness," in *Theorizing Historical Consciousness*, ed. Peter Seixas (Toronto, ON: University of Toronto Press, 2004), 22.
95. Jörn Rüsen, "Historical Consciousness: Narrative Structure, Moral Function, and Ontogenetic Development," in *Theorizing Historical Consciousness*, ed. Peter Seixas (Toronto, ON: University of Toronto Press, 2004): 75.
96. Rüsen, "Historical Consciousness," 77.
97. A.J.P. Taylor, *Origins of the Second World War* (London: Penguin, 1964).
98. Peter Seixas, "Historical Consciousness and Historical Thinking," in *Palgrave Handbook of Research in Historical Culture and Education*, ed. Mario Carretero, Stefan Berger, and Maria Grever, 59–72 (London: Palgrave Macmillan, 2017), 61; Klas-Göran Karlsson, "Processing Time: On the Activation and Manifestation of Historical Consciousness," in *Historicizing the Uses of the Past: Scandinavian Perspectives on History, Culture, Historical Consciousness and Didactics of History Related to World War II*, ed. Helle Bjerg, Claudia Lenz, and Erik Thorstensen, 129–43 (New Brunswick, NJ: Transaction Publishers, 2011).
99. Catherine Duquette, "Relating Historical Consciousness to Historical Thinking Through Assessment," in *New Directions in Assessing Historical Thinking*, ed. Kadriye Ercikan and Peter Seixas, 51–63 (New York and London: Routledge, 2015). Duquette's work has been informed by the work of Christian Laville. See "Historical Consciousness and Historical Education: What to Expect from the First for the Second," in *Theorizing Historical Consciousness*, ed. Peter Seixas, 165–82 (Toronto, ON: University of Toronto Press, 2004) and also Robert Martineau, *L'Histoire a l'Ecole, Matiere a Penser* (Montreal, QC: L'Harmattan, 1999).
100. Seixas, "Historical Consciousness and Historical Thinking," 64.
101. Duquette, "Relating Historical Consciousness to Historical Thinking Through Assessment," 53.
102. Andreas Körber, "German History Didactics: From Historical Consciousness to Historical Competencies—And Beyond?" in *Historicizing the Uses of the Past: Scandinavian Perspectives on History Culture, Historical Consciousness and Didactics of History Related to World War II*, ed. Helle Bjerg, Claudia Lenz, and Erik Thorstensen (Piscataway, NJ: Transaction Publishers, Rutgers University, 2011), 148.

103. Andreas Körber and Johannes Meyer-Hamme, "Historical thinking, Competencies, and Their Measurement: Challenges and Approaches," in *New Directions in Assessing Historical Thinking*, ed. Kadriye Ercikan and Peter Seixas (New York and London: Routledge, 2015), 93–94; see also Carlos Köbl and Lisa Konrad, "Historical Consciousness in Germany: Concept, Implementation, Assessment," in *New Directions in Assessing Historical Thinking*, ed. Kadriye Ercikan and Peter Seixas, 17–28 (New York: Routledge, 2015).
104. Grever and Adriaansen, "Historical Consciousness," 819.
105. This categorization is from Stéphane Lévesque and Penney Clark, "Historical Thinking: Definitions and Educational Applications," in *The Wiley International Handbook of History Teaching and Learning*, ed. Scott Alan Metzger and Lauren McArthur Harris (Hoboken, NJ: Wiley, 2018), 125–26. See Lévesque and Clark for an extensive list of studies that examine these aspects of historical learning.
106. Peter Seixas, "Assessment of Historical Thinking," in *New Possibilities for the Past: Shaping History Education in Canada*, ed. Penney Clark (Vancouver, BC: UBC Press, 2011), 141. These were first articulated by Arie Wilschut, "History Teaching at the Mercy of Politicians and Ideologies," *Journal of Curriculum Studies* 42, no. 5 (2010): 693–723.
107. Hilary Cooper and Jon Nichol, *Identity Trauma, Sensitive and Controversial Issues in the Teaching of History* (Newcastle upon Tyne: Cambridge Scholars Press, 2015); Mario Carretero, Mikel Asensio, and Maria Rodríguez-Moneo, ed., *History Education and the Construction of National Identities* (Charlotte, NC: Information Age, 2012).
108. Keith Barton, "A Sociocultural Perspective on Children's Understanding of Historical Change: Comparative Findings from Northern Ireland and the United States," *American Educational Research Journal* 38 (January 2001): 881–913; Mario Carretero, Cesar Lopez, M.F. González, and M. Rodríguez-Moneo, "Students' Historical Narratives and Concepts About the Nation," in *History Education and the Construction of National Identities*, ed. Mario Carretero, Mikel Asensio, and Maria Rodríguez-Moneo, 153–70 (Charlotte, NC: Information Age, 2012); S. Moller, "Are Family Recollections an Obstacle to History Education? How German Students Make Sense of the East German Dictatorship," in *History Education and the Construction of National Identities*, ed. Mario Carretero, Mikel Asensio, and Maria Rodríguez-Moneo, 281–95 (Charlotte NC: Information Age, 2012); The Pasts Collective: Margaret Conrad, Kadriye Ercikan, Gerald Friesen, Jocelyn Létourneau, Delphin Muise, David Northrup, and Peter Seixas, *Canadians and Their Pasts* (Toronto, ON: University of Toronto Press, 2013); Alan McCully and Fionnuala Waldron, "A Question of Identity? Purpose, Policy and Practice in the Teaching of History in Northern Ireland and the Republic of Ireland,"

in *Identity, Trauma, Sensitive and Controversial Issues in the Teaching of History*, ed. Hilary Cooper and Jon Nichol, 2–24 (Newcastle upon Tyne: Cambridge Scholars, 2015); Edda Sant, Neus González-Monfort, Antoni Santesteban Fernandez, Jorn Pages Blanch, and Montserrat Oller Freixa, "How do Catalan Students Narrate the History of Catalonia When They Finish Primary Education?" *McGill Journal of Education* 50, no. 2/3 (Spring/Fall 2015): 341–62.

109. Indigenous refers to First Peoples of North America and internationally. It is our term of choice in this discussion. We use the term Aboriginal only when we are referring to works that use that term. Aboriginal is recognized in the Canadian Constitution Act of 1982 and incorporates Indians, Métis and Inuit Peoples. We note that First Nations, a term for which there is no legal definition, is widely used now to replace the term Indian and refers to particular groups of "Indians."
110. Andrew Peterson, "Australia," in *Education, Globalization and the Nation*, ed. Eric King Man Chong, Ian Davies, Terrie Epstein, Carla L. Peck, Andrew Peterson, Alistair Ross, Maria Auxiliadora Schmidt, Alan Sears, and Debbie Sonu (Hampshire, UK: Palgrave MacMillan, 2016), 21.
111. Maria Auxiliadora Schmidt, "Brazil," in *Education, Globalization and the Nation*, 41–58.
112. United Nations. "United Nations Declaration on the Rights of Indigenous Peoples" (New York: United Nations, 2008), 7 and 11, https://www.un.org/esa/socdev/unpfii/documents/DRIPS_en.pdf.
113. This commission arose from the Indian Residential Schools Settlement Agreement, the largest class action lawsuit in Canadian history. The commission spent six years travelling across the country hearing from more than 6000 witnesses. It also conducted extensive examinations of archival records.
114. Truth and Reconciliation Commission of Canada, *Final Report of the Truth and Reconciliation Commission of Canada, Vol. 1: Summary: Honouring the Truth, Reconciling for the Future* (Toronto, ON: James Lorimer, 2015), 16.
115. Truth and Reconciliation Commission, *Final Report*, vi.
116. H. Watters, "Truth and Reconciliation Chair Urges Adoption of UN Declaration on Indigenous Peoples," CBC News, June 2, 2015, retrieved April 22, 2019, https://www.cbc.ca/news/politics/truth-and-reconciliation-chair-urges-canada-to-adopt-un-declaration-on-indigenous-peoples-1.3096225.

117. Truth and Reconciliation Commission, *Final Report*, 331, Calls_to_Action_English2.pdf.
118. Faculty of Education, UBC, *The Dean's Distinguished Lecture with Senator Murray Sinclair*, November 19, 2019, retrieved December 1, 2019, https://educ.ubc.ca/deansdistinguishedlecture/.
119. In Canada it is the provinces and territories, rather than the federal government, that have a constitutional responsibility for education.
120. See James Rowinski and Alan Sears, "Unsettled Histories: Transgressing History Education Practice in New Brunswick, Canada," *Historical Encounters*, accepted, for a discussion of the possibilities and challenges of integrating Indigenous knowledge systems into a provincial curriculum.
121. Alberta Education, *Social Studies K-Grade 12*, 2005, retrieved December 9, 2019, http://www.learnalberta.ca/ProgramOfStudy.aspx?lang=en&ProgramId=564423.
122. Alberta Education, *Social Studies K-Grade 12*, revised 2007, social-studies-k-6-pos.pdf.
123. Ontario Ministry of Education, *First Nations, Métis and Inuit Studies Curriculum* (Toronto: Queen's Printer for Ontario, 2019).
124. *First Peoples Principles of Learning*, retrieved December 8, 2019, https://firstpeoplesprinciplesoflearning.wordpress.com/.
125. Osborne, "Teaching Canadian History: A Century of Debate," 56. Also see Timothy J. Stanley, "Whose Public? Whose Memory? Racisms, Grand Narratives and Canadian History," in *To the Past: History Education, Public Memory, & Citizenship in Canada*, ed. Ruth W. Sandwell (Toronto, ON: University of Toronto Press, 2006), 32–49.
126. Penney Clark, "Representations of Aboriginal people in English Canadian History Textbooks: Toward Reconciliation," in *Teaching the Violent Past: History Education and Reconciliation*, ed. Elizabeth A. Cole (Lanham, MD: Rowman & Littlefield and Carnegie Council for Ethics in International Affairs, 2007), 111.
127. Marie Battiste, *Decolonizing Education: Nourishing the Learning Spirit* (Saskatoon, SK: Purich Publishing, 2013), 186.
128. Stéphane Lévesque, *Thinking Historically: Educating Students for the Twenty-First Century* (Toronto, ON: University of Toronto Press, 2004); Peter N. Stearns, Peter Seixas, and Sam Wineburg, ed., *Knowing, Teaching and Learning History: National and International Perspectives* (New York: New York University Press, 2000); Lévesque and Clark, "Historical Thinking," 119–48.
129. Peter Seixas, "A Model of Historical Thinking," *Educational Philosophy and Theory* 49, no. 6 (2017): 593–605, https://doi.org/10.1080/00131857.2015.1101363.

130. Peter Seixas and Tom Morton, *The Big Six Historical Thinking Concepts* (Toronto, ON: Nelson Education, 2013), 4.
131. Peter Seixas and Jill Colyer, *From the Curriculum to the Classroom: More Teachers, More Students, More Thinking: A Report on the National Meeting of the Historical Thinking Project*, Toronto, ON: January 23–25, 2014, available at: http://historicalthinking.ca/sites/default/files/files/docs/HTP2014_EN.pdf; Peter Seixas, "Indigenous Historical Consciousness: An Oxymoron or a Dialogue?" in *History Education and the Construction of National Identities*, ed. Mario Carretero, Mikal Asensio, and Maria Rodríguez-Moneo (Charlotte, NC: Information Age Publishing, 2012), 131.
132. Marie Battiste, ed., *Living Treaties: Narrating Mi'kmaw Relations* (Sydney, NS: Cape Breton University Press, 2016), 3.
133. Michael Marker, "Teaching History from an Indigenous Perspective," in *New Possibilities for the Past: Shaping History Education in Canada*, ed. Penney Clark (Vancouver, BC: UBC Press, 2011), 97–112.
134. In "Indigenous Historical Consciousness," Seixas points to the dangers of over-generalizing by implying that all Indigenous people have these understandings, but does not explore this.
135. Marker, "Teaching History from an Indigenous Perspective," 101.
136. Marker, 100.
137. Michael Marker, "The 'Realness' of Place in the Spiral of Time: Reflections on Indigenous Historical Consciousness from the Coast Salish Territory," in *Contemplating Historical Consciousness: Notes from the Field*, ed. Anna Clark and Carla L. Peck (New York: Berghahn Books, 2019), 193.
138. Seixas, "Indigenous Historical Consciousness," 134.
139. Peter Seixas, "Teaching Rival Histories," *Paedagogica Historica* 48, no. 6 (2012), 871.
140. Seixas, "Indigenous Historical Consciousness," 132.
141. Seixas, "Indigenous Historical Consciousness," 129; Natalie Zemon Davis, *The Return of Martin Guerre* (Cambridge: Harvard University Press, 1983); Carlo Ginzburg, *The Cheese and the Worms: The Cosmos of a Sixteenth-Century Miller*, trans. J.A.A.C. Tedeschi (Baltimore: John Hopkins University Press, 1992); Laurel Thatcher Ulrich, *A Midwife's Tale: The Life of Martha Ballard, Based on Her Diary* (New York: Knopf, 1990).
142. Seixas, "Indigenous Historical Consciousness," 132.
143. Marker, "Teaching History from an Indigenous Perspective," 110–11; 110.
144. Samantha Cutrara, "The Settler Grammar of Canadian History Curriculum: Why Historical Thinking Is Unable to Respond to the TRC's Calls to Action," *Canadian Journal of Education* 41, no. 1 (2018): 253.
145. Cutrara, "The Settler Grammar," 253–54.

146. Seixas, "Indigenous Historical Consciousness," 132.
147. Heather McGregor, "One Classroom Two Teachers? Historical Thinking and Indigenous Education in Canada," *Critical Education* 8, no. 14, October 15, 2017, 13, 13, 5. 14. 14.
148. James Miles, "Teaching History for Truth and Reconciliation: The Challenges and Opportunities of Narrativity, Temporality, and Identity," *McGill Journal of Education* 53, no. 2 (Spring 2018): 302–4, 306.
149. Roger I. Simon, *The Touch of the Past: Remembrance, Learning and Ethics* (New York: Palgrave Macmillan, 2005), 94, quoted in Miles, "Teaching History for Truth and Reconciliation," 296.
150. Miles, "Teaching History for Truth and Reconciliation," 303.
151. Lindsay Gibson and Roland Case, "Reshaping Canadian History Education in Support of Reconciliation," *Canadian Journal of Education* 42, no. 1 (2019): 253.
152. Gibson and Case, "Reshaping Canadian History Education," 255–64.
153. Gibson and Case, 256, 256, 257, 257, 258, 258.
154. Gibson and Case, 254.
155. Gibson and Case, 273.
156. Gibson and Case, 275.
157. Gibson and Case, 276.
158. Jessica Wong, "'Big, Bold, Audacious' Kent Monkman Artworks 'at Home' at the Met, Says Curator," CBC, December 17, 2019, https://www.cbc.ca/news/entertainment/kent-monkman-met-new-paintings-1.5395216.
159. Seixas, "What Is Historical Consciousness?" 21.
160. Seixas, "A Model of Historical Thinking."
161. Seixas, 597.
162. Osborne, "*Knowing Teaching and Learning History*," 554.
163. Osborne, 554.
164. Alan Sears, "Children's Understandings of Democratic Participation: Lessons for Civic Education," in *Civic Education and Youth Political Participation*, ed. Murray Print and Henry Milner, 143–58 (Rotterdam: Sense 2009); Alan Sears, "Historical Thinking and Citizenship Education: It Is Time to End the War," in *New Possibilities for the Past: Shaping History Education in Canada*, ed. Penney Clark, 344–64 (Vancouver, BC: UBC Press, 2011).
165. Stefan Berger, "De-nationalizing History Teaching and Nationalizing it Differently! Some Reflections on How to Defuse the Negative Potential of National(ist) History Teaching," in *History Education and the Construction of National Identities*, ed. Mario Carretero, Mikel Asensio and Maria Rodríguez-Moneo (Charlotte, NC: Information Age, 2012), 43.

166. Keith C. Barton, "History Education and Teacher Preparation in the United States," in *History Teacher Education: Global Interrelations*, ed. Elisabeth Erdmann and Wolfgang Hasberg, 175–89 (Schwalbach/Ts, DE: Wochenschau-Verlag, 2015).
167. Howard Gardner, *The Development and Education of the Mind: The Selected Works of Howard Gardner* (London: Routledge, 2006), 74.
168. Sears, 2009, 145.
169. David Ausubel, Helen Hanesian, and Joseph D. Novak, *Educational Psychology: A Cognitive View* (New York: Holt Rinehart and Winston, 1968); Jean Lave and Etienne Wenger, *Situated Learning: Legitimate Peripheral Participation* (Cambridge: Cambridge University Press, 1991); George Posner, Kenneth A. Strike, Peter W. Hewson, and William A. Gertzog, "Accommodation of a Scientific Conception: Toward a Theory of Conceptual Change," *Science Education* 66 (April 1982): 211–27; Mark Windschitl, "Framing Constructivism in Practice as the Negotiation of Dilemmas: An Analysis of the Conceptual, Pedagogical, Cultural, and Political Challenges Facing Teachers," *Review of Educational Research* 72 (Summer 2002): 131–75.
170. Keith Barton and Linda Levstik, *Teaching History for the Common Good* (Mahwah, NJ: Lawrence Erlbaum 2004).
171. Barton and Levstik, *Teaching History for the Common Good*, 170.
172. Keith Barton and Linda Levstik "'It Wasn't a Good Part of History': National Identity and Students' Explanations of Historical Significance," *Teachers College Record* 99 (1998): 478–513.
173. Peter Lee, "'Walking Backwards into Tomorrow': Historical Consciousness and Understanding of History," *International Journal of Historical Learning, Teaching and Research* 4, no. 1 (2004): 1–46.
174. Bodo von Borries, "Concepts of Historical Thinking and Historical Learning in the Perspective of German Students and Teachers," *International Journal of Education Research* 27, no. 3 (1997): 211–20.
175. Keith Barton, "'Oh, That's a Tricky Piece!' Children, Mediated Action and the Tools of Historical Time," *The Elementary School Journal* 103 (2002): 161–85.
176. Sant, Gonzalez-Monfort, Fernandez, Blanch, and Freixa, "How Do Catalan Students Narrate the History of Catalonia When They Finish Primary Education?" 354.
177. The Pasts Collective, *Canadians and Their Pasts*, 2013.
178. Keith Barton, "History Education and Teacher Preparation in the United States," in *History Education and the Construction of National Identities*, ed. Mario Carretero, Mikel Asensio, and Maria Rodríguez-Moneo (Charlotte, NC: Information Age, 2012); McCully and Waldron, "A Question of Identity?" 2–24.

179. James W. Pellegrino, Nancy Chudowsky, and Robert Glaser, eds., *Knowing What Students Know: The Science and Design of Educational Assessment* (Washington: National Academy Press, 2001), quoted in Seixas, "Assessment of Historical Thinking," 139; see also Kadriye Ercikan and Peter Seixas, ed. *New Directions in Assessing Historical Thinking* (New York: Routledge), 2015.
180. Seixas, "Assessment of Historical Thinking," 152.

Bibliography

Alberta Education. *Social Studies K-Grade 12*, 2005. Retrieved December 9, 2019 at http://www.learnalberta.ca/ProgramOfStudy.aspx?lang=en&ProgramId=564423.

Alberta Education. *Social Studies K-Grade 12*, revised 2007. Retrieved at social-studies-k-6-pos.pdf.

Appleby, Joyce, Lynn Hunt, and Margaret Jacob. *Telling the Truth About History*. New York and London: W. W. Norton, 1994.

Ashenburg, Katherine. "March, to a Different Tune: The Many Modernizations of Alcott's Little Women." *Globe & Mail*, February 8, 2020, R3.

Austen, Jane. *Pride and Prejudice*. London: T. Egerton, 1813, e-book ed., R.W. Chapman, Project Gutenberg, May 9, 2013.

Ausubel, David, Helen Hanesian, and Joseph D. Novak. *Educational Psychology: A Cognitive View*. New York: Holt, Rinehart and Winston, 1968.

Barton, Keith C. "A Sociocultural Perspective on Children's Understanding of Historical Change: Comparative Findings from Northern Ireland and the United States." *American Educational Research Journal* 38 (January 2001): 881–913.

Barton, Keith C. "'Oh That's a Tricky Piece!' Children, Mediated Action, and the Tools of Historical Time." *The Elementary School Journal* 103 (2002): 161–85.

Barton, Keith C. "History Education and Teacher Preparation in the United States." In *History Teacher Education: Global Interrelations*, edited by Elisabeth Erdmann and Wolfgang Hasberg, 175–89. Schwalbach/Ts, DE: Wochenschau-Verlag, 2015.

Barton, Keith C. and Linda Levstik. "'It Wasn't A Good Part of History': National Identity and Students' Explanations of Historical Significance." *Teachers College Record* 99 (1998): 478–513.

Barton, Keith C. and Linda Levstik. *Teaching History for the Common Good*. Mahwah, NJ: Lawrence Erlbaum, 2004.

Battiste, Marie. *Decolonizing Education: Nourishing the Learning Spirit*. Saskatoon, SK: Purich Publishing, 2013.

Battiste, Marie, ed. *Living Treaties: Narrating Mi'kmaw Relations*. Sydney, NS: Cape Breton University Press, 2016.

Berger, Stefan. "De-nationalizing History Teaching and Nationalizing It Differently! Some Reflections on How to Defuse the Negative Potential of National(ist) History Teaching." In *History Education and the Construction of National Identities*, edited by Mario Carretero, Mikel Asensio, and Maria Rodríguez-Moneo, 33–47. Charlotte, NC: Information Age, 2012.

Blight, David W. *Race and Reunion: The Civil War in American History*. Cambridge, MA and London, UK: The Belknap Press of Harvard University Press, 2001.

Bodnar, John. *Remaking America: Public Memory, Commemoration, and Patriotism in the Twentieth Century*. Princeton: Princeton University Press, 1992.

Bonnifield, Paul. *The Dust Bowl: Men, Dirt, and Depression*. Albuquerque: University of New Mexico Press, 1979.

Burke, Peter. *Eyewitnessing: The Uses of Images as Historical Evidence*. Ithaca, NY: Cornell University Press, 2001.

Burke, Peter. *What Is Cultural History?* Second edition. Malden, MA: Polity, 2008.

Burrow, John. *A History of Histories: Epics, Chronicles, Romances & Inquiries from Herodotus and Thucydides to the Twentieth-Century*. London: Penguin, 2009.

Carretero, Mario, Cesar Lopez, M.F. González, and M. Rodríguez-Moneo. "Students' Historical Narratives and Concepts About the Nation." In *History Education and the Construction of National Identities*, edited by Mario Carretero, Mikel Asensio, and Maria Rodríguez-Moneo, 153–70. Charlotte, NC: Information Age, 2012.

Carretero, Mario, Mikel Asensio, and Maria Rodríguez-Moneo, eds. *History Education and the Construction of National Identities*. Charlotte, NC: Information Age, 2012.

Clark, Anna and Carla L. Peck. "Introduction: Historical Consciousness, Theory and Practice." In *Contemplating Historical Consciousness: Notes from the Field*, edited by Anna Clark and Carla L. Peck, 1–15. New York and Oxford: Berghahn Books, 2019.

Clark, Penney. "Representations of Aboriginal People in English Canadian History Textbooks: Toward Reconciliation." In *Teaching the Violent Past: History Education and Reconciliation*, edited by Elizabeth A. Cole, 81–120. Lanham, MD: Rowman & Littlefield and Carnegie Council for Ethics in International Affairs, 2007.

Clark, Penney and Alan Sears. "Fiction, History and Pedagogy: A Double-Edged Sword." *Journal of Curriculum Studies* 49, no. 5 (2017): 620–39.

"Controversial Cornwallis Statue Removed from Halifax Park." CBC News, January 31, 2018. https://www.cbc.ca/news/canada/nova-scotia/cornwallis-statue-removal-1.4511858.
Cooper, Hilary and Jon Nichol, eds. *Identity Trauma, Sensitive and Controversial Issues in the Teaching of History*. Newcastle upon Tyne: Cambridge Scholars Press, 2015.
Cronon, William. "A Place for Stories: Nature, History, and Narrative." *The Journal of American History* 78, no. 4 (March 1992): 1347–76.
Cutrara, Samantha. "The Settler Grammar of Canadian History Curriculum: Why Historical Thinking Is Unable to Respond to the TRC's Calls to Action." *Canadian Journal of Education* 41, no. 1 (2018): 250–75.
Davis, Natalie Zemon. *The Return of Martin Guerre*. Cambridge: Harvard University Press, 1983.
de Groot, Jerome. *The Historical Novel*. London and New York: Routledge, 2010.
Duquette, Catherine. "Relating Historical Consciousness to Historical Thinking Through Assessment." In *New Directions in Assessing Historical Thinking*, edited by Kadriye Ercikan and Peter Seixas, 50–63. Toronto, ON: University of Toronto Press, 2015.
Eliot, George. *Middlemarch*. Oxford: Oxford University Press, 1871/2008.
Ercikan, Kadriye and Peter Seixas, eds. *New Directions in Assessing Historical Thinking*. New York: Routledge, 2015.
Evans, Richard. *In Defence of History*. London: Granta, 2000.
Faculty of Education, UBC. *The Dean's Distinguished Lecture with Senator Murray Sinclair*, November 19, 2019. Retrieved December 9, 2019 at https://educ.ubc.ca/deansdistinguishedlecture/.
First People's Principles of Learning. Retrieved December 8, 2019 at https://firstpeoplesprinciplesoflearning.wordpress.com/.
Fumano, Dan. "Report on Historical Wrongs 'About Now and Future'." *Vancouver Sun*, December 30, 2019, A1.
Gaddis, John Lewis. *The Landscape of History: How Historians Map the Past*. Oxford, UK: Oxford University Press, 2002.
Gardner, Howard. *The Development and Education of the Mind: The Selected Works of Howard Gardner*. London: Routledge, 2006.
Gibson, Lindsay and Roland Case. "Reshaping Canadian History Education in Support of Reconciliation." *Canadian Journal of Education* 42, no. 1 (2019): 252–84.
Ginzburg, Carlo. *The Cheese and the Worms: The Cosmos of a Sixteenth-Century Miller*, trans. J.A.A.C. Tedeschi. Baltimore: John Hopkins University Press, 1992.

Grever, Maria and Robbert-Jan Adraansen. "Historical Consciousness: The Enigma of Different Paradigms." *Journal of Curriculum Studies* 51, no. 6 (2019): 814–30. https://doi.org/10.1080/00220272.2019.1652937.

Halbwachs, Maurice. *The Collective Memory*, trans. Francis J. Didder Jr. and Vida Yazdi Ditter. New York: Harper & Row, 1980.

Harlan, David. "Historical Fiction and the Future of Academic History." In *Manifestos for History*, edited by Keith Jenkins, Sue Morgan, and Alun Munslow, 108–30. London: Routledge, 2007.

Hutton, Patrick. *History as an Art of Memory*. Hanover, NH: University Press of New England, 1993.

"John A. Macdonald Statue Removed from Victoria City Hall," CBC News August 11, 2018. https://www.cbc.ca/news/canada/british-columbia/john-a-macdonald-statue-victoria-city-hall-lisa-helps-1.4782065.

Kansteiner, Wulf. "Finding Meaning in Memory: A Methodological Critique of Collective Memory Studies." *History and Theory* 41, no. 2 (May 2002): 179–97.

Karlsson, Klas-Goran. "Processing Time: On the Activation and Manifestation of Historical Consciousness." In *Historicizing the Uses of the Past: Scandinavian Perspectives on History, Culture, Historical Consciousness and Didactics of History Related to World War II*, edited by Helle Bjerg, Claudia Lenz, and Erik Thorstensen, 129–43. New Brunswick, NJ: Transaction Publishers, 2011.

Köbl, Carlos and Lisa Konrad. "Historical Consciousness in Germany: Concept, Implementation, Assessment." In *New Directions in Assessing Historical Thinking*, edited by Kadriye Ercikan and Peter Seixas, 17–28. New York: Routledge, 2015.

Körber, Andreas. "German History Didactics: From Historical Consciousness to Historical Competencies—And Beyond?" In *Historicizing the Uses of the Past: Scandinavian Perspectives on History Culture, Historical Consciousness and Didactics of History Related to World War II*, edited by Helle Bjerg, Claudia Lenz, and Erik Thorstensen, 145–64. Piscataway, NJ: Transaction Publishers, Rutgers University, 2011.

Körber, Andreas and Johannes Meyer-Hamme. "Historical Thinking Competencies, and Their Measurement: Challenges and Approaches." In *New Directions in Assessing Historical Thinking*, edited by Kadriye Ercikan and Peter Seixas, 89–101. New York and London: Routledge, 2015.

Kremmer, Christopher. "From Dialectics to Dialogue: Bakhtin, White and the 'Moorings' of Fiction and History." *TEXT* 28 (April 2015): 1–16.

Landsberg, Alison. *Prosthetic Memory: The Transformation of American Remembrance in the Age of Mass Culture*. New York: Columbia University Press, 2004.

Lave, Jean and Etienne Wenger. *Situated Learning: Legitimate Peripheral Participation*. Cambridge, UK: Cambridge University Press, 1991.

Laville, Christian. "Historical Consciousness and Historical Education: What to Expect from the First for the Second." In *Theorizing Historical Consciousness*, edited by Peter Seixas, 165–82. Toronto, ON: University of Toronto Press, 2004.

Lee, Peter, "'Walking Backwards into Tomorrow': Historical Consciousness and Understanding of History." *International Journal of Historical Learning, Teaching and Research* 4, no 1 (2004): 1–46.

Lévesque, Stéphane. "Going Beyond 'Narratives' vs. 'Competencies': A Model of History Education." *Public History Weekly* 4 (2016): 12. https://doi.org/10.1515/phw-2016-5918.

Lévesque, Stéphane. *Thinking Historically: Educating Students for the Twenty-First Century*. Toronto, ON: University of Toronto Press, 2008.

Lévesque, Stéphane and Penney Clark. "Historical thinking: Definitions and Educational Applications." In *The Wiley International Handbook of History Teaching and Learning*, edited by Scott Alan Metzger and Lauren McArthur Harris, 119–48. Hoboken, NJ: Wiley, 2018.

Lévesque, Stéphane and Jean-Philippe Croteau. *Beyond History for Historical Consciousness: Students, Narrative, and Memory*. Toronto, ON: University of Toronto Press, 2020.

Lichtenberg, Judith. "The Will to Truth: A Reply to Novick." *The Annals of the American Academy of Political and Social Science* 560 (November 1998): 43–54.

Marker, Michael. "Teaching History from an Indigenous Perspective: Four Winding Paths up the Mountain." In *New Possibilities for the Past: Shaping History Education in Canada*, edited by Penney Clark, 97–112. Vancouver BC: UBC Press, 2011.

Marker, Michael. "The 'Realness' of Place in the Spiral of Time: Reflections on Indigenous Historical Consciousness from the Coast Salish Territory." In *Contemplating Historical Consciousness: Notes from the Field*, edited by Anna Clark and Carla L. Peck, 185–99. New York: Berghahn Books, 2019.

Martineau, Robert. *L'Histoire a l'Ecole, Matiere a Penser*. Montreal: L'Harmattan, 1999.

Maza, Sarah. *Thinking About History*. Chicago: The University of Chicago Press, 2017.

McCully, Alan and Fionnuala Waldon. "A Question of Identity? Purpose, Policy and Practice in the Teaching of History in Northern Ireland and the Republic of Ireland." In *Identity, Trauma, Sensitive and Controversial Issues in the Teaching of History*, edited by Hilary Cooper and Jon Nichol, 2–24. Newcastle upon Tyne: Cambridge Scholars, 2015.

McGregor, Heather. "One Classroom, Two Teachers? Historical Thinking and Indigenous Education in Canada." *Critical Education* 8, no 14 (October 15, 2017): 1–18.

Miles, James. "Teaching History for Truth and Reconciliation: The Challenges and Opportunities of Narrativity, Temporality and Identity." *McGill Journal of Education* 53, no. 2 (Spring 2018): 294–311.

Moller, Sabine. "Are Family Recollections an Obstacle to History Education? How German Students Make Sense of the East German Dictatorship." In *History Education and the Construction of National Identities*, edited by Mario Carretero, Mikel Asensio, and Maria Rodríguez-Moneo, 281–95. Charlotte NC: Information Age, 2012.

Nield, Jonathan. *Guide to the Best Historical Novels and Tales*. Project Gutenberg e-book. www.gutenberg.org/etext/1359.

Nora, Pierre. "Between Memory and History: Les lieux de memoire." *Representations* 26 (Spring 1989): 7–24.

Nora, Pierre. *Realms of Memory: Rethinking the French Past*, trans. Arthur Goldhammer. New York: Columbia University Press, 1996.

Novick, Peter. *That Noble Dream: The "Objectivity Question" and the American Historical Profession*. Cambridge, UK: Cambridge University Press, 1988.

Novick, Peter. "(The Death of) The Ethics of Historical Practice (and Why I Am Not in Mourning." *The Annals of the American Academy of Political and Social Science* 560 (November 1998): 28–42. https://doi.org/10.1177/000271629856000l003.

Novick, Peter. *The Holocaust in American Life*. Boston: Houghton Mifflin Company, 1999.

Ontario Ministry of Education. *First Nations, Métis and Inuit Studies Curriculum*. Toronto, ON: Queen's Printer for Ontario, 2019.

Osborne, Ken. "*Knowing, Teaching and Learning History*, ed. by Peter N. Stearns, Peter Seixas, and Sam Wineburg and *L'histoire à L'école: Matière à Penser* by Robert Martineau (Review)." *Canadian Historical Review* 82, no. 3 (September 2001): 548–54

Osborne, Ken. "Teaching Canadian History: A Century of Debate." In *New Possibilities for the Past: Shaping History Education in Canada*, edited by Penney Clark, 55–80. Vancouver, BC: UBC Press, 2011.

Pellegrino, James W., Nancy Chudowsky, and Robert Glaser, eds. *Knowing What Students Know: The Science and Design of Educational Assessment*. Washington: National Academy Press, 2001.

Peterson Andrew. "Australia." In *Education, Globalization and the Nation*, edited by Eric King Man Chong, Ian Davies, Terrie Epstein, Carla L. Peck, Andrew Peterson, Alistair Ross, Maria Auxiliadora Schmidt, Alan Sears, and Debbie Sonu, 17–40. Hampshire, UK: Palgrave MacMillan, 2016.

Polybius, *The Rise of the Roman Empire*, trans. I. Scott-Kilvert, selected and intro. F. Walbank. London: Penguin, 1979).

Posner, George, Kenneth A. Strike, Peter W. Hewson, and William A. Gertzog. "Accommodation of a Scientific Conception: Toward a Theory of Conceptual Change." *Science Education* 66, no. 2 (April 1982): 211–27.

Rigney, Ann. "Fiction as a Mediator in National Remembrance." In *Narrating the Nation: Representations in History, Media and the Arts*, edited by Stefan Berger, Linas Eriksonas and Andrew Mycock, 79–96. New York: Berghahn, 2008.

Rowinski, James and Alan Sears. "Unsettled Histories: Transgressing History Education Practice in New Brunswick, Canada." *Historical Encounters*. Accepted.

Rüsen, Jörn. "Historical Consciousness: Narrative Structure, Moral Function, and Ontogenetic Development." In *Theorizing Historical Consciousness*, edited by Peter Seixas, 63–85. Toronto, ON: University of Toronto Press, 2004.

Sant, Edda, Neus Gonzalez-Monfort, Antoni Santesteban Fernandez, Jorn Pages Blanch, and Montserrat Oller Freixa. "How Do Catalan Students Narrate the History of Catalonia When They Finish Primary Education?" *McGill Journal of Education* 50, no. 2/3 (Spring/Fall 2015): 341–62.

Schmidt, Maria Auxiliadora. "Brazil." In *Education, Globalization and the Nation*, edited by Eric King Man Chong, Ian Davies, Terrie Epstein, Carla L. Peck, Andrew Peterson, Alistair Ross, Maria Auxiliadora Schmidt, Alan Sears, and Debbie Sonu, 41–58. Hampshire, UK: Palgrave MacMillan, 2016.

Schwartz, Barry. *Abraham Lincoln and the Forge of National Memory*. Chicago: University of Chicago Press, 2000.

Sears, Alan. "Children's Understandings of Democratic Participation: Lessons for Civic Education." In *Civic Education and Youth Political Participation*, edited by Murray Print and Henry Milner, 143–58. Rotterdam: Sense, 2009.

Sears, Alan. "Historical Thinking and Citizenship Education: It Is Time to End the War." In *New Possibilities for the Past: Shaping History Education in Canada*, edited by Penney Clark, 344–64. Vancouver, BC: UBC Press, 2011.

Sears, Alan. "Trends and Issues in History Education in International Contexts." In *Debates in History Teaching*, edited by Ian Davies, 2nd ed., 42–52. London and New York: Routledge, 2017.

Seixas, Peter. "A History/Memory Matrix for History Education." *Public History Weekly* 4, no. 6 (2016). https://doi.org/10.1515/phw-2016-5370.

Seixas, Peter. "A Model of Historical Thinking." *Educational Philosophy and Theory* 49, no. 6 (2017): 593–605. https://doi.org/10.1080/00131857.2015.1101363.

Seixas, Peter. "Assessment of Historical Thinking." In *New Possibilities for the Past: Shaping History Education in Canada*, edited by Penney Clark, 139–53. Vancouver, BC: UBC Press, 2011.

Seixas, Peter. "Author's Reply, A History/Memory Matrix for History Education." *Public History Weekly* 4, no. 6 (2016). https://doi.org/10.1515/phw-2016-5370.

Seixas, Peter. "Historical Consciousness and Historical Thinking." In *Palgrave Handbook of Research in Historical Culture and Education*, edited by Mario Carretero, Stefan Berger and Maria Grever, 59–72. London, UK: Palgrave Macmillan, 2017.

Seixas, Peter. "Historiographies and Historical Consciousness." In *Theorizing Historical Consciousness*, edited by Peter Seixas, 21–24. Toronto, ON: University of Toronto Press, 2004.

Seixas, Peter. "Indigenous Historical Consciousness; An Oxymoron or a Dialogue?" In *History Education and the Construction of National Identities*, edited by Mario Carretero, Mikel Asensio, and Maria Rodríguez-Moneo, 125–38. Charlotte, NC: Information Age Publishing, 2012.

Seixas, Peter. "Teaching Rival Histories." *Paedagogica Historica* 48, no. 6 (2012): 859–72.

Seixas, Peter. "What Is Historical Consciousness?" In *To the Past: History Education, Public Memory, & Citizenship in Canada*, edited by Ruth Sandwell, 11–22. Toronto, ON: University of Toronto Press, 2006.

Seixas, Peter and Jill Colyer. *From the Curriculum to the Classroom: More Teachers, More Students, More Thinking: A Report on the National Meeting of the Historical Thinking Project*. Toronto, ON, January 23–25, 2014. Available at http://historicalthinking.ca/sites/default/files/files/docs/HTP2014_EN.pdf.

Seixas, Peter and Tom Morton. *The Big Six: Historical Thinking Concepts*. Toronto, ON: Nelson Education, 2013.

Simon, Roger I. *The Touch of the Past: Remembrance, Learning and Ethics*. New York: Palgrave Macmillan, 2005.

Somekawa, Ellen and Elizabeth A. Smith. "Theorizing the Writing of History or, 'I Can't Think Why It Should Be so Dull for a Great Deal of It Must Be Invention.'" *Journal of Social History* 22, no. 1 (Fall 1988): 149–61.

Stanley, Timothy J. "Whose Public? Whose Memory? Racisms, Grand Narratives and Canadian History." In *To the Past: History Education Public Memory, & Citizenship in Canada*, edited by Ruth Sandwell, 32–49. Toronto, ON: University of Toronto Press, 2006.

Stearns, Peter N., Peter Seixas, and Sam Wineburg, eds. *Knowing, Teaching and Learning History: National and International Perspectives*. New York: New York University Press, 2000.

Sturken, Marita. *Tangled Memories: The Vietnam War, the AIDS Epidemic, and the Politics of Remembering*. Berkeley: University of California Press, 1997.

Taylor, A.J.P. *Origins of the Second World War*. London: Penguin, 1964.

The Pasts Collective: Conrad, Margaret, Kadriye Ercikan, Gerald Friesen, Jocelyn Létourneau, Delphin Muise, David Northrup, and Peter Seixas. *Canadians and Their Pasts*. Toronto, ON: University of Toronto Press, 2013.

Thompson, Edward. *Making of the English Working Class*. New York: Vintage Books, 1963.

Thucydides. *History of the Peloponnesian War*, trans. R. Warner, intro. and notes M.I. Finley. London: Penguin, 1972.

Truth and Reconciliation Commission of Canada. *Final Report of the Truth and Reconciliation Commission of Canada, Vol.1: Summary: Honouring the Truth, Reconciling for the Future*. Toronto, ON: James Lorimer, 2015.

Tuchman, Barbara. *Practicing History: Selected Essays*. New York: Random House, 1981.

Ulrich, Laurel Thatcher. *A Midwife's Tale: The Life of Martha Ballard, Based on Her Diary*. New York: Knopf, 1990.

United Nations. "United Nations Declaration on the Rights of Indigenous Peoples." New York: United Nations, 2008. https://www.un.org/esa/socdev/unpfii/documents/DRIPS_en.pdf, 7 and 11.

Von Borries, Bodo. "Concepts of Historical Thinking and Historical Learning in the Perspective of German Students and Teachers." *International Journal of Education Research* 27, no. 3 (1997): 211–20.

Watters, H. "Truth and Reconciliation Chair Urges Adoption of UN Declaration on Indigenous Peoples," CBC News, June 2, 2015. https://www.cbc.ca/news/politics/truth-and-reconciliation-chair-urges-canada-to-adopt-un-declaration-on-indigenous-peoples-1.3096225.

Wertsch, James V. "Is It Possible to Teach Beliefs, as Well as Knowledge About History?" In *Knowing, Teaching & Learning History: National and International Perspectives*, edited by Peter N. Stearns, Peter Seixas, and Sam Wineburg, 38–50. New York: New York University Press, 2000.

Wertsch, James V. *Voices of Collective Remembering*. Cambridge: Cambridge University Press, 2002.

Wharton, Edith. *Age of Innocence*. Mineola NY: Dover Publications, 1997.

White, Hayden. "Historical Pluralism." *Critical Inquiry* 12, no. 1 (Spring 1986): 480–93.

White, Hayden V. "The Burden of History." *History and Theory* 5, no. 2 (1996): 111–34.

White, Hayden. "The Public Relevance of Historical Studies: A Reply to Dirk Moses'. *History and Theory* 44, no. 3 (October 2005): 333–38.

Wilschut, Arie. "History Teaching at the Mercy of Politicians and Ideologies." *Journal of Curriculum Studies* 42, no. 5 (2010): 693–721.

Windschitl, Mark. "Framing Constructivism in Practice as the Negotiation of Dilemmas: An Analysis of the Conceptual, Pedagogical, Cultural, and Political Challenges Facing Teachers." *Review of Educational Research* 72 (Summer 2002): 131–75.

Wong, Jessica. "'Big, Bold, Audacious.' Kent Monkman Artworks 'at Home' at the Met, Says Curator." CBC, December 17, 2019. https://www.cbc.ca/news/entertainment/kent-monkman-met-paintings-1.5395216.

Worster, Donald. *Dust Bowl: The Southern Plains in the 1930s*. New York: Oxford University Press, 1979.

Zanazanian, Paul. "History Teaching and Narrative Tools: Towards Integrating English-Speaking Youth into Quebec's Social Fabric." *Minorités linguistiqes et Société/Linguistic Minorities and Society* 7 (2016): 70–96. https://doi.org/10.7202/1036417ar.

CHAPTER 3

Historical F(r)ictions: Fiction and History Education

When 23-year-old Walter Blythe from the village of Glen St. Mary, Prince Edward Island, was killed in action at Courcelette, France, in the year 1916, his family was devastated. But the reaction to this tragic loss of a young life went far beyond the family circle. Many who had never met him wept when they read of his death, including this writer.

Walter Blythe did not, in fact, die because he did not live. He was a fictional character, the second son of the fictional Anne Shirley, protagonist of the iconic Canadian novel, *Anne of Green Gables*.[1] Walter, the character, died in *Rilla of Ingleside*,[2] written shortly after the end of the First World War. This novel was described at the time of its publication in 1920, as "a faithful and worthy picture" of the war years in Glen St. Mary, "that might be written of a thousand communities in Canada."[3] According to a review in *Saturday Night*, "Most Canadians lived and felt those [war] months, very much as did the Blythe family and their friends of Glen St. Mary."[4] For the past century, this compelling novel has made the First World War and its consequences for Canadians, real for its readers in ways that cannot be matched by statistical reports of the numbers of deaths or contemporary newspaper accounts. This novel gives the reader an inside glimpse of how it *felt* on a day-to-day basis to be a part of the events on the home front in Canada.

A 2013 national survey conducted by the Pasts Collective, found that historical fiction is a popular way to engage with the past for many Canadians.[5] These researchers remind us that this interest has even led to the

P. Clark and A. Sears, *The Arts and the Teaching of History*,
https://doi.org/10.1007/978-3-030-51513-3_3

creation of historic sites devoted to imaginary characters.[6] The home of Green Gables in Cavendish, Prince Edward Island (the fictional Avonlea) where the fictional character Anne Shirley lived as a child, is an example. People travel from all over the world to visit this "historic" site. According to Alexander MacLeod, Canadian writer and English and Atlantic Studies professor,

> this dissolving of the border between real and imagined spaces is what makes Cavendish/Avonlea such an important destination for people around the world.... the vast majority of the people who come to Cavendish are attempting to visit the imaginary Avonlea and to put themselves, temporarily at least, into the same shared place where Anne once 'lived' in the real world.... Green Gables functions as a kind of shrine or as a portal between two ways of understanding social space, making the imagined idea of the place and the fact of its physical existence inseparable.[7]

This chapter explores historical fiction in the form of novels, distinguishing between two types of novels with historical content: period novels and historical novels. This is a difference that has significant implications for history pedagogy, a topic that is discussed in Chapter 6.

Period Novels and Historical Novels

We use the term "period novels" for novels that take place in the period in which they are written. They were not intended to be historical, but have become so with the passage of time.[8] We distinguish between these novels and "historical novels," a term we use for works of fiction written across a temporal gap about events that took place in an earlier time. Writers of historical novels deliberately use the past to construct the settings of their novels. We use the term "historical fiction" when we refer to both types of work.

We note that the term "historical novel" is often used for both types of fiction. For example, in "*The Great Gatsby*? Yes, a Historical Novel," historian John Lukacs uses the label for *The Great Gatsby*, a novel written by F. Scott Fitzgerald in 1925 about fictional events set in the 1920s.[9] The failure to make this distinction obscures the significant differences between the two, and by extension, their different implications for history pedagogy.

While literary critics advocate reading historical novels not only for their content, but also their form and style, it is the content on which we focus here because that is what is most relevant for history education.[10] We begin with period novels and discuss their usefulness and also their limitations as primary sources for investigating a time and place. Then we look at historical novels and consider the use of historical evidence in their creation in light of the ways that historians set about creating their accounts.

Period Novels: Fiction as Primary Source

Historian John Lukacs has made the point that, "Certain novels tell us more about a certain time and about certain people than even the best of histories."[11] We agree with Lukacs. A period novel can illuminate details about a place and a time from the perspective of someone immersed in them. It can be treated as a primary source for the period in which it is written and the one which it describes—which are, of course, one and the same. Jerome de Groot points out that "[George] Eliot's historical fictions *Middlemarch*, *Romola* (1853) and *Felix Holt*, all explore historical periods in forensic philosophical, cultural and social detail with a view to understanding political process and change through the experience of a range of ordinary people."[12] Historian Barbara Tuchman gives us two wonderful examples: "When you have read Proust you can see Paris of the nineties, horse cabs and lamplight, the clubman making his calls in white gloves stitched in black and gray top hat lined in green leather."[13] Tuchman also points to *The Edwardians* by British aristocrat Victoria Sackville-West. She says this novel "gave me precise and authoritative information on matters on which the writers of memoirs remain discreet. Like Proust, this author was writing about a world she knew. At the great house parties, one learns, the hostess took into consideration established liaisons in assigning the bedrooms."[14] This hardly seems surprising, but the historian requires evidence. Tuchman found memoirs unsatisfactory in this regard and turned to a novel for the evidence she required.

While any period novel can reveal a great deal about the time and place in which it is written, whether intentionally or incidentally, there are many enduring novels that provide particularly illuminating insights. We will highlight a small, eclectic selection of these as examples, and then focus in more depth on works by British author Jane Austen, Canadian author Lucy Maud Montgomery's World War One novel *Rilla of Ingleside*, and American author F. Scott Fitzgerald's novel about the 1920s, *The Great Gatsby*. We will devote the greatest space to Austen because her novels present life in the Georgian era in England in such exquisite detail.

The Grapes of Wrath by John Steinbeck, about sharecroppers in Oklahoma who move to California in the hopes of a better life, could be read to learn about the devastating effects of the Great Depression and the creation of the Dust Bowl on some people's lives in the United States. The powerful *To Kill a Mockingbird* by Harper Lee reveals the embedded racism in the American South during the period of the Great Depression. *A Passage to India* by E. M. Forster highlights the tensions between the Indian and British colonial communities in 1920s India. *Fathers and Sons*, *Rudin* and other novels by Russian author Ivan Turgenev provide details about life in tumultuous late nineteenth-century Russia.

Novelist Christopher Bram has said, "No writer can underestimate the rigid roles of race, class, and gender in other eras."[15] In *Red and Black*, by Stendahl (Henri Marie Beyle), Julien Sorel, the son of a carpenter, tries in vain to rise through the class structure in France following the French Revolution and the reign of Napoleon Bonaparte. The novel, which presents the class structure as rigid and the aristocracy and the Catholic clergy as hypocritical and materialistic, offers insights into this place and period.

The intersection of class and gender is a common theme, particularly with respect to upper-class women. *Mrs. Dalloway* by Virginia Woolf is one such example. Woolf takes the reader through one day in the life of high-society matron, Clarissa Dalloway, as she prepares for, and hosts, an elegant evening party in her home in post-First World War London. The novel explores, in microcosm, upper-class snobbery and social obligations; expectations for and limitations of, the material and moral circumstances surrounding upper-class women, and men to a lesser degree, at this time and in this place. Henry James contrasts naiveté and experience in the context of class and gender in *Portrait of a Lady*. Isabel Archer, an independent-minded late nineteenth-century American woman inherits wealth, but instead of setting her free, it serves to trap her in an unfortunate marriage to a mercenary man.

Edith Wharton (1862–1937), a member of New York's upper class at the end of the nineteenth and in the early twentieth century, wrote about the milieu in which she lived and the people she knew, exploring the societal expectations placed on both men and women. *Age of Innocence*, *House of Mirth*, and other novels by Wharton are rich sources of information about daily details of life and provide insights about the expectations, the strictures, and the opportunities offered by gender and class position among the old-moneyed, the *nouveau riche*, and those living in genteel poverty, in old New York. For example, in Wharton's *The Age of Innocence*, which takes place in post-Civil-War New York, Newland Archer has inward debates about the mores and expectations of his upper-class environment as he considers abandoning it all to run away with a married Countess. Wharton comments: "It was the old New York way of taking life 'without effusion of blood': the way of people who dreaded scandal more than disease, who placed decency above courage, and who considered that nothing was more ill-bred than scenes, except the behaviour of those who gave rise to them."[16]

In her tragic novel, *The House of Mirth*, which takes place at the beginning of the twentieth century, unmarried socialite Lily Bart embarks on a downward trek through the echelons of old New York society; beginning as the pampered only child of wealthy parents until her father is financially ruined, sojourning for a time in the homes of the rich, and ending as a social pariah, living in a rundown New York boarding house and employed in the workroom of a millinery establishment until she was fired for incompetence. Ultimately, worn out and without options, she dies from an overdose of a sleeping draught (Fig. 3.1).

In a telling indiscretion that launches the novel, Lily accompanies her friend Lawrence Selden to his flat for a cup of tea. In a revealing exchange, she remarks, "How delicious to have a place like this all to one's self! What a miserable thing it is to be a woman." When Selden points out that there are women who do enjoy an independent home such as his, Lily responds that, "Oh, governesses – or widows. But not girls – not poor, miserable, marriageable girls."[17] Ultimately, Lily Bart rejects the option of marriage without love, despite the financial security it offers. However, there are no other possibilities at her disposal and, in so doing, she propels herself further downwards. Ultimately, her tragedy is that she is not fully reconciled to the realities of being a woman of her time and place in history, but does not know how to rebel constructively.

Jane Austen's (1775–1817) six novels, written in Britain in the first two decades of the nineteenth century can be read in order to find compelling details about the day-to-day lives of the country gentry, the seriously

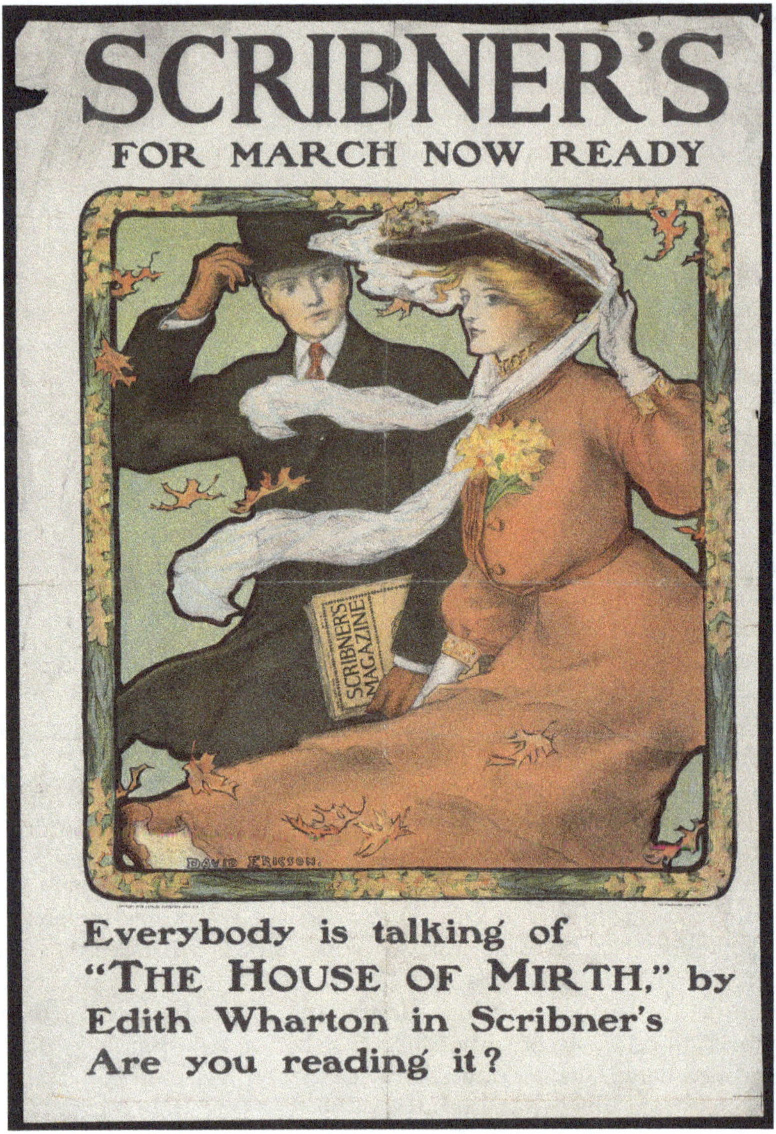

Fig. 3.1 Scribner's for March, now ready. Everybody is talking of the house of mirth by Edith Wharton in Scribner's. Are you reading it? (*Source* Lebrecht Music & Arts/Alamy Stock Photo)

wealthy landowners, and the aristocrats—the lords, the earls, and the baronets. British cultural studies scholar Richard Hoggart has pointed to the value of Austen's novels as "social documents [that give a] sense of the way life was lived 'in the bone' ... that behind people's actions and reactions lay *this* particular sense of England's destiny, *these* assumptions about the relations between the sexes, about class and money and duty" (Fig. 3.2).[18]

Barbara Tuchman made a comment about Proust that is equally as applicable to Austen. "Proust is invaluable because ... it is all confined to a narrow segment of society which he knew personally and intimately; it is like a woman describing her own living room."[19] Jane Austen's conversations never actually took place, but they have verisimilitude. They seem real. She would have experienced such conversations each and every day and she drew on these experiences.

The novels of Jane Austen, and other authors discussed here, provide details about daily life that can be difficult to find in other primary source documents. It is in this gap that period novels can serve as a primary source. From Austen's novels we learn about the functioning of the households of the gentry and the upper classes. She does not reveal the behind-the-scenes activities such as cooking and cleaning, which were carried out by servants; but provides details such as when people ate meals (not a lot about what they ate), the proper protocols to be observed when entertaining guests, and how such people behaved towards their servants. We also learn about the frequency of mail delivery; means of transportation; proper conduct at social events such as balls, formal dinners, and excursions; courtship rituals; means used to manoeuver the intricacies of marriage and family relationships (for example, obligations to penurious relatives); and attitudes about people on other tiers of the class system, and certainly about gender-related expectations.

In *Capital in the Twenty-First Century*, economist Thomas Piketty says: "Jane Austen minutely describes daily life in the early nineteenth century: she tells us what it cost to eat, to buy furniture and clothing, and to travel about."[20] Piketty makes the case for the use of period novels as a source of information about distribution of wealth and relative living standards in the time and place in which the novel is set:

> Film and literature, nineteenth-century novels especially, are full of detailed information about the relative wealth and living standards of different social groups, and especially about the deep structure of inequality, the

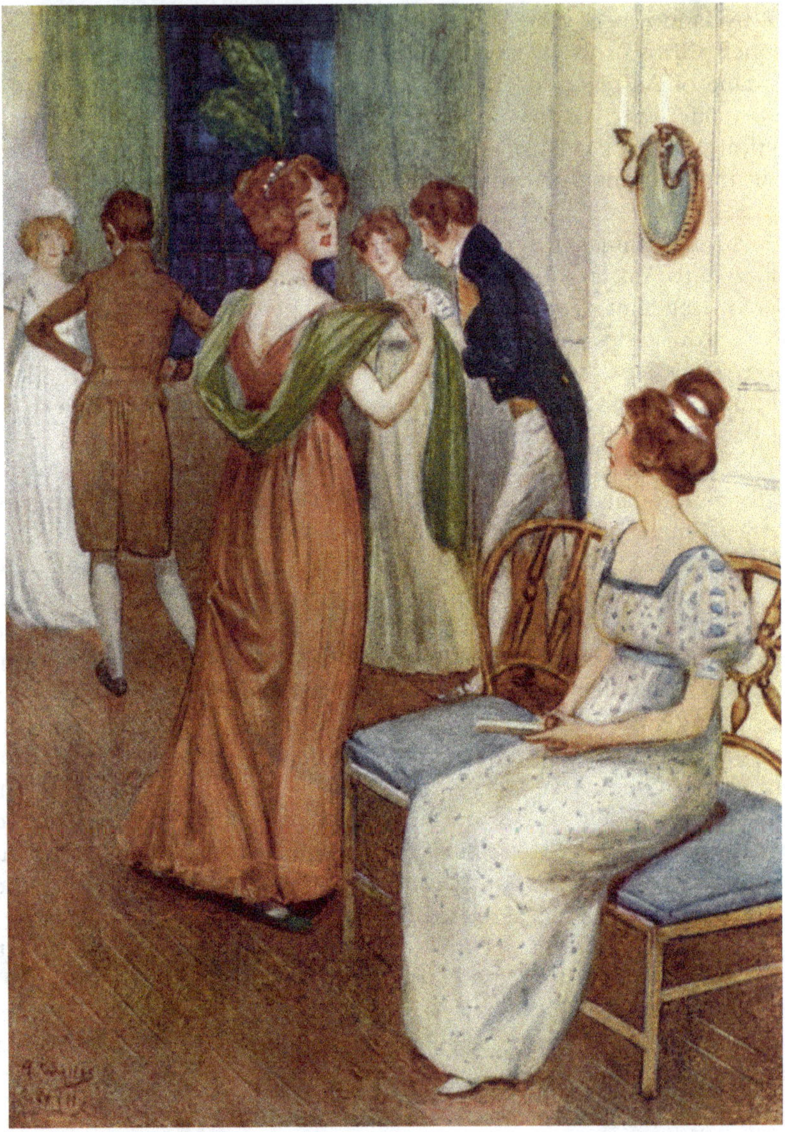

Fig. 3.2 "Pride and Prejudice" by Jane Austen—portrait of Miss Bingley & Elizabeth at Netherfield ball Chapter XVIII Georgian (*Source* Lebrecht Music & Arts/Alamy Stock Photo)

> way it is justified, and its impact on individual lives. Indeed, the novels of Jane Austen and Honoré de Balzac paint striking portraits of the distribution of wealth in Britain and France between 1790 and 1830.... They grasped the hidden contours of wealth and its inevitable implications for the lives of men and women, including their marital strategies and personal hopes and disappointments. These and other novelists depicted the effects of inequality with a verisimilitude and evocative power that no statistical or theoretical analysis can match.[21]

We can learn a great deal about the relationship between primogeniture and marriage from Jane Austen's novels.[22] Primogeniture, the right in law or custom for the eldest legitimate son to inherit his father's estate[23] left daughters and younger sons with limited options. Younger sons could either subsist on any inherited funds that were available to them, find salaried occupations in the church, the military, or less often, the law, or seek to marry an heiress. The only options for women were to marry for money and position or, given that they had no career possibilities, be left with little.

Primogeniture is never absent in Jane Austen's novels. It is either front and centre or lurking in the background. In *Pride and Prejudice*, the estate on which the Bennet family reside is entailed to Mr. Collins, a cousin who will inherit in the event that Mr. Bennet has no male heir. Sadly, with five grown and almost-grown daughters, it is clear that this will be the case. Events in the novel centre around the necessity for the Bennet daughters to marry well—and well means to a man with a high income. In *Persuasion*, the two unmarried sisters, Anne and Elizabeth Elliot, will lose their inheritance if their widowed father remarries and has a son—a compelling reason to be wary of the ubiquitous widow Mrs. Clay. As Piketty points out, "Jane Austen, herself disfavored by inheritance and left a spinster along with her sister, knew what she was talking about."[24]

Of course, primogeniture limited the opportunities available to men, at least those who were not firstborn, as well. In Austen's *Mansfield Park*, Edmund, the younger son, must become a minister in order to secure a comfortable living, albeit one that is far below that in which he grew up. His elder brother Tom (although undeserving from a moral standpoint) will inherit the family estate. In *Pride and Prejudice*, Colonel Fitzwilliam, a younger son of an earl, makes the position of a younger son clear to Elizabeth Bennet. Although attracted to Elizabeth, he cannot consider her as a marriage prospect. He tells her surprisingly directly:

> "A younger son, you know, must be inured to self-denial and dependence."
>
> [Elizabeth responds] "In my opinion the younger son of an Earl can know very little of either. Now, seriously, what have you ever known of self-denial and dependence? When have you been prevented by want of money from going wherever you chose, or procuring any thing you had a fancy for?" …
>
> "… in matters of greater weight, I may suffer from the want of money. Younger sons cannot marry where they like."
>
> "Unless where they like women of fortune, which I think they very often do."
>
> "Our habits of expense make us too dependent, and there are not many in my rank of life who can afford to marry without some attention to money."[25]

Austen clearly lays out the occupational options for younger sons in *Mansfield Park*, when Edmund, the younger Bertram son, who will not inherit the estate, explains to Mary Crawford, who had hoped to marry him, why he has chosen to be a clergyman:

> "Why should it surprise you? You must suppose me designed for some profession and might perceive that I am neither a lawyer, nor a soldier nor a sailor."
>
> "Very true; but, in short, it had not occurred to me. And you know there is generally an uncle or a grandfather to leave a fortune to the second son."
>
> "A very praiseworthy practice … but not quite universal. I am one of the exceptions and *being* one must do something for myself."
>
> "But why are you to be a clergyman? I thought *that* was always the lot of the youngest, where there were many to choose before him."[26]

A century before Edith Wharton's *The House of Mirth* and on the other side of the Atlantic, "the mercenary aspect of marriage"[27] is demonstrated with sharp clarity in Austen's novels. Hence, we have the famous, beautifully expressed, opening lines of Austen's *Pride and Prejudice*: "It is a truth universally acknowledged that a single man in possession of a good fortune, must be in want of a wife."[28] As author Ivor Morris points out, reports of their annual income routinely precede the first appearance of Jane Austen's eligible male characters. In *Pride and Prejudice*, the reader acquires this information within seconds of meeting the wealthy Mr. Darcy. Here we have Mr. Darcy entering the assembly room: "Mr. Darcy soon drew the attention of the room by his fine tall person, handsome features, noble mien; and the report which was in general circulation within five minutes after his entrance, of his having ten thousand a year."[29] As Morris put it, in Jane Austen's world, "knowing a man implies knowledge of his bank balance."[30]

Literary critic Mark Schorer, argues that Jane Austen's *Emma* "is not simply a novel of courtship and marriage, but a novel about the economic and social significance of courtship and marriage."[31] He points out that "the basic situation in all [Austen's] novels arises from the economics of marriage."[32] The values are "of commerce and property, of the counting house and the inherited estate." He goes on to say that "on the surface of the action, this is usually a world of refined sensibility, of concern with moral propriety....

[Yet] we are in a world of peculiarly *material* value, a world of almost instinctive material interests in its basic, intuitive response to experience."[33] It is quite clear that Austen believes that marriages between people of different classes and with different levels of wealth are less than ideal. English Professor Mona Scheuermann expresses it well: "Austen makes fun of class lines and class snobbery, but she arranges her matches so that they conform to those lines."[34]

The harsh reality was, as English professor and novelist Jenny Davidson points out, "Most men of good fortune are *not* in need of wives, and any need in the case can more rationally be apportioned to the young women of little means who seek husbands to mend their fortunes."[35] Gentlewomen had almost no employment prospects and thus relied on marriage for their economic sustenance. Some young women chose to work as a governess as a last-resort option, but with the exception of orphaned Jane Fairfax in the novel *Emma*, this is not an option that is considered by Jane Austen's female characters. It would have been a considerable step down in terms of status for the daughter of a gentleman of property, and, therefore, only a last resort if insufficient family assistance was available and after all prospects of marriage had faded away. This is how Austen describes Jane Fairfax's decision to become a governess: "With the fortitude of a devoted novitiate, she had resolved at one-and-twenty to complete the sacrifice, and retire from all the pleasures of life, of rational intercourse, equal society, peace and hope, to penance and mortification for ever."[36] The obvious irony here makes it quite clear that Austen did not look favourably on such an occupation as a reasonable option for a penurious upper-class single woman unless entirely bereft of other options.

Mrs. Bennet in *Pride and Prejudice* puts the situation in her blunt fashion to her daughter Elizabeth: "But I tell you what, Miss Lizzy, if you take it into your head to go on refusing every offer of marriage in this way, you will never get a husband at all – and I am sure I do not know who is to maintain you when your father is dead."[37] Mrs. Bennet is a shallow, unintelligent woman, whose mind is apparently vacant beyond the considerable thought she gives to her daughters' marriage prospects, but in this she is absolutely correct. Spinsterhood meant penury for women who lacked wealthy relatives who were willing to provide assistance. Austen makes this abundantly clear in *Sense and Sensibility*, when Elinor and Marianne Dashwood, along with their younger sister and mother, are unceremoniously turned out of their home following the death of their father and husband and the passing of the estate to his son by his first marriage.

Elizabeth Bennet's friend Charlotte Lucas, facing at 27, the stark reality of spinsterhood and reliance on her family for sustenance (as was the case with Jane Austen herself and her sister Cassandra), leaps at the chance to marry Mr. Collins, who makes her an offer shortly after being refused by Elizabeth. Elizabeth professes shock at the mercenary nature of Charlotte's action, knowing without a shadow of a doubt, that there is no romantic love on either side, and little respect on the part of Charlotte, who finds his society "irksome."[38] Charlotte is, however, acting on the sure knowledge that marriage is "the only honourable provision for well-educated young women of small fortune and however uncertain of giving happiness, it is their pleasantest preservative from want."[39]

This aspect of the reality of the times is placed squarely in front of readers when they are shown the fates of the three married sisters in Austen's *Mansfield Park*. Lady Bertram's beauty as a young woman had captured the attention of the wealthy and titled Lord Bertram of Mansfield Park and she lived a life of ease and luxury thereafter. Austen informs the reader that Lady Bertram "spent her days sitting nicely dressed on a sofa, doing some long piece of needlework, of little use and no beauty, thinking more of her pug than her children."[40] Mrs. Norris married a clergyman who was provided with a living through the patronage of Lord Bertram. She has a comfortable lifestyle, although far from the level of her sister Lady Bertram and she is dependent upon the patronage of her sister's husband now that her own husband is deceased. The third sister, Mrs. Price, married rashly, for passion, a "Lieutenant of Marines, without education, fortune, or connections."[41] Her husband was "disabled for active service, but not the less equal to company and good liquor, and a very small income to supply their wants."[42] They ultimately had nine children who they were raising in squalid lodgings. The contrast could not be more stark. Not one of these marriages appears particularly successful in terms of mutual love and respect, but in two of them, the women live comfortable lives with stable financial futures. In Jane Austen's world, as Mona Scheuermann points out, "Love is not enough; it must be supported by a social network and adequate financial means to support a comfortable though not necessarily opulent lifestyle."[43]

Men had obligations too. As Jenny Davidson explains, there was an expectation that men who were not wealthy landowners such as Mr. Darcy would use marriage to improve their economic circumstances. Mr. Knightly in *Emma* thought that the yeoman farmer Robert Martin should try to do better than Emma's friend Harriet Smith because Harriet would bring no financial assets to the union. Davidson also points out that, on the other hand, a woman who did not marry well could be a financial drain on her family. The cost of maintaining her in the style to which she was accustomed in her new home could greatly exceed the cost of maintaining a single daughter in the family home.[44]

An Austen novel can teach us a great deal about the class system in early nineteenth-century Britain. The contemporary reader can be taken aback by the nature of this system, with, for example, the strictures it placed on interaction among people of different classes. In *Persuasion*, Anne Elliot's friend casually remarks "and though I did not know his wife previously (her inferior situation in society, indeed, rendered that impossible)…."[45] In *Emma*, Austen shares Emma's thoughts on the possibility of a dinner invitation from her neighbours, the Coles. "The Coles had been settled some years in Highbury, and were very good sort of people—friendly, liberal, and unpretending; but, on the other hand, they were of low origin, in trade, and only moderately genteel … they ought to be taught that it was not for them to arrange the terms on which the superior families would visit them."[46] These casual comments set a contemporary reader back on her heels. It seems unthinkable to us that restrictions on the social interactions of people of different classes were so unyielding, but Jane Austen informs us with utmost clarity that this was the case.

Class is just as central when it goes beyond day-to-day social relations to matters related to marriage. Emma makes the relevance of class distinctions to marriage clear to her illegitimate friend Harriet, informing her in no uncertain terms that, if she had chosen to marry the farmer, Robert Martin, she would have been shut out of Emma's social circle.

> "It would have been the loss of a friend to me. I could not have visited Mrs. Robert Martin, of Abbey-Mill Farm." ...
>
> ....
>
> "Indeed, Harriet it would have been a severe pang to lose you, but it must have been. You would have thrown yourself out of all good society. I must have given you up."[47]

In *Pride and Prejudice*, Lady Catherine De Bourgh, aunt of Elizabeth Bennet's suitor Mr. Darcy, arrives unannounced at Elizabeth's home with the purpose of bullying her into renouncing any claims she may feel she has on the wealthy Mr. Darcy. This exchange succinctly portrays the gaping class divide between the very wealthy and the landed gentry. Lady Catherine is a caricature, but the point is effectively made, nonetheless. In the view of literary critic John Sutherland, "Elizabeth Bennet's final put-down of Lady Catherine de Bourgh ... ranks ... as one of the most memorable scenes in literature."[48]

Elizabeth asks,

> "... why may I not accept him?"
>
> "Because honour, decorum, prudence, nay, interest, forbid it. Yes, Miss Bennet, interest; for do not expect to be noticed by his family or friends, if you wilfully act against the inclination of all. You will be censured, slighted, and despised, by every one connected with him. Your alliance will be a disgrace; your name will never even be mentioned by any of us."
>
> ....
>
> "Neither duty, nor honour, nor gratitude" replied Elizabeth "have any possible claim on me, in the present instance. No principle of either, would be violated by my marriage with Mr Darcy. And with regard to the resentment of his family, or the indignation of the world, if the former *were* excited by his marrying me, it would not give me one moment's concern—and the world in general would have too much sense to join in the scorn"[49]

There is a great deal to be learned about the power and centrality of the class system in Britain at this time from conversations in Austen's novels.

The reader can also learn about *noblesse oblige*, the moral obligation of upper-class people to provide assistance to the poor. We see this in

Emma when she pays a visit to a poor family in the neighbourhood. As Scheuermann notes, the fact that class "stratification is defined not only by privilege but by responsibility is a continuous theme in late eighteenth- and early nineteenth-century writing…."[50] Through the class-conscious Emma, Austen demonstrates how patronizing the upper class could be towards people of the lower classes: Emma "understood their ways, could allow for their ignorance and their temptations, had no romantic expectations of extraordinary virtue from them for whom education had done so little."[51]

That Austen does not question the rigidity of the social system may take a contemporary reader by surprise. As literary critic Arnold Kettle put it: "[T]he question at issue is not Jane Austen's failure to suggest a *solution* to the problem of class divisions but the apparent failure to notice the *existence* of the problem,"[52] The fact that she does not is a window into the attitudes of the upper classes in England at this time. Things were beginning to change but change was not rapid. Austen portrays an orderly and stable society, where people know their place. Scheuermann notes that, "For Austen class is one of the primary ordering devices of society; class distinctions do not keep people separated, but on the contrary they help people to move in society with the least friction possible."[53]

The key to wealth and status was clearly holding title to land. However, there was one important exception and this was naval success during periods of war. Naval officers were able to keep a percentage of the bounty they gained when they captured an enemy ship. The snobbish Sir Walter Eliot, in *Persuasion*, is much disturbed about this opportunity for social mobility, deriding the navy because it is "the means of bringing persons of obscure birth both into undue distinction, and raising men to honours which their father and grandfathers never dreamt of."[54] Captain Frederick Wentworth moves up the social and economic ladder because of his success in the Napoleonic wars. When Wentworth left for war, he was considered a very poor marriage prospect for Anne Elliot, the daughter of Sir Walter Eliot, a baronet. However, as a result of his successful wartime exploits, he became a wealthy man, which transformed him into a worthy marriage partner upon his return. Wentworth's brother-in-law, Admiral Croft, another example of social mobility, was so wealthy as a result of the wars that he was able to rent Kellynch Hall, the ancestral home of Sir Walter Eliot, who could no longer afford to live there. Sir Walter's profligate ways resulted in his displacement by someone from a much lower social background. In this rare case, money decidedly trumped class.

Austen lifts the curtain on prevailing moral views regarding sexual activity, making it clear that it was absolutely essential that a young woman protect her virtue prior to marriage if she wished to keep her place in society. Once soiled, she was no longer marriageable, at least not to a man of wealth and status, and was consigned to the outer limits of society. Austen returns to this theme again and again in her novels. In *Sense and Sensibility*, the worthy Colonel Brandon is supporting a woman and her illegitimate child. The disgraced woman is not allowed to enjoy the comforts of Colonel Brandon's home. He has "removed her and her child into the country, and there she remains."[55] In *Mansfield Park* Maria Rushworth, who leaves her husband for Henry Crawford and then separates from her lover, is banished from good society forever. Her father declares that he would never offer "so great an insult to the neighbourhood as to expect it to notice her."[56] She was forever tainted by her impulsive action, which went so grievously and explicitly against the mores of the society in which she lived. In *Pride and Prejudice*, Elizabeth Bennet's sister Lydia is saved from the social consequences of running off with the charming, but penniless and morally corrupt Wickham, only by means of the intervention of Mr. Darcy. Darcy, acting out of love for Elizabeth (and possibly a degree of humility, his own sister having nearly fallen into the same trap), arranges a small, private wedding and clears Wickham's debts, enabling the couple to assume a reasonably respectable life in military circles.

Another practice which can be jarring for a contemporary reader is the casual way in which Austen's characters expect to use their social connections for purposes of career advancement. Scheuermann takes this a step further, claiming that, in an Austen novel, "using connections to obtain advancement is not only respectable, it is the moral thing to do."[57] In *Mansfield Park*, for example, Fanny's brother William, who has no hope of advancement in the navy without such intervention, is fortunate enough to be introduced to an Admiral. His friend Henry Crawford, who had introduced them in an attempt to ingratiate himself with Fanny, requests that the Admiral write a letter in support of William. The letter does its work and William duly advances to the position of Lieutenant. As Scheuermann points out, this had nothing to do with William's qualifications and everything to do with Crawford's love for Fanny. "William's promotion, then, was entirely contingent on the fact that he and the admiral passed a pleasant evening together. And Austen sees nothing out of the way in this; it is simply the way of the world so natural as to be unremarkable."[58] Austen was very comfortable with this, given that it was the way her own brothers had advanced in their naval careers, with their father interceding on their behalf.[59] Her brother Frances ended his career as Admiral of the Fleet, the navy's highest rank, and Charles was a Rear Admiral, ending his career as Commander-in-Chief of the East Indies and China Station.[60]

For the most part, Jane Austen's characters are confined to the drawing room, the dining room, the library, the ballroom, the manicured gardens, the local assembly rooms, the promenade, and the town square. It seems at first glance that there is little to learn about the broader historical context of the important political or military events that affected Britain during the period of her novels. We, the readers, may meet parliamentarians, naval officers, and slave owners, but do not see them in parliament, at sea, or on their plantations. As Davidson puts it, "it is only the politics of the family, not the politics of the nation, that Austen's fiction renders visible."[61] Davidson goes on to say: "These are serious books about people with real problems, even if they take place in drawing rooms rather than prisons or battlefields or factories or any of the other places, most of them associated more strongly with men's lives than with women's that might be considered the domain of serious literature."[62]

However, a deeper look reveals insights to be gleaned about the broader context in which more narrow events occur. For example, Brian Southam in *Jane Austen and the Navy* comments that historians consider Austen to be "an accurate and dependable eye-witness to the naval matters of her time." He also notes that Sir Walter Elliot of *Persuasion* is quoted in *The Oxford Illustrated History of the Royal Navy* (1995) in a discussion of "naval patronage" and "the social comprehensiveness of the officer corps."[63] The novelist Pritchett has said: "[Austen's work is] [o]ften presented as an example of the felicity of living in a small, cosy world, with one's mind fairly withdrawn from the horror outside. This has always seemed to me untrue, I think of her as a war-novelist formed very much by the Napoleonic wars, knowing directly of prize money, the shortage of men, the economic crisis and change in the value of capital."[64] Clearly, Jane Austen is much more informative about her times than may be immediately obvious. One must dig a bit below the surface.

We now turn to iconic Canadian author Lucy Maud Montgomery (1874–1942). Montgomery's novels and story collections took place mostly on Prince Edward Island and provide a wealth of information about the quotidian details of rural life in Canada's Maritime region in the two decades before and after the turn of the twentieth century. Unlike Jane Austen's novels, which centre on the landed gentry and the upper classes, Montgomery's works are about rural farmers and working- and middle-class people in small towns, people too often ignored in history class. Her books portray the nitty-gritty of daily life in Canadian rural maritime communities, providing details about, for example, putting up preserves for the winter; spring cleaning; appropriate behaviour in various social situations; the place of religion; cultural practices around birth, marriage, illness, and death; behavioural expectations of children; modes of transportation; the education system, including tertiary education[65]; and class and gender relations.

Rilla of Ingleside is the last of the eight novels in the series that began with *Anne of Green Gables*.[66] Rilla, Anne's youngest child, is 15 years old when the novel begins at the start of the First World War. Rilla provides a compelling glimpse into life on the home front in a rural Canadian community during the war.[67] This novel, as journalist Sandra Gwyn has pointed out, is "virtually the only Canadian work of fiction to describe everyday life on the home front from direct personal experience."[68] As Elizabeth Epperly notes, the novel is "invaluable as a social record"[69] of the war period in Canada. Historian Susan Fisher calls *Rilla of Ingleside* "a documentary novel about Canada during the war years."[70] The phrase, "documentary novel," implies that, although it is a novel, which by definition, offers a certain licence to invent, it adheres to the limits of the historical record. In fact, it is one of the few period or historical novels about the Canadian home front in World War One that provides ongoing references to specific battles. Montgomery relied on passages from her own diaries to illuminate the impact of the news of these battles on those at home.[71]

Yes, the novel is peopled with what military historian Jonathan Vance calls "stock characters,"[72] and twenty-first-century novels about the First World War are written from very different perspectives, but that is why it is so useful as a window into the time in which it was written. Published in 1920, shortly after the war, *Rilla* represents the thoughts of many Canadians about the war in the interwar period. This is evident in the positive contemporary reviews, quoted at the beginning of this chapter. Vance has noted that, "by praising the novel's verisimilitude, reviewers shifted *Rilla of Ingleside* from fiction to history: it became a 'true' record of Canada's war and the fictionalization was merely an artistic device that only served to accentuate the book's authenticity."[73] Twenty-seven thousand copies of *Rilla of Ingleside* were sold in Canada in the years between the First and Second World Wars.[74] This is significant, given that the nation's population was only about 11,000,000 at the end of the interwar period.

Montgomery's home front is gendered, centring on the lives of the women of the village of Glen St. Mary and in particular, middle-class women who had some leisure time. As historian Sarah Glassford points out, "What contemporaries called 'war work' – women's unpaid labour for voluntary organizations and war charities – is an integral part of Montgomery's vision of the Canadian home front, as depicted in *Rilla of Ingleside*."[75]

> In church groups, family groups, and on their own, or through large national organizations such as the Women's Institutes, Imperial Order Daughters of the Empire (IODE), Canadian Red Cross Society, and Canadian Patriotic Fund, women raised millions of dollars and created tens of millions of comfort items, supplementary hospital supplies and prisoner of war food parcels.[76]

Thus, 15-year-old Rilla starts a Junior Red Cross league and her mother, with her friend Miss Cornelia, establishes a local Red Cross Society. According to Glassford, this was representative of what actually went on, as the Canadian Red Cross Society "expanded from a handful of branches to hundreds across Canada, including many on Prince Edward Island."[77] The women spend a great deal of time knitting and sewing for the soldiers overseas. Rilla, too, knits (an activity she detests). She remarks, "I just think of Jem [her brother] joking about the mud on Salisbury Plain and I go at them."[78] Rilla also organizes a patriotic entertainment to raise funds for Belgian refugees. Most centrally, she raises a war baby, a tiny boy whose mother has died and whose father has gone off to war. Above and beyond all of these activities, Montgomery highlights the agony of waiting at home for news of the action overseas. "There were moments when waiting at home, in safety and comfort, seemed an unendurable thing."[79] As Susan Fisher puts it, women on the home front, "reveal their courage not through battlefield derring-do but by carrying on despite their fear and their grief."[80] Over the course of the novel we see Rilla transform from a selfish adolescent to a mature, thoughtful young woman who puts aside her own petty concerns for the greater good. As Epperly says, "By the end of the novel we find that the apparently passive, apparently secondary role the women take is essential to the war effort and, equally importantly, to the continuation of a life of values and vision after the war."[81] Ultimately, "Montgomery's novel shows that women's work is often sacrificial, distasteful, and difficult, and frequently downplayed by members of the larger community."[82]

Rilla is an exception among Montgomery's novels. While *Rilla* examines the impact of a world war on people at home in Canada, other Montgomery novels rarely venture beyond local events. As one example, we do not read in *Anne of Green Gables* about a transformation in land ownership that took place during the time frame of that novel. The 1875 Land Purchase Act forced British absentee landowners, who owned the majority of land on the island, to sell it to the provincial government, who, in turn, sold it to the people who were living on it and paying rent. By 1880, most of the land in the province was owned by the people who occupied it. These events do not appear in the novel. It is important to make students aware that a novel depicts only selected aspects of life in a particular time and place. But then, we must remember that there is more happening at any time than can possibly be revealed by any single primary source.

Like *Rilla*, *The Great Gatsby*, by American author F. Scott Fitzgerald, is hugely informative about the period in which it was written. (Fig. 3.3). Historian John Lukacs tells us that he put it on the reading list for an American history course in lieu of readings on the politics of the 1920s or biographies of influential political leaders. He chose to do this because, in his view, the social and cultural changes during the period were both more consequential and more interesting than the governmental and political activities that took place during the same timespan.[83]

We include discussion of this novel here to indicate a caution about the use of period novels as the only source for an historical period. It is always important to corroborate with other sources. Lukacs quotes a literary critic, who said: "*The Great Gatsby* has become an international source for American social history and is read as a record of American life at an actual time and place."[84] However, there is a proviso. A historian using such novels must be aware of the limitations of the source because there is much that a writer does not explain and much that is not included. Lukacs references *Another Part of the Twenties*, published in 1973, in which historian Paul A. Carter, makes the point that not everyone living in the 1920s in the United States had the sort of experiences described in

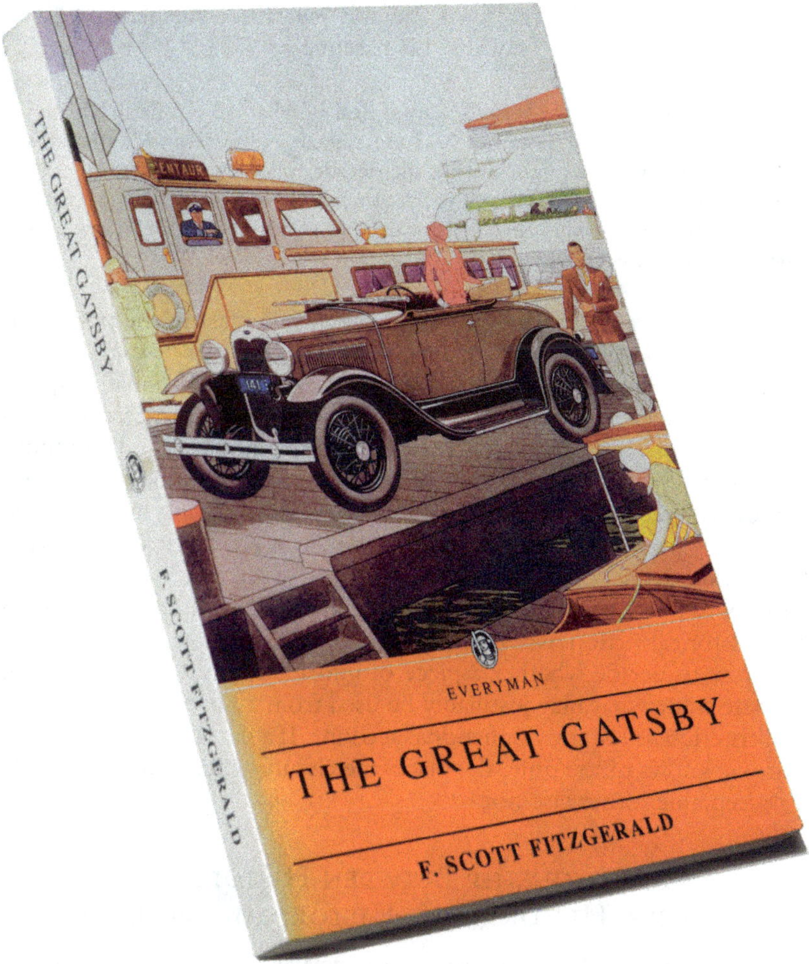

Fig. 3.3 *The Great Gatsby* by F. Scott Fitzgerald (*Source* CBW/Alamy Stock Photo)

Gatsby. He notes that his father could not have afforded a raccoon coat. About his mother, he says, "Snapshots and a portrait of her from the twenties show a strikingly attractive, high-spirited woman, but she was hardly a flapper as that term is ordinarily employed. Her idea of fun was a church social, and for vacations she and my father inexpensively went camping." He goes on to say that his parents:

> were not alone in having missed a good deal of what we ordinarily characterize as 'The Roaring Twenties'.... In fact, gazing away from Manhattan's Great White Way any night during the decade following 1920, one could have seen wide, dark stretches of the continent where the roar of the Twenties was muted indeed; where life was lived in a rhythm in which there was not the faintest echo of jazz.[85]

Lukacs acknowledges the validity of this, while making the point that, "This was (and still is) a big country. And *The Great Gatsby* is still a near-perfect period piece—and more: a description of a small segment of American society but also something beyond that: a concern with the insubstantial essence of what so many Americans thought (and still think) reality is."[86] So, a proviso is that we cannot naively assume that a novel is necessarily representative of the majority of people living in a particular place and a particular time. Nevertheless, it can represent one reality in illuminating detail.

As mentioned earlier, historian Barbara Tuchman is an advocate of using historical fiction as a primary source. She provides valuable advice as to how to decide whether a piece of information can be used or not. "To determine what may justifiably be used from a novel, one applies the same criterion as for any nonfictional account: If a particular item fits with what one knows of the time, the place, the circumstances, and the people, it is acceptable; otherwise not."[87]

Relationship Between Historical Novels, History, and Historical Evidence

In contrast to period novels, historical novels are fictional narratives that take place during a period in which the writer does not live. They cannot be used as primary sources for the time in which the events of the novel occur because they are not first-hand accounts; although they could be used as such for novelists' interpretations in the time in which they are written.

Authors of historical novels have a more complex task than do authors of period novels. As Renée Hulan has pointed out, "In its classic form, the historical novel creates a world which is sufficiently different to seem historical to the reader yet similar enough to make the past seem relevant to the present."[88] In creating her fictional narrative, the writer of the period novel has no need to concern herself with creating a world that is historical. The world the period novelist creates only becomes historical with the passage of time, something that is beyond the novelist's control.

> Fiction is based on historiography. It benefits from the quiet work done by historians in the shadows, which never reaches the large audiences for works of fiction. Novelists and writers read historians carefully, some of them going as far as detailing the sources and bibliographical references they used. History inspires and nurtures fiction. However, the former is not servile with respect to the latter. Fiction plays an essential role in the construction of imagination, especially by showing us lost worlds and by giving substance to what is no longer. Thus, fiction inspires and nurtures history.[89]

As discussed in Chapter 2 in the scholarly conversation pertaining to history and the arts, the essential difference between an historian and an author of historical novels is that the historian has a scholarly obligation to ground interpretations in the extant evidence. Many historical novelists also make extensive use of primary sources. However, novelists may feel far less constraint about departing from the historical record than do historians. It is useful for teachers to pose the question to their students: To what extent should the author of a historical novel be responsible for adhering to the extant historical evidence? It is revealing to consider the range of responses to this question on the part of authors of historical novels. We note that we don't need to ask this question about period novels. Because the authors of period novels are writing about their own time they don't have to research the details. They are swimming in them. It would be more relevant to ask to what extent the authors can see beyond the milieu in which they are immersed—but that is not our concern here.

For writers of historical novels history can be a source of inspiration and material for their art. British author Hilary Mantel found inspiration for her Man Booker Prize-winning characterization of Henry VIII's advisor Thomas Cromwell in *Wolf Hall*, not only in the history of the period but in historiography as well. In her research she became very aware of the contested interpretations of Cromwell presented by historians over the years and quite consciously developed her work to fit with some of the revisionist work on the man.[90]

While history is a source and inspiration, it can also raise challenges for an author. Mantel feels obligated to adhere to available historical evidence in order to make her stories as historically accurate as possible and, while free to fill in the gaps, she feels bound not to distort facts to make for more compelling art. She says, "I cannot describe to you what revulsion it inspires in me when people play around with the facts. If I were to distort something just to make it more convenient or dramatic, I would feel I'd failed as a writer.... you should be drawing the drama out of real life, not putting it there, like icing on a cake."[91]

Canadian author Margaret Atwood talks about the challenge of unearthing information about mundane quotidian details that have not been recorded because they were simply so taken for granted. She cites "how to clean a chamber pot, what footgear would have been worn in winter, the origins of quilt-pattern names, and how to store parsnips"[92] as examples of information which had to be researched for her novel *Alias Grace*, which took place in Canada West (now the Canadian province of Ontario) during the 1840s and was based on an actual murder and real people. Atwood developed a set of principles to guide her writing:

> when there was a solid fact, I could not alter it; long as I might to have Grace witness McDermott's execution, it could not be done, because, worse luck, she was already in the Penitentiary on that day.... but in the parts left unexplained—the gaps left unfilled—I was free to invent. Since there were a lot of gaps, there is a lot of invention. *Alias Grace* is very much a novel rather than a documentary.[93]

Mantel and Atwood are at one end of a lengthy continuum. The relationship between an author of historical novels and her evidence varies considerably from one writer to another and it can be a troubled one. Some authors have few qualms about altering the historical record for the sake of the story. Margaret Sweatman, author of *Fox* (Winnipeg, Canada, General Strike), has commented, "It is always kind of creepy when you do depart and steal and lie when you're working with the public domain. So I am an embezzler, you know, in public property, the history.... you need to depart from the historical record in order to create [your characters] on your own..."[94] For Charles Frazier, author of *Cold Mountain* (American

Civil War), this is not an issue. When asked which was more important, his clear-cut response was, "Let the fiction drive and the history ride."[95]

Sofia Grant (Littlewood) is closer to the middle of the continuum. She states that "historical accuracy is paramount," but adds that "we historical authors must cheat a bit in service of the story."[96] In a blog in which she gives advice to other authors, she advocates the use of a note to the reader to explain why changes from the historical record have been made. She remarks that a reviewer noted that she had included an ice maker in one of her novels two years before they were available in the United States. She had been aware of the anachronism, but needed it for her plotline, and assumed no one would notice. They did.

Michael Crummy, author of *River Thieves* (the extinct Beothuk of Newfoundland) takes a stance that could also be placed somewhere in the middle of the continuum: "You can't write it exactly as it was, because as a novel that would fail. So there were many places where I had to make decisions that collapsed characters into one another, changed the historical record slightly, to deal with aesthetic writerly questions like, 'How do I speed this up? How do I hold these things together?'"[97]

Ian Weir, author of *Will Starling*, which takes place in London, England in 1816, has commented, "If you've signed on to write a script based on true events, then you honour the principle of AMSU: Avoid Making Shit Up." He goes on to say, "Historical fiction implies a promise to the reader; this is a glimpse of what it was actually like." He describes spending two years researching *Will Starling*, commenting that, "it's … about scavenging shards of fact. The schedule of surgeries at Guy's Hospital and the occupation of Half-Hanged Smith, the going rates for exhumed cadavers and the bill of fare at the Coal Hole Tavern. All the thousands of shiny nails that a writer can use to hammer his planks together. By the time I'd finished, I had a platform that would hold the weight of a novel." So far so good, but, he goes on to say that "the [AMSU] principle remains sacred, right up to the point at which the script gets boring. Then, of course you make shit up."[98]

Historical novelist Guy Vanderhaeghe describes the relationship between historians and historical fiction authors as prickly:

> [W]riters of fiction sin … egregiously, blithely pronounce the unspoken thoughts of historical characters, and cavalierly ignore awkward facts or interpret them in ways a historian would never countenance. In the opinion of many historians, writers of historical fiction are nothing but magpies

> that pick up all the shiny, entertaining bits from the past, tart them up even more, and pass off their gaudy, cheap trinkets on an unsuspecting public. In prickly self-defence, historical novelists are likely to retort that the autopsies academic historians perform on the past drain all the blood from it....[99]

Vanderhaeghe reveals that historians and writers of fiction may have different purposes in mind when they construct their accounts, resulting in narratives that tell different truths. In *The Englishman's Boy* Vanderhaeghe described a rape that occurred after the Cypress Hills Massacre.[100] He was accused by an historian of "diminishing the atrocity by minimizing the number of Aboriginal women raped." Vanderhaeghe explains his decision by pointing to "My novelist's intuition [that] led me to focus all the violence and indignity inherent in an act of rape on one individual because I felt that in doing so, the scene would be more visceral, more repugnant, and more atrociously brutal."[101] He was not seeking to diminish the act but rather to allow the reader to understand it more profoundly and personally.

According to historical novelist Fred Stenson, "Historians can't invent in the gaps, so they wind up just building the structure all full of holes."[102] Yet, historian Jonathan Spence points out that historians too may in fact invent in the gaps, without necessarily being conscious of doing so.

> And yet, even being scrupulous, we may draw conclusions that are equivalent to filling gaps. For instance, we may assume that a missing conversation or memo in a sequence has no particular importance; we may take it for granted that something laying [sic] in the in tray on a desk was read by the intended recipient; we may assume someone noticed a sunset, or meant what they said about being in love. We may juxtapose pieces of information in such a way to imbue them with new meanings or at least hint at their interconnections.[103]

Artists, on the other hand, invent in the gaps with impunity. As Spence puts it: "It is true that the novelist can have a snowfall or earthquake virtually whenever he or she chooses, given certain constraints of verisimilitude, whereas the historian seeks clear proof that snow did fall on such and such a day or that the earth did quake and open."[104]

Conclusion

In his introduction to a 2005 issue of *Rethinking History* primarily devoted to historical fiction, historian David Harlan posed three central questions based on the discussions in the articles in the Forum section of the issue. These were: In what sense can historical novels be called histories? What can we learn from historical novels that we can't learn from academic histories? What does the growing popularity of historical fiction mean for the future of academic history?[105] These three questions provide a useful way to frame our concluding discussion for this chapter. We note that Harlan seems to use the terms historical novels and historical fiction interchangeably since he uses "historical novels" in his first two questions and then switches to "historical fiction" in his third question. We, therefore, take the liberty to refer to "historical fiction" (period and historical novels) rather than merely "historical novels" in all three questions.

In what sense can historical fiction be called history?

Historian John Demos has described the boundary between history and fiction as "less a boundary than a borderland of surprising width and variegated topography."[106] In the same issue of *Rethinking History* historian James Goodman makes the point that "The thing itself, the past, eludes us. But we never give up our faith in the chase."[107] Historians construct histories in an effort to come as close to past actualities as possible, but they can never replicate the past. He adds that "Fictional historians share that faith. Even when they take great leaps—when they imagine dialogue and interior monologues, when they fill gaps in the historical record with words—they leap to get closer to the past, the world outside the novel."[108]

As discussed in Chapter 2, histories are constructed accounts based on interpretations of the available evidence. Historical fiction authors vary in their adherence to the historical evidence, as discussed in this chapter, but they also construct accounts using evidence. Some authors of historical fiction feel at liberty to invent only in the gaps. Others allow themselves greater freedom to exercise their imagination. Therefore, the reader should corroborate a fictional account by comparing it to other historical sources and secondary accounts. As Demos says, "Fiction is fiction and history is history, but they do share a capacious borderland."[109]

What can we learn from historical fiction that we can't learn from academic histories?

Richard Hoggart sums up the value of novels by highlighting:

> their intrinsic power, their power as works of literature.... read in and for themselves, with an openness to the author's imagination and art—works of literature give an insight into the life of an age, a kind and intensity of insight, which no other source can give. They are not a substitute for these other sources, and to think so would be foolish. But it is just as foolish to think that these other sources can be sufficient in themselves. Without the full literary witness the student of society will be blind to the fullness of a society's life.[110]

James Goodman ended his contribution to the issue of *Rethinking History* with the words, "Novels arise out of the shortcomings of history."[111] John Demos talks about the way in which he gradually began to appreciate the value to historians of reading novels and refers to the ways in which history could benefit from the same concern with details demonstrated by novelists. He says, "Only thus can we do justice to all the textural (as opposed to structural) qualities of the life of the past." He also notes that, "But just as historians might well follow novelists in 'wrestling' more fully with the minutiae, so, too, might they follow in engaging more directly the foundations of (dare we say) the human condition.... Should we continue to leave the most basic, universal, and personally significant parts of all our lives to novelists, poets, philosophers, religious leaders, and their like? I hope not."[112]

Demos is pointing to two aspects of the value of historical fiction. The first involves the details it can provide about life as it was lived "in the bone"[113] as Richard Hoggart has put it. These are details that historians often fail to provide. Demos' second point is that novelists explore what he calls "the foundations of ... the human condition"—motivations, aspirations, loyalties, and the full range of human emotions. The licence that novelists have allows them to explore infinite possibilities. Demos contends that historians should also engage with these "foundations" because they are central to human experience and at the core of human choices and behaviour. Historian Herbert Butterfield made this point very well in 1924. Butterfield said "history cannot come so near to human hearts and human passions as a good novel can; its very fidelity to facts makes it not perhaps less true to life but further away from the heart of things."[114]

Renée Hulan says that "historical writing that renders an aesthetic experience of the past does not merely create an illusion of reality ... nor is it necessarily the death rattle of History ... rather ... it is the dialectical relation of material evidence and imagination."[115] Historical novels take the reader underneath and beyond the "facts" about a place and time. They can portray "the fullness of a society's life,"[116] giving the reader a sense of what it was actually like to live there. They can convey the daily details as to how people behaved in particular situations, class differences, expectations regarding gender, how people dressed, and so on. History lacks the imagination piece. It is the dialectical relation between material evidence and the ability to make intelligent interpretations based on prior knowledge and logical inferences. History can't take things as far or go as deep as historical fiction.

Jerome de Groot provides an analysis of the work of theorist Georg Lukacs and his view of the value of historical novels. He says

> For Lukacs, then, the historical novel is keenly important for various reasons. It represents historical process.... The realism of the novel allows the reader to engage with and empathize with historical individuals and thence gain a sense of their own historical specificity. It is able to communicate to people a sense of their own historicity and the ways that they might be able to construct historically inflected identities for themselves. The historical novel has a humanist impulse to teach and educate, and this pedagogical element is crucial for Lukacs; it is the movement to historicised revelation and understanding which is the point of the exercise.[117]

What does the growing popularity of historical fiction mean for the future of academic history?

Historical fiction certainly does not place academic history in jeopardy. On the contrary, fiction might inspire different questions on the part of historians that could lead to new ways of encountering the past. Historical and period novels may compel readers to find out more about life in the time and place they are reading about. They may wish to delve deeper and thus turn to secondary sources written by academic historians in order to do so. The growing popularity of historical fiction in the form of novels could lead to greater interest in reading historical accounts, viewing historical documentaries, or accessing depositories of historical remains such as museums, historic sites, art galleries, and archives. It could also invigorate interest in historical fiction in the form of films and plays. Novelists may be "exploiting the allure of history,"[118] but historical fiction and history can thrive in sync. As historian and archivist Sarah Glassford put it, with regard to fully understanding Canadian women's wartime experiences, "we must keep both our history books and our copies of *Rilla of Ingleside* close to hand."[119] This is such an apt way of expressing it: historical fiction and history both matter.

Notes

1. L.M. Montgomery, *Anne of Green Gables* (Philadelphia, PA: Running Press, 1993/1908).
2. L.M. Montgomery, *Rilla of Ingleside* (Toronto, ON: McClelland & Stewart), 1920.
3. "A Faithful and Worthy Picture," *The Globe* (Toronto, ON), in *The L.M. Montgomery Reader, Vol. 3: A Legacy in Review*, ed. Benjamin Lefebvre (Toronto, ON: University of Toronto Press, 2015), 229.
4. "May Be Read by Others Than Girls," *Saturday Night* (Toronto, ON), in *The L.M. Montgomery Reader, Vol. 3*, 234.
5. The Pasts Collective: Margaret Conrad, Kadriye Ercikan, Gerald Friesen, Jocelyn Létourneau, Del Muise, David Northrup and Peter Seixas, *Canadians and Their Pasts* (Toronto, ON: University of Toronto Press, 2013).
6. The Pasts Collective, *Canadians and Their Pasts*, 17.
7. Alexander MacLeod, "On the Road from Bright River: Shifting Social Space in *Anne of Green Gables*," in *Anne's World: A New Century of Anne of Green Gables*, ed. Irene Gammel and Benjamin Lefebvre (Toronto, ON: University of Toronto Press, 2010), 139.
8. Historical art fits within this category. It was not created to be "historical," but has become so over time.
9. John Lukacs, "The Great Gatsby? Yes, A Historical Novel," in *Remembered Past, John Lukacs on History, Historians, and Historical Knowledge: A Reader*, ed. M. G. Malvasi and J. O. Nelson, 721–26 (Washington, DC: ISI, 2005). Some of the material in this chapter first appeared in Penney Clark and Alan Sears, "Fiction, History and Pedagogy: A Double-Edged Sword," *Journal of Curriculum Studies* 49, no. 5 (2017): 620–39. http://doi.org/19.1080/00220272.2016.1238108, https://www.tandfonline.com/toc/tcus20/49/5?nav=tocList. It is used here with permission.
10. See Renée Hulan, "The Past is an Imagined Country," in *Settling and Unsettling Memories: Essays in Canadian Public History*, ed. Nicole Neatby and Peter Hodgins, 591–614 (Toronto, ON: University of Toronto Press, 2012).
11. Lukacs, "The Great Gatsby? Yes, A Historical Novel," 721.
12. Jerome de Groot, *The Historical Novel* (London: Abingdon, Oxon, 2010), 38.

13. Barbara Tuchman, "History by the Ounce," in *Practicing History: Selected Essays* (New York: Random House, 2014), 43.
14. Tuchman, "History by the Ounce," 43–44.
15. Christopher Bram, *The Art of History; Unlocking the Past in Fiction and Nonfiction* (Minneapolis, MN: Graywolf Press, 2016), 55.
16. Edith Wharton, *Age of Innocence* (New York: W. W. Norton, 2003/1920), 278.
17. Edith Wharton, *The House of Mirth* (New York: W. W. Norton, 1990/1905), 8.
18. R. Hoggart, "Literature and Society," in *A Guide to the Social Sciences*, ed. Norman Mackenzie (London: George Weidenfeld & Nicolson, 1966), 230.
19. Tuchman, *Practicing History*, 43.
20. Thomas Piketty, *Capital in the Twenty-First Century* (Cambridge, MA: The Belknap Press of Harvard University Press, 2014), 415.
21. Piketty, *Capital in the Twenty-First Century*, 2.
22. It is interesting to note that primogeniture is a significant plot driver in the popular contemporary period drama *Downton Abbey*—about the early twentieth century. The drama opens with news of the sinking of the Titanic and the death of Lord Grantham's closest male heir, putting his estate and his daughters' futures in jeopardy. Primogeniture continues to drive dramatic plots and interest contemporary audiences.
23. This law was intended to prevent estates from being broken up. The Statute of Wills (1540) permitted the eldest son to be cut off, but primogeniture remained the custom. It was abolished in 1925 as the governing rule when an individual died intestate. For an extended discussion of primogeniture in English literature, see Zouheir Jamoussi, *Primogeniture and Entail in England: A Survey of Their History and Representation in Literature* (Tunis, TN: Centre de Publication Universitaire, 1999).
24. Piketty, *Capital in the Twenty-First Century*, 362.
25. Jane Austen, *Pride and Prejudice* (London: T. Egerton, 1813, e-book ed., R.W. Chapman, Project Gutenberg, May 9, 2013), 372. See Mona Scheuermann, "Jane Austen: *Pride and Prejudice* and *Emma*," in *Her Bread to Earn: Women, Money and Society from Defoe to Austen* (Lexington, KY: The University Press of Kentucky, 1993), 209–10 for a brief discussion of this conversation and its explication of the status of a younger son in an aristocratic family.
26. Jane Austen, *Mansfield Park* (London: T. Egerton, 1814, e-book ed., Project Gutenberg, May 25, 2008), 48.
27. Ivor Morris, *Mr Collins Considered: Approaches to Jane Austen* (London and New York: Routledge & Kegan Paul, 1987), 51.
28. Austen, *Pride and Prejudice*, 10.
29. Jane Austen, *Pride and Prejudice*, 25.

30. Morris, *Mr Collins Considered*, 35.
31. Mark Schorer, "The Humiliation of Emma Woodhouse," *The Literary Review* 2, no. 4 (Summer 1959): 550.
32. Schorer, "Humiliation," *The Literary Review*, 550.
33. Schorer, 548, 549.
34. Scheuermann, "Jane Austen: *Pride and Prejudice* and *Emma*," 225.
35. Jenny Davidson, *Reading Jane Austen* (Cambridge, UK: Cambridge University Press, 2017), 20.
36. Jane Austen, *Emma* (London: John Murray, 1815, e-book ed., Project Gutenberg, May 25, 2008), 86.
37. Austen, *Pride and Prejudice*, 231.
38. Austen, *Pride and Prejudice*, 251.
39. Austen, *Pride and Prejudice*, 251.
40. Austen, *Mansfield Park*, 9.
41. Austen, *Mansfield Park*, 1.
42. Austen, *Mansfield Park*, 3.
43. Mona Scheuermann, *Reading Jane Austen* (New York: Palgrave Macmillan, 2009), 35.
44. Davidson, *Reading Jane Austen*, 131.
45. Jane Austen, *Persuasion* (London: John Murray, 1818, e-book ed., Project Gutenberg, June 20, 2019), 383.
46. Austen, *Emma*, 108.
47. Austen, *Emma*, 27.
48. John Sutherland, *Who Betrays Elizabeth Bennet? Further Puzzles in Classic Fiction* (Oxford: Oxford University Press, 1999), 17.
49. Austen, *Pride and Prejudice*, 718–24.
50. Scheuerman, *Reading Jane Austen*, 125.
51. Austen, *Emma*, 47.
52. Arnold Kettle, *An Introduction to the English Novel* (New York: Harper & Row, 1951), 99, quoted in Scheuermann, *Her Bread to Earn*, 279.
53. Scheuermann, "Jane Austen: *Pride and Prejudice* and *Emma*," 238.
54. Austen, *Persuasion*, 36.
55. Jane Austen, *Sense and Sensibility* (London: T. Egerton, 1811, e-book ed., Project Gutenberg, May 25, 2008), 397.
56. Austen, *Mansfield Park*, 238.
57. Scheuermann, *Reading Jane Austen*, 35.
58. Scheuermann, *Reading Jane Austen*, 62.
59. Scheuermann, *Reading Jane Austen*, 201.
60. See Brian Southam, *Jane Austen and the Navy* (London and New York: Hambledon and London, 2000) for an extended discussion of the careers of Austen's brothers Frances and Charles and their relationship with their sister Jane.
61. Davidson, *Reading Jane Austen*, 142.

62. Davidson, *Reading Jane Austen*, 142–43.
63. Southam, *Jane Austen and the Navy*, 10. Here is an example of period fiction informing an historical account.
64. V.S. Pritchett, *George Meredith and English Comedy* (New York: Random House, 1970), quoted in Brian Southam, *Jane Austen and the Navy*, 10.
65. For a discussion of child-centred education in *Anne of Green Gables* see Jennifer Henderson, "At Normal School: Seton, Montgomery and the New Education," in *Home-work: Postcolonialism, Pedagogy, and Canadian Literature*, ed. C. Sugars, 461–85 (Ottawa, ON: University of Ottawa Press, 2004).
66. Montgomery, *Rilla of Ingleside*. This novel is the eighth and last in terms of the chronology of the Anne narrative. It was the sixth that L.M. Montgomery wrote.
67. See Andrea McKenzie and Jane Ledwell, eds., "Introduction," in *L.M. Montgomery and War* (Montreal, QC and Kingston, ON: McGill-Queen's University Press, 2017), 18 for a discussion of the depiction of war in *Rilla*. McKenzie and Ledwell point out that *Rilla* "is the only novel about the First World War by a Canadian author who experienced it to still be in print in a trade edition," 18, and yet it did not appear on any of the lists of war novels recommended by mainstream Canadian cultural institutions in 2014 to mark the centenary of the beginning of the war. Their view is that the novel should have been included and they contend that "she can be considered as a forerunner of later Canadian authors who challenge the male, battle-centred vision of Canada's war or who question the myth of a unified Canada," 18. They point out that *Rilla* is often considered to be a children's book, which may have been one reason it was disqualified. They also point out, with reference to English professor Donna Coates, that "women's wartime writing has been completely ignored" (Donna Coates, "The Best Soldiers of All: Unsung Heroines in Canadian Women's Great War Fictions," *Canadian Literature* 151 (1996): 66). Finally, they note that Montgomery's views (which were more nuanced than has been recognized) were not in keeping with present-day attitudes towards war.
68. Sandra Gwyn, *Tapestry of War: A Private View of Canadians in the Great War* (Toronto, ON: Harper*Perennial*Canada, 1992), 144.
69. Elizabeth Rollins Epperly, *The Fragrance of Sweet-Grass: L.M. Montgomery's Heroines and the Pursuit of Romance* (Toronto: University of Toronto Press, 2014/1993), 114.
70. Susan Fisher, *Boys and Girls in No Man's Land: English-Canadian Children and the First World War* (Toronto: University of Toronto Press, 2011), 213.
71. Epperly, *The Fragrance of Sweet-Grass*, 113.

72. Jonathan Vance, *Death So Noble: Memory, Meaning, and the First World War* (Vancouver, BC: UBC Press, 1997), 175.
73. Vance, *Death So Noble*, 176.
74. Vance, 176.
75. Sarah Glassford, "'I Must Do Something to Help at Home': *Rilla of Ingleside* in the Context of Real Women's War Work," in *L.M. Montgomery and War*, ed. Andrea McKenzie and Jane Ledwell (Montreal, QC and Kingston, ON: McGill-Queen's University Press, 2017), 131.
76. Glassford, "'I Must Do Something to Help at Home'," 130.
77. Glassford, 132.
78. Montgomery, *Rilla of Ingleside*, 79.
79. Montgomery, 144.
80. Fisher, *Boys and Girls in No Man's Land*, 213.
81. Epperly, *The Fragrance of Sweet-Grass*, 114.
82. Laura M. Robinson, "L.M. Montgomery's Great War: The Home as Battleground in *Rilla of Ingleside*," in *L.M. Montgomery and War*, 114.
83. Lukacs, "The Great Gatsby? Yes, a Historical Novel," 722–23.
84. Lukacs, 721–26.
85. Paul A. Carter, *Another Part of the Twenties* (New York: Columbia University Press, 1977), Lukacs, 724–25.
86. Lukacs, "The Great Gatsby? Yes, a Historical Novel," 725.
87. Tuchman, "History by the Ounce," 44.
88. Hulan, "The Past is an Imagined Country," 596.
89. Nadine Fink, "The Force of Fiction," *Public History Weekly* 6, 2018. https://doi.org/10.1515/phw-2018-11199.
90. Larissa MacFarquhar, *The Dead Are Real: Hilary Mantel's Imagination*. Retrieved from http://www.newyorker.com/magazine/2012/10/15/the-dead-are-real.
91. Quoted in MacFarquhar.
92. Margaret Atwood, "In Search of Alias Grace: On Writing Canadian Historical Fiction," *The American Historical Review* 103: 1514.
93. Atwood, "In Search of Alias Grace," 1515.
94. Herb Wyile, "Ghosts Are Our Allies, Margaret Sweatman," interview in *Speaking in the Past Tense: Canadian Novelists on Writing Historical Fiction* (Waterloo, ON: Wilfrid Laurier University Press, 2007), 171.
95. Charles Frazier, "Some Remarks on History and Fiction," in *Historians and Novelists Confront America's Past (and Each Other)*, ed. M.C. Carnes (New York: Simon & Schuster, 2001), 313.
96. Sofia Grant, "6 Keys to Writing a Compelling Historical Novel," *The Writer's Dig*, July 26, 2017. http://www.writersdigest.com/online-editor/6-keys-writing-compelling-historical-novel.
97. Wyile, 301.
98. Ian Weir, "Scaling the Mountain," *Quill & Quire* 80 (2014): 42.

99. Guy Vanderhaeghe, "Apprehending the Past: History Versus the Historical Novel," *The Trudeau Foundation Papers*, 11, 2010, 76. Retrieved from http://www.trudeaufoundation.ca/sites/default/files/u5/trudeaupapers2010.pdf.
100. This event, which occurred on June 1, 1873, involved the murder of 20 or more Indigenous men by a group of mainly American men. It occurred in the Cypress Hills area of the Northwest Territories (now Saskatchewan).
101. Vanderhaeghe, 83.
102. Wyile, "History 'from the Workingman's End of the Telescope', Fred Stenson," interview in *Speaking in the Past Tense*, 201.
103. J.D. Spence, "Margaret Atwood and the Edges of History," *The American Historical Review* 103, no. 5 (1998): 1523–524.
104. Spence, "Margaret Atwood and the Edges of History," 1522.
105. David Harlan, "In This Issue," *Rethinking History: The Journal of Theory and Practice* 9, nos. 2/3 (June/September 2005): 143. https://doi.org/10.1080/13642520500148980.
106. John Demos, "Afterword: Notes From, and About, the History/Fiction Borderland," *Rethinking History* 9, nos. 2/3 (June/September 2005): 329. https://doi.org/10.1080/1362520500149178.
107. James Goodman, "Fictional History," *Rethinking History: The Journal of Theory and Practice* 9, nos. 2/3 (June/September 2005): 246. https://doi.org/10.1080/1362520500149178.
108. Goodman, "Fictional History," 246–47.
109. Demos, "Afterword," 334–35.
110. Hoggart, "Literature and Society," 226.
111. Goodman, "Fictional History," 253.
112. John Demos, "In Search of Reasons for Historians to Read Novels," *The American Historical Review* 103 (December 1998): 1526–529.
113. Hoggart, "Literature and Society," 230.
114. Herbert Butterfield, *The Historical Novel: An Essay* (Cambridge: Cambridge University Press, 1924), 18.
115. Renée Hulan, "Preface," in *Canadian Historical Writing: Reading the Remains* (New York: Palgrave Macmillan, 2014), xvii.
116. Hoggart, "Literature and Society," 226.
117. de Groot, Jerome, *The Historical Novel*, 29.
118. Herb Wyile, *Speculative Fictions: Contemporary Canadian Novelists and the Writing of History* (Montreal, QC and Kingston, ON: McGill-Queen's University Press, 2002), 255.
119. Glassford, "I Must Do Something to Help at Home," 142.

Bibliography

"A Faithful and Worthy Picture." *The Globe* (Toronto, ON). In *The L.M. Montgomery Reader, Vol. 3: A Legacy in Review*, edited by Benjamin Lefebvre. Toronto, ON: University of Toronto Press, 2015.

Atwood, Margaret. "In Search of Alias Grace: On Writing Canadian Historical Fiction." *The American Historical Review* 103 (1998): 1503–516.

Austen, Jane. *Emma*. London: John Murray, 1815, e-book ed., Project Gutenberg, May 25, 2008.

Austen, Jane. *Mansfield Park*. London: T. Egerton, 1814, e-book. Project Gutenberg, May 25, 2008.

Austen, Jane. *Persuasion*. London: John Murray, 1818, e-book ed., Project Gutenberg, June 20, 2019.

Austen, Jane. *Pride and Prejudice*. London: T. Egerton, 1813, e-book ed., R.W. Chapman, Project Gutenberg, May 9, 2013.

Austen, Jane. *Sense and Sensibility*. London: T. Egerton, 1811, e-book ed., Project Gutenberg, May 25, 2008.

Bram, Christopher. *The Art of History: Unlocking the Past in Fiction and Nonfiction*. Minneapolis, MN: Graywolf Press, 2016.

Butterfield, Herbert. *The Historical Novel: An Essay*. Cambridge: Cambridge University Press, 1924.

Carter, Paul A. *Another Part of the Twenties*. New York: Columbia University Press, 1977.

Clark, Penney and Alan Sears. "Fiction, History and Pedagogy: A Double-Edged Sword." *Journal of Curriculum Studies* 49, no. 5 (2017): 620–39.

Coates, Donna. "The Best Soldiers of All: Unsung Heroines in Canadian Women's Great War Fictions." *Canadian Literature* 151 (1996): 66–99.

Davidson, Davidson. *Reading Jane Austen*. Cambridge, UK: Cambridge University Press, 2017.

de Groot, Jerome. *The Historical Novel*. London: Abingdon, Oxon, 2010.

Demos, John. "In Search of Reasons for Historians to Read Novels." *The American Historical Review* 103 (December 1998): 1526–529.

Demos, John. "Afterword: Notes From, and About, the History/Fiction Borderland." *Rethinking History: The Journal of Theory and Practice* 9, nos. 2/3 (June/September 2005): 329–35. https://doi.org/10.1080/136252050014 9178.

Eliot, George. *Romola*. London: Smith, Elder, 1863.

Eliot, George. *Felix Holt, the Radical*. London: Blackwood and Sons, 1866.

Eliot, George. *Middlemarch*. Oxford: Oxford University Press, 1871/2008.

Epperly, Elizabeth Rollins. *The Fragrance of Sweet-Grass: L.M. Montgomery's Heroines and the Pursuit of Romance*. Toronto, ON: University of Toronto Press, 2014/1993.

Fink, Nadine. "The Force of Fiction." *Public History Weekly* 6, 2018. https://doi.org/10.1515/phw-2018-11199.

Fisher, Susan. *Boys and Girls in No Man's Land: English-Canadian Children and the First World War*. Toronto, ON: University of Toronto Press, 2011.

Fitzgerald, F. Scott. *The Great Gatsby*. New York: Scribner, 1925.

Forster, E.M. *A Passage to India*. London: Edward Arnold, 1924.

Frazier, Charles. "Some Remarks on History and Fiction." In *Historians and Novelists Confront America's Past (and Each Other)*, edited by M.C. Carnes, 311–15. New York: Simon & Schuster, 2001.

Glassford, Sarah. "'I Must Do Something to Help at Home': *Rilla of Ingleside* in the Context of Real Women's War Work." In *L.M. Montgomery and War*, edited by Andrea McKenzie and Jane Ledwell, 128-45. Montreal, QC and Kingston, ON: McGill-Queen's University Press, 2017.

Goodman, James. "Fictional History." *Rethinking History: The Journal of Theory and Practice* 9, nos. 2/3 (June/September 2005): 246. https://doi.org/10.1080/1362520500149178.

Grant, Sofia. "6 Keys to Writing a Compelling Historical Novel." *The Writer's Dig*, July 26, 2017. http://www.writersdigest.com/online-editor/6-keys-writing-compelling-historical-novel.

Gwyn, Sandra. *Tapestry of War: A Private View of Canadians in the Great War*. Toronto, ON: Harper Perennial Canada, 1992.

Harlan, David. "In This Issue." *Rethinking History: The Journal of Theory and Practice* 9, nos. 2/3 (June/September 2005): 143. https://doi.org/10.1080/13642520500148980.

Henderson, Jennifer. "At Normal School: Seton, Montgomery and the New Education." In *Home-work: Postcolonialism, Pedagogy and Canadian Literature*, edited by C. Sugars, 461–85. Ottawa, ON: University of Ottawa Press, 2004.

Hoggart, Richard. "Literature and Society." In *A Guide to the Social Sciences*, edited by Norman MacKenzie, 225–48. London: George Weidenfeld & Nicolson, 1966.

Hulan, Renée. "The Past is an Imagined Country." In *Settling and Unsettling Memories: Essays in Canadian Public History*, edited by Nicole Neatby and Peter Hodgins, 591–614. Toronto, ON: University of Toronto Press, 2012.

Hulan, Renée. "Preface." In *Canadian Historical Writing: Reading the Remains*. New York: Palgrave Macmillan, 2014.

James, Henry. *Portrait of a Lady*. New York: Collier, 1917.

Jamoussi, Zouheir. *Primogeniture and Entail in England: A Survey of Their History and Representation in Literature*. Tunis, TN: Centre de Publication Universitaire, 1999.

Kettle, Arnold. *An Introduction to the English Novel*. New York: Harper & Row, 1951.

Lee, Harper. *To Kill a Mockingbird*. Philadelphia: J.B. Lippincott, 1960.

Lukacs, John. "The Great Gatsby? Yes, A Historical Novel." In *Remembered Past, John Lukacs on History, Historians, and Historical Knowledge: A Reader*, edited by M.G. Malvasi and J.O. Nelson, 721–26. Washington, DC: ISI, 2005.

MacFarquhar, Larissa. *The Dead Are Real: Hilary Mantel's Imagination*, October 8, 2012. Retrieved from http://www.newyorker.com/magazine/2012/10/15/the-dead-are-real.

MacLeod, Alexander. "On the Road from Bright River: Shifting Social Space in *Anne of Green Gables*." In *Anne's World: A New Century of Anne of Green Gables*, edited by Irene Gammel and Benjamin Lefebvre, 134–49. Toronto, ON: University of Toronto Press, 2010.

"May Be Read by Others Than Girls." *The Globe* (Toronto, ON). In *The L.M. Montgomery Reader, Vol. 3: A Legacy in Review*, edited by Benjamin Lefebvre, 233-34. Toronto, ON: University of Toronto Press, 2015.

McKenzie, Andrea and Jane Ledwell, ed. "Introduction." In *L.M. Montgomery and War*, 3–37. Montreal, QC and Kingston, ON: McGill-Queen's University Press, 2017.

Montgomery, L.M. *Anne of Green Gables*. Philadelphia, PA: Running Press, 1993/1908.

Montgomery, L.M. *Rilla of Ingleside*. Toronto, ON: McClelland & Stewart, 1920.

Morris, Ivor. *Mr Collins Considered: Approaches to Jane Austen*. London and New York: Routledge & Kegan Paul, 1987.

Piketty, Thomas. *Capital in the Twenty-First Century*. Cambridge, MA: The Belknap Press of Harvard University Press, 2014.

Pritchett, V.S. *George Meredith and English Comedy*. New York: Random House, 1970.

Robinson, Laura M. "L.M. Montgomery's Great War: The Home as Battleground in *Rilla of Ingleside*." In *L.M. Montgomery and War*, edited by Andrea McKenzie and Jane Ledwell, 113–27. Montreal, QC and Kingston, ON: McGill-Queen's University Press, 2017.

Sackville-West, Victoria. *The Edwardians*. London: Hogarth, 1930.

Saturday Night (Toronto, ON). In *The L.M. Montgomery Reader, Vol. 3*, edited by Benjamin Lefebvre. Toronto, ON: University of Toronto Press.

Scheuermann, Mona. "Jane Austen: *Pride and Prejudice* and *Emma*." In *Her Bread to Earn: Women, Money and Society from Defoe to Austen*. Lexington, KY: The University Press of Kentucky, 1993.

Scheuermann, Mona. *Reading Jane Austen*. New York: Palgrave Macmillan, 2009.

Schorer, Mark. "The Humiliation of Emma Woodhouse." *The Literary Review* 2, no. 4 (Summer 1959): 547–63.

Southam, Brian. *Jane Austen and the Navy.* London and New York: Hambledon and London, 2000.

Spence, J.D. "Margaret Atwood and the Edges of History." *The American Historical Review* 103, no. 5 (1998): 1523–524.

Steinbeck, John. *The Grapes of Wrath.* New York: Viking, 1939.

Stendahl (Henri Marie Beyle). *The Red and the Black.* New York: Modern Library, 1984/1830.

Sutherland, John. *Who Betrays Elizabeth Bennet? Further Puzzles in Classic Fiction.* Oxford: Oxford University Press, 1999.

The Pasts Collective: Conrad, Margaret, Kadriye Ercikan, Gerald Friesen, Jocelyn Létourneau, Del Muise, David Northrup and Peter Seixas. *Canadians and Their Pasts.* Toronto, ON: University of Toronto Press, 2013.

Tuchman, Barbara. "History by the Ounce." In *Practicing History: Selected Essays*, 35–47. New York: Random House, 2014.

Turgenev, Ivan Sergeevich. *Rudin.* Baltimore, MD: Penguin, 1974/1856.

Turgenev, Ivan Sergeevich. *Fathers and Sons.* New York: Norton, 1989/1862.

Vance, Jonathan F. *Death so Noble: Memory, Meaning, and the First World War.* Vancouver, BC: UBC Press, 1997.

Vanderhaeghe, Guy. "Apprehending the Past: History Versus the Historical Novel." *The Trudeau Foundation Papers*, 11, 2010. Retrieved from http://www.trudeaufoundation.ca/sites/default/files/u5/trudeaupapers2010.pdf.

Weir, Ian. "Scaling the Mountain." *Quill & Quire* 80 (2014): 42.

Wharton, Edith. *The House of Mirth.* New York: W. W. Norton, 1990/1905.

Wharton, Edith. *Age of Innocence.* New York: W. W. Norton, 2003/1920.

Woolf, Virginia. *Mrs. Dalloway.* New York: Harcourt Brace, 1925.

Wyile, Herb. *Speculative Fictions: Contemporary Canadian Novelists and the Writing of History.* Montreal, QC and Kingston, ON: McGill-Queen's University Press, 2002.

Wyile, Herb. *Speaking in the Past Tense: Canadian Novelists on Writing Historical Fiction.* Waterloo, ON: Wilfrid Laurier Press, 2007.

CHAPTER 4

Beyond Adornment: Visual Art as Source and Account in History Classrooms and Public Spaces

A visitor arriving at the railway station in Strasbourg, Germany in late 1883 passed under two mural paintings designed to show the benevolent and enduring nature of German rule in the region. The "paintings connected the new Reich with the old Reich of the twelfth century: one of them depicted a visit by the medieval emperor Barbarossa to Alsace, the other one showed the visit of emperor Wilhelm I in 1877, with Alsatian women in folk dress welcoming him."[1] The continuity portrayed in these murals belied the tenuous and shifting relationship the region of Alsace had with the German state. Until 1870 the region and its capital of Strasbourg had been part of France. It was annexed to Germany in 1871 as part of the settlement of the Franco-Prussian War, one of a number of such shifts of control of the area that occurred between 1681 and 1945.

This annexation of the region to Germany "was not welcome in Alsace" and this resistance led the Germans to attempt "thoroughly Germanising Alsace."[2] These "Germanisation measures which at times were both vexatious and ridiculous encompassed the elimination of anything reminiscent of the French past of Alsace"[3] in public spaces, and the imposition of a thoroughly German past through images such as the ones portrayed in the railway station murals, statues of iconic German figures in public spaces, and the suppression of French as a public language.

Just as art was a key aspect of the programme of Germanization, it was also an important part of resistance to it. Irish scholar Detmar

P. Clark and A. Sears, *The Arts and the Teaching of History*,
https://doi.org/10.1007/978-3-030-51513-3_4

Klein argues this began after the annexation when Alsatians realized political agitation "had a detrimental effect on their material interests,"[4] and turned to more subtle forms of resistance. This originated when "French artists such as Alsatian-born Jean-Jacques Henner started displaying the iconic figure of l'Alsacienne, the Alsatian woman in her traditional folk costume with her butterfly-shaped headdress, the coiffe."[5] It later morphed into far more edgy portrayals of the German occupiers including the "openly uncompromising Germanophobia displayed in the caricatures and satirical writings of Hansi (Jean-Jaques Waltz) and Henri Zislin."[6] These artists employed iconography as a weapon portraying Germans as "ugly, bespectacled and badly dressed, they are supercilious and have militaristic mannerisms – in short, they are a ridiculous species."[7] One of Hansi's posters from 1915, for example, shows a German soldier in uniform with, what one assumes, are the fruits of his looting of French homes (a grandfather clock, umbrella, teapot, bottle of wine, ladies' boots, etc.) strapped to his back, under his arms, or dangling from his hands. The slogan "Armée Allemande: soldat du regiment du Kronprinz tenue de campagne" (field dress of a soldier of the German Army, regiment of the Crown Prince) adorns the bottom of the poster.[8]

This image of the ugly, uncouth, and kleptocratic German is contrasted in Hansi and Zislin's art by the "archetypal Alsacienne—in her folk costume with the coiffe."

> She is pure and untainted by the opportunism and collaboration chosen by many men out of economic necessity or political expediency; she fights a battle against the Germans and her Function as a mother, imbues her children with the same spirit of resistance.[9]

American researcher Laird Boswell contends this "myth of Alsace and Lorraine" spread far beyond the region to become "a constituent part of French identity and patriotism."[10]

We chose these examples of German and Alsatian visual culture to open this chapter because they illustrate well key elements of our case for using visual art in the teaching and learning of history. First, they show the ubiquitous nature of images related to the past. These images were part of everyday life for Alsatians during the period between 1870 and the end of the Second World War and, the Alsatian ones at least, remain so today. Dissident artists like Hansi endure as folk heroes in the region and copies of their art adorn many public spaces and much of the tourist kitsch sold in local shops.

Philosopher Fred Evans reminds us that public art is pervasive in all societies. It shows up in public spaces, museums, galleries, the posters on our classroom and bedroom walls, and, particularly interesting from a teaching point of view, in school textbooks. Evans also makes the point that its presence is neither neutral nor benign. It is certainly true, he argues, that public art is conceived of and shaped by members of the public, but it also plays a role in shaping the public, in creating a particular type of citizen. "Art," he writes, "does more than merely provide a lesson or entertainment. It often sends a condensed shock of recognition through us that provokes us to repeat in thought, language, or action what its more immediate presence is suggesting."[11] It therefore seems to us important for citizens to understand how art operates to shape historical consciousness and, consequently, social organization and public policy.

Second, art is an important source of information about the past and is often used by historians in their own work. Related to our opening example, contemporary scholars "have explored the notion of a specific Alsatian consciousness and identity that developed in the course of the Reichsland period,"[12] and the art of the time has been an important source for that project. Historian Matthew Sears makes the point that "art objects represent a complex and difficult category of evidence for the historian."[13] Sears studies the ancient world and a dearth of written sources enhances the importance of visual and material sources for his work, but even historians of more contemporary times draw extensively on art as a source as we discuss in more detail below.

Third, art provides important and diverse accounts of the past that should be studied and interrogated alongside more traditional accounts from books, articles, or film. The murals adorning the train station in Strasbourg discussed above provided an account of the past of the region which was disrupted by the dissident accounts provided by local artists. We discuss several more examples of both officially sanctioned, or iconic, artistic accounts as well as visual counter narratives below. Engaging with multiple perspectives on the past is a key aspect of good history teaching and art provides one vehicle for doing this.

Finally, engaging with art potentially enriches and extends the history curriculum. The shifting relationship between France and Germany was central to the history of Europe and the world in the nineteenth and twentieth centuries, and the Rhineland regions of Alsace and Lorraine were a key focus of the tension between the two countries. Virtually every school history student in Europe and North America will study topics like the unification of Germany, the Franco-Prussian War, and the two world wars of the twentieth century. In doing so they will hear about the several transfers of sovereignty over Alsace and Lorraine. The art described here provides a potential window to take students beyond the macro view of European geopolitics into how these events were experienced by ordinary people, a focus that has great potential for fostering interest and enhancing historical understanding.

The Ubiquitous Presence of Art

Visual art on historical themes is everywhere, in art galleries, museums, in and around public spaces, on the walls of our houses and classrooms, in textbooks, on the internet, on money, and in the television shows and movies we watch. We suspect, though, that while it is ever-present, it is often just background noise and almost never examined closely or interrogated in the way historical sources or accounts should be. We note that visual art already has a prominent place in history classrooms. Teachers habitually have posters or prints on their walls and textbooks often use paintings and other visual imagery to support their textual content. Unfortunately, research indicates that students do not necessarily attend to this visual information, viewing it as superfluous to the content of the written text.[14]

When overt attention is paid to art, it is often not the kind of critical readings required to foster complex historical understandings. We know, for example, that people generally regard historical information and narratives presented in visual displays at museums and galleries to be much more reliable than history teachers. They believe that in encountering artefacts and pictures from the past they are getting a direct and unmediated presentation of history. They do not recognize the curatorial processes involved in mounting displays or the inadequacies, perspectives, or biases inherent in visual materials.[15]

There is wide agreement among those who study visual culture that these images exert considerable influence over us in a number of ways. Literary scholar Sherrill Grace puts it this way,

> I take it for granted that the arts matter and that they exert considerable power in, as well as bringing great pleasure to, our lives. Moreover, I assume that, collectively, they have and continue to represent, illustrate, narrate, shape, and inform identity, our personal identities and the identities of any number of social groups or physical places to which we might belong...[16]

Arts and media educator Karen Stanworth agrees and pushes further, arguing that the images around us largely reflect and determine relations of power and influence in a society. She points out that "Normative images that dominate everyday culture are not normal they are normalized by and through visual practices that are the result of uneven relations of power."[17] In other words, public visual culture defines, or at least tries to, who is included, marginalized, or excluded in any society.

In his discussion of Benjamin West's eighteenth-century painting *The Death of General Wolfe*, public historian Simon Schama illustrates the power of art to set normative parameters for a society (see Fig. 4.9). He argues that West's painting became "an icon of the British Empire," and that "when British children of future generations grew up drilled in the pieties of imperial history, it was West's scene they imagined rather than any more literal account."[18]

Treating visual art as simply an adornment in public spaces or history classrooms, as something that pretties up rooms or makes textbook pages a little more inviting, is a disservice both to the art and to students of history. As we have shown above and argue more fully below, artistic images are important vehicles for conveying historical information and "truths" and, as such, it is important that young people be taught to pay close attention to them and read them in critical ways. As David Harlan points out: "if our students are to become thoughtful and resourceful readers of the past...they will have to become adept at finding their way between competing but equally valid truth claims made in distinct and often divergent modes of historical representation."[19] We now turn to some specific ways for doing just that.

Visual Art as Primary Source

Ludmilla Jordanova cautions that some historians may have reservations about the use of visuals as primary sources because "compared to documents and printed matter, they are less weighty and historically significant. They can be deemed trivial." She goes on to say that this

> simply mean[s] that, as is always the case, we have to define clearly what phenomena they can and cannot testify to. Since people have always experienced the world through their eyes and given weight to the resulting experiences, it follows that what is artfully made is especially culturally, socially, politically, and economically dense. It is unreasonable to marginalize certain kinds of sources a priori without first thinking hard about what they do and do not reveal.[20]

Leon Battista Alberti (1991/1435) eloquently articulated the point we are going to make now in 1435. He said: "Painting possesses a truly divine power in that not only does it make the absent present (as they say of friendship), but it also represents the dead to the living many centuries later." Of course, the same could be said of any primary source. Visual art is a primary source for the time and place in which it was created, and historians have long made use of it in this way. In the chapter, "What Were They Thinking?" in *The War That Ended Peace*, historian Margaret MacMillan used visual art to construct her account of culture and social mores in Europe just prior to the First World War. One way she demonstrates how old institutions and values were under attack is by describing how young Austrian painters no longer tried to represent the world as it actually was, but "probe[d] beneath the surface into the life of instinct and emotion."[21]

MacMillan is arguing that art can provide a sense of the spirit or ethos of an age that is often missing in other sources. In Chapter 3 we make a similar case about fiction which, we argue, can provide information about the worldviews and perspectives of whole classes of people in visceral, engaging, and wholistic ways. It provides the opportunity to immerse oneself in other times and places in an affective rather than strictly analytical way. We think that visual art has the same potential to provide a deeper experience of the past that connects students to two elements of historical thinking: perspective taking and wrestling with the ethical dimension of history. Canadian war art affords a good example of this.

The war artist programme was initiated by Max Aitkin, later known as Lord Beaverbrook, in 1916. Beaverbrook hired over 116 artists in Canada and Great Britain to document scenes of Canada at war. Beginning with the Great War and continuing through the Second World War, the Korean Conflict, and more recent engagements in the Arabian Gulf region, Kosovo, Bosnia, Canada and other Commonwealth countries sent artists to war to document aspects of the conflicts in painting. The last Canadian war artist, Ted Zuber, who illustrated aspects of conflicts from Korea, Europe, and the Gulf, died in October of 2018.[22] Canada now has a repository of hundreds of artistic representations of war made by some of its best known artists. Many of these are held by public museums such as the Canadian War Museum or the National Gallery and pictorial representations of them are available online.

All of this begs the question, why send artists to war to paint? This question seems especially relevant in the twentieth and twenty-first centuries when major conflicts are comprehensively documented in film and photographs. What can painters possibly add to this visual record? Grace addresses this question arguing artists (including writers, painters, and photographers) deal with the human experience of war and the ethical dimensions of conflict in ways that are not adequately explored in other sources. She approvingly quotes documentary film-maker Terrance McKenna who claimed that until "documentary film was created, only our painters were telling us the truth."[23] We contend that even after the advent of documentary films, painters have something unique to contribute to the historical record. Alexandra Walton illustrates this point when writing about the collection of British war art held at the Imperial War Museum in London.

> For as long as people have waged wars, they have also responded to conflict through visual art forms, such as painting, sculpture, drawing, printmaking, and photography. This response was driven by the desire to understand their war experience and to communicate that understanding to others.[24]

It follows then, that if subsequent generations want to understand not only the conflicts of the past, but also how peoples of the time experienced and thought about them, this visual record becomes an important source.

A striking example of the unique truth telling of artists commended by Grace is the 1946 painting by Lieutenant Jack Nichols titled *Drowning Sailor*. This painting, worked up from a sketch done in 1944 when

Nichols was serving on a Canadian warship, is a dark and disturbing portrayal of the horror of being swallowed up in a cold, unforgiving sea. Eyes wide open, mouth agape in a primal scream, body constrained by swirling currents, the sailor is sucked down into oblivion. Canada lost 24 warships during the Second World War and more than 2000 sailors perished. As well, the Canadian navy participated in the sinking of 32 enemy vessels and, therefore, the death of thousands of adversaries. Interestingly, Nichols' sailor is painted with no indication of nationality. As the artist commented later, "When you are drowning you lose your nationality, don't you?" This is not a celebration of Canadian courage or a lament for national loss, it is, as the Canadian War Museum says of all of Nichols' work, a study of "the human experience of war."[25] It confronts observers with powerful truths about the arbitrariness of war in a way that is emotionally and aesthetically impactful.

Grace recognizes this kind of truth telling is not always comfortable or welcome. She documents shifts in Canadians' attitudes towards war and commemoration over time, writing that

> Canadians have gone from celebrating war, however cautiously, to realistic depictions of battle, followed by a period (during the Cold War) of repressing war trauma and downplaying former military activities, to our recent painful rediscovery of the meaning of both world wars for the development of the country and, lastly, to attempts to understand our latest experiences abroad as peacekeepers and combatants.[26]

These changing times impacted the ways in which officials treated Canadian war art. For years the collection was largely hidden away because, Grace argues, it is so strikingly effective and did not fit the propagandistic inclinations of officials and institutions more interested in nationalistic and patriotic depictions. It was finally "rescued from the oblivion of storage vaults" for a "national touring exhibition between 2000 and 2004, and then hung (some of it at least) on permanent display in the Canadian War Museum when it opened in 2005."[27]

Elsewhere we have written about the power of this kind of visceral source to engage people and provide insights into history not available from other sources. We have also cautioned that the very force of art is like a "double-edged sword" which cuts both ways. It opens up potentially new historical understandings but also has the potential to draw observers in, blinding them to alternative readings offered by other sources.[28] This is not a reason to avoid artistic sources in history classrooms, but does call for their careful treatment by well-prepared teachers. In Chapter 6 we explore some specific ways to do this.

The overall aesthetic force or impact of painting is only one point of interest to historians. The content of a painting is also revealing. Karen Stanworth makes the case that visual culture is fundamental to understanding Canada in the nineteenth century, writing "that a close and detailed analysis of pictorial imagery can shed light on a number of issues in Canadian socio-cultural history." She goes on to make the point that "sometimes the only source of documentation is pictorial" because there is no surviving written documentation.[29] For historians of more distant pasts where written sources were nonexistent or the materials on which they were written have long since turned to dust, this is even more true. For example, Paul Cartledge calls iconography "the keynote of my penultimate class of evidence for the history of ancient Greek democracy and specifically democracy at Athens."[30]

British Renaissance scholar Jerry Brotton agrees that paintings often provide a window into a particular time and context. He demonstrates this in his discussion of Hans Holbein the Younger's painting, *The Ambassadors*, which depicts two French diplomats to the court of Henry VIII (see Fig. 4.1). The painting, Brotton argues, uses the placement of objects to "illustrate the commercial and religious discord of the time."[31] For example, one of the objects in the painting is a globe including the controversial dividing line defined by the Treaty of Tordesillas that separated the world into Portuguese and Spanish spheres of influence. It is not simply the placement of objects, however, but the objects themselves that are revealing, and Brotton shows how close attention to the painting can reveal important and specific aspects of the Renaissance that are sometimes glossed over or forgotten.

> Yet if we look even more closely at the objects in Holbein's painting, they lead us to quite another version of the Renaissance. On the lower shelf one of the strings on the lute is broken, a symbol of discord. Next to the lute is an open hymn book, identifiable as the work of the religious reformer Martin Luther. On the [left-hand] edge of the painting, the curtain is slightly pulled back to reveal a silver crucifix. These objects draw our attention to religious debate and discord in the Renaissance. When Holbein painted it, Luther's Protestant ideas were sweeping through Europe, defying the established authority of the Roman Catholic Church.

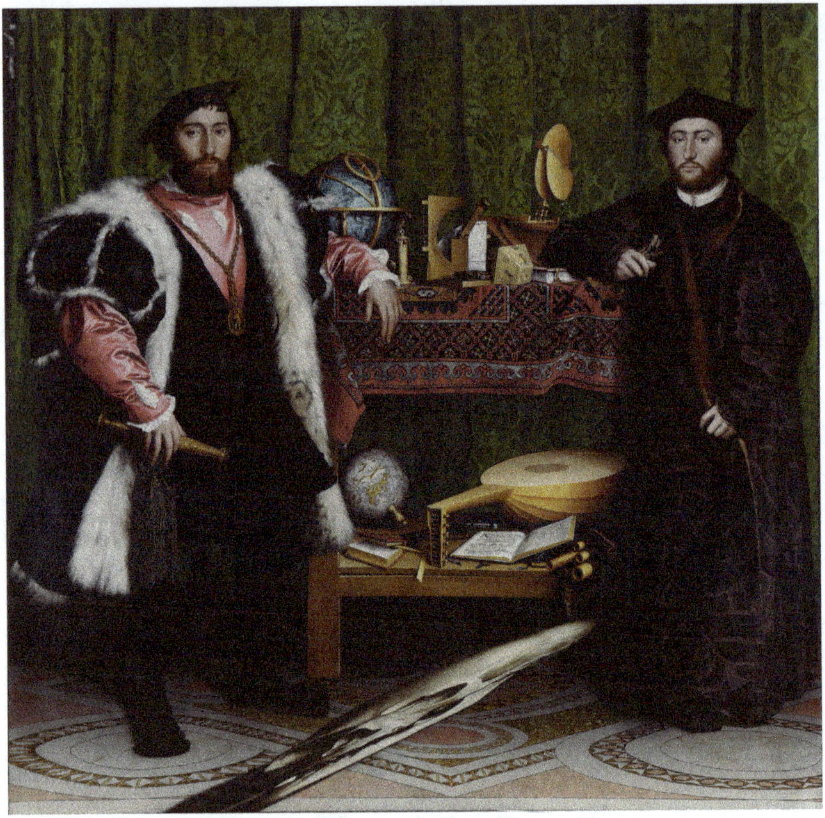

Fig. 4.1 *The Ambassadors* (1533) painting by Hans Holbein the younger (*Source* Antiquarian images/Alamy stock photo)

> The broken lute is a powerful symbol of the religious conflict characterized by Holbein in his juxtaposition of Lutheran hymn book and Catholic crucifix.[32]

For Brotton, the real power of the painting as a source, however, lies in its depiction of an important human turning point. Holbein breaks with the tradition of including religious objects in this type of painting, replacing them with "globes, scientific instruments and mercantile textbooks." This is key evidence of "a world in transition, caught between the religious certainties of the past and the political, intellectual and commercial excitement of a rapidly changing present. Religion is quite literally sidelined, its remaining presence that of a silver crucifix barely visible behind a curtain in the top left-hand corner."[33]

In his fascinating book, *Vermeer's Hat*, historian Timothy Brook uses several paintings by Dutch painter Johannes Vermeer of life in Holland, created in mid-seventeenth century, to demonstrate his points about world trade and cultural exchange at the time. He contends, for example, that Vermeer's painting *Officer and Laughing Girl* is "an almost generic account of the new rules governing how young men and women in polite Dutch society courted in the late 1650s" (see Fig. 4.2).[34]

He points out that only a few decades earlier a young woman of high station and an officer would not have been allowed the opportunity for a private flirtation such as this. The painting depicts a shift in gender relations that involved the acquisition of a great deal more social power by young women. Then Brook takes the reader beyond what is easily evident in the painting to its global connections, specifically to Champlain and the fur trade (which was fuelled by the European demand for beaver hats such as the one the officer is wearing), and the dream of finding a route to China; the officer's fur hat being a by-product of that search.

Vermeer painted during a time when the Dutch were dominant players in world trade, not only of furs from North America but also of spices from the so-called Spice Islands of the South Pacific. He painted not only the material items of that trade, but he was also fascinated with maps which he recreated in precise detail in several of his paintings. In *Officer and Laughing Girl*, for example, Vermeer "depicts a map of Holland and West Friesland" which is "as visually arresting as the painting's main subjects."[35] Jerry Brotton argues that in the reproduction of this map Vermeer is making a political statement, joining "his artistic contemporaries in displaying popular pride at the political and geographical unity of the recently independent Republic."[36] The map is not merely background, but is a source for important information about political and social sensibilities of the period.

For Brotton, maps connect to art not simply as subjects reproduced by painters like Vermeer and others, but as works of art themselves. Throughout his book, *The History of the World in Twelve Maps*, he argues that maps are not only attempts to represent the physical world more or less accurately, but creative works that are infused with the world-views of the people and times that produced them. "A map," he writes,

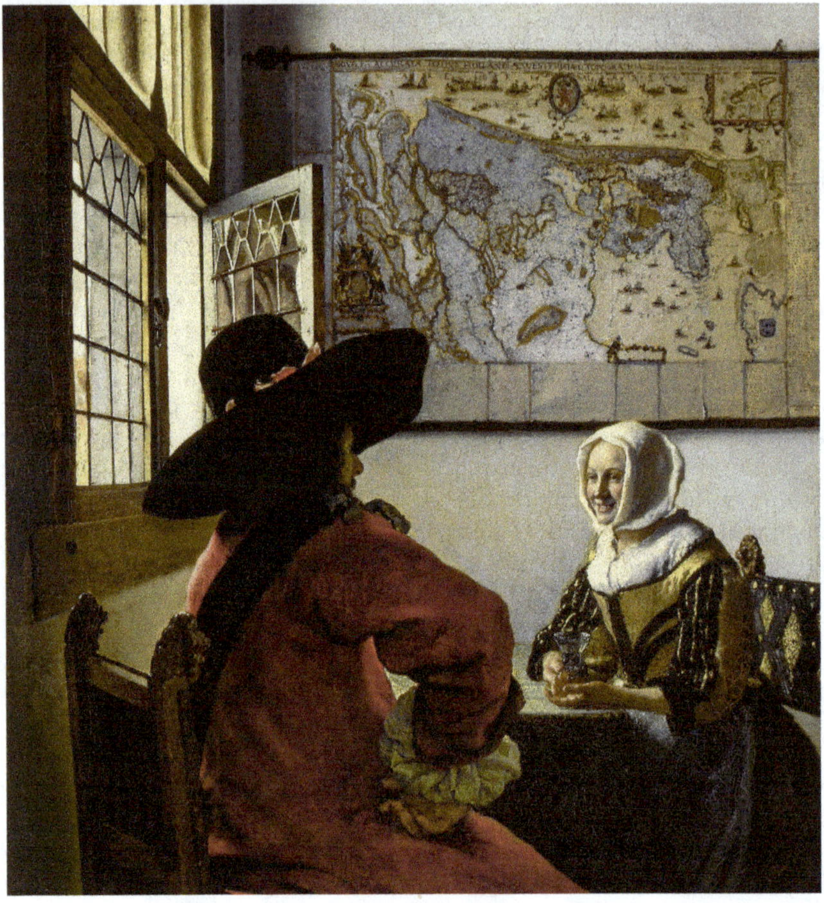

Fig. 4.2 *Officer and Laughing Girl* painting by Johannes Vermeer (*Source* Incamerastock/Alamy stock photo)

"draws on artistic methods of execution to create an ultimately imaginative representation of an unknowable object (the world)..."[37] This is well illustrated in a map from the turn of the fourteenth century called the *Hereford Mappa Mundi*. It gets the first part of its name from the cathedral in England where it hangs but the second literally means "cloth of the world" (see Fig. 4.3). Brotton calls it "one of the most important

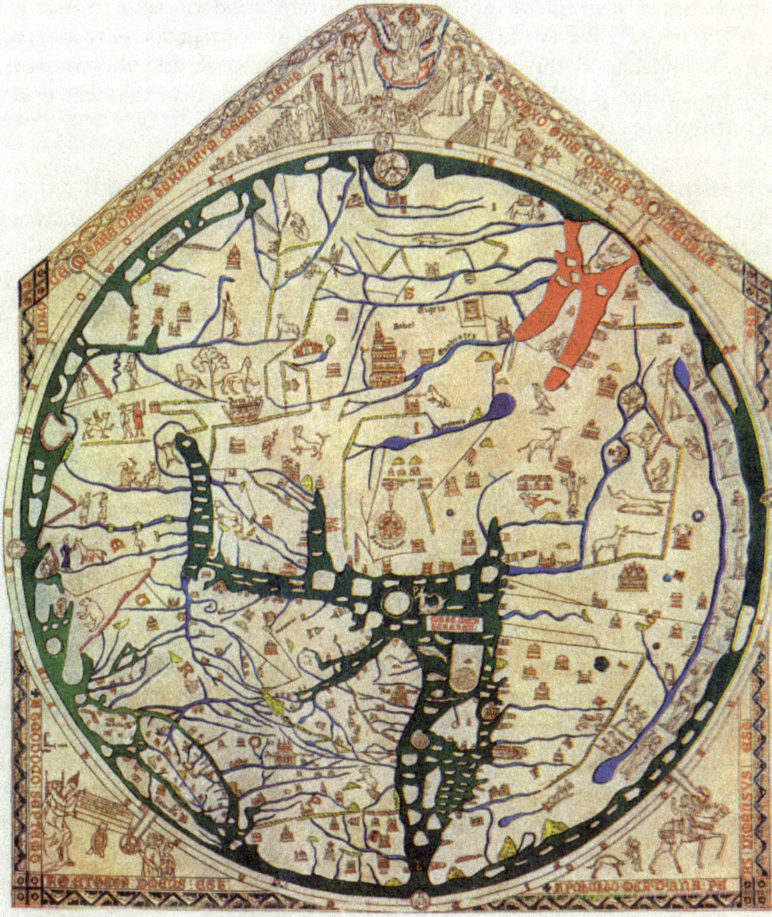

Fig. 4.3 *Hereford Mappa Mundi* of 1280 showing Jerusalem at the centre Europe is lower left Africa is lower right (*Source* North wind picture archives/Alamy stock photo)

maps in the history of cartography" offering "an encyclopedic vision of what the world looked like to a thirteenth century Christian."[38] He goes on to write,

> This is not a map as we understand it in any modern sense. Instead, it is an image of a world defined by theology, not geography, where place is understood through faith rather than location, and the passage of time according to biblical events is more important than the depiction of territorial space.[39]

This is such a potentially important source for understanding the period in which it was created that the BBC subtitled its documentary of *Mappa Mundi*, "Mapping the Medieval Mind."[40]

Sherrill Grace also makes a compelling argument that maps are indeed artistic creations that engage with perspective and form to provide an image of the world and help us imagine, or reimagine, places and times.[41] She uses the example of the map *Inuit View of the South* which is part of the front matter for Canadian author Rudy Wiebe's book, *Playing Dead: A Contemplation Concerning the Arctic*.[42] In the book Wiebe contrasts Inuit and Western worldviews and how those contrasts have played out over time in the Canadian Arctic. A key example for him is the ill-fated Franklin Expedition of the mid-nineteenth century. The map is a fairly standard cartographic representation of part of Canada except that its orientation on the page is quite different than normal. The view is looking down on the country with the northern coastline of the Arctic ocean at the centre with the southern, and usually more prominent regions, fading to relative insignificance at the periphery of the map. Its placement at the front of the book is a visual cue that historical perspective taking is a key theme of the work. As one reviewer puts it, through encountering the map at the front of the book readers "are immediately, and aptly, invited to consider an Arctic perspective."[43] This disrupting of the traditional representation of the geography of Canada pushes Wiebe's point about considering alternative perspectives, and also illustrates the constructed and creative character of maps. The map is now part of the collection of the Virtual Museum of Canada and can be accessed online there.[44] Thinking about maps as works of art that reflect the worldview and perspective of peoples, places, and times has the potential to foster much more sophisticated student engagement with historical sources and ideas.

Visual Art as Account

There is another layer of complexity. A painting, sculpture, or memorial site can accurately depict an historical period and, in doing so, can provide the historian with information about that time and place. However, as with other sources, there are limitations to the use of visual art and students must be made aware of those limitations. Visual representations are not simply traces of the past to be accepted as evidence but are constructed accounts that reflect the perspective and purposes of the artist. Artistic products can even be "fiction" in the same way that a novel is fiction. Historical reality may have been deliberately altered in order to please a wealthy patron or potential purchaser. Or, important historical details may have been omitted because they were not aesthetically pleasing to the artist, or because they were deemed to be irrelevant to, or countered the particular narrative the artist intended to communicate.

Sometimes, like novelists, painters distort reality or use metaphors not to hide the truth but to reveal it more fully. Picasso's greatest historical piece, *Guernica* is not a straightforward depiction of the bombing of a sleepy Spanish town in the civil war, but it certainly evokes a deep sense of the horror of that event beyond, perhaps, what a more realistic image might evoke (see Fig. 4.4). Picasso noted that the bull represented brutality and darkness and the horse the people of Guernica.

Of course, reading art as an historical account in any of these ways is a complex task that requires particular skills and knowledge. While visual material adorns school textbooks and other educational materials as well as sites of public history, it often remains unexamined. The works included are what Stanworth calls "normative images" and are, she argues, critical to the construction of social identities. The problem is, "normative images that dominate everyday culture are not normal, they are normalized by and through visual practices that are the result of uneven relations of power."[45] Paintings like Benjamin West's *The Death of General Wolfe* reveal a great deal about what was considered to be important in the eighteenth century (see Fig. 4.9). They "depict white men in political action – Englishmen vanquish Frenchmen; they all conquer the aboriginal population: women are not a factor."[46] She argues we should move beyond the passive acceptance of these images as background noise to recognize "the visual is politicized and the political is visual."[47] It seems to us just this kind of recognition is, or should be, an important part of history education.

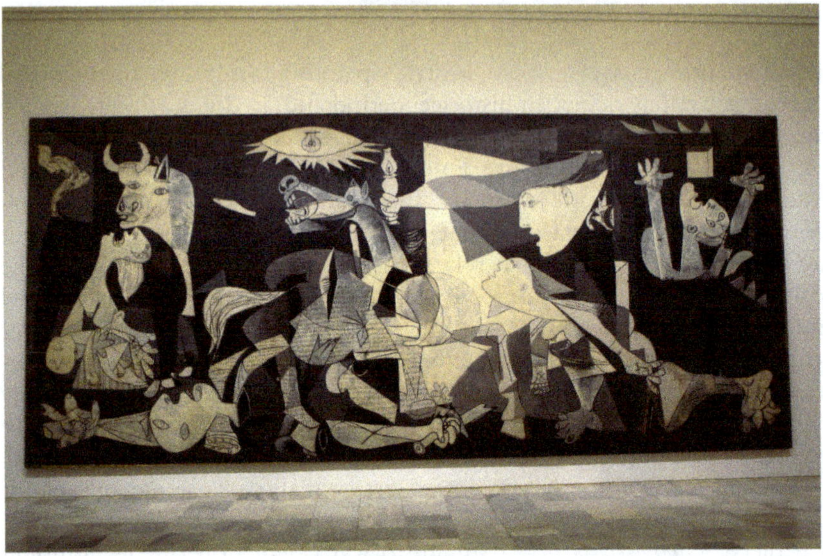

Fig. 4.4 *Guernica* painting by Pablo Picasso at the Centro de Arte Reina Sofia in Madrid Spain (*Source* Greek photonews/Alamy stock photo)

There is perhaps no more iconic and "normalized" image in Canada than *The Fathers of Confederation*. The painting was originally commissioned in 1883 to depict the 23 attendees at the Charlottetown Conference of September 1864, where the idea of British North American colonies uniting to form what was to become Canada was first discussed. Before the painting was complete the artist, Robert Harris, was asked to change the location to Québec where a subsequent conference was held later in the same year. This larger venue allowed Harris to add ten figures (all European men) to the 23 originally proposed. Harris's painting was lost when the Parliament buildings were destroyed by fire in 1916. In the mid-1960s Rex Woods was commissioned by a private insurance company to recreate the painting in honour of Canada's impending centennial year celebrations in 1967 (see Fig. 4.5). Woods did that, adding three additional figures who attended the London Conference of 1866 where the final deal for Canada was sealed.[48]

The picture presents a widely accepted account of the creation of Canada grounded on the idea that visionary men assembled in various

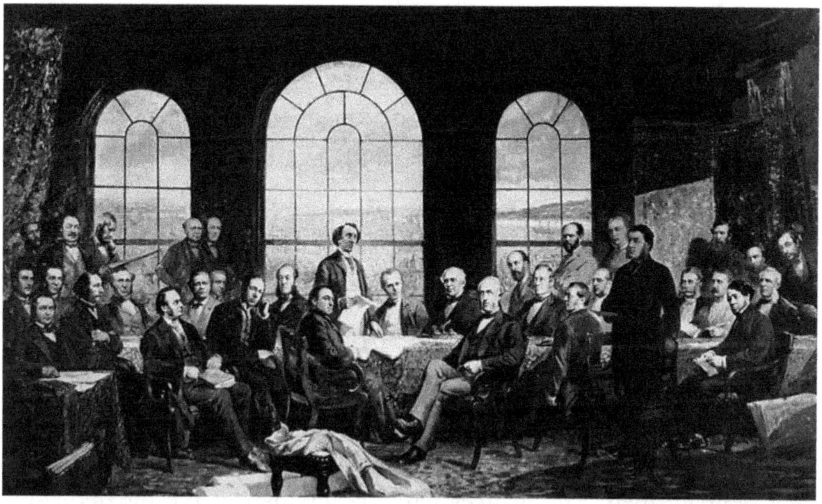

Fig. 4.5 *Fathers of Confederation* painting by Rex Woods (*Source* © House of Commons Collection, Ottawa)

locations during the middle part of the 1860s and created an unlikely country out of disparate, reluctant, and often quarrelling colonies. They did so with a combination of visionary insight, Machiavellian strategy, and tenacious persistence. The same narrative is reflected in the work of popular historians such as Christopher Moore whose book *1867: How the Fathers Made a Deal* sets out to restore the sense of the immense accomplishment of "the Fathers" in the face of what he saw as contemporary neglect or cynicism about their role in establishing Canada.[49] Moore's book was published with the famous painting on the cover. Journalist and historian Richard Gwyn narrows the focus even further to the "Father" who became the first prime minister calling him "the man who made us."[50] For these historians, and others, "the Fathers," in spite of all their faults, created what became one of the best countries on earth.

In response to this progress narrative of Canadian greatness, Indigenous artist Kent Monkman uses art to present a counter or dissident narrative. Evans argues that "dissident public art counts as an act of citizenship when it reflects a democratic ethos and corrects the government's support of art that implicitly or explicitly promotes autocratic values."[51]

The painting *The Fathers of Confederation* and, we argue, the narrative it sustains, certainly enjoy government support. The work hangs in the Parliament of Canada and adorns many Canadian history textbooks which are virtually all government sanctioned. In the eyes of many from the Indigenous community, and others, this narrative, at least implicitly, promotes autocratic values by downplaying or even ignoring the immense injustices perpetrated on Indigenous Peoples as a result of the original deal and the unfolding of Confederation from 1867 onwards.

Monkman counters this narrative directly in his painting *The Daddies* which was created as part of a series of works in response to the 150th commemoration of Confederation in 2017 (see Fig. 4.6). In *The Daddies* Monkman reproduces core elements of the Harris painting of *The Fathers* but includes the trickster Miss Chief Eagle Testickle sitting naked before John A. Macdonald and the other "Daddies," reclining on a Hudson's Bay Company blanket. Miss Chief is clearly holding forth to instruct the assembled men. The blanket symbolically invokes the fur trade, and other exploitive aspects of Indigenous-Settler relations. The intrusion of Miss Chief into this iconic image "is a characteristic move by the 51-year-old Mr. Monkman, whose work constantly messes with accepted

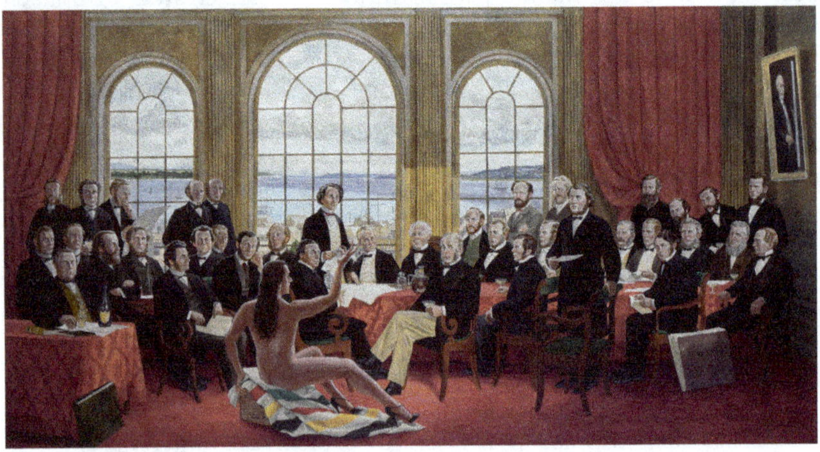

Fig. 4.6 *The Daddies*, Kent Monkman 2016. Acrylic on canvas 60" x 112.5" (*Source* Image courtesy of the artist)

visual codes."[52] Among other things it raises questions about the traditional narratives of Canadian Confederation, including consideration of who is not included in the original picture and the events it is meant to commemorate.

Monkman draws on traditional and widely known aspects of the Western art canon to present "transgressive narratives" that "set up a provocative friction between Canadian national myths, aboriginal experience and traditional European art practices."[53] In his work *The Scream*, Monkman intentionally invokes the name of the nineteenth-century painting by Expressionist artist Edvard Munch (see Fig. 4.7). The British Museum calls Munch's painting "art's most haunting and iconic face. A universal symbol of anxiety."[54] In this case Monkman does not reproduce the image but draws on the name's universal evocation of extreme angst to make his point. His painting depicting the abduction of Indigenous children by members of the Royal Canadian Mounted Police (RCMP) as well as Roman Catholic priests and nuns is foregrounded by a scream: the terrified expression of an Indigenous mother held back by two Mounties

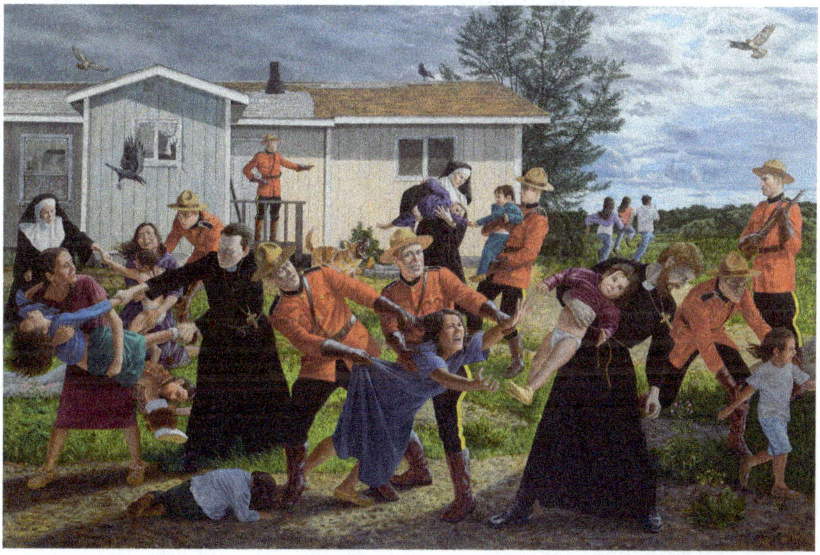

Fig. 4.7 *The Scream*, Kent Monkman 2017. Acrylic on canvas 84" x 126" (*Source* Collection of the Denver Art Museum. Image courtesy of the artist)

in their iconic red serge uniforms while a priest carries away her child into the residential school system. Around this central motif several other mothers grapple with police and representatives of the Church while their children are ripped from their arms and the Mountie in charge directs attention to three children trying to run away.

As he was with *The Daddies,* Monkman is again presenting a powerful counter narrative to more mainstream depictions of the past. Michael Dawson points out that the image of the Mountie (the nickname for an individual member of the RCMP) is ubiquitous in Canadian popular culture, appearing on everything from baby clothing to coffee mugs and shot glasses. This widespread affiliation with all things Mountie is, he argues, "the tangible product of individual achievements and the force's central role in the expansion of Canada's western and northern frontiers."[55] In the middle years of the twentieth century this regard for the Mounties made its way into popular histories and a series of Hollywood films which portrayed the national police force as purveyors of good against a set of formidable enemies including "Indigenous peoples, French Canadians, Eastern European immigrants and, occasionally, Americans."[56] In these accounts, Mounties effectively tamed the frontier and made it safe for civilized and modern settlement. In the face of shifting public sensibilities in the 1970s the force mounted an aggressive public relations effort to remake its image. In Dawson's view, "this involved a highly selective approach to history, one that would emphasize (and at times simply invent) elements of its past that were likely to win over an increasingly skeptical public, such as ethnic harmony and a positive relationship with Indigenous people."[57]

It is as a counter point to this official history that Monkman presents *The Scream* and a number of other paintings that depict the role of the RCMP in abducting children for the residential school system. These paintings do not depict actual events and are often inaccurate in specific ways, for example, members of the RCMP do not wear their red dress uniforms on regular patrols, but the works do present a powerful and compelling challenge to widely accepted popular history. We are not suggesting that teachers should replace one narrative with another, rather we advocate engaging students in reading both in sophisticated ways in order to understand the story being advocated and the ways in which the artists present their work to make their points. Students can also be led to consider the relative merits of the accounts in light of other primary and secondary sources they have encountered.

Beyond Adornment: Visual Art in the Classroom

We conclude this chapter by examining three examples of visual art often found in textbooks or other classroom materials and exploring their potential both as sources and accounts in the study of history. The three are: the Bayeux Tapestry, Benjamin West's *The Death of Wolfe*, and Canadian war artist William Roberts' *The First German Gas Attack at Ypres*. All of these raise questions about the value and limitations of paintings both as primary sources and as accounts.

The Bayeux Tapestry, actually an embroidery, has been called "a primary source for the history of England" which "deserves to be studied alongside the accounts in the Anglo-Saxon Chronicle and in William of Poitiers" (see Fig. 4.8).[58] This tapestry, which is about 70 metres long, depicts the Norman Conquest of England led by William the Conqueror in 1066.

The Tapestry, now held in its own museum in Bayeux, France, is included in UNESCO's Memory of the World registry. There it is recognized as an exceptional work of art, but also as valuable as both historical source and account.

> The Tapestry is a historical account, but also an essential source of information on the way of life in the Middle Ages in general, and the eleventh century in particular: it is therefore a documentary record which employs

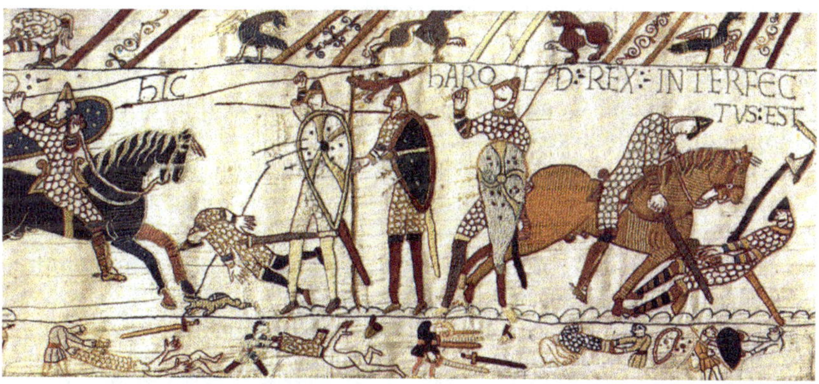

Fig. 4.8 *Bayeux Tapestry* depicting The Battle of Hastings (*Source* GL archive/Alamy stock photo)

> particular narrative techniques and makes use of symbolism, as do many literary and artistic works of the Romanesque period.[59]

French historian François Neveux agrees, writing that "the Embroidery is not only an historical account; it is also an essential source of knowledge of medieval life in general, and of the eleventh century in particular."[60]

Over the years a generally accepted historical consensus emerged about the cloth, including ideas about who commissioned it and why. Michael Crafton summarizes aspects of that consensus:

> Most modern scholarship on the Bayeux Tapestry tends to work under some key assumptions about its provenance: the tapestry was created in England, not long after the Conquest, under the patronage of Bishop Odo, half-brother to William and bishop of the city of Bayeux in France, where its existence was first recorded in 1476 and where it remains today.[61]

In addition to general agreement about where, when, and by whom it was made, scholars have also tended to agree that it was produced to justify William's conquest, present him as the legitimate king, and reveal the defeated Harold as a usurper. Cultural historian Peter Burke calls it "a spectacular example of history written by the victors."[62]

While there is considerable scholarly consensus that accords with the points made here by Crafton and Burke, virtually every element of that consensus is challenged by other academics who charge the tapestry has been read too narrowly by researchers who "ignored its various gaps, silences, and ambiguities."[63] Some of the major interpretive understandings of the work have suggested that: (1) It takes a decidedly pro English view of the Conquest portraying Harold as the legitimate king of England; (2) It takes a decidedly pro Norman view portraying William as the legitimate heir to Edward and Harold as a conniving usurper; (3) A revisionist view posits that Bishop Odo commissioned it to do both of the above, to help the English feel better about the heroic Harold and accept the conqueror William. It was, in other words, an attempt at reconciliation and nation building.[64]

Elizabeth Pastan and Stephen White have been at the forefront of a view that rejects "the notion that the hanging was commissioned by an external patron and deny that it should be 'read' as a text, a legal justification for regime change in England, or a reliable historical record of events."[65] They argue the interpretive lens of previous historians focused too much on the main panels and not enough on the surrounding material that appears to be representations of fables which have largely been regarded as decorative and not central to the work. White contends that "although the embroidery never specifies the relationship of the fables to the narrative in the main frieze, some of the fable-images are so neatly coordinated with certain scenes that viewers seem to be encouraged to seek such relationships."[66] He and his colleagues argue that attention to these aspects of the tapestry reveals a religious rather than secular-political interpretation of the events depicted. They posit that the cloth was most likely created by the monks of St. Augustine's Abbey, Canterbury to hang in the Abbey itself for the edification of the monks. In the view of these historians, the tapestry does not present an explanation of or justification for political events, but rather an account of God's judgement on England for its waywardness.

This complexity serves to make the tapestry interesting both as a potential source and account for use with students. While the sections of the Tapestry often appear in school history textbooks (most notably the scene that seems to show King Harold with an arrow in his eye), there is no evidence students are asked to engage the Tapestry as either a secondary account of the Norman invasion or a primary source of aspects of life in the twelfth century, including the religious sensibilities of the time. It offers all kinds of potential for engaging students more deeply in the nature of history and historical sources.

The Death of General Wolfe by Benjamin West is an oft-cited example of a painting that was deliberately presented in a particular way for nationalistic and monetary gain (see Fig. 4.9). This painting, which depicts the dying breaths of British General Wolfe on the battlefield of the Plains of Abraham in Quebec, is iconic because it shaped the founding myth of English Canada and has appeared in countless school textbooks. This battle signalled the triumph of the British Empire over the claims of the French in British North America. As one historian put it:

> The awful contrast of dark and light in the sky, the great folds of the flag above Wolfe's head, the men-of-war lying at anchor, and the lamenting officers grouped in circle—all told the solemn importance of the occasion. The various expressions on the faces of Wolfe's attendants gave depth and veracity to the emotional effect of a hero's death in his moment of victory, and served to draw the spectator by sympathy into the company. Each character makes his own contributions: the impersonal grief of the grenadier

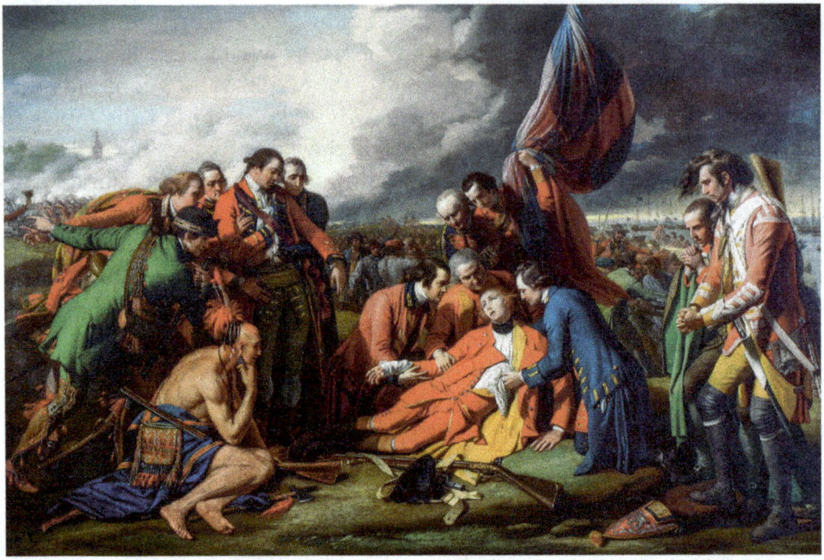

Fig. 4.9 *The Death of General Wolfe*, Benjamin West, 1770 (*Source* Incamerastock/Alamy stock photo)

> standing on the right with folded hands; the anxious solicitude of the surgeon wiping Wolfe's brow; the mixed emotions of Sir William Howe stretching out his hand to welcome the victory and regretting that Wolfe will not live to enjoy it; the unwitting eagerness of the soldier running up with the news; and the aloof calm of the Cherokee Indian, indifferent to victory and lost in contemplation of mortality.[67]

Iconic as this painting has become, and as powerfully evocative as it was when it first appeared (it moved people to tears when they went to view it), it is not historically accurate. One author has called it "grotesquley false."[68] Not one of the people depicted in the scene was actually present. There were only three people present and they are not depicted. Second, those who were on the Plains of Abraham that morning would have been occupied with fighting (Wolfe died in the midst of battle) and not free to gather around the dying general. Third, there is a great deal of Christian iconography in the painting, which serves a metaphorical purpose rather than one of historical documentation. The scene is deliberately composed as a Pieta (the Virgin Mary mourning over the body of Christ). The

Indigenous person is the epitome of the "noble savage," which conveys a message of, as historian Jonathan Vance puts it, "death so noble."[69] Ironically, when criticized for not dressing his people in classical garb, as was the custom at the time, West replied, "the same truth that guides the pen of the historian should govern the pencil of the artist. I consider myself as undertaking to tell this great event to the eye of the world; but if, instead of the facts of the transaction, I represent classical fictions, how shall I be understood by posterity!"[70]

Now we turn to a third example of an historical account. *The First German Gas Attack at Ypres* painted by war artist William Roberts, as part of the Canadian War Memorials programme discussed above.

Canadian war artists were hired to create accounts that were intended to preserve events for posterity. Unlike Benjamin West, they were actually part of the war, although they may not have been at every one of the scenes they depicted. As Dean Oliver and Laura Brandon (2000) put it in *Canvas of War*:

> the artists had painted from their own personal experiences the history of a generation. Like the soldiers they depicted, may of the artists too had seen comrades and brothers die. They had marched their corpses, suffered through deafening bombardments and endured inhumane conditions. Today, the survival of these painters' work ensures for all Canadians a vivid, first-hand account of 'how it was.'[71]

They were soldiers themselves and travelled with and endured the same conditions as other soldiers. What they saw was not glorious and they did not choose to depict it in that way.

Painted in 1918, three years after the event, *The First German Gas Attack at Ypres* depicts the point during the Battle of Gravenstafel Ridge when chlorine gas was unleashed on the French frontline units composed mainly of Algerian troops, causing these soldiers to retreat through the Canadian support trenches. As Maria Tippett *in Art at the Service of War* has put it: "the twisted faces and writhing bodies of the 45th Algerian Division meet the surprised soldiers of the First Canadian brigade…Like no other painting in the CWMF collection, 'The First German Gas Attack at Ypres' conveys the confusion and the horror of modern war."[72]

This is another example of art as a metaphor because the material images have meanings beyond the evident. Tippett points out that the painter has drawn on "traditional images of the Last Judgment and in particular, on Michelangelo's rendition in the Sistine Chapel with its cascade of falling, twisted bodies descending into an unknown hell" (p. 28). She notes that, "this imagery as a visual metaphor for gas warfare makes a terrible weapon immediately comprehensible in all its horror."[73]

According to art historian Jules Prown, "a metaphor is by definition a lie—a person is not a snake in the grass, an idea is not a bombshell—and the same is true of…tropes of all sorts. And yet literary fictions [and we would add art]…can arrive at large, even profound truths that resonate with our own experience of life as lived in this world, and they can move us deeply."[74]

In his seminal work comparing the way historians and high school students engage with historical sources, Sam Wineburg demonstrated that, for historians, what is important is "not what the text says, but what it does." He goes on to write:

> It is not the literal text, or even the inferred text (as that word is commonly used), that this historian comprehends, but the subtext, a text of hidden and latent meanings. Subtexts of historical documents can be divided into two distinct but related spheres: the text as a rhetorical artifact and the text as a human artifact.[75]

Students are much more functional in their reading of sources, focusing on extracting specific information rather than understanding how the text operates as a social construction. As Wineburg (2001) puts it, "In sum, students failed to see the texts as a social instrument skillfully crafted to a social end."[76] But many historical sources are just that, social instruments crafted to a social end. Traditional historical understandings of the Bayeux Tapestry focus not on the events surrounding the Battle of Hastings but on the cloth as an attempt to legitimize William's reign over England. As Burke points out, "the scenes which represent Harold's mission to William culminating in his famous oath of fealty sworn on holy relics, have been described as 'deliberately framed' to display William's power and Harold's obligations to him."[77] In similar ways *The Death of General Wolfe* attempts to legitimate a particular political and social regime and the relations of power within it.

While students' natural inclination is to engage with the historical sources purely as repositories of information rather than as human constructions with their attendant subliminal messages, Wineburg and other history educators argue that a key purpose of history education is to develop students' capacities to do the latter: in their language, to contextualize sources.[78] As Peter Seixas and Tom Morton put it, helping "students realize that identifying the worldviews and perspectives (or mindset) of a creator [of an historical source] can only enrich their understanding of a period of history."[79] All three of the works discussed here, as well as the other art examined in the chapter, offer rich opportunities to do just this with students.

Our central point here is that students should learn not only history, understood as accounts of particular events from the past, but also how history works to shape personal and collective identity and therefore views of the present and the future. Public history, of which some of the works discussed here are well known examples, is often an attempt to bolster a particular regime's legitimacy and/or foster a sense of collective identity and social cohesion. That was the case in twelfth-century England and Normandy, eighteenth-century British North America, early twentieth-century Canada, and remains the case today. As Stanworth points out, "For at least two hundred years, Canadians have been obsessed with who they are," and for most of that period "this obsession has been worked out in part in the visual realm."[80] It was for just this reason a former Conservative Government mandated changes to many of Canada's cultural institutions including rebranding the Museum of Civilization as the Canadian Museum of History. Bruce Curtis characterized this as "a de-Liberalization of Canadian public space and memory."[81] Of course, if this is true, Canadian public space and memory was "Liberalized" in the first place which is no less political. It seems to us that educated citizens need to recognize how public art contributes to a sense of our collective past and how that shapes the contemporary context.

Conclusion

From the 1930s to the 1990s visitors moving through the rotunda of the provincial legislative assembly building in Victoria, British Columbia, Canada passed by four murals commissioned to highlight aspects of the colonial history of the province (see Fig. 4.10). The paintings, also discussed in Chapters 5, 6, and 7, represented four qualities necessary for the establishment of a civilization[82]: courage, enterprise, labour, and justice. Similar to the murals in the Strasbourg train station with which we opened this chapter, the murals in Victoria were designed to present

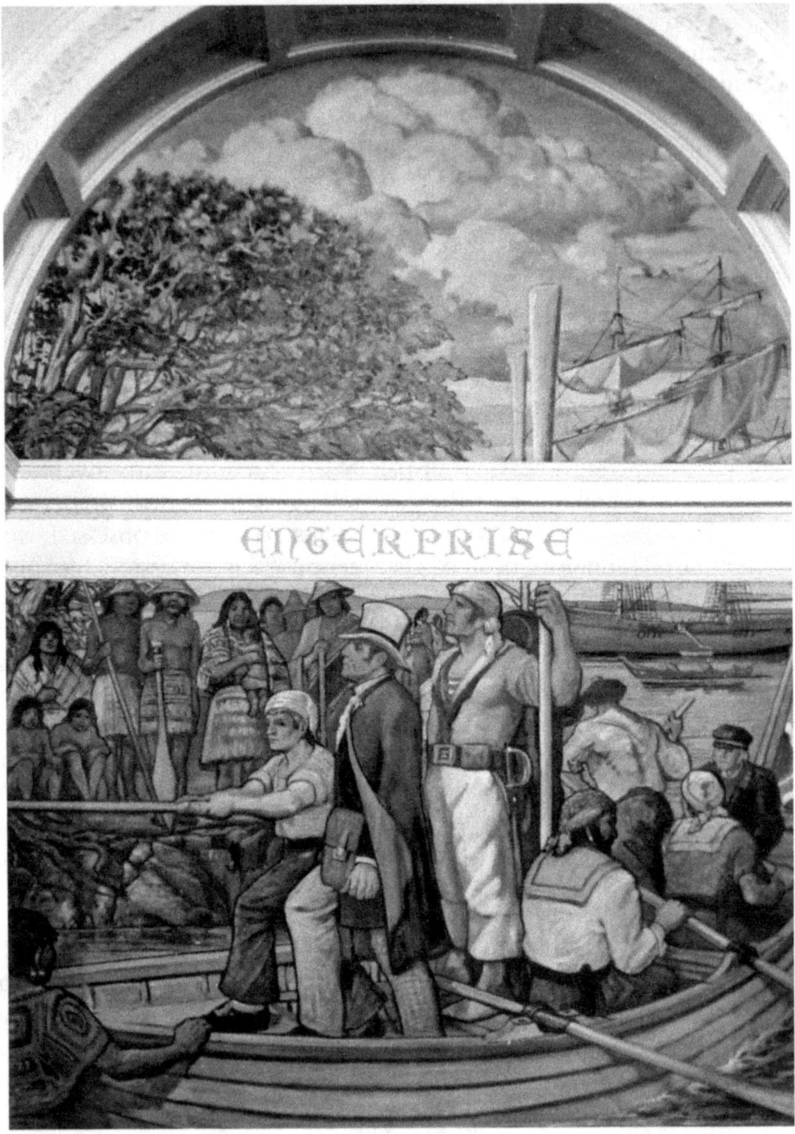

Fig. 4.10 Mural painting by George Southwell (*Source* Image *Enterprise*, B-06675, Courtesy of the Royal BC Museum and Archives) The image shows Hudson's Bay Co. Chief Factor James Douglas landing from the Cadboro at Clover Point to select the site for Fort Victoria (1873)

a particular narrative of the history of the province, and as "pedagogical sites whose messages are intended to convey values to the next generation."[83]

A key aspect of the narrative presented was the centrality of European peoples to the building of the province and the peripheral role of Indigenous Peoples. Three of the four paintings (*Courage*, *Enterprise*, and *Justice*) centre on European actors with Indigenous people observing from the sidelines or, in the case of Justice, as the recipients of European benevolence. The painting titled *Labour* does centre on Indigenous people, but here they are working as labourers unloading cargo under the supervision of European managers.

This visual characterization of Canadian history and, in particular, Settler—Indigenous relations is quite consistent with the one presented in school history textbooks.

> The narrative in Canadian history textbooks is overwhelmingly one of progress—progress in taming the wilderness and the people who lived in it at the time of European arrival; progress in establishing orderly (European) systems of law and government; progress in building efficient networks of transportation, communication and trade.[84]

There too, Indigenous People "are outside the real action of textbooks because they are seen as outside the narrative of progress that is Canadian history. They were not part of the story of the taming of the wilderness, the settling of the land, the building of the cities, the story of production and commerce."[85]

In a letter to the provincial Attorney General written in the 1990s, a group of Indigenous leaders pointed out that "these paintings of bare-breasted Aboriginal women and of Aboriginal persons in subservient positions are, as we are sure you will understand, highly offensive, demeaning and degrading to First Nations people in the province."[86] These leaders understood that these images were not just colourful adornments of the provincial legislature, but powerful teaching tools that communicated a skewed narrative of the history of the region, a narrative that presented their ancestors as marginal to the story and passive. They believed that narrative should be critically examined and countered with new evidence and alternative renderings of the past. We return to an examination of these murals in both Chapters 5 and 6.

Artistic representations like these from and of the past surround students in their everyday lives and are peppered throughout history textbooks and other source material. In both cases they remain largely unexamined as historical sources, and, in our view, this is a significant pedagogical mistake. As we have argued throughout this chapter, history education should equip students to do just what those Indigenous leaders did: to recognize the underlying assumptions and narratives in visual representations of the past, critique those, and set them in the context of other evidence and alternative accounts.

Notes

1. Detmar Klein, "Folklore as a Weapon: National Identity in German-Annexed Alsace, 1890–1914," in *Folklore and Nationalism in Europe During the Long Nineteenth Century*, ed. David M. Hopkin and Timothy Baycroft (Leiden and Boston: Brill, 2012), 169.
2. Detmar Klein, "Battleground of Cultures: 'Politics of Identities' and the National Question in Alsace under German Imperial Rule (1870–1914)," *Revue d'Alsace*, no. 132 (September 1, 2006), 1 & 3, https://doi.org/10.4000/alsace.1565.
3. Klein, "Battleground of Cultures," 3.
4. Klein, "Folklore as a Weapon," 163.
5. Klein, "Folklore as a Weapon," 166.
6. Klein, "Folklore as a Weapon," 171.
7. Klein, "Folklore as a Weapon," 162.
8. Jean Paule Deldeau, "L'Oncle Hansi, de son vrai nom Jean-Jacques Waltz. 2015 116," accessed October 24, 2019, https://www.xn--unregarddiffrentsurlanature-moc.com/2015/11/loncle-hansi-de-son-vrai-nom-jean.html.
9. Klein, "Folklore as a Weapon," 172.
10. Laird Boswell, "From Liberation to Purge Trials in the 'Mythic Provinces': Recasting French Identities in Alsace…," *French Historical Studies* 23, no. 1 (Winter 2000), 131–32, https://doi.org/10.1215/00161071-23-1-129.
11. Fred Evans, *Public Art and the Fragility of Democracy: An Essay in Political Aesthetics* (New York: Columbia University Press, 2019), 17.
12. Klein, "Folklore as a Weapon," 162.
13. Matthew A. Sears, *Athens, Thrace, and the Shaping of Athenian Leadership* (Cambridge: New York: Cambridge University Press, 2013), 25.
14. Walter Werner, "Reading Visual Texts," *Theory and Research in Social Education* 30, no. 3 (2002), 401–28.

15. Veronica Boix-Mansilla, "Commentary: What Is the Purpose of a History Museum in the Early 21st Century?" in *History Education and the Construction of National Identities*, ed. Mario Carretero, Milel Asensio, and Maria Rodríguez-Moneo (Charlotte, NC: Information Age Publishing, 2012), 269–77; Stéphane Lévesque and Paul Zanazanian, "Developing Historical Consciousness And A Community Of History Practitioners: A Survey Of Prospective History Teachers Across Canada," *McGill Journal of Education* 50, no. 2/3 (2015), 389–412; The Pasts Collective, *Canadians and Their Pasts* (Toronto: University of Toronto Press, 2013). David Lowenthal, *The Past Is a Foreign Country Revisited* (Cambridge and New York: Cambridge University Press, 2015); James W. Loewen, *Lies Across America: What Our Historic Sites Get Wrong* (New York: Simon and Schuster, 1999).
16. Sherrill Grace, *On the Art of Being Canadian* (Vancouver, BC: University of British Columbia Press, 2009), 7.
17. Karen Stanworth, *Visibly Canadian: Imagining Collective Identities in the Canadas, 1820–1910* (Montreal, QC & Kingston, ON: McGill-Queen's University Press, 2014): 9. See also, Michael Dawson, Catherine Gidney, and Donald Wright, *Symbols of Canada* (Between the Lines, 2018).
18. Simon Schama, *Dead Certainties, Unwarranted Speculations* (New York: Knopf, 1991), 32, 37.
19. David Harlan, "Historical Fiction and the Future of Academic History," in *Manifestos for History*, ed. Keith Jenkins, Sue Morgan, and Alun Munslow (New York & London: Routledge, 2007), 122.
20. Ludmilla Jordanova, "Approaching Visual Materials," in *Research Methods for History*, ed. Simon Gunn and Lucy Faire (Edinburgh: Edinburgh University Press, 2011), 42.
21. Margaret MacMillan, *The War That Ended Peace: The Road to 1914* (Toronto, ON: Allen Lane, 2013), 247.
22. Gloria Galloway, "Korean War Vet Ted Zuber Became Canada's Last Official War Artist," *The Globe and Mail*, accessed November 10, 2018, https://www.theglobeandmail.com/arts/art-and-architecture/article-korean-war-vet-ted-zuber-became-canadas-last-official-war-artist/.
23. Grace, *On the Art*, 70.
24. Alexandra F. Walton, "Art and Learning at the Imperial War Museum (IWM), London," *Australian Art Education* 38, no. 1 (2017), 158.
25. Canadian War Museum, "Painting, Drowning Sailor," *Canadian War Museum*, n.d., https://www.warmuseum.ca/collections/artifact/1016750/.
26. Grace, *On the Art*, 37
27. Grace, 94.

28. Penney Clark and Alan Sears, "Fiction History and Pedagogy: A Double-Edged Sword," *Journal of Curriculum Studies* 49, no. 1 (2017), 620–39, https://doi.org/10.1080/00220272.2016.1238108.
29. Stanworth, *Visibly Canadian*, 12.
30. Paul Cartledge, *Democracy: A Life*, Reprint edition (Oxford & New York: Oxford University Press, 2018), 31–32.
31. Jerry Brotton, *A History of the World in 12 Maps* (New York: Penguin, 2014), 215.
32. Jerry Brotton, *The Renaissance: A Very Short Introduction*, Very Short Introductions (Oxford & New York: Oxford University Press, 2006), 4.
33. Brotton, *The Renaissance*, 216.
34. Timothy Brook, *Vermeer's Hat: The Seventeenth Century and the Dawn of the Global World*, Reprint edition (Bloomsbury Publishing, 2009), 27.
35. Jerry Brotton, *A History of the World*, 272.
36. Jerry Brotton, 273.
37. Jerry Brotton, 5.
38. Jerry Brotton, 84.
39. Jerry Brotton, 89.
40. BBC, "BBC Four—The Beauty of Maps, Medieval Maps—Mapping the Medieval Mind," BBC, accessed November 1, 2019, https://www.bbc.co.uk/programmes/b00s3v0t.
41. Grace, *On the Art*.
42. Rudy Wiebe, *Playing Dead: A Contemplation Concerning the Arctic* (Edmonton: NeWest, 1989).
43. W.J. Keith, "Arctic Perspectives," *University of Toronto Quarterly* 59, no. 2, 361.
44. Rudy Wiebe, Rudy, "Inuit View to the South," *virtualmuseum.ca*, 1989. http://www.virtualmuseum.ca/Exhibitions/Holman/english/includes/popup.php3?needle=P36.
45. Stanworth, *Visibly Canadian*, 9.
46. Stanworth, 9.
47. Stanworth, 10.
48. Parliament of Canada, "The Fathers of Confederation," *History, Arts and Architecture*, n.d., https://www.ourcommons.ca/About/HistoryArtsArchitecture/fine_arts/historical/609-e.htm.
49. Christopher Moore, *1867: How the Fathers Made a Deal* (Toronto, ON: M&S, 1997).
50. Richard Gwyn, *John A, The Man Who Made Us: The Life and Times of John A. Macdonald Volume 1: 1815–1867* (Toronto, ON: Vintage Canada, 2008).
51. Evans, *Public Art*, 11.

52. Robert Everett-Green, "Kent Monkman: A Trickster with a Cause Crashes Canada's 150th Birthday Party," 2017, http://www.theglobeandmail.com/news/national/canada-150/kent-monkman-shame-and-prejudice/article33515775/.
53. Robert Everett-Green, "Kent Monkman."
54. British Museum, "10 Things You May Not Know about The Scream," *The British Museum Blog* (blog), March 5, 2019, https://blog.britishmuseum.org/10-things-you-may-not-know-about-the-scream/.
55. Michael Dawson, "Mountie," in *Symbols of Canada*, ed. Michael Dawson, Catherine Gidney, and Donald Wright, 129–31 (Toronto, ON: Between the Lines Press, 2018), 129.
56. Dawson, "Mountie," 131.
57. Dawson, 133–34.
58. Quoted in, Peter Burke, *Eyewitnessing: The Uses of Images as Historical Evidence* (Cornell University Press, 2001), 10.
59. UNESCO, "Bayeux Tapestry," Memory of the World, 2016, http://www.unesco.org/new/en/communication-and-information/memory-of-the-world/register/full-list-of-registered-heritage/registered-heritage-page-1/bayeux-tapestry/.
60. François Neveux, "Introduction," in *The Bayeux Tapestry: Embroidering the Facts of History*, ed. Pierre Bouet, Brian Levy, and François Neveux (Caen: Presses Universitaires de Caen, 2004), 11–14.
61. Michael Crafton, "Elizabeth Carson Pastan and Stephen D. White with Kate Gilbert, The Bayeux Tapestry and Its Contexts: A Reassessment," *Speculum* 91, no. 2 (2016), 550, https://doi.org/10.1086/685438. See also, Pierre Bouet, Brian Levy, and François Neveux, ed. *The Bayeux Tapestry: Embroidering the Facts of History* (Caen: Presses universitaires de Caen, 2004).
62. Burke, *Eyewittnessing*, 154.
63. Elizabeth Carson Pastan and Stephen D. White with Kate Gilbert, *The Bayeux Tapestry and Its Contexts: A Reassessment* (Woodbridge: The Boydell Press, 2014), 4.
64. Pastan, White, and Gilbert, *The Bayeux Tapestry*.
65. Pastan, White, and Gilbert, xvii.
66. Pastan, White, and Gilbert, 54.
67. Charles Mitchell, "Benjamin West's 'Death of General Wolfe' and the Popular History Piece," *Journal of the Warburg and Courtauld Institutes* 7 (1944), 30.
68. J. Clarence Webster, "Pictures of the Death of Major-General James Wolfe," *Journal of the Society for Army Historical Research* 6, no. 23 (January 1927), 34.
69. Jonathan Vance, *Death So Noble: Memory, Meaning, and the First World War* (Vancouver, BC: UBC Press, 1997).

70. Mitchell, "Benjamin West's Death," 20.
71. Dean Frederick Oliver and Laura Brandon, *Canvas of War: Painting the Canadian Experience, 1914 to 1945*, First Edition (Vancouver, BC: Douglas & McIntyre Ltd, 2000), 70.
72. Maria Tippett, *Art at the Service of War: Canada, Art, and the Great War* (Toronto, ON: University of Toronto Press, Scholarly Publishing Division, 2013), 70.
73. Tippett, *Art at the Service of War*, 28.
74. Jules David Prown, *Art as Evidence: Writings on Art and Material Culture* (New Haven, CT: Yale University Press, 2002), 255.
75. Samuel S. Wineburg, *Historical Thinking and Other Unnatural Acts: Charting the Future of Teaching the Past* (Philadelphia: Temple University Press, 2001), 65.
76. Samuel S. Wineburg, *Historical Thinking*, 69.
77. Burke, *Eyewitnessing*, 154.
78. Wineburg, *Historical Thinking*.
79. Peter Seixas and Tom Morton, *The Big Six Historical Thinking Concepts* (Toronto, ON: Nelson Education, 2013), 59.
80. Stanworth, *Visibly Canadian*, 3.
81. Bruce Curtis, "Debate on the Teaching of History: Historical: Epistemology Meets Nationalist Narrative," *Historical Studies in Education* 25, no. 2 (2013), 125.
82. Peter Seixas and Penney Clark, "Obsolete Icons and the Teaching of History," in *New Possibilities for the Past Shaping History Education in Canada*, ed. Penney Clark (Vancouver, BC: UBC Press, 2011), 287.
83. Seixas and Clark, "Obsolete Icons and the Teaching of History," 282.
84. Penney Clark, "Representations of Aboriginal People in English Canadian History Textbooks: Toward Reconciliation," in *Teaching the Violent Past: History Education and Reconciliation*, ed. Elizabeth A. Cole (Lanham, MD: Rowman & Littlefield, 2007), 111.
85. Clark, "Representations of Aboriginal," 104.
86. Quoted in Peter Seixas and Penney Clark, "Obsolete Icons," 284.

Bibliography

BBC. "BBC Four—The Beauty of Maps, Medieval Maps—Mapping the Medieval Mind." *BBC*. Accessed November 1, 2019. https://www.bbc.co.uk/programmes/b00s3v0t.

Boix-Mansilla, Veronica. "Commentary: What Is the Purpose of a History Museum in the Early 21st Century?" In *History Education and the Construction of National Identities*, edited by Mario Carretero, Milel Asensio, and Maria Rodríguez-Moneo, 269–77. Charlotte, NC: Information Age Publishing, 2012.

Boswell, Laird. “From Liberation to Purge Trials in the ‘Mythic Provinces’: Recasting French Identities in Alsace...” *French Historical Studies* 23, no. 1 (Winter 2000): 129–62. https://doi.org/10.1215/00161071-23-1-129.

Bouet, Pierre, Brian Levy, and François Neveux, ed. *The Bayeux Tapestry: Embroidering the Facts of History*. Caen: Presses universitaires de Caen, 2004.

British Museum. “10 Things You May Not Know about The Scream.” *The British Museum Blog* (blog), March 5, 2019. https://blog.britishmuseum.org/10-things-you-may-not-know-about-the-scream/.

Brook, Timothy. *Vermeer's Hat: The Seventeenth Century and the Dawn of the Global World*. Reprint edition. Bloomsbury Publishing, 2009.

Brotton, Jerry. *The Renaissance: A Very Short Introduction*. Very Short Introductions. Oxford & New York: Oxford University Press, 2006.

Brotton, Jerry. *A History of the World in 12 Maps*. New York: Penguin, 2014.

Burke, Peter. *Eyewitnessing: The Uses of Images as Historical Evidence*. Cornell University Press, 2001.

Canadian War Museum. “Painting, Drowning Sailor.” *Canadian War Museum*, n.d. https://www.warmuseum.ca/collections/artifact/1016750/.

Cartledge, Paul. *Democracy: A Life*. Reprint Edition. Oxford & New York: Oxford University Press, 2018.

Clark, Penney. “Representations of Aboriginal People in English Canadian History Textbooks: Toward Reconciliation.” In *Teaching the Violent Past: History Education and Reconciliation*, edited by Elizabeth A. Cole, 81–120. Lanham, MD: Rowman & Littlefield, 2007.

Clark, Penney and Alan Sears. “Fiction History and Pedagogy: A Double-Edged Sword.” *Journal of Curriculum Studies* 49, no. 1 (2017): 620–39. https://doi.org/10.1080/00220272.2016.1238108.

Crafton, Michael. “Elizabeth Carson Pastan and Stephen D. White with Kate Gilbert, The Bayeux Tapestry and Its Contexts: A Reassessment.” *Speculum* 91, no. 2 (2016): 550–51. https://doi.org/10.1086/685438.

Curtis, Bruce. “Debate on the Teaching of History: Historical Epistemology Meets Nationalist Narrative. *Historical Studies in Education* 25, no. 2 (2013): 115–128.

Dawson, Michael. “Mountie.” In *Symbols of Canada*, edited by Michael Dawson, Catherine Gidney, and Donald Wright, 129–31. Toronto, ON: Between the Lines Press, 2018.

Dawson, Michael, Catherine Gidney, and Donald Wright. *Symbols of Canada*. Between the Lines, 2018.

Deldeau, Jean Paule. “L'Oncle Hansi, de son vrai nom Jean-Jacques Waltz. 2015 116.” Accessed October 24, 2019. https://www.xn--unregarddiffrentsurlanature-moc.com/2015/11/loncle-hansi-de-son-vrai-nom-jean.html.

Evans, Fred. *Public Art and the Fragility of Democracy: An Essay in Political Aesthetics*. New York: Columbia University Press, 2019.

Everett-Green, Robert. "Kent Monkman: A Trickster with a Cause Crashes Canada's 150th Birthday Party," 2017. http://www.theglobeandmail.com/news/national/canada-150/kent-monkman-shame-and-prejudice/article33515775/.

Galloway, Gloria. "Korean War Vet Ted Zuber Became Canada's Last Official War Artist." *The Globe and Mail.* Accessed November 10, 2018. https://www.theglobeandmail.com/arts/art-and-architecture/article-korean-war-vet-ted-zuber-became-canadas-last-official-war-artist/.

Grace, Sherrill. *On the Art of Being Canadian.* Vancouver, BC: UBC Press, 2009.

greatwar.co.uk. "Cemeteries and Locations on the WW1 Ypres Salient Battlefields, Belgium," n.d. http://www.greatwar.co.uk/places/ypres-salient-cemeteries.htm.

Gwyn, Richard. *John A, The Man Who Made Us: The Life and Times of John A. Macdonald Volume 1: 1815–1867.* Toronto, ON: Vintage Canada, 2008.

Harlan, David. "Historical Fiction and the Future of Academic History." In *Manifestos for History*, edited by Keith Jenkins, Sue Morgan, and Alun Munslow, 108–30. New York & London: Routledge, 2007.

Jordanova, Ludmilla. "Approaching Visual Materials." In *Research Methods for History*, edited by Simon Gunn and Lucy Faire, 30–47. Edinburgh: Edinburgh University Press, 2011.

Keith, W.J. "Arctic Perspectives." *University of Toronto Quarterly* 59, no. 2 (90 1989): 361–62.

Klein, Detmar. "Battleground of Cultures: 'Politics of Identities' and the National Question in Alsace under German Imperial Rule (1870–1914)." *Revue d'Alsace*, no. 132 (September 1, 2006): 503–9. https://doi.org/10.4000/alsace.1565.

Klein, Detmar. "Folklore as a Weapon: National Identity in German-Annexed Alsace, 1890–1914." In *Folklore and Nationalism in Europe During the Long Nineteenth Century*, edited by David M. Hopkin and Timothy Baycroft, 161–91. Leiden and Boston: Brill, 2012.

Lévesque, Stéphane and Paul Zanazanian. "Developing Historical Consciousness And A Community Of History Practitioners: A Survey Of Prospective History Teachers Across Canada." *McGill Journal of Education* 50, no. 2/3 (2015): 389–412.

Loewen, James W. *Lies Across America: What Our Historic Sites Get Wrong.* New York: Simon and Schuster, 1999.

Lowenthal, David. *The Past Is a Foreign Country Revisited.* Cambridge and New York: Cambridge University Press, 2015.

MacMillan, Margaret. *The War That Ended Peace: The Road to 1914.* Toronto, ON: Allen Lane, 2013.

Mitchell, Charles. "Benjamin's West's 'Death of General Wolfe' and the Popular History Piece." *Journal of the Warburg and Courtauld Institutes* 7 (1944): 20–33.

Moore, Christopher. *1867: How the Fathers Made a Deal*. Toronto, ON: M&S, 1997.

Neveux, François. "Introduction." In *The Bayeux Tapestry: Embroidering the Facts of History*, edited by Pierre Bouet, Brian Levy, and François Neveux, 11–14. Caen: Presses universitaires de Caen, 2004.

Oliver, Dean Frederick and Laura Brandon. *Canvas of War: Painting the Canadian Experience, 1914–1945*. First edition. Vancouver, BC: Douglas & McIntyre Ltd, 2000.

Parliament of Canada. "The Fathers of Confederation." *History, Arts and Architecture*, n.d. https://www.ourcommons.ca/About/HistoryArtsArchitecture/fine_arts/historical/609-e.htm.

Pastan, Elizabeth Carson, Stephen D. White, with Kate Gilbert. *The Bayeux Tapestry and Its Contexts: A Reassessment*. Woodbridge, UK: The Boydell Press, 2014.

Prown, Jules David. *Art as Evidence: Writings on Art and Material Culture*. New Haven, CT: Yale University Press, 2002.

Schama, Simon. *Dead Certainties, Unwarranted Speculations*. New York: Knopf, 1991.

Sears, Matthew A. *Athens, Thrace, and the Shaping of Athenian Leadership*. Cambridge and New York: Cambridge University Press, 2013.

Seixas, Peter and Penney Clark. "Obsolete Icons and the Teaching of History." In *New Possibilities for the Past Shaping History Education in Canada*, edited by Penney Clark, 282–301. Vancouver, BC: UBC Press, 2011.

Seixas, Peter and Tom Morton. *The Big Six Historical Thinking Concepts*. Toronto, ON: Nelson Education, 2013.

Stanworth, Karen. *Visibly Canadian: Imagining Collective Identities in the Canadas, 1820–1910*. Montreal, QC & Kingston, ON: McGill-Queen's University Press, 2014.

Tippett, Maria. *Art at the Service of War: Canada, Art, and the Great War*. Toronto, ON: University of Toronto Press, Scholarly Publishing Division, 2013.

The Pasts Collective: Conrad, Margaret, Kadriye Ercikan, Gerald Friesen, Jocelyn Létourneau, Delphin Muise, David Northrup, and Peter Seixas. *Canadians and Their Pasts*. Toronto, ON: University of Toronto Press, 2013.

UNESCO. "The Bayeux Tapestry," 2007. http://www.unesco.org/new/en/communication-and-information/flagship-project-activities/memory-of-the-world/register/full-list-of-registered-heritage/registered-heritage-page-1/bayeux-tapestry/.

Vance, Jonathan. *Death So Noble: Memory, Meaning, and the First World War*. Vancouver: UBC Press, 1997.
Walton, Alexandra F. "Art and Learning at the Imperial War Museum (IWM), London." *Australian Art Education* 38, no. 1 (2017): 158–69.
Webster, J. Clarence. "Pictures of the Death of Major-General James Wolfe." *Journal of the Society for Army Historical Research* 6, no. 23 (January 1927): 30–36.
Werner, Walter. "Reading Visual Texts." *Theory and Research in Social Education* 30, no. 3 (2002): 401–28.
Wiebe, Rudy. *Playing Dead: A Contemplation Concerning the Arctic*. Edmonton, AB: NeWest, 1989.
Wiebe, Rudy. "Inuit View to the South." *Virtualmuseum.ca*, 1989. http://www.virtualmuseum.ca/Exhibitions/Holman/english/includes/popup.php3?needle=P36.
Wineburg, Samuel S. *Historical Thinking and Other Unnatural Acts: Charting the Future of Teaching the Past*. Philadelphia: Temple University Press, 2001.

CHAPTER 5

Points of Convergence: Public Commemorative Art and the Teaching of History

In or around 514 BCE the Athenian brothers Harmodius and Aristogeiton killed the Tyrant Hippias in an effort to overturn aristocratic government and establish democracy in the city. Harmodius was killed during the assassination by palace guards, while Aristogeiton was captured and died after a period of torture and interrogation. For this self-sacrificial act of democratic resistance, the brothers "were transformed into icons of liberty and democracy and were the first humans to have named bronze statues erected in their honour in the Athenian Agora."[1] Unfortunately, the original statues have not survived as they were carried off to Persia by "the ultimate tyrant" Xerxes after he sacked and burned the city in 480 BCE.[2] The heroic story transcended the Persian wars, however, and the statues were copied a number of times in the ancient world with several Roman marble versions on display in museums today (see Fig. 5.1). Like the originals, the copies were intended to be powerful symbols of democratic action.

Twenty-five centuries later another iconic representation of the march for freedom and democracy was unveiled in Kelly Ingram Park in Birmingham, Alabama. This statue, titled *Foot Soldier*, depicts an austere Birmingham police officer siccing his ferocious German shepherd dog on a young African American civil rights protester (see Fig. 5.2). The statue was fashioned based on a news photograph taken on 3 May 1963, during a large civil rights march led by Martin Luther King Jr. American writer Malcolm Gladwell calls the incident "one of the most iconic moments in

P. Clark and A. Sears, *The Arts and the Teaching of History*,
https://doi.org/10.1007/978-3-030-51513-3_5

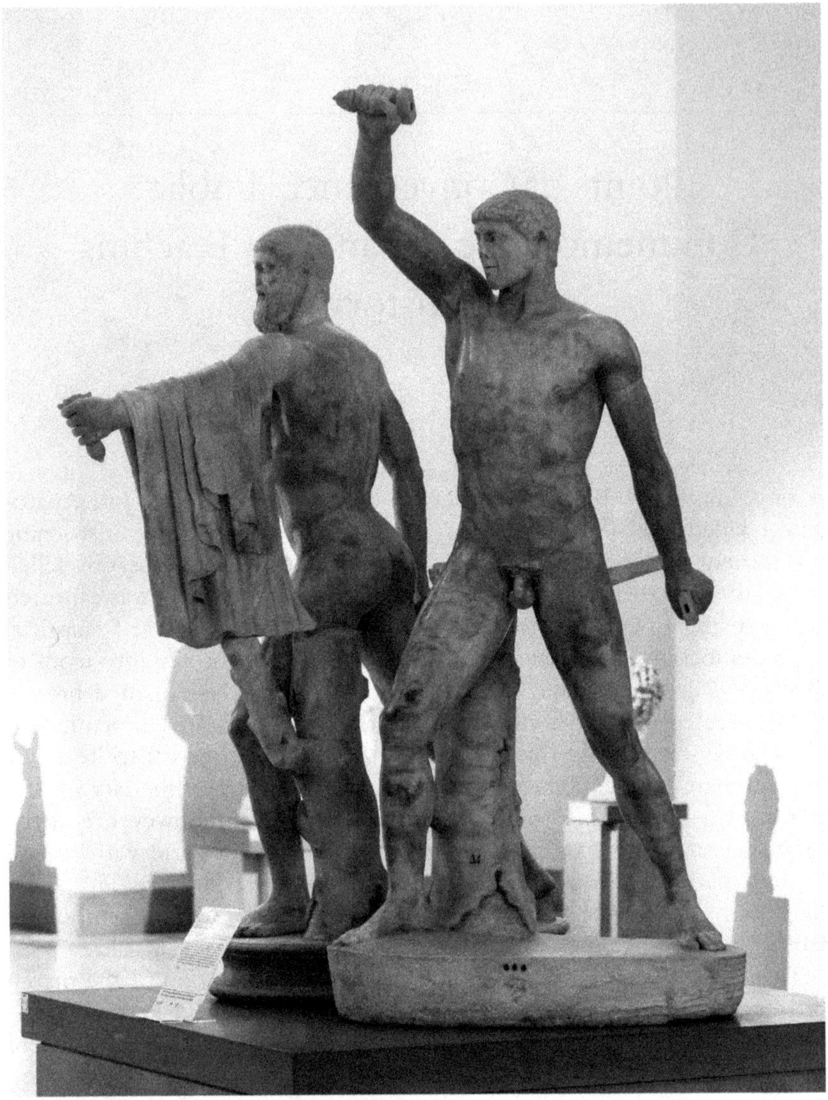

Fig. 5.1 *The Tyrannicides*, sculpture depicting Harmodius (right) and Aristogeiton (left). Second-century Roman copy of a Greek Original (*Source* Adam Eastland/Alamy Stock Photo)

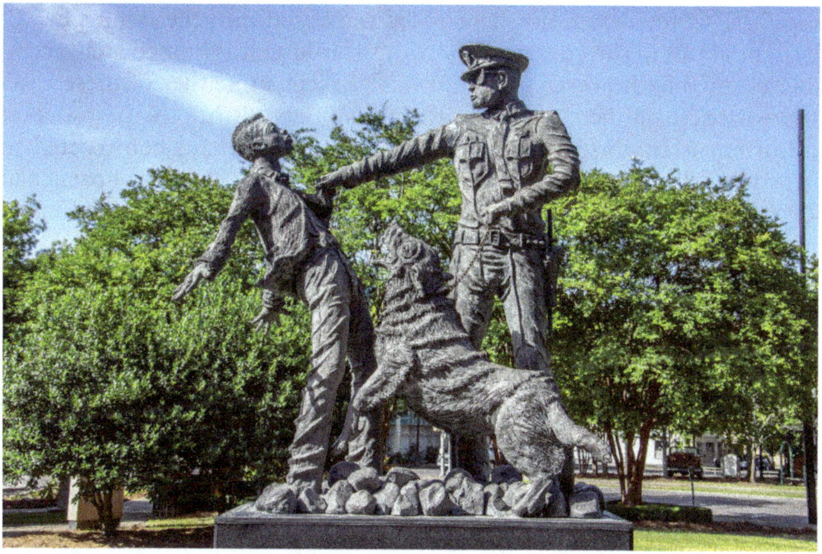

Fig. 5.2 *The Foot Soldier*, statue sculpted by Ronald S McDowell, Kelly Ingram Park, Birmingham, Alabama, USA (*Source* dbimages/Alamy Stock Photo)

civil rights history," and makes the point that both the photograph and the statue powerfully shaped understandings of the history of the civil rights struggle in Birmingham specifically, and the United States more broadly.[3] The original photograph went viral, appearing in newspapers and magazines across the United States and around the world. Just a year later Congress passed The Civil Rights Act, giving rise to the common phrase, "The Civil Rights Act was written in Birmingham."[4] To keep the memory of the confrontation between police officer, dog, and protestor alive a later mayor of Birmingham commissioned *Foot Soldier*, and in 1995 it took its place among the other monuments of the civil rights movement scattered throughout the park. Gladwell calls it "the most powerful statue in Kelly Ingram Park. Nothing else comes close."[5]

These two iconic monuments demonstrate the power of public commemorative art to record history, capture important ideas, and artistically embody the spirit of an age or the dynamic energy of an historical turning point. They are vivid examples of visual portrayals of history that David Lowenthal argues popularize the past. "History seen rather than read," he writes, "does not have to be translated into the mind's eye or thought about in the context of previous learning; it is immediately accessible to anyone, however unschooled."[6] Except in neither of these cases is history actually being seen; both monuments distort the past at best and invent it at worst. Both present ideological accounts constructed to shape the collective memories and consciousnesses of citizens of particular polities. They are not really meant to portray past events, but rather to shape the present and the future.

In the case of the so-called tyrannicides, Harmodius and Aristogeiton, the event commemorated by their statues never happened. They did not kill the tyrant Hippias but his younger brother Hipparchus, and their motivation was most likely a lovers' quarrel rather than political liberation. Hippias ruled Athens for several more years and the attack motivated him to institute even harsher measures to control the population.[7]

A police officer's dog did lunge at Walter Gadsden during the civil rights march in Kelly Ingram Park in May of 1963 and a photograph of that incident accurately portrays the interaction. But the story that grew from that photograph to inspire a nation, and later a sculptor, is not at all accurate. Walter Gadsden was a high school student who skipped school to get a look at Martin Luther King Jr. and the other marchers. He was cutting across the park to avoid the oncoming demonstration when he strayed close to the police dog who jumped at him. The officer handling the dog was most likely trying to restrain it, not use it as a weapon against the young man. The real irony is that Gadsden himself rejects both the idea that he was a marcher that day or involved in the civil rights movement at all. In fact, years later when asked by an interviewer what benefits he, his family, and the community gained from the movement his reply was, "none."[8]

A close comparison of the photograph and the sculpture reveals a number of stark differences. For example, in the photograph Gadsden is taller and larger than the police officer, but the sculpture presents him as much smaller. The dog in the sculpture is distinctly more wolf-like than the one in the photograph. Finally, the positioning of both Gadsden and the police officer is different, creating a much more menacing scene. The artist, Ronald McDowell, is worth quoting at length on this. In describing his reaction to the photograph and the translation of it into his sculpture, he says, in part:

> Well, I saw that the boy was being about 6′4, the officer was maybe 5′10, 5′9. And I said, 'This is a movement about power.' So, I made the little boy younger and smaller, and the officer taller and stronger. The arm of the law is so strong, that's why his arm is almost, like, straight. And the dog is more like a wolf than a real dog. Because if I'm a little boy, that's what I would see. I would see like this superman hovering over me, putting this big old giant monster of a dog in my groin area, in my private area. And so, that's what I envisioned when I first saw the photograph.[9]

McDowell created a work that Gladwell argues "has historical authority; it's in the shadow of 16th Street Baptist Church, inside Kelly Ingram Park, at the actual site of the Birmingham marches. But it's a work of imagination. It's not a literal representation; it's art."[10]

In both cases the works are indeed art, but they are also, in important ways, history in the sense that they narrate the past for public consumption. While their connection to actual events is tenuous, their relationship to important historical themes, ideas, and even truths, is not. For several centuries political life in Athens was characterized by the tension between tyranny and democracy, with government moving back and forth between the two at various points. This is illustrated by another famous piece of Athenian public art. Almost a century after the supposed killing of Hippias by the "tyrannicides," and in response to incursions into Greece by the Macedonian king Philip II and his son Alexander, the assembly of Athens passed the Law Against Tyranny. It appeared on a marble stele capped by a relief sculpture showing the goddess Democracy crowning the Demos—the people of Athens. The law read, in part: "If anyone should rise up against the Demos for tyranny or join in establishing the tyranny or overthrow the Demos of the Athenians or the democracy in Athens, whoever kills him who does any of these things shall be blameless."[11] While the statues to Harmodius and Aristogeiton and the story that grew up around them do not present events as they happened, they do communicate important historical ideas about political life and governance in classical Athens.

Similarly, while the sculpture *Foot Soldier* is not an accurate portrayal of the events involving Walter Gadsden and the Birmingham police in May of 1963, it does encapsulate important historical elements of the struggle for civil rights in the US. Unarmed and philosophically non-violent protesters, or foot soldiers as they were called, did march repeatedly to advocate for equal rights. They were frequently subjected to extreme violence either directly from the police or because of police complicity in allowing counter protestors to perpetrate acts of brutality. That extreme violence did prompt revulsion among many Americans and help lay the groundwork for the kind of shift in attitudes that led to the passing of the Civil Rights Act and other progressive legislation.

We chose these two pieces of public commemorative art to open this chapter because they aptly illustrate the potential of this realm to bring together key aspects of history education, and foster student progress towards what Ken Osborne calls "historical mindedness." As we discuss in Chapter 1, historical mindedness is a broader understanding of the past that "is a way of looking, not so much at history, but at the world at large, that derives from a familiarity with the past and with trying to understand and interpret it."[12] History education has been dominated by a focus on what historians know (the names, dates, narratives, and counter narratives of the discipline of history—often referred to as content), and, second, developing facility with how historians know (the processes and procedures of doing history—often referred to as historical thinking). Historical mindedness includes facility with these but also with understanding the role historical consciousness and public memory play in shaping understandings of the past. We believe engaging with public, commemorative art provides the opportunity to bring together these aspects of history education and foster other important points of convergence.

Bringing Together the Past and History

Central to the idea of historical consciousness is that people, as individuals and collectivities, live temporally narrated lives. That is, they have stories of their own pasts and use those to frame how they understand the present and think about possibilities for the future. Anna Clark and Carla Peck describe historical consciousness as "the ways people orient themselves in time, and how they are bound by the historical and cultural contexts which shape their sense of temporality and collective memory."[13]

The way most people and groups engage with the past is neither the same as, nor particularly connected to, the disciplinary study of history. People draw on family lore, community stories, historic sites, and fictional accounts in books and movies. A national study of how Canadians encounter and think about the past, for example, found "the majority of Canadians rely primarily on family history to anchor themselves in time and place."[14] In their study of historical understandings among high school students in Northern Ireland, Alan McCully and Keith Barton documented the power of public art in shaping historical consciousness and identity. They write, "Marches, banners, commemorations, and wall murals display sectional loyalty through the use of imagery associated with historical events and figures of the past."[15] Similarly, James Loewen argues that most Americans learn their history from "historical novels, Oliver Stone movies - but surely most of all from the landscape [of historical sites and commemorations]."[16] As Lowenthal points out, academic "history is merely one among many versions of the past, and to most no more veracious than any other."[17]

There is a substantial body of research around the world examining how young people narrate their own histories as well as the history of their religious, ethnocultural, or national groups and what impact that has on how they see the present and the future. The work of Jocelyn Létourneau and others in Québec, for example, demonstrates that young Francophones in that province have a largely shared sense of their history and place in the larger nation of Canada that is not particularly consistent with the thinking of many professional historians. Létourneau calls the students' narratives "mythistories," and argues these need to be examined and disrupted as part of history education.[18] Edda Sant and her colleagues conducted research in the Catalan region of Spain that also found a largely shared narrative that was different from those found by researchers elsewhere.[19]

What this research makes clear is that young people in Québec, Catalonia, and elsewhere come to school with a strong sense of their own and their collective's history. That sense shapes how they engage with school history, interpret current events, and think about possibilities for the future. There is evidence, for example, that American students are deeply committed to freedom and progress as the twin pillars of the national narrative of their country. The history of the United States, they believe, is one of continual movement towards more of both. So powerful is this frame that students resist considering alternatives and "distort the historical evidence to fit their preconceptions."[20] Students of the same age from Northern Ireland, however, are much more fatalistic, believing that the appearance of social progress, particularly related to the so-called Troubles, is an illusion because history shows things do not change for the better. Barton and Levstik argue that both of these stances are largely unexamined, and neither is particularly healthy for a democratic polity.[21]

People do not only narrate their own history; they also narrate the history of other groups or nations. When someone makes a comment about an identified group of people such as, "immigrants have made an important contribution to Canada," it is most often an expression of that sense of historical consciousness: a strongly held, and often superficial and unexamined, sense of another's story.

These competing historical narratives are clearly illustrated in high profile debates about public history and commemorative art around the world. One example of this occurred on July 1, Canada Day, of 2017 when a small group of Indigenous protestors gathered around a statue of Edward Cornwallis in Halifax, the capital of the province of Nova Scotia. Cornwallis, an eighteenth-century British governor of Nova Scotia credited with founding Halifax, is a controversial figure. While governor he issued a bounty on Mi'kmaq scalps in response to aggression against colonists. The Indigenous people gathered there on Canada's national holiday to perform a ceremony of mourning for the lives lost as a result of Cornwallis's decree, and to continue long standing protests about the placement of his statue in such a prominent location. Soon after the ceremony began, a small group of men in matching shirts entered the park carrying a Red Ensign flag (the flag of Canada until 1965 that includes a Union Jack in one corner) and singing *God Save the Queen*. These so-called "Proud Boys" took issue with Indigenous protests at the injustices of colonial rule, claiming Canada had a proud and honourable British heritage that should be celebrated rather than disparaged.[22] After a brief exchange between the groups, the young men moved off and the incident ended. Press coverage and calls for action, particularly sanctions against the men, some of whom were serving military members, continued for some time afterwards.

Both the Indigenous people and the "Proud Boys" in this example had a strong sense of their own and Canada's history. News reports made it clear they each also made assumptions about the history and present orientation of the other group. From that dual sense of historical consciousness—perhaps better termed historical unconsciousness because understandings like this most often exist as tacit and unexamined—flowed their attitudes towards each other, the Cornwallis statue, and what they thought needed to be done to or with it.[23]

Public commemorative art has been and is contentious around the world including debates about the presence and placement of statues to leaders of the Confederacy in the United States, or calls to remove a statue of John A. Macdonald, Canada's first prime minister, from the front of city hall in Victoria, B.C., or protests in Korea and China whenever a Japanese politician visits the Yasukuni Shrine which honours Japanese war dead from Second World War, including some designated as war criminals. All these cases involve iconic historical symbols and deeply held and highly divergent views about particular historical figures and events. All also have the potential to bring together different aspects of history education in ways that enrich students' experiences.

Bringing Together Multiple Historical Eras

On a geographic feature called the Lorette Spur in the Artois region of France just outside the city of Arras sit two compelling examples of public commemorative art. The first is the Ablain St.-Nazaire French Military Cemetery also known as Notre Dame de Lorette. This is the largest French military cemetery in the world containing the remains of more than 40,000 French soldiers killed in action in the area during First World War (1914–1918). It is anchored by a large Romanesque basilica and a compelling lantern tower that contains selected remains of unknown soldiers from all French wars after the so-called Great War of 1914–1918. Surrounding the basilica and tower are eight ossuaries containing the remains of unidentified dead and seemingly endless rows of grave markers (almost all crosses) marking the individual graves of identified dead.

On November 11 of 2014 François Hollande, then president of France, accompanied by German Chancellor Angela Merkel and British Prime Minister David Cameron, inaugurated a new memorial across the parking lot from Notre Dame de Lorette. The Anneau de la Mémoire, or Ring of Remembrance, is "a 328-metre ring of dark, lightweight concrete barely touching and, as if by magic, projecting over a plateau… Inside the ring, 500 sheets of bronzed stainless steel list 579,606 names"[24] of soldiers killed in the Nord Pad de Calais region of France during the Great War (see Fig. 5.3). These very different memorials commemorate the same past but from the perspective of very different eras and with a view to alternative futures.

In their examination of debates about the appropriate public policy response to four controversial historical murals in the main rotunda of the Provincial Legislature in British Columbia, Canada, Peter Seixas and Penney Clark point out that commemorative art installations speak to

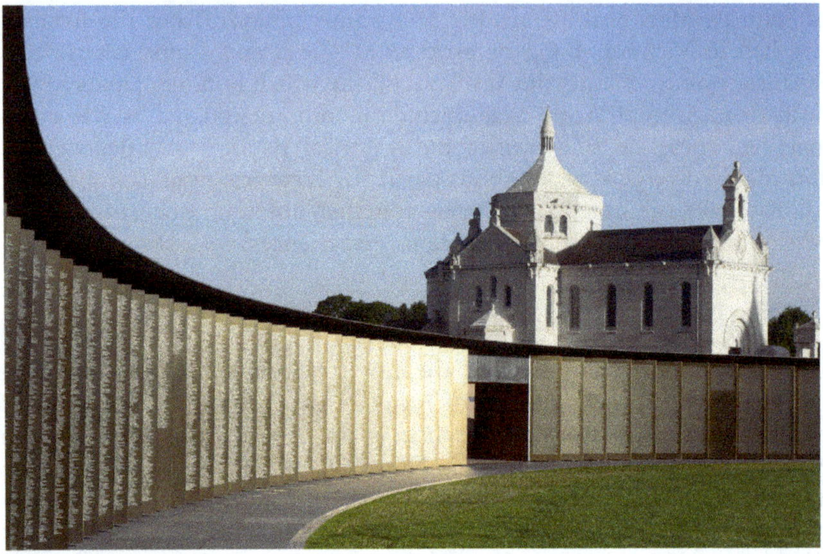

Fig. 5.3 *The Ring of Remembrance* with Notre Dame de Lorette Basilica in the background. Ablain-Saint-Nazaire, Pas-de-Calais, France (*Source* Chandelle/Alamy Stock Photo)

at least three "temporal moments:" the period represented or commemorated by the piece; the period in which the piece was commissioned and created; and the present. In the case of the murals at the centre of their work, "The first temporal moment involved the colonial past, the time portrayed in the murals between 1792 and the 1860s ... The second temporal moment focused on the 1930s paintings themselves as pictorial representations of the past. The third temporal moment is the present."[25] In addition to these three, Seixas and Clark acknowledge that public commemorative art is also very much about imagined futures, writing, "These moments potentially offer an opportunity to examine how people are thinking about their collective pasts and, thus, how they seek to position themselves for the future."[26]

The contrasting war memorials on the Lorette Spur provide the same convergence of multiple pasts, the present, and alternative futures. They offer the opportunity for history educators and their students to explore the complexities of memory, identity formation, and public policy. They share the first temporal moment of the period of the Great War, 1914–1918. The second temporal moment is different for each; the early 1920s for Notre Dame de Lorette and the early 2010s for the Ring of Remembrance. They both attempt to lay the commemorative groundwork for particular, and very different, futures.

In terms of the first moment, both memorials focus on loss, and both use names to emphasize the enormity of the tragedy. While the Ancient Athenians regularly used individual names in the public commemoration of war dead the practice had fallen out of fashion in the 2000 years between them and the First World War. In the intervening years there were monuments to particular engagements or great men, but ordinary soldiers were largely forgotten. Matthew Sears makes the case that "the memorials of the Great War, especially those overseen by the Imperial War Graves Commission, were directly inspired by Classical Athenian monuments and practices,"[27] and one aspect of that inspiration was the listing of names "to foster memory, mourning, and sober reflection on war's costs."[28]

In the listing of names, however, there is a significant difference. Notre Dame de Lorette is a fiercely national memorial listing only the names of French soldiers with each grave marker bearing the declaration: "Mort Pour La France" (Died for France). In its nationalistic character, the monument is consistent with others of the era such as the Canadian memorial at Vimy Ridge or the British one at Thiepval. All of these emphasize national loss through the exclusive listing of the names of soldiers of the relevant nation; the names of allies and enemies are nowhere to be seen.

The Ring of Remembrance, on the other hand, "seeks to challenge the hegemonic national discourses on Great War heritage," and "unite former enemies, as more than 580,000 names from both sides of the war are etched onto the walls of the memorial, arranged not by nationality or regiment or rank but in alphabetical order."[29] These differences speak to the second temporal moment, and help us understand the times when the memorials were created.

The 1920s in the shadow of the losses of the war, and the international tensions around the remaking of Europe and much of the world through the making of the Treaty of Versailles were a time for projecting nationalism at home and abroad through colonial activities. Early twenty-first-century Europe, on the other hand, was a very different place. The European Union united former enemies and was seeking through a number of means to create pan-European attachments. That project was very much on the mind of Philippe Proust, the architect who designed the Ring, in his words, "To give shape to brotherhood, to unite yesterday's enemies." He goes on:

> I chose the ring as a figure to bring together the names of the soldiers, thinking of the circle formed by people holding hands. The ring is synonymous with unity and eternity. Unity, because the names form a sort of human chain, and eternity because the letters are joined without an end, in alphabetical order without any distinction of nationality, rank or religion.[30]

Proust's comment about religion indicates another profound difference in the memorials that is illustrative of the times in which they were created. Notre Dame de Lorette "with its hulking Romanesque basilica and cruciform tower, presents an unabashedly Catholic vision of death and resurrection, implicitly blaming the war on the sins of a secular republic."[31] Daniel Sherman argues even the ossuaries were designed "to inculcate in visitors not only a commemorative discourse with which they were already familiar but also more traditional Catholic doctrine."[32] Sherman contends the Catholic church of the early 1920s engaged significantly in memorializing the war at Lorette and elsewhere as part of its attempts to reassert its waning legitimacy in France. This monument, and others like it, helps us understand something of the struggle for the soul, or souls, of France in the early twentieth century. In contrast, *The Ring of Remembrance* eschews religious symbols and is much more consistent with contemporary Europe generally and secular France in particular. It too provides a window into the spirit and spirituality of the age.

In terms of the present, the very recent one hundredth anniversary of the Great War provided the impetus for rethinking and reimagining both the war itself and how it should be commemorated. Romain Fathi, for example, argues that there has been a long standing and widely shared collective memory in France that saw the war as "a boucherie, a futile slaughter and a pointless European civil war in which row after row of men were mown down by machine guns. In short, it was a bloody mistake."[33] The anniversary, however, provided an opportunity to reshape commemoration in the service of the present and the future. Through public art and commemorative ceremony, the French government, and other governments across Europe, sought to challenge growing anomie towards the EU and the idea of pan-European cooperation. For Fathi,

> It seems clear that there are key political messages shaping the commemoration: namely peace, reconciliation and Europe, all of which promote the European ideal ...
>
> The Elysée Palace has thus used the centenary of the First World War as relevant commemorative ground on which to remind people of European stability and successes in order to repopularise the European ideal.[34]

This is not unique to France. Rafiq Ahmed and Anne Hertzog trace what they call "the shifting regimes of remembrance tourism" across the so-called Western Front of the Great War. The Ring of Remembrance is just one of several commemorative initiatives that seek to narrate "the war from a transnational perspective and putting forward the concept of 'shared memory' of the war."[35] This trend, they argue, is rooted solidly in contemporary sensibilities that challenge older ways of thinking about this particular past. This new approach to commemoration seeks to "establish a new regime of memory, based on globalised 'post-modern' ideas and values: memory of minorities, victims, civilians and 'dominated groups' at large."[36]

Our key point here is that public commemorative art provides an important point of convergence for investigating and understanding multiple historical eras and the evolution and contested nature of collective memory and national understanding. We concur with Karel Van Nieuwenhuyse and Kaat Wils who argue that "Commemoration and remembrance are integral elements of postmodern western culture" and, while different from "scientific historiography" in important ways, should be a key component of history education.[37] As discussed above, we know that public art plays a key role in shaping peoples' sense of the past. The trouble is, however, public art is rarely engaged as part of an inquiry-oriented approach to history education.

Bringing Together History and Heritage

Public commemorative art provides not only a point of convergence for bringing together consideration of different eras, but also two very different approaches to the past: heritage and history. James Loewen points out, "history and heritage are not the same; indeed the two are often at odds."[38] Peter Seixas contrasts "celebratory heritage and critical history,"[39] arguing the former is designed to foster national or community cohesion around a shared memory of a triumphal past largely grounded on a number of iconic stories, symbols, or representations. In their book, *The Vimy Trap*, Ian McKay and Jamie Swift show how one Great War battle and the stories, symbols, and monuments constructed to commemorate it, play just this kind of role in Canada. They refer to the phenomenon as Vimyism and write,

> By Vimyism we mean a network of ideas and symbols that centre on how Canada's Great War experience somehow represents the country's supreme triumph - a scaling of a grand height of honour and bravery and maturity, a glorious achievement - and affirm that the war itself and anyone who fought and died in it should be unconditionally revered and commemorated - and not least because it marked the country's birth... Vimyism thus offers Canadians an uplifting and sacred story of their origins-something to believe in.[40]

In contrast to the myth making of celebratory heritage, critical history uses the disciplinary process of the academic discipline to engage with evidence, ask questions, and consider different perspectives in constructing historical accounts that are complex, nuanced, and evolving.

This tension between celebratory heritage and critical history animates debates about school history and citizenship curricula around the world. A recent book examining citizenship education in the context of globalization in a number of jurisdictions around the world including countries in Asia, South America, North America, and Europe found all of the jurisdictions profiled "are attempting to forge a sense of national citizenship amongst populations of disparate peoples."[41] Curriculum planners and educators in all of these nations felt the tension between critical disciplinary approaches to history and a more heritage-oriented focus on nation building. Policy and practice in public education in all jurisdictions fell somewhere on the continuum between them. This is similar to the findings of Alan Reid and his colleagues who examined 12 countries around the world and found the issue of fostering cohesion in diverse societies to be a central concern of public education. They found that the curriculum in most countries fell somewhere along the continuum between jingoistic patriotism and diverse, critical citizenship, but concluded that the focus of most was on fostering a common sense of national identity.[42] While trends in curricula and policy related to school history education over the past 30 years, in Western democracies at least, have been towards the critical disciplinary study of history, evidence indicates that classroom practices are often not consistent with this emphasis.

As important as it is, formal history education is not the only way, or the most influential way, people encounter the past. Compared to public history it is quite limited in terms of its presence in people's lives. Most people get a few hours of it a week at best while in school, and once graduating rarely if ever encounter it again. Heritage, on the other hand, is ubiquitous, it surrounds us every day and in most places. It shows up in symbols on our money, in the regular singing of the national anthem or other patriotic ceremonies in schools or at sporting events, in media portrayals of the past, and in the commemorative art that adorns our legislatures, other public buildings, and landscapes. As pointed out above, a number of studies from Canada and around the world demonstrate the power of this kind of public history to shape understandings of the past and impact how citizens think about themselves, their cultural or ethnic group, their nations, and the other groups and nations which they encounter. Research from Northern Ireland, for example, illustrates the power of communal histories to shape the historical consciousness of even very young children, demonstrating that "even by the age of three, many children in Northern Ireland have already acquired an embryonic framework of sectarian identification."[43]

Lowenthal characterizes the kind of heritage illustrated by Vimyism and present in most communities as promoting "possessive and partisan pasts," which are "akin to a sacred possession to be passed on from generation to generation." They are partisan in that a key purpose is to "distinguish *us* from *others*."[44] These limited and parochial accounts shape how we think about ourselves, others, and the world at large and act as a powerful frame for excluding new and nuanced ideas. They are not a good basis for democratic citizenship in diverse societies and a globalized world. As Margaret Conrad and her colleagues argue, "The absence of ongoing critical perspectives on the past can leave citizens prey to phony arguments manufactured by demagogues."[45]

This is not an argument for doing away with heritage even if that were possible. It is ubiquitous partly because it is a necessary part of life. All of us narrate our lives temporally both as individuals and communities. Part of that narration is putting down markers as ways of remembering the past, orienting ourselves for the present, and imagining possible futures. As Loewen puts it, historic sites are important first because of "the role that stories play in human culture. Human beings live by stories."[46]

Keith Barton and Linda Levstik describe a number of stances that history education and public history take including "the analytic stance" that best corresponds with disciplinary approaches to history education and the "moral response stance" that, among other things, seeks to makes sense of "coercive or divisive elements of the past" in thinking through the kind of society desired in the presence.[47] Political leaders apologizing for the past wrongs committed by their nation and committing to acting differently in the future, is an example of drawing moral lessons from the past and applying them to the present. Barton and Levstik also lay out the "identification stance" which is a form of heritage education and focuses on history taught for identification with family, community, and nation. They are careful to point out the dangers of this approach to history education but also argue, "Some form of identification is necessary for democratic life, because without attachment to community individuals would be unlikely to take part in the hard work of seeking the common good."[48]

The key then, is not to ignore or disparage heritage or the sites of memory it gives rise to, but to subject them to critical interrogation. Much more will be said about this in Chapter 6 where we explore in some depth the implications of the ideas in this book for the classroom, but we will make some brief observations here. First, as shown above, commemorative art installations and heritage sites are important sources for understanding both past and contemporary societies. Students should be taught to engage them as historical sources asking questions not only about the ideas and values they are designed to disseminate, but also about who made them, for what purposes, and in what contexts.

Second, we do not engage with public commemorative art to make it iconic but we do so because it already is iconic and a key role for historians and history education, in the words of Margaret MacMillan, "is to challenge and even explode national myths ."[49] History teachers should not be icon makers but, rather, icon breakers, engaging students with critical questions about the meaning and messages of commemorative installations and spaces and, just as important, asking about the people, events, or ideas that are not memorialized.

Third, commemorative art is everywhere, making it easily accessible for teachers and students. Engaging with commemorative art in public spaces moves history education beyond the classroom and into the community. It can help students move past taken for granted assumptions about their community's history and be more attentive to how public spaces frame and define their lives and the lives of others including considerations of who is included and excluded and how. It is vital for challenging the "possessive and partisan pasts" described by Lowenthal that are so problematic as a basis for democratic citizenship.

Finally, public commemorative art is often contested, opening up the opportunity for students to understand the contested and multiperspective nature of history. Contemporary controversies over commemorative statues in a range of places illustrate something that should be seen as good news for history teachers: people care very much about the past. In fact, they care about it enough to demonstrate, deface public property, and, sadly, to commit acts of slander or violence in defending their perspectives. We argue in Chapter 7 that substantial history education has the potential to help us move beyond screaming at or harming each other in defence of our feelings about past actors and events by providing meaningful historical context for understanding those feelings and fostering the skills to make nuanced arguments that transcend sloganeering.

One important aspect of context is the knowledge that contests over public commemoration are not a new feature of an age soaked in so-called political correctness, but an enduring reality of human societies. For example, most Canadian communities have war memorials that were built by citizens a hundred years ago following the First World War. Establishing these almost always involved disputes about where they should be located, what themes they should embody (e.g. loss, triumph, sacrifice), or who should be commemorated (e.g. all soldiers from the community who served or only the dead). Thomas Littlewood, for example, describes the public process of memorializing the war in Saint John, NB as "a contentious and tense three years."[50] This contention centred around questions of whether a previously installed memorial commemorating Loyalist women should be moved to make way for one commemorating the men who fought in the war. Matthew Sears shows this penchant for contesting public commemorative art extends at least as far back as Ancient Greece.[51] For history educators, these enduring tensions over public commemorative art are not a problem but an opportunity to foster the final point of convergence we discuss in this chapter; the links between history and citizenship education.

Bringing Together History and Citizenship Education

Around the world the portion of public school curricula dedicated to social education is divided into often competing sectors including history, civic or citizenship education, social studies, geography, and others. The National Curriculum for England and Wales, for example, includes separate programmes for citizenship, history, and geography, while the Humanities and Social Sciences section of the Australian Curriculum includes separate attention to history, civics and citizenship, geography, and economics and business.[52] In North America there tends to be a single curriculum area called social studies, but within it similar clusters of subjects compete for curricular priority. A number of books and articles from around the world illustrate the contested nature of this curricular territory including titles such as: *The Social Studies Wars: What Should We Teach the Children?*, *History on Trial: The Culture Wars and the Teaching of the Past*, *History Wars and the Classroom: Global Perspectives, The Disuniting of America*, and *Who Killed Canadian History?*, just to name a few.[53]

One of us has written extensively elsewhere about the often vociferous contest between history education and civics or citizenship education for curricular priority.[54] In jurisdictions around the world, these two subject areas maintain rigid boundaries and proponents of each characterize the other area in disparaging ways. History, for example, is portrayed by civic educators as conservative, nationalistic, disconnected from student lives or concerns, irrelevant to understanding contemporary society, and often taught in a didactic way that emphasizes its irrelevance and makes it boring. Citizenship education, on the other hand, is said by history educators to be soft, non-academic, and overly focused on trendy contemporary issues while offering no sense of context for understanding those more deeply. Alan Sears has characterized this rhetoric as “based on false premises – on specific truths turned into general lies.”[55] In other words, many of the claims made are true in specific instances but not inherently true of the subject areas targeted. School history is too often conservative, nationalistic, and boring, but it is not necessarily so. Citizenship education is routinely overly focused on the issue of the month with little investigation of historical antecedents that might help contextualize it, but, again, this approach is not intrinsic to the field.

Sears makes the case there are considerable areas of overlap between history and citizenship education and the contest between them is particularly destructive to social education as a whole. He writes, "social education around the world continues to lose curricular ground vis-à-vis subjects considered more relevant and economically practical, such as literacy, math, science, and career planning."[56] It is time, he argues, to end the war and recognize the potential for productive collaboration between history and civic educators. Historian Cecilia Morgan argues that "studying commemorative practices - the putting up of a statue, or the staging of a historical pageant - has often been a way of bringing together and integrating cultural, social, and political history, fields that at times may appear unconnected."[57] We agree and would add citizenship to these areas of convergence.

Across the democratic world citizenship education has a distinctly civic republican character that focuses on fostering two key dispositions in young citizens: agency and responsibility.[58] Agency combines the belief they can make a difference with the knowledge and skills to enact that belief, while responsibility is the sense that engagement is an expected part of civic life. One recent international report describes globally competent citizens as those who can "examine local, global and intercultural issues, to understand and appreciate the perspectives and world views of others, to engage in open, appropriate and effective interactions with people from different cultures, and to act for collective well-being and sustainable development."[59] Engagement around public commemorative art provides substantial opportunity for achieving these outcomes.

As outlined above, public commemorations go to the centre of how communities and nations understand themselves and their aspirations for the future. They seek to portray who we are today and what we see as constituting the common good in the future. Wrestling with the nature of the common good and seeking to work towards it are at the very core of citizenship and citizenship education. There are some who would claim commemoration is apolitical, a simple remembering of the past, but as Sherman points out, this is hardly the case.

> The attempt of commemoration to appear apolitical, moreover, only masks the depth of its political engagement. The competing narratives of

> commemoration construct and disseminate knowledge about the nation, making judgments, assigning blame, prescribing obligations. To this extent, commemoration always involves a contest over power. Regardless of the similarities to contemporary phenomena, historians studying commemoration should keep in mind that, as with any form of representation, its real stakes lie below the surface, and involve the present and future as much as the past.[60]

As another writer puts it, "the monument war [is] not just about history."[61]

Seixas and Clark take this up in their work about the controversial set of murals in the rotunda of the legislature in British Columbia mentioned earlier. These murals were commissioned in 1932 with the artist being asked to "illustrate 'the historical qualities necessary for the establishment of a civilization.'"[62] The paintings, representing the themes of courage, enterprise, labour, and justice, hung uncontested in a central place of government for the province for more than fifty years (see Fig. 5.4). In the 1990s a group of Indigenous people wrote to the attorney general of the province making the point that "these paintings of bare-breasted Aboriginal women and of Aboriginal persons in subservient positions are, as we are sure you will understand, highly offensive, demeaning and degrading to First Nations people in the province."[63] In response to this, and other criticism of the murals, the province tasked a commission with deciding what to do with them.

Seixas and Clark used this incident as an opportunity to study how high school students think about the history and politics of commemoration. To get at this they used an essay question in a national history contest examination. The question read:

> There is currently a controversy about the way First Nations people are portrayed in four paintings found in the Legislative buildings in Victoria, BC. Consider the titles of the paintings and identify the elements that likely caused the controversy. Write a paragraph supporting either the retention or the removal of the paintings or suggesting some way to resolve the problem.[64]

The co-authors examined a sample of the 553 responses and delineated a number of analytical categories for understanding the approaches students took to the problem. We explore these categories in some detail in Chapter 6, but here we want to make the point that students can

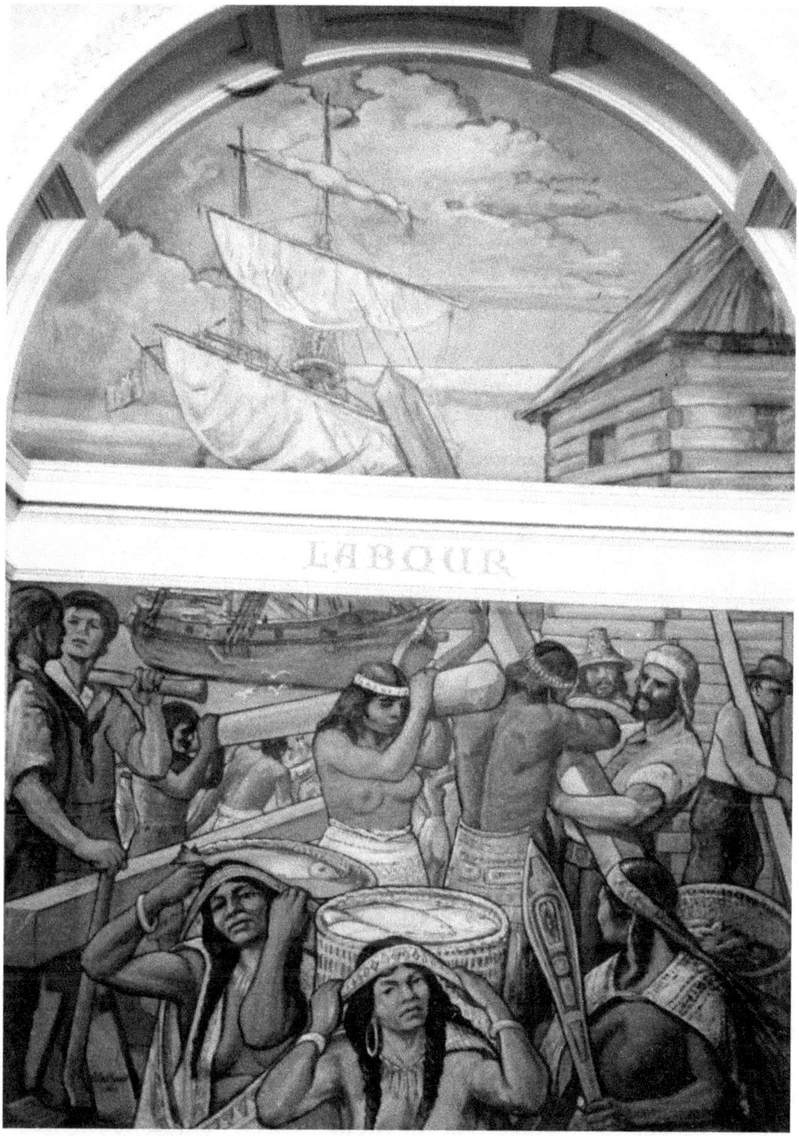

Fig. 5.4 Mural painting by George Southwell (*Source* Image *Labour*, B-06669, Courtesy of the Royal BC Museum and Archives). The image has been described as the building of Fort Victoria (1843) and, alternatively, as the building of Fort Langley (late 1820s)

engage with this important public policy controversy in a range of ways demonstrating various kinds of thinking about both the past and present, some of which mirrored elements of the thinking of the expert panel commissioned with dealing with the problem. More importantly, perhaps, "These young people were apparently fairly comfortable with the idea of controversy over historical representations," and "were at ease judging the murals on the basis of moral baggage that the pictures carry forward into the present."[65] Based on their findings, Seixas and Clark make a compelling argument for engaging students in these kinds of public issues.

> Where there is public controversy over the meaning of the past, where the definitions of the nation, civilization, and moral progress are contested, lieux de memoire become central nodes in the debates. In this age, it will not serve us well to conceive of the central obligation of the older to the younger generation as the handing down of knowledge of the past in the form of memorial narratives.[66]

Similarly, when a group of grades 6–8 students in Port Williams, Nova Scotia investigated the issues around the statue of Edward Cornwallis in Halifax described above, they developed a detailed and innovative proposal which they sent to the committee in Halifax charged with dealing with the issue. One Indigenous leader responded by writing that the students' project was an example of the kind of collaboration and dialogue he was hoping to see.[67] It is also a strong example of substantial engagement with history and citizenship education. In Chapter 6 we say much more about specific ideas for using art to engage students with important questions related to citizenship and civic life.

Conclusion

In the introduction to his book *Monument Wars* Kirk Savage tells the story of American congressman Nathaniel Macon who in 1800 led the legislative charge against the construction of a monument to commemorate George Washington. For Macon such a thing would be antithetical to the ideals of the United States in particular and democracy in general. He proclaimed, "Democracy has no monuments. It strikes no medals; it bears the head of no man upon its coin; its very essence is iconoclastic." Savage makes the point that Macon was hardly a lone voice, his views fit with key cultural trends of the time and place.

> In the United States, the iconoclastic sentiment had strong cultural support from a variety of sources: The Revolutionary critique of monarchy, the Puritan hostility toward graven images, and the Renaissance belief, seemingly verified by the ruins of antiquity, that words always outlived the grandest handiworks of sculpture and architecture.[68]

Macon and the iconoclasts won the battle but lost the war. It was almost 50 years before construction started on the Washington Monument and for that period the National Mall remained, for the most part, a forested park. Following that, however, the dam burst and

> The nation's memorial landscape has expanded relentlessly, reaching even outside the territorial borders of the United States, with major monuments on battlefields in Europe, North Africa, and Asia, and now into the solar system, with a monument on Mars to the fallen crew of the space shuttle Columbia. In Washington, the monumental core of the nation, the National Mall has become more densely filled with memorials and visitors than ever.[69]

What is true of the United States is also true of virtually every nation, territory, city, town, or village on earth: people create artistic representations to reflect who they are, or perceive themselves to be, what they value today, and who they want to be in the future. Like the proposed monument to Washington, those representations emerge from particular perspectives on and orientations to the past and are fraught with problematic particularities and absences. Virtually all commentators agree they play a significant role in shaping the collective memory of groups and nations. For all of these reasons—their ubiquitousness, representativeness, particularity, and power—they are rich fodder for history educators. Comprehensive history education then, must teach students with artistic representations of the past, learn how they work to shape understanding, mine them for evidence and new perspectives, and consider the role they do and should play in civic life.

Catriona Pennell illustrates the importance of this in her study with groups of English students who went on tours of key memorial sites on the Western Front in 2015, 2016, and 2017. The programme was centred "around three key enquiry questions: (1) How did the First World War affect ordinary people? (2) Was the Somme 1916 a disaster? (3) Is remembrance more or less important 100 years on?" and, in theory at least, grounded on the disciplinary approach to history advocated in the English national curriculum.[70] In spite of this critical orientation, Pennell found that key elements of the tour such as the presence of active and past military members, the sacred nature of the sites visited, and the overwhelming British view presented mitigated against the students developing critical and nuanced understandings of the events commemorated or the nature of remembrance itself. She concluded:

> Yet, there remains an inherent contradiction at the heart of the programme's "marrying" of education and remembrance, an inevitable result of the programme's timing: during the war's centenary, with the inevitable emphasis that state funders have placed on remembrance. Government-sponsored battlefield tours during the centenary are potentially contributing to the convergence – or even replacement – of history education with a military-centered concept of citizenship where hierarchies of Britishness based on gender, ethnicity, race and military service are prioritised over alternative war experiences."[71]

In a similar, but smaller scale, study, Barnaby Nemko found the students he studied "failed to recognize that every monument or museum contained its own interpretation," "failed to apply a critical eye to the monuments," and "appeared to find the battlefields of the First World War beyond the scope of critical analysis."[72] Neither of these studies is an argument for not engaging with commemorative sites, but they are illustrations of how difficult and complex that process will be. People will continue to visit historic sites and engage with public commemorative art and commemorative installations will continue to play a central place in debates about public policy. Because of this, we concur with Nemko who argues, "if we want to avoid bringing back coachloads of historical tourists who refuse to think critically about what they have seen, then we must invest time in devising tasks which force pupils to consider the context in which the monuments they visit were created."[73] We will take this up in more detail in Chapter 6.

Notes

1. Paul Cartledge, *Democracy: A Life*, Reprint edition (Oxford and New York: Oxford University Press, 2018), 83.
2. Matthew Sears, "A Tale of Two Statues," *The Art Newspaper*, 2018, http://theartnewspaper.com/comment/a-tale-of-two-statues.

3. Malcolm Gladwell, "The Foot Soldier of Birmingham," Revisionist History Season 2, accessed June 2, 2019, http://revisionisthistory.com/seasons?selected=season-2.
4. Gladwell, "The Foot Soldier."
5. Gladwell, "The Foot Soldier."
6. David Lowenthal, *The Past Is a Foreign Country Revisited* (Cambridge and New York: Cambridge University Press, 2015), 14.
7. See, Cartledge, *Democracy* and Sears, "A Tale."
8. Gladwell, "The Foot Soldier."
9. Gladwell, "The Foot Soldier."
10. Gladwell, "The Foot Soldier."
11. American School for Classical Studies in Athens, "Law Against Tyranny," Athenian Agora Excavations, n.d., http://www.agathe.gr/democracy/marble_stele.html.
12. Ken Osborne, "*Knowing, Teaching, and Learning History* ed. by Peter N. Stearns, Peter Seixas, Sam Wineburg, and: *Ľhistoire à Ľécole: Matière à Penser* by Robert Martineau (Review)," *Canadian Historical Review* 82, no. 3 (2001): 553.
13. Anna Clark and Carla L. Peck, "Introduction: Historical Consciousness, Theory and Practice," in *Historical Consciousness: Notes from the Field*, ed. Anna Clark and Carla L. Peck, Making Sense of History (New York and Oxford: Berghahn Books, 2019), 2.
14. The Pasts Collective: Margaret Conrad, Kadriye Ercikan, Gerald Friesen, Jocelyn Létourneau, Delphin Muise, David Northrup, and Peter Seixas, *Canadians and Their Pasts* (Toronto, ON: University of Toronto Press, 2013), 5.
15. Alan McCully and Keith C. Barton, "Schools, Students, and Community History in Northern Ireland," in *Contemplating Historical Consciousness: Notes from the Field*, ed. Anna Clark and Carla L. Peck (New York and Oxford: Berghahn Books, 2019), 20.
16. James W. Loewen, *Lies Across America: What Our Historic Sites Get Wrong*, Touchstone (New York: Simon and Schuster, 1999), 1.
17. Lowenthal, *The Past*, 14.
18. Jocelyn Létourneau, "Remembering Our Past: An Examination of the Historical Memory of Young Québécois," in *To the Past: History Education, Public Memory, and Citizenship in Canada*, ed. R.W. Sandwell (Toronto, ON: University of Toronto Press, 2006), 71.
19. Edda Sant et al., "How Do Catalan Students Narrate The History of Catalonia When They Finish Primary Education?," *McGill Journal of Education* 50, nos. 2/3 (2015): 354. See also, Keith Barton and Linda Levstik, "'It Wasn't a Good Part of History': National Identity and Students' Explanations of Historical Significance," *Teachers College Record* 99, no. 3 (1998): 478–513; Keith Barton, "'Oh, That's a Tricky

Piece!' Children, Mediated Action, and the Tools of Historical Time," *The Elementary School Journal* 103, no. 2 (2002): 161–85; Bodo von Borries, "Concepts of Historical Thinking and Historical Learning in the Perspective of German Students and Teachers," *International Journal of Educational Research* 27, no. 3 (1997): 211–20; and Peter Lee, "'Walking Backwards into Tomorrow': Historical Consciousness and Understanding of History," *International Journal of Historical Learning, Teaching and Research* 4, no. 1 (2004): 1–46.

20. Keith Barton and Linda Levstik, *Teaching History for the Common Good* (Mahwah, NJ: Lawrence Erlbaum Associates, 2004), 170.
21. Barton and Levstik, *Teaching History*.
22. Adina Bresage, "2 Navy Members Linked to Canada Day Incident at Indigenous Ceremony in Halifax | CBC News," CBC, July 4, 2017, https://www.cbc.ca/news/canada/nova-scotia/canada-day-halifax-indigenous-ceremony-proud-boys-1.4189020.
23. Alan has written more extensively about this incident in, Alan Sears, "Issues Facing the Field: Public History Goes to School," in *Learning to Inquire in History, Geography, and Social Studies: An Anthology for Secondary Teachers*, 4th ed., ed. Roland Case and Penney Clark (Vancouver, BC: The Critical Thinking Consortium, 2020), 11–13.
24. Jonathan Glancey, "The Ring of Remembrance, Notre Dame de Lorette," *The Telegraph*, 2014, https://www.telegraph.co.uk/culture/art/architecture/11220393/The-Ring-of-Remembrance-Notre-Dame-de-Lorette.html.
25. Peter Seixas and Penney Clark, "Obsolete Icons and the Teaching of History," in *New Possibilities for the Past Shaping History Education in Canada*, ed. Penney Clark (Vancouver, BC: UBC Press, 2011), 288. See also, Peter Seixas and Penney Clark, "Murals as Monuments: Students' Ideas About Depictions of Civilization in British Columbia," *American Journal of Education* 110, no. 2 (2004): 146–71, https://doi.org/10.1086/380573.
26. Seixas and Clark, "Murals," 147.
27. Matthew A. Sears, "Mother Canada and Mourning Athena: From Classical Athens to Vimy Ridge," *Arion* 25, no. 3 (2018): 48.
28. Sears, "Mother Canada." See also, Daniel J. Sherman, "Bodies and Names: The Emergence of Commemoration in Interwar France," *The American Historical Review* 103, no. 2 (1998): 443–66, https://doi.org/10.2307/2649775.
29. Rafiq Ahmad and Anne Hertzog, "Itineraries of the Great War and the Rise of the Local on the Western Front: Memory, Commemoration and the Shifting Regimes of Remembrance Tourism," *Memory Studies* (July 16, 2018): 5, 1750698018784117.
30. Quoted in Glancey, "The Ring of Remembrance."

31. Sherman, "Bodies," 449.
32. Sherman, 461.
33. Romain Fathi, "French Commemoration: The Centenary Effect and the (Re)Discovery of 14–18," *Australian Journal of Political Science* 50, no. 3 (July 3, 2015): 545–52, https://doi.org/10.1080/10361146.2015.1079940, 546.
34. Fathi, "French Commemoration," 550.
35. Ahmad and Hertzog, "Itineraries," 8.
36. Ahmad and Hertzog, 9.
37. Karel Van Nieuwenhuyse and Kaat Wils, "Remembrance Education between History Teaching and Citizenship Education," *Citizenship Teaching and Learning* 7, no. 2 (2012): 151–71.
38. Loewen, *Lies*, 16.
39. Peter Seixas, "History and Heritage: What's the Difference?," *Canadian Issues Thèmes Canadiens*, (Fall 2014): 14.
40. Ian McKay and Jamie Swift, *The Vimy Trap, or, How We Learned to Stop Worrying and Love the Great War* (Toronto, ON: Between the Lines Press, 2016), 9, 257.
41. King Man Chong et al., *Education, Globalization and the Nation* (Hampshire, UK: Palgrave Macmillan, 2016), 12.
42. Alan Reid, Judith Gill and Alan Sears, eds., *Globalization, the Nation-State and the Citizen: Dilemmas and Directions for Civics and Citizenship Education* (New York and London: Routledge, 2010).
43. Alan McCully and Fionnuala Waldron, "A Question of Identity? Purpose, Policy and Practice in the Teaching of History in Northern Ireland and the Republic of Ireland," in *Identity, Trauma, Sensitive and Controversial Issues in the Teaching of History*, ed. Hilary Cooper and Jon Nichol (Newcastle upon Tyne: Cambridge Scholars Publishing, 2015), 2–24.
44. Lowenthal, *The Past*, 502, 503. Emphasis in the original.
45. The Pasts Collective, *Canadians and Their Pasts*, 3. See also Margaret MacMillan, *The Uses and Abuses of History* (Toronto, ON: Viking, 2008).
46. Loewen, *Lies*, 11.
47. Barton and Levstik, *Teaching History*, 69, 95.
48. Barton and Levstik, *Teaching History*, 46.
49. MacMillan, *The Uses*, 39.
50. Thomas M. Littlewood, "Conflicting Commemorations: The Saint John War Memorial and the Women's Christian Temperance Union Fountain, 1922–1925," *Journal of New Brunswick Studies / Revue d'études Sur Le Nouveau-Brunswick* 10 (November 1, 2018), https://journals.lib.unb.ca/index.php/JNBS/article/view/28717.
51. Matthew Sears, "The Monument War: Not Just About 'History,'" *ActiveHistory.Ca* (blog), 2017, http://activehistory.ca/2017/10/the-monument-war-not-just-about-history/.

52. Department for Education, "National Curriculum," GOV.UK, 2014, https://www.gov.uk/government/collections/national-curriculum. Australian Curriculum, Assessment and Reporting Authority, "Humanities and Social Sciences," Australian Curriculum, n.d., https://www.australiancurriculum.edu.au/f-10-curriculum/humanities-and-social-sciences/.
53. Ronald W. Evans, *The Social Studies Wars: What Should We Teach the Children?* (New York: Teachers College Press, 2004); Gary B. Nash, Charlotte Crabtree and Ross Dunn, *History on Trial: Culture Wars and the Teaching of the Past* (New York: Knopf, 1997); Tony Taylor and Robert Guyver, eds., *History Wars and the Classroom: Global Perspectives* (Charlotte, NC: Information Age Publishing, 2012); Arthur Schlesinger Jr., *The Disuniting of America* (New York: Norton, 1992); and Jack Granatstein, *Who Killed Canadian History?* (Toronto, ON: Harper-Collins, 1998).
54. Alan Sears, "Historical Thinking and Citizenship Education: It Is Time to End the War," in *New Possibilities for the Past: Shaping History Education in Canada*, ed. Penney Clark (Vancouver, BC: UBC Press, 2011), 344–64.
55. Sears, "Historical Thinking," 346.
56. Sears, 359–60.
57. Cecilia Morgan, *Commemorating Canada: History, Heritage, and Memory, 1850s–1990s* (Toronto, ON: University of Toronto Press, 2016).
58. Andrew Peterson, *Civic Republicanism and Civic Education* (Basingstoke, England: Palgrave MacMillan, 2011); Andrew S. Hughes and Alan Sears, "The Struggle for Citizenship Education in Canada: The Centre Cannot Hold," in *The Sage Handbook of Education for Citizenship and Democracy*, ed. James Arthur, Ian Davies and Carole Hahn (London: Sage, 2008), 124–38.
59. OECD, "Preparing Our Youth For an Inclusive and Sustainable World the OECD Pisa Global Competence Framework" (Paris: Directorate for Education and Skills, 2018).
60. Sherman, "Bodies and Names," 466.
61. M. Sears, "The Monument War."
62. Seixas and Clark, "Murals," 149.
63. Quoted in Seixas and Clark, "Obsolete," 284.
64. Seixas and Clark, "Murals," 151.
65. Seixas and Clark, "Murals," 168.
66. Seixas and Clark, "Murals," 168.
67. Nina Corfu, "Kids Propose Solution to Cornwallis Statue Woes," CBC News, accessed January 26, 2018, http://www.cbc.ca/news/canada/nova-scotia/edward-cornwallis-statue-halifax-park-students-solution-1.4483005.
68. Kirk Savage, *Monument Wars: Washington, D.C., the National Mall, and the Transformation of the Memorial Landscape*, First edition (Berkeley, CA: University of California Press, 2011), 1.

69. Savage, *Monument Wars*, 2, 4.
70. Catriona Pennell, "Taught to Remember? British Youth and First World War Centenary Battlefield Tours," *Cultural Trends* 27, no. 2 (2018): 87. https://doi.org/10.1080/09548963.2018.1453449.
71. Pennell, "Taught to Remember?" 93–94.
72. Barnaby Nemko, "Are We Creating a Generation of 'Historical Tourists'? Visual Assessment as a Means of Measuring Pupils' Progress in Historical Interpretation," *Teaching History*, no. 137 (December 2009), 34, 36.
73. Nemko, "Are We Creating," 38.

Bibliography

Ahmad, Rafiq and Anne Hertzog. "Itineraries of the Great War and the Rise of the Local on the Western Front: Memory, Commemoration and the Shifting Regimes of Remembrance Tourism." *Memory Studies* (July 16, 2018): 1750698018784117. https://doi.org/10.1177/1750698018784117.

American School for Classical Studies in Athens. "Law Against Tyranny." Athenian Agora Excavations, n.d. http://www.agathe.gr/democracy/marble_stele.html.

Australian Curriculum, Assessment and Reporting Authority. "Humanities and Social Sciences." Australian Curriculum, n.d. https://www.australiancurriculum.edu.au/f-10-curriculum/humanities-and-social-sciences/.

Barton, Keith. "'Oh, That's a Tricky Piece!' Children, Mediated Action, and the Tools of Historical Time." *The Elementary School Journal* 103, no. 2 (2002): 161–85.

Barton, Keith and Linda Levstik. "'It Wasn't a Good Part of History': National Identity and Students' Explanations of Historical Significance." *Teachers College Record* 99, no. 3 (1998): 478–513.

Barton, Keith and Linda Levstik. *Teaching History for the Common Good*. Mahwah, NJ: Lawrence Erlbaum Associates, 2004.

Borries, Bodo von. "Concepts of Historical Thinking and Historical Learning in the Perspective of German Students and Teachers." *International Journal of Educational Research* 27, no. 3 (1997): 211–20.

Bresage, Adina, "2 Navy Members Linked to Canada Day Incident at Indigenous Ceremony in Halifax | CBC News." CBC, July 4, 2017. https://www.cbc.ca/news/canada/nova-scotia/canada-day-halifax-indigenous-ceremony-proud-boys-1.4189020.

Cartledge, Paul. *Democracy: A Life*. Reprint edition. Oxford and New York: Oxford University Press, 2018.

Chong, King Man, Ian Davies, Terrie Epstein, Carla L. Peck, Andrew Peterson, Alistair Ross, Maria Auxiliadora Schmidt, Alan Sears and Debbie Sonu. *Education, Globalization and The Nation*. Hampshire, UK: Palgrave Macmillan, 2016.

Clark, Anna and Carla L. Peck. "Introduction: Historical Consciousness, Theory and Practice." In *Historical Consciousness: Notes from the Field*, edited by Anna Clark and Carla L. Peck, 1–5. Making Sense of History. New York and Oxford: Berghahn Books, 2019.

Corfu, Nina. "Kids Propose Solution to Cornwallis Statue Woes." CBC News. Accessed January 26, 2018. http://www.cbc.ca/news/canada/nova-scotia/edward-cornwallis-statue-halifax-park-students-solution-1.4483005.

Department for Education. "National Curriculum." GOV.UK, 2014. https://www.gov.uk/government/collections/national-curriculum.

Evans, Ronald W. *The Social Studies Wars: What Should We Teach the Children?* New York: Teachers College Press, 2004.

Fathi, Romain. "French Commemoration: The Centenary Effect and the (Re)Discovery of 14–18." *Australian Journal of Political Science* 50, no. 3 (July 3, 2015): 545–52. https://doi.org/10.1080/10361146.2015.1079940.

Gladwell, Malcolm. "The Foot Soldier of Birmingham." Revisionist History Season 2. Accessed June 2, 2019. http://revisionisthistory.com/seasons?selected=season-2.

Glancey, Jonathan. "The Ring of Remembrance, Notre Dame de Lorette." *The Telegraph*, 2014. https://www.telegraph.co.uk/culture/art/architecture/11220393/The-Ring-of-Remembrance-Notre-Dame-de-Lorette.html.

Granatstein, Jack. *Who Killed Canadian History?* Toronto, ON: HarperCollins, 1998.

Hughes, Andrew S. and Alan Sears. "The Struggle for Citizenship Education in Canada: The Centre Cannot Hold." In *The Sage Handbook of Education for Citizenship and Democracy*, edited by James Arthur, Ian Davies and Carole Hahn, 124–38. London: Sage, 2008.

Lee, Peter. "'Walking Backwards into Tomorrow': Historical Consciousness and Understanding of History." *International Journal of Historical Learning, Teaching and Research* 4, no. 1 (2004): 1–46.

Létourneau, Jocelyn. "Remembering Our Past: An Examination of the Historical Memory of Young Québécois." In *To the Past: History Education, Public Memory, and Citizenship in Canada*, edited by R.W. Sandwell, 71–87. Toronto, ON: University of Toronto Press, 2006.

Littlewood, Thomas M. "Conflicting Commemorations: The Saint John War Memorial and the Women's Christian Temperance Union Fountain, 1922–1925." *Journal of New Brunswick Studies / Revue d'études Sur Le Nouveau-Brunswick* 10 (November 1, 2018). https://journals.lib.unb.ca/index.php/JNBS/article/view/28717.

Loewen, James W. *Lies Across America: What Our Historic Sites Get Wrong*. Touchstone. New York: Simon and Schuster, 1999.

Lowenthal, David. *The Past Is a Foreign Country Revisited*. Cambridge and New York: Cambridge University Press, 2015.

MacMillan, Margaret. *The Uses and Abuses of History*. Toronto, ON: Viking, 2008.

McCully, Alan and Fionnuala Waldron. "A Question of Identity? Purpose, Policy and Practice in the Teaching of History in Northern Ireland and the Republic of Ireland." In *Identity, Trauma, Sensitive and Controversial Issues in the Teaching of History*, edited by Hilary Cooper and Jon Nichol, 2–24. Newcastle upon Tyne: Cambridge Scholars Publishing, 2015.

McCully, Alan and Keith C. Barton. "Schools, Students, and Community History in Northern Ireland." In *Contemplating Historical Consciousness: Notes from the Field*, edited by Anna Clark and Carla L. Peck, 19–31. New York and Oxford: Berghahn Books, 2019.

McKay, Ian and Jamie Swift. *The Vimy Trap, or, How We Learned to Stop Worrying and Love the Great War*. Toronto, ON: Between the Lines Press, 2016.

Morgan, Cecilia. *Commemorating Canada: History, Heritage, and Memory, 1850s–1990s*. Toronto, ON: University of Toronto Press, 2016.

Nash, Gary B., Charlotte Crabtree and Ross Dunn. *History on Trial: Culture Wars and the Teaching of the Past*. New York: Knopf, 1997.

Nemko, Barnaby. "Are We Creating a Generation of 'Historical Tourists'? Visual Assessment as a Means of Measuring Pupils' Progress in Historical Interpretation." *Teaching History*, no. 137 (December 2009): 32–39.

OECD. "Preparing Our Youth for an Inclusive and Sustainable World the OECD Pisa Global Competence Framework." Paris: Directorate for Education and Skills, 2018.

Osborne, Ken. "*Knowing, Teaching, and Learning History* ed. by Peter N. Stearns, Peter Seixas, Sam Wineburg, and: *Lhistoire à Lécole: Matière à Penser* by Robert Martineau (Review)." *Canadian Historical Review* 82, no. 3 (2001): 548–54.

The Pasts Collective: Conrad, Margaret, Kadriye Ercikan, Gerald Friesen, Jocelyn Létourneau, Delphin Muise, David Northrup and Peter Seixas. *Canadians and Their Pasts*. Toronto, ON: University of Toronto Press, 2013.

Pennell, Catriona. "Taught to Remember? British Youth and First World War Centenary Battlefield Tours." *Cultural Trends* 27, no. 2 (2018): 83–98. https://doi.org/10.1080/09548963.2018.1453449.

Peterson, Andrew. *Civic Republicanism and Civic Education*. Basingstoke, UK: Palgrave MacMillan, 2011.

Reid, Alan, Judith Gill and Alan Sears, eds. *Globalization, the Nation-State and the Citizen: Dilemmas and Directions for Civics and Citizenship Education*. New York and London: Routledge, 2010.

Sant, Edda, Neus González-Monfort, Antoni Santisteban Fernández, Joan Pagès Blanch and Montserrat Oller Freixa. "How Do Catalan Students Narrate the History of Catalonia When They Finish Primary Education?" *McGill Journal of Education* 50, nos. 2/3 (2015): 341–62.

Savage, Kirk. *Monument Wars: Washington, D.C., the National Mall, and the Transformation of the Memorial Landscape*. First Edition. Berkeley: University of California Press, 2009.

Schlesinger, Arthur, Jr. *The Disuniting of America*. New York: Norton, 1992.

Sears, Alan. "Historical Thinking and Citizenship Education: It Is Time to End the War." In *New Possibilities for the Past: Shaping History Education in Canada*, edited by Penney Clark, 344–64. Vancouver, BC: UBC Press, 2011.

Sears, Alan. "Issues Facing the Field: Public History Goes to School." In *Learning to Inquire in History, Geography, and Social Studies: An Anthology for Secondary Teachers*, 4th ed., edited by Roland Case and Penney Clark, 11–13. Vancouver, BC: The Critical Thinking Consortium, 2020.

Sears, Matthew A. "The Monument War: Not Just About 'History.'" *ActiveHistory.Ca* (blog), 2017. http://activehistory.ca/2017/10/the-monument-war-not-just-about-history/.

Sears, Matthew A. "A Tale of Two Statues." *The Art Newspaper*, 2018. http://theartnewspaper.com/comment/a-tale-of-two-statues.

Sears, Matthew A. "Mother Canada and Mourning Athena: From Classical Athens to Vimy Ridge." *Arion* 25, no. 3 (2018): 43–66.

Seixas, Peter. "History and Heritage: What's the Difference." *Canadian Issues Thèmes Canadiens* (Fall 2014): 12–16.

Seixas, Peter and Penney Clark. "Murals as Monuments: Students' Ideas About Depictions of Civilization in British Columbia." *American Journal of Education* 110, no. 2 (2004): 146–71. https://doi.org/10.1086/380573.

Seixas, Peter and Penney Clark. "Obsolete Icons and the Teaching of History." In *New Possibilities for the Past Shaping History Education in Canada*, edited by Penney Clark, 282–301. Vancouver, BC: UBC Press, 2011.

Sherman, Daniel J. "Bodies and Names: The Emergence of Commemoration in Interwar France." *The American Historical Review* 103, no. 2 (1998): 443–66. https://doi.org/10.2307/2649775.

Taylor, Tony and Robert Guyver, eds. *History Wars and the Classroom: Global Perspectives*. Charlotte, NC: Information Age Publishing, 2012.

CHAPTER 6

Engaging the Fray: Preparing Teachers and Students for Critical Encounters with the Past

In the mid-1930s Patrick Leigh Fermor, a young Englishman, decided to walk across Europe from the Hook of Holland to Constantinople. The continent was living in the shadow of the Great War and experiencing the political, social, and economic upheavals that were setting the stage for the second global conflict that began a few years after Fermor's journey. He chronicled his experiences in a trilogy of books that include fascinating reflections on how the people he met engaged with and used the past in their personal, community, and national lives.[1]

In early 1934 Fermor found himself traversing Transylvania which was then part of Rumania. It had been carved out of the disassembled Austro-Hungarian Empire and given to that state as part of the settlement mandated by the Treaty of Versailles in 1919. Ethnic Rumanians Fermor encountered were thrilled, but Hungarians living both in Transylvania and Hungary saw the situation as a travesty. Both groups drew on community memories of the past extending to pre-Roman times to make the case for their claim on the territory. The historical record was, in fact, spotty for much of the period considered, but this lack of evidence was not a detriment to either side when it came to drawing on the past to justify or critique present realities. Fermor describes how the very paucity of reliable sources provided fodder for turning ethnic myth into settled history:

P. Clark and A. Sears, *The Arts and the Teaching of History*,
https://doi.org/10.1007/978-3-030-51513-3_6

> ... the advantage of this void to the rival controversialists is enormous. Theories can be evolved in a void, as it were, and the occasional fragments of hard fact – linguistic, geographical, ethnological or religious – need not fit into any jigsaw; indeed they are unable to do so, because all the other pieces are missing; and within certain loose bounds they can be arranged in whatever pattern suits the speaker best. The interpretations are as different as the work of two paleontologists, one of whom would construct a dinosaur and the other a mastodon from the same handful of bone-fragments...'Let us assume' turns in a few pages into 'We may assume', which, in a few more, is 'As we have shown'; and after a few more pages yet, the shy initial hypothesis has hardened into a brazen established landmark, all the time with not an atom of new evidence being adduced.[2]

Fermor's musings make several important points that are central to the arguments we make in this book, and to exploring implications for using the arts to enrich consideration of the past in educational contexts. First, and perhaps most importantly, the past is hotly contested terrain. This is true not just for academic historians but also for ordinary people. The Rumanians and Hungarians Fermor met on his travels came from all classes of society from peasants to aristocrats and almost none of them were trained historians. All of them, however, cared deeply about the past and its implications for the present and the future. The thousands of people calling for the removal or retention of controversial monuments or other commemorative installations around the world also care very much about their versions of the past as do those who work to establish historical societies, community museums, and memorial sites in virtually every town, village, or hamlet in the world.

Second, people's engagement with the past is not restricted to academic history, in fact academic history, including its subsidiary school history, plays a relatively minor role in the way people think about and connect with the past. As we have shown in the earlier chapters of this book, the past is a ubiquitous presence in the lives of individuals and communities. It surrounds us in our built heritage, the historic sites that embellish the landscape, the books we read, the movies we watch, and the community and family celebrations in which we engage. It is not only central to how we think about ourselves, but also to how we think about others; our families, our ethnic and community groups, our nations. This use of the past in thinking about who we are, how we got here, and where we are going is often called historical consciousness but, as we argue in Chapter 5, it might better be termed historical unconsciousness because it is rarely thought about overtly and almost never examined critically, but exists at the level of tacit assumption.

Third, people's engagement with the past is profoundly shaped by their community's collective memory and those memories often have an ambivalent relationship with academic history. Peter Seixas elaborates the distinction between memory and history: "memory is deeply felt; it affirms community ties, collective identities, and common foes; and it thrives on preservation and enhancement. History is analytic and intellectual; it belongs to 'everyone and no one' (in Pierre Nora's phrase) and thrives on evidence-based critique and revision." Seixas argues that school history is often focused on one or the other of these orientations emphasizing either a disciplinary approach or is "unabashedly aimed at shaping public memory."[3]

Fourth, and finally, people's engagement with the past is often not about the past at all but focused on the present and the future. The Rumanians and Hungarians pushing different versions of Transylvania's past on Patrick Leigh Fermor were not primarily concerned with correcting the historical record, they were, however, very concerned about the present sociopolitical arrangements in the region and how those might be preserved or altered in the future. They believed that getting the past right would lead to a better present and future. They were devotees of the Party slogan from George Orwell's *1984*, "Who controls the past controls the future."[4] We use these points to frame our discussion of the pedagogical implications of using the arts as a vehicle for engaging with the past.

The Past as Contested Terrain

In the spring of 2018, the American Museum of Natural History in New York City (AMNH) asked Indigenous visual historian and curator Bradley Pecore to help them with a dilemma. A large diorama in the museum's Roosevelt Hall depicted an artist's conception of a seventeenth-century meeting between Dutch colonials and representatives of the Lenape, an Indigenous nation from the territory that now includes Manhattan.[5] The diorama created in 1939 was both historically inaccurate and contested. In particular its depiction of the Lenape was rife with stereotypes that showed them as primitive, subservient, and led exclusively by the males of the group. These effects were achieved through a range of features in the visual display including the relative positioning of individuals, their demeanour and dress, and their placement relative to the meeting of the Settlers and Indigenous People. A key feature of the diorama that illustrates several of these elements is the placement of women in the background and their portrayal as half-dressed labourers with no role in the foregrounded meeting. In fact, women regularly took leadership roles in Lenape society and the historical record shows that at least one participated in treaty negotiations with the Dutch during the period depicted. As Pecore points out, this and other stereotypes in the work are not only inaccurate but powerful and "shape the American public's understandings of Indigenous people."[6]

Beginning in 2016 a civil society group called Decolonize this Place began pushing the museum to rethink many of its displays which the organization argued "perform the daily work of reinforcing racist legacies that reside in the minds of the AMNH's visitors."[7] This challenge was partly responsible for the Museum engaging Pecore and others in thinking about what to do with the diorama including considering altering it or taking it out completely. In the end, they decided to keep the image and add interpretive materials designed to both call visitors' attention to the ways in which the image portrayed both Indigenous People and settlers and to offer alternative historical accounts to the ones implied in the work. One example is a panel titled Women in the Background. It reads:

> These Lenape women are shown as subservient and only engaged in physical labour – and they would not have been dressed in this way. In reality women in Lenape society, both in the past and today, hold leadership roles, are knowledge keepers and help maintain cultural continuity. The female sachem (leader) Mamanuchqua was active in treaty negotiations in the mid 1600s.[8]

The purpose of the new interpretive materials is, in Pecore's view, "to offer an Indigenous perspective" and "begin a conversation" about this contested and difficult past.[9]

This controversy over an artistic instillation at the AMNH is an example of how history is—or could be—contested in public spaces around the world. Virtually every community has examples of public art and commemorative spaces that reflect particular perspectives on the past; perspectives that often marginalize or demean some actors, leave others out completely, and present archaic and limited views of the events or people represented. Public history, including school history, is often designed to forge or solidify social consensus, to present a view of the world that affirms and valorizes the status quo. It is critical that students be engaged in understanding the often static and conformist nature of public history and considering alternative perspectives.

One interesting way into this would be to assign students to do a critical audit of the historical art that exists in their local context including their school, local museums and galleries, community public spaces, and even their own homes. This audit should address a number of questions including, but not necessarily limited to:

1. What events, individuals, and groups are represented in the art surveyed?
2. What are the main ideas, themes, or accounts conveyed through the art?
3. What creative techniques or approaches have the artists used to convey those ideas, themes, or accounts?
4. How does the placement of the works (i.e. in or near important buildings and central locations or more hidden away) impact the ideas, themes, accounts portrayed?
5. Are there individuals, groups, or events marginalized, misrepresented, or missing from this artistic record?
6. What do the works tell us about the times and peoples they represent as well as the times in which they were created?
7. What individuals, groups, or organizations were responsible for commissioning, generating, and approving the works and their placement in the community?
8. What individuals, groups, or organizations are responsible for preserving and promoting the works?
9. Are there individuals, groups, or organizations who have raised or are raising concerns about the art (i.e. that it misrepresents or distorts the past or is not sufficiently inclusive of peoples and events)?
10. Are there issues with this historical record that you think need to be addressed? What are those? Why are they important? How might they be addressed? Who should address them?
11. How do the issues and concerns about historical art in your community compare with those across different times and contexts?[10]

This exercise uses an anchored instruction approach to studying history. Anchored instruction is premised on using critical incidents or examples as vehicles for probing important ideas and concepts. It is grounded on the idea that matters of social consequence in any society are contested and fluid; that is, they are argued about and operationalized differently across time and contexts. Teachers select critical incidents or stories that will engage students and launch a deeper probe of the important ideas and concepts involved. Understanding or working out solutions for the single example are not the end game, developing a more complex understanding of how the concepts and ideas have played out over time and how we might think of them in our own context is the ultimate goal. Elsewhere one of us has proposed design criteria for the examples or prompts. They are:

1. They should be authentic;
2. They should be presented in a vivid rendering that will catch and hold student interest and enthusiasm;
3. They should be succinct as the prompt is not a self-contained case but rather a stimulus for wider study;
4. They should be multidimensional in that they promote the consideration of ideas from a number of perspectives;
5. They should be deliberately ambiguous as their purpose is not to provide answers but to raise questions; and
6. They should be representative in that they include within them ideas, concepts, and even events that are common across a number of situations or contexts.[11]

In this case the critical incidents or prompts are authentic as they are those that exist in the community. It may be that they have largely been uncontested, but it is unlikely that important and contested questions cannot be raised about them. One example might be Humberside Collegiate, a high school in Toronto. The school is home to what has been called the largest mural in Canada painted by the eminent artist and Group of Seven member, Arthur Lismer. It was commissioned in 1925 and painted and installed in the school's auditorium over the subsequent seven years. One website describes it this way:

> This ambitious composition represented the themes of heritage, nationhood and optimism through a central panel depicting allegorical representations of civilization's virtues and ideals. These included Motherhood, Childhood, Youth, Courage, Beauty, and Wisdom with Truth. Two panels honoured the explorers of the Old World; a fourth panel symbolized the pioneers and builders of the new world and the fifth panel, the future with science and engineering.[12]

The mural "was dismantled, damaged and partially lost during school reconstruction," but efforts spearheaded by a teacher in the late 1990s and early 2000s led to the restoration of the work which now "hangs in its full majesty in the school auditorium, renamed Lismer Hall."[13]

As the description above makes clear, the mural draws on historical themes to represent the "virtues" of settler-colonial society in the territory now called Canada. Indigenous People, although present in the painting, are not mentioned in the description. In the painting they are peripheral and passive, the recipients of the "virtues" not the authors of them. The depiction is fraught with problematic and widespread stereotypes about both Settler and Indigenous Peoples. It provides an opportunity for a teacher to involve students in investigating the problematic ideas, themes, and accounts, comparing them to others elsewhere, and exploring alternative perspectives. The final question in the audit proposed above is what makes this more than a parochial exercise in community naval gazing. The issues inherent in the Lismer mural are closely related to the ones raised about the diorama at the AMNH, the murals that once adorned the rotunda of the British Columbia Legislature, and those in St. Stephen's Hall in the Palace of Westminster in London discussed in Chapters 4, 5, and 7.

As discussed in Chapter 5, Peter Seixas and Penney Clark drew on the controversial murals at the BC Legislature to conduct a study of how high school students might engage with this type of question. They analyzed responses to a short essay question dealing with the murals that was included in a national test competition for Canadian high school students. The researchers found that student responses varied across three categories: "Preserve the Monument: Antiquarian Type;" "Destroy the Monument: The Critical Type;" and "Historicize the Monument: The Modern Type."[14] Considering the relatively brief time (10 minutes) students had to respond to the test question and the lack of prior context, they demonstrated clear capacity to think deeply about the issues and to engage with important historical questions. As Seixas and Clark argue,

> These sites become particularly interesting at the moment when they inspire debate and contention. Such moments offer pedagogical opportunity: rather than seeking to resolve the controversies before they make their way into classrooms and textbooks, the debates themselves might be mobilized to help develop young people's capacities to construct meanings of the past in a conflict-ridden present.[15]

Historical art installations provide many opportunities to engage with contested and controversial areas of history in addition to the history of colonialism and settlement. For example, from ancient to contemporary times, nations and communities around the world have erected war memorials. In Chapter 5 we discuss some areas of controversy such as where they should be located, what themes they should embody (e.g., loss, triumph, sacrifice), or who should be commemorated (e.g. all soldiers from the community who served or only the dead). We also point out that the nature and purposes of commemoration often shift over time reflecting changing social sensibilities about past events. These shifts are reflected in the creation of new commemorative works or sites and the removal or altering of old ones. Virtually all of these changes cause controversy and require the consideration of diverse perspectives.

At one level the teaching of contested and controversial issues in history class is a settled question. Across much of the world official policy and curricula not only allow for teaching controversial topics, they mandate it. For example, Jonathan Zimmerman and Emily Robertson point out that, "teaching controversial issues has become the official 'best practice' in American schools."[16] The English National Curriculum for citizenship puts it this way, "Teaching should equip pupils with the skills and knowledge to explore political and social issues critically, to weigh evidence, debate and make reasoned arguments."[17] And, finally, the Australian national curriculum for history emphasizes a number of elements of historical knowledge and understanding including "contestability."

> Contestability is an inescapable characteristic of history, emerging from the essential nature of the discipline. History is the study and description of something ('the past') that no longer exists. Reconstructing the past

> depends on the surviving fragments of the past – themselves 'problematic'; involves processes of interpretation; disciplined imagination; and judgement by historians who bring to the task their various abilities, experiences, perspectives, foibles and fallibilities. Contestability occurs when particular interpretations about the past are open to debate, for example as a result of a lack of evidence or different perspectives, with debate often remaining intractable. Some students might question the value of a discipline that seems incapable of producing 'the truth'. But contestability gives history a distinctive strength and value. In history, as in life, certainty remains elusive – but nonetheless worth the pursuit.[18]

While scholarship on teaching and official policy, including school curricula, emphasizes engaging students with important and contested issues in history class, evidence from around the world indicates that teachers largely avoid dealing with controversy. A comprehensive national study conducted by A. B. Hodgetts in Canada more than 50 years ago described students in history class as "bench-bound listeners"[19] studying "a dry-as-dust chronological story of uninterrupted political and economic progress without the controversy that is an inherent part of history."[20] Many years later Anna Clark reported on her national study of history teaching in Australian schools which included extensive interviews with students and teachers. Her findings were similar to Hodgetts' indicating Australian students were being taught a superficial, unsystematic, uncontested, and heroic version of the nation's past.[21] Seeking to situate her findings in a comparative context, Clark replicated her work in Canada and found similar approaches dominated history teaching across that country. Diana Hess and Paula McAvoy conducted a longitudinal study of history and social studies teaching that included more than 1000 students, 35 teachers, and 21 schools across three states in the United States. The researchers divided the classes they saw into three types: "lecture," "discussion," and "best-practice discussion." Only in the latter, which was a small percentage of the overall number, did students engage in substantial consideration of controversial issues at least 20% of the time.[22]

There are a number of reasons teachers do not engage students in contested and controversial issues in history, or any other subject for that matter. These include lack of professional preparation; fear of criticism from colleagues, parents, and community members; and lack of good resources for the kind of in-depth investigation necessary for a substantial study.[23] Using art as a vehicle for fostering controversial historical questions potentially mitigates some of these issues in a number of ways:

- The sources are materially accessible. Public art on historical themes exists in virtually every community and, as pointed out above, sometimes in the school itself. As well, most museums, galleries, and public historical sites have websites or other resources that make images of works accessible for teachers and students.
- It is intellectually and pedagogically accessible. An issue related to using primary source material in history is students' ability to read it. That depends on a number of factors including student reading levels and the nature of the source. Many primary sources are written using cursive writing or archaic language and these can prove challenging for even the best readers. Visual artistic works, on the other hand, are often readable by students who find text difficult. The use of artistic forms also offers opportunities for students to present ideas in different media offering another opportunity for differentiating instruction to include a wider range of learners.
- It deals with important ideas, themes, and accounts. Historical art is often iconic in that it is associated with foundational ideas and events for groups, communities, and nations. We engage with it in history class not to add to its iconic nature but, rather, to understand and raise questions about the ideas and themes that motivated those who created it. As Margaret MacMillan points out in *The Uses and Abuses of History,* an important role for history education "is to challenge and even explode national myths."[24]
- While some art helps establish and perpetuate iconic and widely shared views of the past, artistic representations can also present powerful counter narratives that challenge iconic and widely accepted "official" histories. The work of Canadian Indigenous artist Kent Monkman discussed extensively in Chapter 4 is one example of this. In that chapter we write about two of Monkman's paintings, *The Daddies* and *The Scream*, that intentionally disrupt key components of Canadian collective memory. The power of Monkman's work was recently recognized by the Metropolitan Museum of Art in New York City which commissioned him to respond to its collection by creating two very large murals to be displayed in its Great Hall, the main entrance to the Museum. In contrast to the settler-focused

diorama at the American Museum of Natural History (AMNH) (just a short walk away across Central Park) described above, Monkman says he wants his works to "authorize Indigenous experience, both historic and contemporary, into this canon of art history. We've been erased from the art history of this continent. The settler artists that came here, had their own vision of this continent, which was essentially an empty landscape."[25] He argues his work "reverses the colonial gaze to challenge received notions of history and Indigenous peoples."[26] It is important for teachers to include artistic representations that present a range of perspectives on the past.

- It broadens the range of topics, events, and peoples considered in history class. As we make clear in Chapter 3, an important aspect of both historical and period fiction is that they deal with interpersonal human elements, parlour conversations, or internal family dynamics, for example, not often encountered in other sorts of historical evidence or accounts. This offers the potential both to capture the interest of a wider range of students and to provide them with a fuller sense of the complexity of the past.
- It provides a vehicle for deepening students' understanding of, and facility with using, both historical evidence and secondary accounts. As will be discussed more fully below, skillful reading of artistic works and installations as historical sources and accounts is a sophisticated process that is largely similar to the reading of other types of source material but with a number of nuances that require careful attention in history education. The power of compelling art, written or visual, to sweep those who encounter it up in particular views of the past is one of those distinctive elements that should be addressed.
- The kind of study proposed in the audit above will, by nature, be contested. That helps to move students from being simply consumers of historical truths to understanding the discipline as a contested and fluid enterprise and participating in those parts of it. Historian James J. O'Donnell puts it this way, "History as the historian practices it is in constant motion, but history as the general reader remembers it is held down by inertia. Like Tolkien's hobbits, we like to hear stories we already know, after all."[27] Historical study in school should help move students from being passive recipients of received truths to becoming active interrogators and producers of historical accounts.

- Finally, this kind of study has the potential to connect students more deeply to their communities. Not only will they know more about the art that inhabits public spaces where they live, they will understand some of the ideas and perspectives that inspired it as well as those that question or challenge it. They will learn about individuals and institutions that sponsor, produce, maintain, and challenge specific art works and the underlying ideas and perspectives and how those individuals and institutions operate in the civic sphere.

Before moving on to the next section it is important to emphasize that empirical research from around the world demonstrates that engaging students in the contested nature of history works at a number of levels. First of all, they find the subject far more interesting and engaging. In her work with Australian and Canadian students, Clark found them bored and disengaged from the study of their national history. Even given this disillusionment with the way history was being taught, however, they were supportive and recognized the importance of teaching national history, they simply wanted it to be approached differently. Clark concluded that "students overwhelmingly appreciated the opportunity to study history that was contested, changeable, and not restricted to core national knowledge."[28]

In the American research by Hess and McAvoy described above, students were interviewed five years after the initial study. Those who had been involved in "best-practice discussion" classes felt they learned more and were more connected with their peers. They "spoke about discussions, debates and group work and named specific issues that they talked about such as gay marriage and abortion. They also remembered learning from their peers and about multiple perspectives on issues even though students in their class were ideologically similar."[29]

Second, there is a plethora of research from around the world demonstrating that engaging students with important and contested questions fosters an array of positive educational outcomes. Hess and McAvoy's study, for example, found that,

> students in classes with rich and frequent discussion of controversial political issues describe these courses as engaging, become more confident in their ability to participate competently in discussions, demonstrate increased political knowledge, and display more interest in politics. They follow the news more regularly, are more likely to engage in political

> discussions with people with whom they disagree ideologically, and are more interested in listening to opinions different from their own.[30]

Similarly, a meta-analysis of more than 100 studies of civic education from a number of countries found that an "open classroom climate"—a classroom where students encounter ideas from different perspectives, are encouraged to express their own points of view, and develop well thought out arguments and positions—was the most common predictor of positive learning outcomes. The authors write, "a single finding consistently emerged across countries, contexts, times and groups: that an open, participatory and respectful discussion climate is associated with civic knowledge and engagement." They go on to point out that "across a number of countries, researchers have connected this experience of open classroom climates to a variety of positive outcomes: civic knowledge, expected political behaviour and supportive attitudes regarding gender, ethnic and immigrant rights."[31]

Drawing on the arts to present history as a contested and fluid discipline, then, not only enhances student engagement with the subject but also has the potential to enhance learning across the areas of knowledge, skills, and dispositions. It also pays attention to the diverse nature of people's interest with the past and engages their prior knowledge in ways that accord with a growing body of scholarship in these areas.

Meeting Students Where They Are in Order to Take Them Someplace New

In Chapter 2 we discuss the five scholarly conversations to which this book contributes. Elements of several of these can be closely linked in thinking through the pedagogical implications of using the arts in engaging students with the past; collective memory and historical consciousness; and the aspects of the constructivist nature of contemporary approaches to history education. As we discuss in that chapter, a central tenet of constructivism is the importance of what the literature calls prior knowledge in shaping learning.[32] Howard Gardner puts it this way:

> The key idea put forth by cognitivists is that there are important entities within the mind/brain – and these are called mental representations. Individuals do not just react to or perform in the world; they possess minds and

> these minds contain images, schemes, pictures, frames, languages, ideas, and the like.[33]

Gardner goes on to point out that cognitive science demonstrates "these early representations are extremely powerful and prove very difficult to change… If one wants to educate for genuine understanding, then, it is important to identify these early representations, appreciate their power, and confront them directly and repeatedly."[34]

As we point out in Chapter 2, researchers from around the world have investigated the historical understandings of students and found them to have well-formed and diverse historical narratives or frameworks that are often substantially different from those emphasized by academic historians or in school history.[35] The Rumanians and Hungarians discussed at the beginning of this chapter are an example of just that: they had a clear sense of their region's history that, like the cognitive frames learners bring to history class, was tenacious and resistant to change.

A very recent study of 600 students in Francophone high schools in several regions of the Canadian provinces of Ontario and Québec found students from the two provinces, and even in different regions of the same province, had developed diverse but powerful shared narratives of the history of Francophones in Canada. Québec students, for example, had a distinct provincial orientation to their accounts, paying little attention to Canada as a whole. Conversely, in Ontario, "over half (52%) of their narratives present a story situated in the country of Canada while slightly less than one third (30%) are located in the province of Ontario."[36] In addition to situating their sense of the nation (a common focus of school history) differently, these students focus on different events and themes to provide diverse historical accounts. As the authors put it, "after the fall of New France [1759-60], Ontario and Quebec students no longer tell a common history."[37]

A central point of Lévesque and Croteau's book length treatment of this study is that history teachers must engage students' prior conceptions/narratives if they want to foster growth in understanding the complex past. They write:

> … unless we engage the meaningful learning experiences of students, it is unlikely that our formal history teaching will disrupt the powerful memories, emotions, and experiences that they acquire in practical life and too often take for granted. History education needs to problematize

> this cultural knowledge so as to help learners develop more complex types of historical consciousness – particular ways of conceiving the world as a complex, multidimensional space open to changes and new forms of traditions, memories, identities, and narrative representations.[38]

In other words, good teachers must meet students where they are before they can start the process of moving them on to someplace new. This means engaging with the collective memories and historical constructions students bring with them to class. Educators have generally deemed these to be "irrelevant to students' scholastic experiences"[39] but that needs to change. Historians and history educators have only recently begun to grapple with the implications of broadening engagement with the past in history class to include collective memory and historical consciousness. In Chapter 2 we discuss in detail different, and in some ways contrasting, models developed by Peter Seixas and Stéphane Lévesque.[40] Seixas proposes a purple zone where educators can bridge the gulf by engaging "the memorial cultures of students" through subjecting them to "critical historical scrutiny, feeding back into public memory."[41] Lévesque and Croteau affirm the idea of recognizing the need to include attention to both disciplinary history and memory in school history classrooms but take issue with putting them in a single, intersecting framework for a couple of reasons. First, they argue that attention to disciplinary concepts and processes in schools is different from that of academic historians and, second, they contend the domains of academic history and collective memory are too substantially different to be contained in a single system. They propose an alternative that holds the spheres as separate with school history drawing from both and enhancing student understanding of both without the requirement they inform one another.[42]

It is important to note that both models are important attempts to begin the discussion of how to include attention to disciplinary history and historical culture in history education. We concur with these authors that this is an important next step for history education. We do think, however, that the Lévesque/Croteau matrix is a more helpful way to think about the issue at this point, particularly because of concerns from Indigenous Peoples that the inclusion of their approaches to the past in a way that subjects them to "critical historical scrutiny," as proposed by Seixas, ultimately means undermining both them and the cultural frameworks they sustain.

As we discuss in more detail in Chapter 2, a number of Indigenous and non-Indigenous scholars make the point that Indigenous approaches to the past are distinct from those of the Western disciplinary tradition of history.[43] While many of these would concur with calls from bodies like the Truth and Reconciliation Commission of Canada for the inclusion of more attention to Indigenous themes and issues in history education in Canada, most also argue that inclusion of Indigenous content is not enough. That inclusion most often takes place "within the dominating Eurocentric" framework which seeks to subsume Indigenous knowledge.[44] For them, a balanced education system should be "trans-systemic," paying attention to both the distinct epistemologies and knowledges of Indigenous Peoples and the underlying assumptions and premises of Western approaches to historical knowledge.[45] As we argue in Chapter 2, discussions about finding ways to balance these approaches to the past in history education are in their beginning stages.

In Chapter 5 we argue that school history education has been dominated by two themes: teaching students what historians know (content); and teaching students how historians know (historical thinking). What has been missing is attention to how history—or the past—works to shape individual and collective identities, ways of being in the world, and approaches to thinking about the future. It is incredibly important for citizens to develop facility with all three of these as they all have implications for how we understand ourselves, our fellow citizens, and others in the world as well as how we interact. History education must allow students the opportunity to engage with their own and others' collective memories and develop understandings of how those operate in shaping the world. That is not to downplay the study of academic or disciplinary history, it is also not to argue that collective memory should never be challenged by the findings and processes of academic history, but rather to acknowledge that historical mindedness, as described in Chapter 1, involves much more than facility with the knowledge and skills of academic history.

Pedagogical engagement with historical consciousness can and should begin with teachers exploring with their students the historical consciousness and collective memories they hold themselves and, in particular, understanding them as culturally and temporally embedded: as products of particular times and places and not universally true. In a study of how Canadian elementary school teachers think about ethnic diversity researchers began by asking participants to describe their own sense of ethnicity "in a way that made sense to them."[46] Interestingly, a number of teachers were flummoxed by the assignment saying they really did not have an ethnic identity, they were just Canadian, as if that were somehow neutral and devoid of the kinds of collective understandings and cultural practices associated with identified ethnicity. Furthermore, they had very superficial views of ethnicity seeing it as encapsulated in food, fun, and festivals rather than deeply engrained ways of seeing and engaging with the world. Participants largely saw ethnicity as an accessory that one could put on and take off at will.

A parallel study of grade six students' understandings of ethnic identity had similar findings. Students responded to prompts that pushed them to talk about issues related to cultural diversity across important areas of public policy in Canada. Like the teachers, students saw expressions of diversity as largely superficial aspects of a person's life and very few showed any evidence of understanding that groups might have deep linguistic and cultural collective identities that were recognized in Canadian law and which they wanted to enhance and protect.[47]

An overwhelming number of participants in both studies identified themselves with the majority ethno-cultural group in Canada, White Anglophones. They lived in a world that largely reflected their cultural identity, perspective, and collective memory, and consequently assumed their sense of identity to be both normal and normative. This finding is consistent with other work on collective identity and race. It is the manifestation of structural inequality and exclusion. It is often not the overt exclusion of the other, rather the widespread assumption that embedded cultural beliefs, practices, and institutions are the only, or at least the right, alternative. This results in what James Banks calls a "liberal assimilationist" approach to education which is generally hostile to significant variations in language, culture, and worldview.[48]

Following from this, a key to help students begin to understand different perspectives on historical consciousness and collective memory and how those operate in the world is not to teach them about other perspectives, but to have them recognize their own as limited, contingent, and culturally embedded. Before they can develop empathetic understandings of other perspectives on the past, they must recognize the underlying assumptions and implications of their own perspective and how it is manifested in the structures of society. In more theoretical language, we need to help them problematize what they now take for granted.

As we have discussed at several points in this book, history education researchers around the world have begun to build a substantial body of knowledge about the narrative frameworks or historical consciousness/collective memories of young people. The study by Lévesque and Croteau described in detail above and in Chapter 2 is one recent example of this. Familiarity with that knowledge base, particularly where it relates to students in their own regions, is critical for history teachers in planning ways to engage with students' cognitive frames in class.

Teachers can also use the techniques employed by researchers to assess the cognitive frameworks of the students in their own classes. Researchers have used a range of what Keith Barton calls "elicitation techniques" to surface the ways in which young people think about the past.[49] These have included asking students to write historical accounts, respond to interview questions, create timelines, assess the relative significance of historical events, sort or classify historical images, and draw pictures or graphic illustrations of the past.[50] All of these approaches have potential as pedagogical techniques for helping teachers get at the frames of their students and for students to begin to grapple with the contingent nature of their historical narratives. For example, in her research on high school students' conceptions of historical significance, Carla Peck asked participants to select the ten most significant events in Canadian history from picture cards illustrating thirty possible events.[51] She then asked them to explain their choices and found students working from a limited number of narrative frameworks in making their selections. The same exercise can be employed as a teaching technique in the classroom and provides a window into the narrative frames of students and demonstrates to the students that there are a number of ways to understand the history of their country.

Keith Barton and Linda Levstik demonstrate how important it is to engage with this kind of teaching by providing a compelling example of how pre-existing frameworks shape new knowledge. A significant body of research demonstrates that American students have a conception of the history of the United States framed by the twin themes of freedom and progress. This view allows for slight deviations, but the overall understanding of American history is of progress towards greater freedom and prosperity. As part of their work Barton and Levstik exposed students to historical material that countered these preconceptions and found, "so powerful was the narrative of progress that it led students to distort the historical evidence to fit their preconceptions."[52]

This illustrates the central implication of research on prior knowledge; in order to be effective curricula and teaching must take the cognitive schema of students into account and operate to create the cognitive dissonance necessary to foster the reframing of the schema in line with more accurate and sophisticated understandings of the concepts and/or processes being studied. If this is not done, teaching all the right information in the world will be largely ineffective.

The arts provide an excellent vehicle for getting students to think about dominant and marginalized expressions of collective identity. The community or school audit described above asks students to engage with the stories that are told about the past in and through public visual culture. The work of artists like Kent Monkman offers powerful counter narratives to official histories. Like Monkman, Indigenous photographer and curator Jeff Thomas whose work has been shown across Canada and the United States sets out to address "significant absences" from the historical record, including "photographs depicting aboriginal people living in cities and the absence of images produced by aboriginal people."[53]

The art of protest, what Philosopher Fred Evans calls "dissident public art," also exists in communities around the world and both reflects the collective memory of groups within societies and offers counter narratives to state histories.[54] We began Chapter 4 with the example of the protest art of Alsace during the 1871–1918 period of German rule in the region. Like all effective protest art, it was public, accessible, and reflected a challenge to official narratives of the communal past.

A 2016 peace agreement brought at least partial resolution to a decades long insurgency in Colombia. A central issue in the conflict was land rights for campesinos, peasant farmers displaced for a number of reasons including opening land for mining. Street art in various parts of the country, including downtown Bogota, about the period called La Violencia presents a devastating account of the impact of that displacement on ordinary people (see Fig. 6.1). It provides an interesting and accessible opportunity for teachers to engage their students in investigating and comparing collective memories of that period.

Similarly, in Northern Ireland visual culture plays a big role in the formation of historical consciousness and identity. As Alan McCully and Keith Barton point out, "Marches, banners, commemorations, and wall murals display sectional loyalty through the use of imagery associated with historical events and figures of the past."[55] McCully and Barton go on to

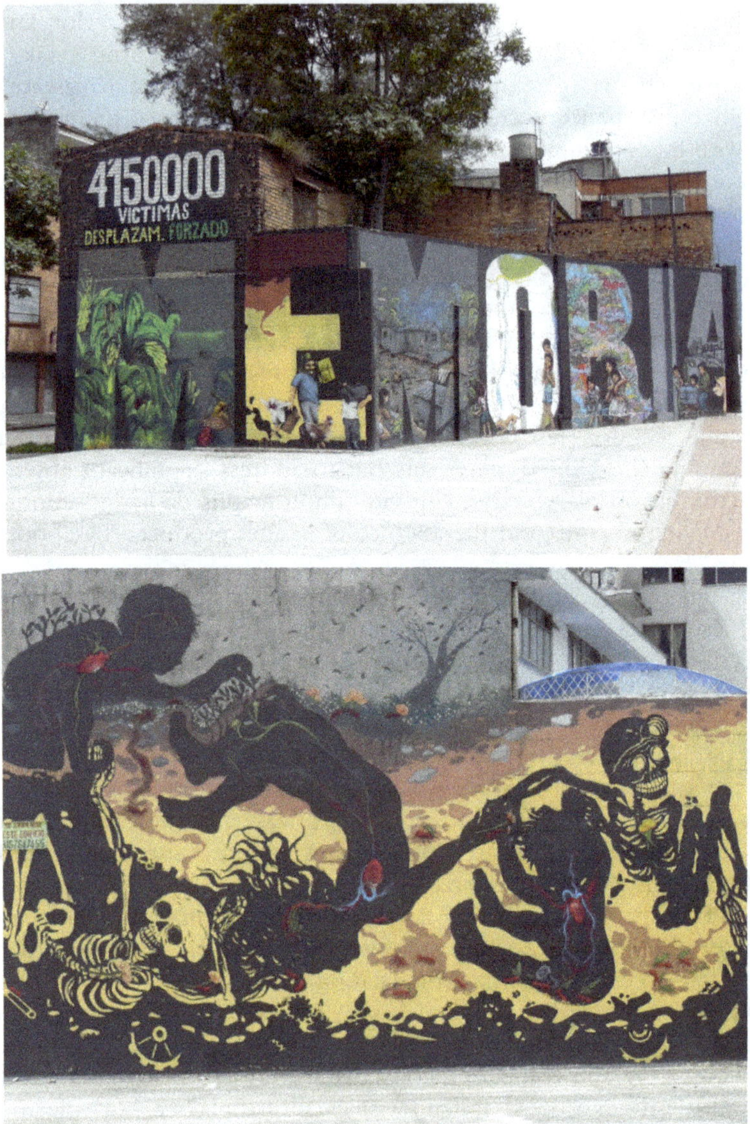

Fig. 6.1 Protest Art in Bogota Columbia (*Source* Photographs by Alan Sears)

argue this visual material can be one source to help engage students in "a meta-cognitive process whereby they can take account of the various factors shaping their ideas."[56]

Well-structured lessons can raise questions about the accuracy, comprehensiveness, and perspective represented in artistic works. Research in cognitive change makes it clear that well-entrenched frames or narratives are persistent and resistant to change and require the creation of cognitive dissonance—the feeling of being uncomfortable or uncertain about current knowledge and beliefs—before they will begin to be reconsidered. Written or visual art often evokes just the kind of visceral response necessary to foster significant cognitive dissonance. In addition to examples of evocative visual art discussed above, compelling fictional accounts can also be cognitively disruptive. The powerful pathos and helplessness that permeate the life of the Joad family in John Steinbeck's *The Grapes of Wrath* or the palpable anomie pervading the war poetry of Siegfried Sassoon, for example, offer powerful challenges to narratives of national progress or virtue often propagated in official histories. Again, cognitive frames resist change and single encounters are inadequate to foster growth, but art does offer educators a powerful pedagogical resource in the long-term project.

Engaging Artistic Works as Resources for Historical Analysis

In addition to emphasizing the contested nature of history and providing an entry point for thinking about collective memory, the arts also have considerable potential as sources for fostering student growth in historical thinking; the disciplinary work of doing history. Artistic works, for example, have great potential as historical evidence. For example, Peter Seixas makes the case that Canadian novelist Lawrence Hill's *The Book of Negroes* is a useful source for raising questions related to the ethical dimension of history.[57] He cautions, however, that this source is a "double-edged sword" arguing that the narrative force that draws the reader in and connects him or her to the experience of the characters also mitigates against alternative readings of the situation and "can trump our attempts to historicize and take into account the foreignness of the people of the past."[58]

Elsewhere we take up this idea of the "double-edged sword" as a useful metaphor for the pedagogical use of fiction in teaching history.[59] Here we argue it applies to the arts more generally. Artistic works are designed to engage people at a range of levels but, in particular, to have visceral impact; to appeal not primarily to the analytical but to the emotive parts of our intellect. That visceral power enhances interest and draws us in, making it an effective tool for captivating student interest. However, as Seixas argues, that very power to captivate has potential to narrow our analytic vision. Disciplinary work in history, while not antithetical to more emotive concerns, is primarily an analytic exercise. This means that works of art should be treated differently in history class from the ways they are treated in literature or art classes.

Linda Levstik's body of research on how children engage with narrative is a helpful guide for using fiction, and art more broadly, in the classroom.[60] Her interest in the subject began during her doctoral work when she discovered that despite considerable advocacy for using narrative, including fiction and mythical stories, as a vehicle for teaching history to young children, "there wasn't much empirical evidence" to support that approach.[61] Her subsequent research clearly illustrates our point about narrative generally and fiction in particular being a double-edged sword. "Classroom observation," she writes, "suggests narrative is a potent spur to historical investigation."[62] In a yearlong study with one grade five student Levstik found that "historical fiction provided a number of satisfactions not available from a textbook" including spurring the student "to look for causation and morality, and to ponder the complexity of events as perceived by the characters in historical fiction."[63] Writing in another place, Levstik and a colleague sum up some of the benefits of using fiction in teaching history to children,

> Through historical fiction, students learn that people in all times have faced change and crisis, that people in all times have basic needs in common, and that these needs remain in our time. Students can discover some of the myriad ways in which humans depend on each other. They will also discover the consequences of human failure in relationships, both personal and historical.[64]

In several of her studies, however, Levstik reported that the power of fiction in helping students identify with characters and situations in the past also inhibited their ability to recognize authorial perspective or choice in shaping accounts. "Narrative transmitted a sense of truth that overpowered the reader's concern for historical accuracy. A good story appears to outweigh historical accuracy."[65] It is not enough, she argues, to simply assign a piece of good fiction in history class. "Rather, the use of historical fiction requires careful selection, opportunity for discussion and reflection, the provision of time and resources for further inquiry, and a teacher willing to encourage careful analysis of books from the dual perspectives of literature and history."[66] Two central components of using fiction or other artistic works in the history classroom, then, will be first, to help students develop an understanding of what the particular art form is and how it operates and, second, to teach them strategies for interrupting and interrogating the story.

In visual and commemorative art the authorial perspective is often even more hidden than in fiction because the artist's name often does not appear on works, or is not obvious if it does. Ronald McDowell, the sculptor who created the famous *Foot Soldier* statue in Kelly Ingram Park in Birmingham, Alabama, discussed extensively in Chapter 5, had a clear account of the civil rights movement that he wanted to portray through his work and fashioned the sculpture accordingly. His artistic choices are not obvious in viewing the work but are effectively communicated using a technique called hieratic scale. Hieratic scale uses size and relative positioning to communicate important ideas about the relationship of people and things, showing relative importance, influence, power, etc. As McDowell said about his work on *Foot Soldier*, he wanted to portray the law, as viewed through the police officer and his dog, as powerful, threatening, and arbitrary, and the protesters, represented by the young man, as innocent and vulnerable. He did this even though it involved intentionally changing, some might say distorting, the actual people and events supposedly depicted in the work.[67]

James Loewen makes the point that hieratic scale and other artistic devices like relative position, colour, and the use of symbol are used in historical monuments to communicate important ideas, themes, and narratives in ways that are often unexamined; they are the instruments of authorial intent. Loewen contends that "since memory is an intensely visual medium, the images monuments show us often linger in memory long after we have forgotten the words they tell us."[68] History teaching must engage students in considering the positioning and purpose of authors relative to the stories they write or art works they create, and investigating how their works were constructed. Fortunately, fiction authors and artists themselves often speak or write about the creative process or, when they do not, others sometimes do it for them.

As we have discussed in Chapter 3 one element in the process of writing fiction, particularly what we call historical novels, is attention and fidelity to historical knowledge and sources. The same is, of course, also true of the makers of visual and commemorative art. Students should be taught that writers and artists approach this differently and should engage in consideration of why this might be so and what difference it makes for assessing a story as a historical account. Working on historical thinking makes the point that when encountering sources historians consider a number of factors external to the source itself, including trying to understand the motivations and methods of the creators of the sources. Questions of the credibility of evidence often hang on knowing who created particular sources, why, and in what contexts. Students can investigate the background of particular writers and artists, asking questions such as: What was the creator's own social position? What relationship did the creator have to the kinds of people, phenomena, or events described or depicted? And, what do we know about the creator's social and political views and how might these have shaped the development of the work? There are, of course, many specific elements of artistic technique that contribute to the force of a particular story, image, or installation and students should be taught to recognize these and understand how they work to convey some important ideas and obscure others.

While history, like art, is concerned with significant themes related to transcendent questions about the human condition, it is also necessarily rooted in detailed attention to actual events, sources, and consideration of alternative accounts of the same phenomena. Engagement with art forms in history class then, should be much different than engagement in art forms for pleasure or personal development. It ought to be interrupted with questions about the events and persons described or depicted, the sources used to construct those depictions, and consideration of alternative accounts. There are many ways teachers might scaffold these kinds of interruptions. One is to use portions of fictional stories and set those against other accounts of the same events or themes, asking students to assess the similarities and differences and make judgments about the historical accuracy of both. Another is to present a work of fiction or visual art as an example of primary source evidence and have students work through the analysis of it much like they would with any other source. In both cases the artistic work is being used in the service of developing more sophisticated historical understandings, not simply to tell a compelling story.

A significant line of research in history education has been to map how historians and young people encounter and make use of sources of various kinds, including fiction, maps, and illustrations.[69] Drawing on Wineburg's work, William Boerman-Cornell summarizes some of the key operations historians undertake in dealing with sources. "History-specific strategies" include being able to contextualize, corroborate, and source across multiple sources.

> *Contextualization* refers to the reader's ability to locate historical actors and actions in space and time. The reader must go beyond merely comprehending the individual words in the document and be able to connect to a fuller awareness and familiarity with the historical period in question. *Corroboration* occurs when the reader can use intertextual links to check different accounts against each other to determine the validity of the arguments those accounts make. *Sourcing* involves identifying and understanding the opinions, positioning, and bias of the author of a particular document. Sourcing can also be a term meant to refer to how trustworthy the reader considers the document in question.[70]

Research clearly demonstrates that while historians do these things spontaneously, students do not readily take them up: they are "unnatural acts."[71] Research also demonstrates that "with careful teacher scaffolding and ongoing attention to the use of sources, students demonstrate a surprisingly advanced understanding of abstract concepts like perspective and reliability."[72]

Artistic representations as historical sources often illuminate areas of life not addressed well, if at all, in other kinds of sources. Artistic accounts cannot, however, be taken at face value but must be subject to the same kind of scrutiny as other sources. Seixas and Morton set out five guideposts, similar to the elements outlined by Boerman-Cornell above, which describe important elements of a sophisticated understanding of the ways in which historians use sources. In all of these areas artistic sources can be used to develop more sophisticated understandings.[73]

A key element of using sources is the ability to move beyond the basic information in a source to draw significant inferences about the period and context.[74] Throughout this book we have written about a number of roughly contemporaneous visual depictions of Settler—Indigenous/Native relations in North America and India. These were all created and displayed in the 1920s and 1930s in four different contexts: St. Stephen's Hall, Westminster; The BC Legislature, an Ontario

High School, and the Museum of Natural History in New York. They are secondary accounts of the colonial periods depicted but important primary sources for the era in which they were commissioned, created, and first displayed. Students can be taught to use them to draw inferences about how the dominant culture in disparate parts of the Western world of the 1920s and 1930s thought about colonialism and the relative social and moral positioning of the peoples involved.

In good art the creator often disappears, becoming lost in the power of the ideas being communicated. Lucy Maud Montgomery becomes swallowed up in *Anne of Green Gables*, Lawrence Hill is obscured by the voice of Aminata Diallo, the protagonist in his novel *The Book of Negroes*, and painter Kent Monkman is subsumed by his trickster character Miss Chief Eagle Testickle. Understanding who creators are and how they think (or thought), however, is a critical element of learning to work with primary sources. Students need to learn to ask who created sources, how and why they created them, and explore "the author's purposes, values and worldview."[75] Again, the nature of art provides a different context for assessing the role of originators in creating sources and thus adds a potential level of sophistication to student work in the area.

Artistic works, it seems to us, provide an excellent opportunity for teachers to explore with students the ways in which creators use sources in constructing accounts. Students can examine what fiction writers and artists say, and they often say lots, about what sources they use and how and compare that to how historians write and talk about using sources. The discussion of sources is a common feature of the acknowledgements or afterword section of many novels and most histories include a substantial discussion of sources. Artists also often discuss the inspirations and sources for their work. Students can be asked to compare how the sources are treated and to assess what artists say about what they do when there are no specific sources for what they want to describe.

Developing sophisticated understandings of and facility working with primary sources is a complex and multifaceted enterprise. It is, at least at some levels, among the most concrete aspects of historical thinking as it often involves engagement with things that can be read, touched, and examined. The related historical thinking concepts of the ethical dimension of history and historical perspective taking present a much greater challenge for educators. These are inherently more abstract and difficult for people to grasp. Indeed, the tendency towards presentism, interpreting the past using contemporary values or frameworks, is often frustrating for historians as is the drawing of simplistic lessons from the past without a complex sense of perspective.

There is considerable work on how fictional narratives are an effective means for engaging younger children with times and places different from their own as well as with compelling moral and ethical ideas. Drawing on the work of Kieran Egan, Linda Levstik, and others on children's facility with narrative, a team of researchers in New Brunswick, Canada implemented a story-based approach to teaching about the ancient and medieval world to primary school students. Teachers used stories to engage young students with topics, themes, and issues from Ancient Greece to Yuan China, medieval Ireland and Northern Africa, and several other places. The children demonstrated growing understanding that the contexts they were examining were much different than their own, the first step in perspective taking, and enjoyed encountering and working through contested ethical questions about issues of courage, heroism, and the importance of religion and spirituality in human affairs.[76]

For older students, historical fiction provides similar potential for exploring perspective and the ethical questions that permeate human history. After all, presenting stories consistent with the perspectives of particular times and contexts is exactly what authors of historical fiction attempt to do. Having high school students consider the degree to which novelists get it right would be a good exercise in developing their own sense of perspective. Using primary and secondary sources of the period as well as considering other works of fiction in making their assessment would also build on their abilities to evaluate and contextualize sources.

Time Travel: Attention to Multiple Pasts, the Present, and the Future Through the Arts

Visual reminders of the American Civil War have been contentious for years, but recently that contention has spilled out into the wider public sphere. Debates about flying the Confederate flag on state legislatures and other official buildings and about statues and historic sites memorializing Confederate generals and politicians have resulted in mass demonstrations, violence, and even the murder of at least one protester.[77] The visual history of the war was largely constructed in the post-Reconstruction period from 1876 to 1930. Historian Jill Lepore argues that "the seedy compromises, underhanded dealings, personal viciousness, and outright fraud of small-minded and self-gratifying men" at the beginning of that period "abandoned a century long fight for civil rights" and surrendered the nation to segregationist propaganda and policy.[78]

Writing towards the end of the flurry of monument making, African American scholar and civil rights advocate W. E. B. Du Bois argued that "the facts of the American history have in the last half century been falsified because the nation was ashamed."[79] That shame led to a reworking of American history to show African Americans as "ignorant …lazy, dishonest, and extravagant" as well as incapable of self-government.[80] This "propaganda of history" also made the Civil War about states' rights and other causes much more noble than the retention of slavery.[81] According to Loewen the essential purpose of this historical revisionism, particularly in public commemorative art, was "to continue the Civil War by other means" and justify the so-called Jim Crow legal framework for segregation.[82] A key component in propagating this history was the construction and installation of public art across the United States. As Loewen points out, "the history written on the American landscape is largely the history of the federal governments - United States of America and Confederate States of America - and particularly of their wars."[83]

For Loewen it is particularly important that those encountering historical public art recognize it is "always a tale of two eras," the time it is meant to commemorate or illustrate and the time in which it was created.[84] As he goes on to point out, the context of the latter often mitigates accurate portrayal of the former. "Too often our historic sites related inaccurate and misleading history owing to the ideological demands of the time and the purpose of their erection or preservation."[85]

In their research with students' thinking about the historical murals in the British Columbia Legislature discussed earlier in this chapter and in Chapters 4, 5, and 7 Peter Seixas and Penney Clark identify three relevant temporal moments: "the colonial past, the time portrayed in the murals between 1792 and the 1860s;" the 1930s when the paintings were commissioned, painted, and installed; and the present when the paintings were being debated and their fate decided.[86] Evans adds a fourth temporal moment to the mix in his recognition that public art is as much about shaping the future as it is in commemorating the past. For Evans, public commemorative art sets out public values that are portrayed as normative for moulding collective consciousness as well as public practices and institutions. He argues that the public art works of the Reconstruction era discussed above, for example, were designed to terrorize Blacks, erode their civil rights, and exclude them from power in order to preserve a segregated society.[87]

It is essential for teachers when engaging students with public art to structure lessons to call attention to these intersecting temporal periods. In the research they did with students about the B.C. murals, Seixas and Clark found the majority of participants did not draw on knowledge of the colonial past in making their judgements about how to deal with the murals. Most "exhibited a critical historical consciousness advocating the destruction of the monumental status of the murals."[88] While they did not demonstrate knowledge about or awareness of the multiple eras bearing on the controversy about the murals, the "young people were apparently fairly comfortable with the idea of controversy over historical representation" and "were at ease judging the murals on the basis of moral baggage that the pictures carry forward into the present."[89] For Seixas and Clark, this indicates the opportunity public controversies about art installations provide for opening up more in-depth study of the intersecting eras and elements of history and public memory inherent in these disputes.

This provides a way to connect history to the present lives of students and their communities and to recognize the contribution of history to citizenship education. Building on the audit of community art outlined earlier in this chapter, students can be engaged in important public discussions about the kind of public art that exists in the community, how well it represents the pasts of which it speaks, what it tells us about the eras in which it was created, and what preserving, altering, or removing it means for the present and the future. In Chapter 5 we provide one example of a middle school teacher in Nova Scotia, Canada who engaged her students in making proposals to a commission struck to deal with controversies over a statue to British colonial governor Edward Cornwallis in that city. The students learned not only about Cornwallis and the contemporary controversy but about the different groups who had lived in colonial Nova Scotia and the relationships between and among them. They also wrestled with contemporary questions including thinking about the kind of values they thought public art should convey for the future of the city and the province.[90]

Both Fred Evans and Kirk Savage have written extensively about American public art, and both did so because they see a civic purpose in having people engage in deliberation both about existing works but also about possible new works.[91] Evans argues that public art is an act of citizenship "when it reflects a democratic ethos and corrects the government's support of art that implicitly or explicitly promotes autocratic values."[92] His book sets out to help citizens think through criteria for both judging existing works of public art and proposing new ones. Savage also advocates civic engagement with public commemorative art. He documents the changing artistic landscape of the National Mall in Washington, D.C. making the point that "no matter how compelling" particular monuments are, "people and history get in the way and force the commemorative landscape to change." "For that," he argues, "we should be grateful: change keeps the monuments alive."[93] He goes on to write that "one of the hopes of this book is that readers may become empowered not just to 'stand in silence' at Washington's shrines but to follow the example of citizens before them and shape a different future."[94] We see a key purpose of history education as preparing citizens to do exactly that in their own contexts.

Conclusion

St. Stephen's Hall is part of the Palace of Westminster or Houses of Parliament in London. It sits on the location of the former St. Stephen's Chapel which was the first permanent home of the House of Commons. That building was destroyed by fire in 1834 and rebuilt in its current form. Today, St. Stephen's Hall serves as the primary entrance for visitors to Parliament.

In the mid-1920s, just about the time Arthur Lismer was commissioned to paint the mural at Humberside Collegiate in Toronto, George Southwell painted the four murals in the Rotunda of the BC Legislature, and just a decade before the creation of the diorama in New York's AMNH discussed above, a series of paintings was commissioned for St. Stephen's Hall to focus on eight important turning points in British history. According to Sir Henry Newbolt, a key advisor to the project, "only such scenes could be chosen as would be of the highest and most far-reaching significance, and that the period they were to cover must be the eight centuries which began with King Alfred and end with Queen Anne [877-1707]." "The series," he continued, "is concerned with a single subject – the building of Britain – and the eight pictures given striking examples of this process."[95]

Consistent with a key argument that pervades this book, Newbolt recognized the power of art to deeply impact how people think about the past. It is often, he argued, far more powerful than more typical prose accounts.

> Historical pictures, if they are really works of art, are not designed to give information on points of fact: they are not merely literal illustrations to a prosaic narrative. The present series in particular is intended to go beyond fact, and to symbolize the inner meaning of certain events – to awake us to the greatness and wonder of our growth as a nation, our evolution from a group of tribal societies to a world-wide Commonwealth.[96]

In other words, Newbolt intended these paintings to have a profound educational impact on those who passed through the hall; an impact that would shape their perspectives on Britain's past and present and lay the basis for a particular view of her future. There is no doubt that kind of educational purpose was also true of those who commissioned the murals for Humberside Collegiate, the BC Legislature, the diorama for AMN, and many other works of art that adorn our public and private spaces.

Newbolt intended that educational impact to be both unmediated and unexamined. In other words, it would be delivered by the images alone without the intervention of a teacher, and would not, should not, in fact, be subject to critique. We argue in this chapter, and throughout this book, that art is extraordinarily powerful as an educational medium, but that power should be mediated by skillful teachers and examined critically in the context of alternative sources of knowledge about and perspectives on the particular aspects of the past being portrayed.

Notes

1. Patrick Leigh Fermor and Jan Morris, *A Time of Gifts: On Foot to Constantinople: From the Hook of Holland to the Middle Danube*, First edition (New York: NYRB Classics, 2005); Patrick Leigh Fermor, *Between the Woods and the Water: On Foot to Constantinople: The Middle Danube to the Iron Gates*, Kindle (London: John Murray, 1986); Patrick Leigh Fermor, *The Broken Road: From the Iron Gates to Mount Athos*, ed. Colin Thubron and Artemis Cooper (NYRB Classics, 2015).
2. Fermor, *Between the Woods*, Location 1500–1505.
3. Peter Seixas, "A History/Memory Matrix for History Education," *Public History Weekly—The International Blogjournal* (blog), 2016,

https://public-history-weekly.degruyter.com/4-2016-6/a-historymemory-matrix-for-history-education/.
4. George Orwell, *Nineteen Eighty-Four* (Markham, ON: Penguin Books, 1949), 31.
5. There is a longer description of this in Ana Fota, "What's Wrong With This Diorama? You Can Read All About It," *The New York Times*, March 21, 2019, sec. Arts, https://www.nytimes.com/2019/03/20/arts/design/natural-history-museum-diorama.html.
6. Quoted in Fota, "What's Wrong."
7. Decolonize This Place, "Indigenous People's Day 2018" (Deconlonize this Place, 2018), http://www.decolonizethisplace.org/content/post/indigenous-peoples-day/dtp_amnh-action_brochure_2018.pdf. See also, Decolonize This Place, "Decolonize This Place," Decolonize This Place, n.d., http://www.decolonizethisplace.org/.
8. Fota, "What's Wrong."
9. American Museum of Natural History, *Behind the Updates to Old New York Diorama* (New York, 2018), https://www.youtube.com/watch?v=ndj59hGuSSY.
10. See also James W. Loewen, *Lies Across America: What Our Historic Sites Get Wrong* (New York: Simon & Schuster, 1999). Appendix B is titled "Ten Questions to Ask at an Historic Site." Our list is partly an adaptation of his.
11. Adapted from Andrew S. Hughes and Alan Sears, "Situated Learning and Anchored Instruction as Vehicles for Social Education," in *Challenges and Prospects for Canadian Social Studies*, ed. Alan Sears and Ian Wright (Vancouver, BC: Pacific Educational Press, 2004), 268–69.
12. Radical Reform, "Humerside Mural Panel—Allegory of Virtues," Radical Reform: Education and Society 1845–1945, n.d., http://www.1845rr1945.ca/timeline/decades/1920s/event/the_humberside_mural?assetnodeid=1137.
13. Spacing, "Mel Greif," Spacing, n.d., http://spacing.ca/jane-jacobs-prize/jane-jacobs-prize-winners/mel-greif/.
14. Peter Seixas and Penney Clark, "Murals as Monuments: Students' Ideas about Depictions of Civilization in British Columbia," *American Journal of Education* 110, no. 2 (2004): 155–56, https://doi.org/10.1086/380573.
15. Peter Seixas and Penney Clark, "Obsolete Icons and the Teaching of History," in *New Possibilities for the Past Shaping History Education in Canada*, ed. Penney Clark (Vancouver, BC: UBC Press, 2011), 283.
16. Jonathan Zimmerman and Emiy Robertson, *The Case for Contention: Teaching Controversial Issues in American Schools* (Chicago and London: University of Chicago Press, 2017), 94.

17. Department for Education, "National Curriculum in England: Citizenship Programmes of Study for Key Stages 3 and 4," GOV.UK, accessed December 20, 2019, https://www.gov.uk/government/publications/national-curriculum-in-england-citizenship-programmes-of-study/national-curriculum-in-england-citizenship-programmes-of-study-for-key-stages-3-and-4.
18. Australian Curriculum, Assessment and Reporting Authority (ACARA), "Structure: Historical Knowledge and Understanding Strand," n.d., https://www.australiancurriculum.edu.au/f-10-curriculum/humanities-and-social-sciences/history/structure/.
19. A.B. Hodgetts, *What Culture? What Heritage? A Study of Civic Education in Canada* (Toronto, ON: OISE Press, 1968), 121.
20. Hodgetts, *What Culture?* iii.
21. Anna Clark, *History's Children: History Wars in the Classroom* (Sydney: University of New South Wales Press, 2008).
22. Diana Hess and Paula McAvoy, *The Political Classroom: Evidence and Ethics in Democratic Education* (New York and London: Routledge, 2015), 47–48.
23. A number of sources deal with these issues in depth including, Zimmerman and Robertson, *The Case for Contention*; Hess and McAvoy, *The Political Classroom*; Hilary Claire and Cathie Holden, eds., *The Challenge of Teaching Controversial Issues* (Stoke on Kent, UK: Trentham Books, 2007); Diana E. Hess, *Controversy in the Classroom: The Democratic Power of Discussion*, First edition (New York: Routledge, 2009); Meira Levinson, *No Citizen Left Behind* (Cambridge, MA: Harvard University Press, 2012).
24. Margaret MacMillan, *The Uses and Abuses of History* (Toronto, ON: Viking, 2008), 39.
25. Quoted in, Jessica Wong, "'Big, Bold, Audacious' Kent Monkman Artworks 'at Home' at the Met, Says Curator," CBC, December 17, 2019, https://www.cbc.ca/news/entertainment/kent-monkman-met-new-paintings-1.5395216.
26. Quoted in Kate Taylor, "At the Met, Cree Artist Kent Monkman Asks Visitors to Confront North America's Colonial Past," The Globe and Mail, 2019, https://www.theglobeandmail.com/arts/art-and-architecture/article-at-the-met-cree-artist-kent-monkman-asks-visitors-to-confront-north/.
27. James J. O'Donnell, *Pagans: The End of Traditional Religion and the Rise of Christianity* (New York: HaperCollins, 2015), 13.
28. Anna Clark, "Teaching the Nation's Story: Comparing Public Debates and Classroom Perspectives of History Education in Australia and Canada," *Journal of Curriculum Studies* 41, no. 6 (2009): 756.
29. Hess and McAvoy, *The Political Classroom*, 51

30. Hess and McAvoy, 46.
31. Ryan T. Knowles, Judith Torney-Purta, and Carolyn Barber, "Enhancing Citizenship Learning with International Comparative Research: Analyses of IEA Civic Education Datasets," *Citizenship Teaching and Learning* 13, no. 1 (2018): 12–13, https://doi.org/10.1386/ctl.13.1.7_1.
32. In addition to chapter two, see Alan Sears, "Children's Understandings of Democratic Participation: Lessons for Civic Education," in *Civic Education and Youth Political Participation*, ed. Murray Print and Henry Milner (Rotterdam, Boston, and Taipei: Sense, 2009), 143–58; Alan Sears, "Historical Thinking and Citizenship Education: It Is Time to End the War," in *New Possibilities for the Past: Shaping History Education in Canada*, ed. Penney Clark (Vancouver: UBC Press, 2011), 344–64; Mark Windschitl, "Framing Constructivism in Practice as the Negotiation of Dilemmas: An Analysis of the Conceptual, Pedagogical, Cultural, and Political Challenges Facing Teachers," *Review of Educational Research* 72, no. 2 (2002): 131–75.
33. Howard Gardner, *The Development and Education of the Mind: The Selected Works of Howard Gardner*, World Library of Educationalists Series (London and New York: Routledge, 2006), 76.
34. Gardner, *The Development*, 77.
35. Keith Barton, "A Sociocultural Perspective on Children's Understanding of Historical Change: Comparative Findings from Northern Ireland and the United States," *American Educational Research Journal* 38, no. 4 (2001): 881–914; Mario Carretero, Milel Asensio, and Maria Rodríguez-Moneo, eds., *History Education and the Construction of National Identities* (Charlotte, NC: Information Age Publishing, 2012); The Pasts Collective, *Canadians and Their Pasts* (Toronto, ON: University of Toronto Press, 2013); Alan McCully and Fionnuala Waldron, "A Question of Identity? Purpose, Policy and Practice in the Teaching of History in Northern Ireland and the Republic of Ireland," in *Identity, Trauma, Sensitive and Controversial Issues in the Teaching of History*, ed. Hilary Cooper and Jon Nichol (Newcastle upon Tyne: Cambridge Scholars Publishing, 2015), 2–24; Edda Sant et al., "How Do Catalan Students Narrate the History of Catalonia When They Finish Primary Education?," *McGill Journal of Education* 50, no. 2/3 (2015): 341–62.
36. Stéphane Lévesque and Jean-Philippe Croteau, *Beyond History for Historical Consciousness: Students, Narrative, and Memory* (Toronto, ON: University of Toronto Press, 2020), 63, 64.
37. Lévesque and Croteau, *Beyond History*, 78.
38. Lévesque and Croteau, 20.
39. Lévesque and Croteau, 20.
40. Peter Seixas, "A History/Memory Matrix for History Education." Lévesque first articulated his model in Stéphane Lévesque, "Going

Beyond 'Narratives' Vs. 'Competencies:' A Model of History Education," *Public History Weekly* 4 (2016): 12, https://doi.org/10.1515/phw-2016-5918. There is an elaborated discussion of it, particularly its relationship to Seixas's model, in Lévesque and Croteau, *Beyond History.*

41. Seixas, "A History/Memory Matrix."
42. Lévesque and Croteau, *Beyond History*.
43. Marie Battiste, *Decolonizing Education: Nourishing the Learning Spirit* (Saskatoon: Purich Publishing Limited, 2013); Marie Battiste, "Reframing the Humanities: From Cognitive Assimilation to Cognitive Justice," in *Visioning a Mi'kmaw Humanities: Indigenizing the Academy* (Sydney, NS: Cape Breton University Press, 2016), 1–18; Michael Marker, "Teaching History from an Indigenous Perspective," in *New Possibilities for the Past: Shaping History Education in Canad*, ed. Penney Clark (Vancouver, BC: UBC Press, 2011), 97–112; Michael Marker, "The 'Realness' of Place in the Spiral of Time: Reflections on Indigenous Historical Consciousness from the Coast Salish Territory," in *Contemplating Historical Consciousness: Notes from the Field*, ed. Anna Clark and Carla L. Peck (New York: Berghahn Books, 2019), 185–99; Samantha Alana Cutrara, "The Settler Grammar of Canadian History Curriculum: Why Historical Thinking Is Unable to Respond to the TRC's Calls to Action," *Canadian Journal of Education/Revue Canadienne de l'éducation* 41, no. 1 (April 5, 2018): 250–75.
44. Battiste, *Decolonizing*, 102; Truth and Reconciliation Commission of Canada, "Honouring the Truth, Reconciling for the Future: Summary of the Final Report of the Truth and Reconciliation Commission of Canada" (Truth and Reconciliation Commission of Canada, 2015), http://www.trc.ca/websites/trcinstitution/File/2015/Findings/Calls_to_Action_English2.pdf.
45. Battiste, *Decolonizing*, 101. See also, Marie Battiste, *Visioning a Mi'kmaw Humanities.*
46. Carla Lee Peck and Alan Sears, "Teachers' Understandings of Ethnic Diversity: After 40+ Years of Official Multiculturalism in Canada, Are We Any Further Ahead?" (American Educational Research Assoication Annual Conference, Philadelphia, 2014).
47. Lyle Hamm, Carla Lee Peck, and Alan Sears, "'Don't Even Think About Bringing That to School': New Brunswick Students' Understandings of Ethnic Diversity," *Education, Citizenship and Social Justice* 13, no. 2 (2018): 101–19, https://doi.org/10.1177/1746197917699219.
48. James A. Banks, "Diversity, Group Identity, and Citizenship Education in a Global Age," *Educational Researcher* 37, no. 3 (April 2008), 129.
49. Keith C. Barton, "Elicitation Techniques: Getting People to Talk About Ideas They Don't Usually Talk About," *Theory and Research in Social*

Education 43, no. 2 (2015): 179–205, https://doi.org/10.1080/00933104.2015.1034392.

50. Linda S. Levstik and Keith Barton, *Researching History Education* (New York: Routledge, 2008); B. Jewsiewicki and Jocelyn Létourneau, eds., *Les Jeunes à l'ère de La Mondialisation. Quête Identitaire et Conscience Historique* (Sillery: Septentrion [with the assistance of Irène Hermann], 1998); Jocelyn Létourneau and Sabrina Moisan, "Young People's Assimilation of a Collective Historical Memory: A Case Study of Quebeckers of French-Canadian Heritage," in *Theorizing Historical Consciousness*, ed. Peter Seixas (Toronto, ON: University of Toronto Press, 2004), 109–28; Carla Lee Peck, "'It's Not like [I'm] Chinese and Canadian. I Am in Between': Ethnicity and Students' Conceptions of Historical Significance," *Theory and Research in Social Education* 38, no. 4 (2010): 575–617; Peter Seixas, "Historical Understanding among Adolescents in a Multicultural Setting," *Curriculum Inquiry* 23, no. 3 (1994): 301–27.
51. Peck, "'It's Not like [I'm] Chinese and Canadian.'"
52. Keith Barton and Linda Levstik, *Teaching History for the Common Good* (Mahwah, NJ: Lawrence Erlbaum Associates, 2004), 170.
53. Jeff Thomas, "Artist Statement," Jeff Thomas, 2020, https://jeff-thomas.ca/artist-statement-2/.
54. Fred Evans, *Public Art and the Fragility of Democracy: An Essay in Political Aesthetics* (New York: Columbia University Press, 2019).
55. Alan McCully and Keith C. Barton, "Schools, Students, and Community History in Northern Ireland," in *Contemplating Historical Consciousness: Notes from the Field*, ed. Anna Clark and Carla L. Peck (New York and Oxford: Berghahn Books, 2019), 21.
56. McCully and Barton, "Schools, Students, and Community History," 23.
57. Lawrence Hill, *The Book of Negroes* (Toronto: HarperCollins, 2007). This is published in some countries with the title, *Someone Knows My Name.*
58. Peter Seixas, "Looking for History," in *Joined-Up History: New Directions in History Education and Research*, ed. Arthur Chapman and Arie Wilschut (Charlotte, NC: Information Age, 2015), 255–76.
59. Penney Clark and Alan Sears, "Fiction History and Pedagogy: A Double-Edged Sword," *Journal of Curriculum Studies* 49, no. 1 (2017): 620–39, https://doi.org/10.1080/00220272.2016.1238108.
60. Some of the material in this chapter first appeared in Penney Clark and Alan Sears, "Fiction, History and Pedagogy: A Double-Edged Sword," *Journal of Curriculum Studies* 49, no. 5 (2017): 620–39. http://doi.org/19.1080/00220272.2016.1238108, https://www.tandfonline.com/toc/tcus20/49/5?nav=tocList. It is used here with permission.

61. Linda S. Levstik, "Narrative as a Primary Act of Mind," in *Researching History Education: Theory, Method, and Context*, ed. Linda S. Levstik and Keith C. Barton (New York: Routledge, 2008), 3.
62. Linda S. Levstik, "The Relationship Between Historical Response and Narrative in a Sixth Grade Classroom," in *Researching History Education: Theory, Method, and Context*, ed. Linda S. Levstik and Keith C. Barton (New York: Routledge, 2008), 11.
63. Linda Levstik, "Historical Narrative and the Young Reader," *Theory into Practice* 89, no. 2 (1989): 115, 117.
64. Evelyn B. Freeman and Linda Levstik, "Recreating the Past: Historical Fiction in the Social Studies Curriculum," *The Elementary School Journal* 88, no. 4 (1988): 330.
65. Levsitk, "Historical Narrative," 118.
66. Freeman and Levstitk, "Recreating," 330.
67. Malcolm Gladwell, "The Foot Soldier of Birmingham," Revisionist History Season 2, accessed June 2, 2019, http://revisionisthistory.com/seasons?selected=season-2. See also the discussion of this work in Chapter 5.
68. James W. Loewen, *Lies Across America*, 29.
69. Keith Barton, "'I Just Kinda Know': Elementary Students' Ideas About Historical Evidence," *Theory and Research in Social Education* 25, no. 4 (1997): 407–30, https://doi.org/10.1080/00933104.1997.10505821; Samuel S. Wineburg, *Historical Thinking and Other Unnatural Acts: Charting the Future of Teaching the Past* (Philadelphia: Temple University Press, 2001).
70. William Boerman-Cornell, "Using Historical Graphic Novels in High School History Classes: Potential for Contexualization, Sourcing and Corroborating," *The History Teacher* 48, no. 2 (2015): 211.
71. Wineburg, *Historical Thinking*.
72. Barton and Levstik, *Teaching History*, 192.
73. Peter Seixas and Tom Morton, *The Big Six Historical Thinking Concepts* (Toronto, ON: Nelson Education, 2013).
74. Seixas and Morton, *The Big Six*, 40.
75. Seixas and Morton, 40.
76. Gerry Clarke et al., "Voyages in Primary Social Studies: A Story-Based Approach," *Thresholds in Education* 19, no. 4 (1993): 13–16.
77. Gary Robertson, "Neo-Nazi Gets Second Life Sentence in Murder of Protester in Virginia," News, Reuters, July 15, 2019, https://www.reuters.com/article/us-virginia-protests-idUSKCN1UA0TV.
78. Jill Lepore, *These Truths: A History of the United States*, First edition (New York: W. W. Norton & Company, 2018), 329.
79. William Edward Burghardt Du Bois, *Black Reconstruction in America 1860–1880* (New York: Antheneum, 1992), 711.

80. Du Bois, *Black Reconstruction*, 711–712. See also Lepore, *These Truths*.
81. Du Bois, 71.
82. Loewen, *Lies Across America*, 25.
83. Loewen, 5.
84. Loewen, 21.
85. Loewen, 21.
86. Seixas and Clark, "Obsolete Icons," 288.
87. Evans, *Public Art*, 2. See also, Lepore, *These Truths*; Du Bois, *Black Reconstruction*.
88. Seixas and Clark, "Murals as Monuments," 164.
89. Seixas and Clark, "Murals as Monuments," 164.
90. Nina Corfu, "Kids Propose Solution to Cornwallis Statue Woes," CBC News, accessed January 26, 2018, http://www.cbc.ca/news/canada/nova-scotia/edward-cornwallis-statue-halifax-park-students-solution-1.4483005. See also, Alan Sears, "Public History Goes to School," in *Learning to Inquire in History, Geography, and Social Studies: An Anthology for Secondary Teachers*, 4th ed., ed. Roland Case and Penney Clark (Vancouver, BC: The Critical Thinking Consortium, 2020).
91. Evans, *Public Art*; Kirk Savage, *Monument Wars: Washington, D.C., The National Mall, and the Transformation of the Memorial Landscape*, First edition (Berkeley: University of California Press, 2009).
92. Evens, *Public Art*, 11.
93. Savage, *Monument Wars*, 7.
94. Savage, 22.
95. Henry Newbolt, *The Building of Britain: A Series of Paintings in St. Stephen's Hall, Westminster* (London: Thomas Nelson and Sons, 1927), 3.
96. Newbolt, *The Building*, 4.

Bibliography

American Museum of Natural History. *Behind the Updates to Old New York Diorama*. New York, 2018. https://www.youtube.com/watch?v=ndj59hGuSSY.

Australian Curriculum, Assessment and Reporting Authority (ACARA). "Structure: Historical Knowledge and Understanding Strand." n.d. https://www.australiancurriculum.edu.au/f-10-curriculum/humanities-and-social-sciences/history/structure/.

Banks, James A. "Diversity, Group Identity, and Citizenship Education in a Global Age." *Educational Researcher* 37, no. 3 (April 2008): 129–39.

Barton, Keith. "'I Just Kinda Know': Elementary Students' Ideas About Historical Evidence." *Theory and Research in Social Education* 25, no. 4 (1997): 407–30. https://doi.org/10.1080/00933104.1997.10505821.

Barton, Keith. "A Sociocultural Perspective on Children's Understanding of Historical Change: Comparative Findings from Northern Ireland and the United States." *American Educational Research Journal* 38, no. 4 (2001): 881–914.

Barton, Keith C. "Elicitation Techniques: Getting People to Talk About Ideas They Don't Usually Talk About." *Theory and Research in Social Education* 43, no. 2 (2015): 179–205. https://doi.org/10.1080/00933104.2015.1034392.

Barton, Keith and Linda Levstik. "'It Wasn't a Good Part of History': National Identity and Students' Explanations of Historical Significance." *Teachers College Record* 99, no. 3 (1998): 478–513.

Barton, Keith and Linda Levstik. *Teaching History for the Common Good.* Mahwah, NJ: Lawrence Erlbaum Associates, 2004.

Battiste, Marie. *Decolonizing Education: Nourishing the Learning Spirit.* Saskatoon, SK: Purich Publishing Limited, 2013.

Battiste, Marie. "Reframing the Humanities: From Cognitive Assimilation to Cognitive Justice." In *Visioning a Mi'kmaw Humanities: Indigenizing the Academy*, 1–18. Sydney, NS: Cape Breton University Press, 2016.

Boerman-Cornell, William. "Using Historical Graphic Novels in High School History Classes: Potential for Contexualization, Sourcing and Corroborating." *The History Teacher* 48, no. 2 (2015): 209–24.

Carretero, Mario, Milel Asensio, and Maria Rodríguez-Moneo, ed. *History Education and the Construction of National Identities.* Charlotte, NC: Information Age Publishing, 2012.

Claire, Hilary and Cathie Holden, ed. *The Challenge of Teaching Controversial Issues.* Stoke on Kent, UK: Trentham Books, 2007.

Clark, Anna. *History's Children: History Wars in the Classroom.* Sydney: University of New South Wales Press, 2008.

Clark, Anna. "Teaching the Nation's Story: Comparing Public Debates and Classroom Perspectives of History Education in Australia and Canada." *Journal of Curriculum Studies* 41, no. 6 (2009): 745–62.

Clark, Penney and Alan Sears. "Fiction, History and Pedagogy: A Double-Edged Sword." *Journal of Curriculum Studies* 49, no. 1 (2017): 620–39. https://doi.org/10.1080/00220272.2016.1238108.

Clarke, Gerry, Alan Sears, Joanne Smyth, and Shirley-Dale Easley. "Voyages in Primary Social Studies: A Story-Based Approach." *Thresholds in Education* 19, no. 4 (1993): 13–16.

Corfu, Nina. "Kids Propose Solution to Cornwallis Statue Woes." CBC News. Accessed January 26, 2018. http://www.cbc.ca/news/canada/nova-scotia/edward-cornwallis-statue-halifax-park-students-solution-1.4483005.

Cutrara, Samantha Alana. "The Settler Grammar of Canadian History Curriculum: Why Historical Thinking Is Unable to Respond to the TRC's

Calls to Action." *Canadian Journal of Education/Revue Canadienne de l'éducation* 41, no. 1 (2018): 250–75.
Decolonize This Place. "Decolonize This Place." Decolonize This Place, n.d. http://www.decolonizethisplace.org/.
Decolonize This Place. "Indigenous People's Day 2018." Deconlonize This Place, 2018. http://www.decolonizethisplace.org/content/post/indigenous-peoples-day/dtp_amnh-action_brochure_2018.pdf.
Department for Education. "National Curriculum in England: Citizenship Programmes of Study for Key Stages 3 and 4." GOV.UK. Accessed December 20, 2019. https://www.gov.uk/government/publications/national-curriculum-in-england-citizenship-programmes-of-study/national-curriculum-in-england-citizenship-programmes-of-study-for-key-stages-3-and-4.
Du Bois, William Edward Burghardt. *Black Reconstruction in America 1860–1880*. New York: Antheneum, 1992.
Evans, Fred. *Public Art and the Fragility of Democracy: An Essay in Political Aesthetics*. New York: Columbia University Press, 2019.
Fermor, Patrick Leigh. *Between the Woods and the Water: On Foot to Constantinople: The Middle Danube to the Iron Gates*. Kindle. London: John Murray, 1986.
Fermor, Patrick Leigh. *The Broken Road: From the Iron Gates to Mount Athos*. Edited by Colin Thubron and Artemis Cooper. NYRB Classics, 2015.
Fermor, Patrick Leigh and Jan Morris. *A Time of Gifts: On Foot to Constantinople: From the Hook of Holland to the Middle Danube*. First Edition. New York: NYRB Classics, 2005.
Fota, Ana. "What's Wrong With This Diorama? You Can Read All About It." *The New York Times*, March 21, 2019, sec. Arts. https://www.nytimes.com/2019/03/20/arts/design/natural-history-museum-diorama.html.
Freeman, Evelyn B. and Linda Levstik. "Recreating the Past: Historical Fiction in the Social Studies Curriculum." *The Elementary School Journal* 88, no. 4 (1988): 329–37.
Gardner, Howard. *The Development and Education of the Mind: The Selected Works of Howard Gardner*. World Library of Educationalists Series. London and New York: Routledge, 2006.
Gladwell, Malcolm. "The Foot Soldier of Birmingham." Revisionist History Season 2. Accessed June 2, 2019. http://revisionisthistory.com/seasons?selected=season-2.
Hamm, Lyle, Carla Lee Peck, and Alan Sears. "'Don't Even Think About Bringing That to School': New Brunswick Students' Understandings of Ethnic Diversity." *Education, Citizenship and Social Justice* 13, no. 2 (2018): 101–19. https://doi.org/10.1177/1746197917699219.
Hess, Diana E. *Controversy in the Classroom: The Democratic Power of Discussion*. First edition. New York: Routledge, 2009.

Hess, Diana and Paula McAvoy. *The Political Classroom: Evidence and Ethics in Democratic Education.* New York and London: Routledge, 2015.

Hill, Lawrence. *The Book of Negroes.* Toronto, ON: HarperCollins, 2007.

Hodgetts, A.B. *What Culture? What Heritage? A Study of Civic Education in Canada.* Toronto, ON: OISE Press, 1968.

Hughes, Andrew S. and Alan Sears. "Situated Learning and Anchored Instruction as Vehicles for Social Education." In *Challenges and Prospects for Canadian Social Studies*, edited by Alan Sears and Ian Wright, 259–73. Vancouver, BC: Pacific Educational Press, 2004.

Jewsiewicki, B. and Jocelyn Létourneau, ed. *Les Jeunes à l'ère de La Mondialisation. Quête Identitaire et Conscience Historique.* Sillery: Septentrion (with the assistance of Irène Hermann), 1998.

Knowles, Ryan T., Judith Torney-Purta, and Carolyn Barber. "Enhancing Citizenship Learning with International Comparative Research: Analyses of IEA Civic Education Datasets." *Citizenship Teaching and Learning* 13, no. 1 (2018): 7–30. https://doi.org/10.1386/ctl.13.1.7_1.

Létourneau, Jocelyn and Sabrina Moisan. "Young People's Assimilation of a Collective Historical Memory: A Case Study of Quebeckers of French-Canadian Heritage." In *Theorizing Historical Consciousness*, edited by Peter Seixas, 109–128. Toronto, ON: University of Toronto Press, 2004.

Lévesque, Stéphane. "Going Beyond 'Narratives' Vs. 'Competencies': A Model of History Education." *Public History Weekly* 4 (2016): 12. https://doi.org/10.1515/phw-2016-5918.

Lévesque, Stéphane and Jean-Philippe Croteau. *Beyond History for Historical Consciousness: Students, Narrative, and Memory.* Toronto, ON: University of Toronto Press, 2020.

Levinson, Meira. *No Citizen Left Behind.* Cambridge, MA: Harvard University Press, 2012.

Levstik, Linda. "Historical Narrative and the Young Reader." *Theory into Practice* 89, no. 2 (1989): 114–19.

Levstik, Linda S. "Narrative as a Primary Act of Mind." In *Researching History Education: Theory, Method, and Context*, edited by Linda S. Levstik and Keith C. Barton, 1–9. New York: Routledge, 2008.

Levstik, Linda S. "The Relationship Between Historical Response and Narrative in a Sixth Grade Classroom." In *Researching History Education: Theory, Method, and Context*, edited by Linda S. Levstik and Keith C. Barton, 10–29. New York: Routledge, 2008.

Levstik, Linda S. and Keith Barton. *Researching History Education: Theroy, Method, and Context.* New York: Routledge, 2008.

Loewen, James W. *Lies Across America: What Our Historic Sites Get Wrong.* New York: Simon & Schuster, 1999.

MacMillan, Margaret. *The Uses and Abuses of History*. Toronto, ON: Viking, 2008.

Marker, Michael. "Teaching History from an Indigenous Perspective." In *New Possibilities for the Past: Shaping History Education in Canada*, edited by Penney Clark, 97–112. Vancouver, BC: UBC Press, 2011.

Marker, Michael. "The 'Realness' of Place in the Spiral of Time: Reflections on Indigenous Historical Consciousness from the Coast Salish Territory." In *Contemplating Historical Consciousness: Notes from the Field*, edited by Anna Clark and Carla L. Peck, 185–99. New York: Berghahn Books, 2019.

McCully, Alan and Fionnuala Waldron. "A Question of Identity? Purpose, Policy and Practice in the Teaching of History in Northern Ireland and the Republic of Ireland." In *Identity, Trauma, Sensitive and Controversial Issues in the Teaching of History*, edited by Hilary Cooper and Jon Nichol, 2–24. Newcastle upon Tyne: Cambridge Scholars Publishing, 2015.

McCully, Alan and Keith C. Barton. "Schools, Students, and Community History in Northern Ireland." In *Contemplating Historical Consciousness: Notes from the Field*, edited by Anna Clark and Carla L. Peck, 19–31. New York and Oxford: Berghahn Books, 2019.

Newbolt, Henry. *The Building of Britain: A Series of Paintings in St. Stephen's Hall, Westminster*. London: Thomas Nelson and Sons, 1927.

O'Donnell, James J. *Pagans: The End of Traditional Religion and the Rise of Christianity*. New York: HaperCollins, 2015.

Orwell, George. *Nineteen Eighty-Four*. Markham, ON: Penguin Books, 1949.

The Pasts Collective: Conrad, Margaret, Kadriye Ercikan, Gerald Friesen, Jocelyn Létourneau, Delphin Muise, David Northrup, and Peter Seixas. *Canadians and Their Pasts*. Toronto: ON: University of Toronto Press, 2013.

Peck, Carla Lee. "'It's Not like [I'm] Chinese and Canadian. I Am in Between': Ethnicity and Students' Conceptions of Historical Significance." *Theory and Research in Social Education* 38, no. 4 (2010): 575–617.

Peck, Carla Lee and Alan Sears. "Teachers' Understandings of Ethnic Diversity: After 40+ Years of Official Multiculturalism in Canada, Are We Any Further Ahead?" American Educational Research Association Annual Conference, Philadelphia, 2014.

Radical Reform. "Humerside Mural Panel—Allegory of Virtues." Radical Reform: Education and Society 1845–1945, n.d. http://www.1845rr1945.ca/timeline/decades/1920s/event/the_humberside_mural?assetnodeid=1137.

Robertson, Gary. "Neo-Nazi Gets Second Life Sentence in Murder of Protester in Virginia." News. Reuters, July 15, 2019. https://www.reuters.com/article/us-virginia-protests-idUSKCN1UA0TV.

Sant, Edda, Neus González-Monfort, Antoni Santisteban Fernández, Joan Pagès Blanch, and Montserrat Oller Freixa. "How Do Catalan Students Narrate the

History of Catalonia When They Finish Primary Education?" *McGill Journal of Education* 50, no. 2/3 (2015): 341–62.

Savage, Kirk. *Monument Wars: Washington, D.C., the National Mall, and the Transformation of the Memorial Landscape*. First Edition. Berkeley: University of California Press, 2009.

Sears, Alan. "Children's Understandings of Democratic Participation: Lessons for Civic Education." In *Civic Education and Youth Political Participation*, edited by Murray Print and Henry Milner, 143–58. Rotterdam, Boston, and Taipei: Sense, 2009.

Sears, Alan. "Historical Thinking and Citizenship Education: It Is Time to End the War." In *New Possibilities for the Past: Shaping History Education in Canada*, edited by Penney Clark, 344–64. Vancouver, BC: UBC Press, 2011.

Sears, Alan. "Issues Facing the Field: Public History Goes to School." In *Learning to Inquire in History, Geography, and Social Studies: An Anthology for Secondary Teachers*, edited by Roland Case and Penney Clark, 11–13. Vancouver, BC: The Critical Thinking Consortium, 2020.

Seixas, Peter. "Historical Understanding Among Adolescents in a Multicultural Setting." *Curriculum Inquiry* 23, no. 3 (1994): 301–27.

Seixas, Peter. "Looking for History." In *Joined-Up History: New Directions in History Education and Research*, edited by Arthur Chapman and Arie Wilschut, 255–76. Charlotte, NC: Information Age, 2015.

Seixas, Peter. "A History/Memory Matrix for History Education." *Public History Weekly—The International Blogjournal* (blog), 2016. https://public-history-weekly.degruyter.com/4-2016-6/a-historymemory-matrix-for-history-education/.

Seixas, Peter and Penney Clark. "Murals as Monuments: Students' Ideas About Depictions of Civilization in British Columbia." *American Journal of Education* 110, no. 2 (2004): 146–71. https://doi.org/10.1086/380573.

Seixas, Peter and Penney Clark. "Obsolete Icons and the Teaching of History." In *New Possibilities for the Past Shaping History Education in Canada*, edited by Penney Clark, 282–301. Vancouver, BC: UBC Press, 2011.

Seixas, Peter and Tom Morton. *The Big Six Historical Thinking Concepts*. Toronto, ON: Nelson Education, 2013.

Spacing. "Mel Greif." Spacing, n.d. http://spacing.ca/jane-jacobs-prize/jane-jacobs-prize-winners/mel-greif/.

Taylor, Kate. "At the Met, Cree Artist Kent Monkman Asks Visitors to Confront North America's Colonial Past." The Globe and Mail, 2019. https://www.theglobeandmail.com/arts/art-and-architecture/article-at-the-met-cree-artist-kent-monkman-asks-visitors-to-confront-north/.

Thomas, Jeff. "Artist Statement." Jeff Thomas, 2020. https://jeff-thomas.ca/artist-statement-2/.

Truth and Reconciliation Commission of Canada, *Final Report of the Truth and Reconciliation Commission of Canada, Vol. I: Summary: Honouring the Truth, Reconciling for the Future* (Toronto, ON: James Lorimer, 2015). http://www.trc.ca/websites/trcinstitution/file/2015/Findings/Calls_to_ActionEnglish2.pdf.

Windschitl, Mark. "Framing Constructivism in Practice as the Negotiation of Dilemmas: An Analysis of the Conceptual, Pedagogical, Cultural, and Political Challenges Facing Teachers." *Review of Educational Research* 72, no. 2 (2002): 131–75.

Wineburg, Samuel S. *Historical Thinking and Other Unnatural Acts: Charting the Future of Teaching the Past*. Philadelphia: Temple University Press, 2001.

Wong, Jessica. "'Big, Bold, Audacious' Kent Monkman Artworks 'at Home' at the Met, Says Curator." CBC, December 17, 2019. https://www.cbc.ca/news/entertainment/kent-monkman-met-new-paintings-1.5395216.

Zimmerman, Jonathan and Emiy Robertson. *The Case for Contention: Teaching Controversial Issues in American Schools*. Chicago and London: University of Chicago Press, 2017.

CHAPTER 7

The Humanizing and Civic Missions of History Education

In this book we have explored the possibilities of using various art forms: fiction, visual art, and public commemorative art in history education. We have set our work in the context of five scholarly conversations: the nature of history and historical truths and the role of interpretation in history; connections between history and the arts; the phenomena of collective memory and historical consciousness and how they work to integrate the past into our sense of the present and future; the relationship between Indigenous worldviews and approaches to the past and Western disciplinary perspectives on history; and new scholarly work in history education.

All of this begs a number of questions including: Why study the past at all? What contribution does, or can, history make to a person's education? Aren't other areas of school curricula much more important for people's real lives? Making connections between the arts and teaching about the past might make the latter more interesting, but does it have any value beyond that? The past is after all past, so why pay any attention to it at all?

In an era where many subjects compete for curricular attention these questions are not just academic, and whether they have been asked explicitly or not, history has not fared well in the decisions of curriculum policymakers around the world. In recent years it has consistently lost ground to other subjects deemed more economically relevant such as

P. Clark and A. Sears, *The Arts and the Teaching of History*,
https://doi.org/10.1007/978-3-030-51513-3_7

literacy (not literature) and the so-called STEM subjects (science, technology, engineering, and mathematics). In recent years there has been an attempt to add the arts to the latter mix, creating the acronym STEAM, but the arts in this case are usually in service to the technology, being used to enhance skills in computer-based graphic design, video game development, and other career-oriented pursuits.

One reaction to this curricular narrowing has been to make the case that studying history does foster knowledge and skills important to many career paths. In a 2019 letter to the president of the Public Service Commission of Canada, the president of the Canadian Historical Association made the case that students of history were well prepared for many jobs in the public service. She highlighted the relevant skills learned in the study of history including "excellent research skills," "analytical skills and the organization of complex materials," and "interpersonal skills," and closed her letter by requesting that the Commission "add History as a qualifying degree in your standard advertisement for analysts and related positions."[1]

While we concur that the study of history is good preparation for many professional careers, central to the arguments of this book is that studying the past has value well beyond a narrow focus on career development. Facility with the past is critical to develop a full sense of who we are as human beings both individually and collectively, who the other people are who share the world with us, and how we might engage together in working toward the common good. Studying the past, in other words, is both a humanizing and a civic mission and it has never been more critical than it is today.

How the Past Permeates Our Present

From the time of Australia's Federation as an independent nation-state in 1901, political and social leaders conceived of the idea of creating a national history museum to preserve elements of the past and help explain the country to itself and others. Political bickering, financial contingencies, and historical controversies delayed the project for 100 years. A key issue centred around the purpose for this national museum: should it portray "an agreed upon sense of national identity" or be more focused on presenting complex and contested aspects of the past?[2]

After a century of discussion and wrangling, the National Museum of Australia opened in March 2001 as part of the celebrations of the centenary of Australian nationhood. With the opening of its doors the controversies that had dogged the project for years spilled out into the public realm. Criticism of the museum's focus and displays came from professional historians, members of the Museum Council, the popular press, and prominent politicians including Prime Minister John Howard. Iconoclastic writer and historian Keith Windschuttle led the charge claiming the museum "had been hijacked by postmodern and postcolonial theorists and social historians and consequently the museum overemphasized past injustices." In particular, he argued, it paid far too much attention to colonial injustice perpetrated upon Indigenous Peoples and excluded the views and contributions of mainstream historians, political leaders, and ordinary citizens.[3] Other historians countered with the argument that the museum "should encourage debate and not shy away from controversy."[4]

The debate quickly migrated to the wider public realm becoming part of what Stewart Macintyre and Anna Clark call "the history wars" in Australia.[5] These wars were fought on a number of fronts including academic conferences and publications, the mainstream press, sites of public history, and schools.[6] They were characterized by personal attacks and polemical language such as the description of the approach the museum had taken as "black armband history" designed to promote sorrow and guilt about the past. That was countered by claims that traditional approaches constituted "three cheers history" focused on blind adherence to nation grounded on a narrow and overly positive presentation of its past.[7] As Macintyre and Clark point out, these debates were not characterized by a search for understanding but by a desire "to vanquish the enemy."[8] The combatants, they argue, demonstrated very little desire to convince the other side but set out to "caricature their opponents and impugn their motives" through appeals "to loyalty, hope, fear and prejudice."[9]

On the other side of the world in March of 2015, Canadian politician and future prime minister Justin Trudeau gave a speech at Montreal's McGill University. In the speech Trudeau addressed a prominent public controversy about whether or not a female Muslim immigrant to Canada should be required to remove her niqab (face veil) at the forthcoming ceremony where she would swear allegiance to Canada and become a citizen. Stephen Harper, the prime minister at the time, felt strongly that she should be required to show her face for the oath, Mr. Trudeau disagreed. In responding to the prime minister's position,

Trudeau invoked three specific historical incidents important in Canadian collective memory. He said, "This is not the spirit of Canadian liberty, my friends. It is the spirit of the *Komagata Maru*. Of the *St. Louis*. Of 'none is too many.'"[10]

The first refers to a shipload of mostly Sikh migrants from India which arrived in Vancouver Harbour in March of 1914. The migrants were seeking refuge in Canada from nationalist and anti-colonialist struggles in India. Of the 376 passengers only 24 were admitted to Canada and the rest were returned to India. Some of the returnees were arrested or shot by police on arrival there. The incident became a symbol of racist and exclusionary immigration policies in early twentieth-century Canada and two later prime ministers, both Mr. Harper and Mr. Trudeau, apologized for the Canadian government's response.[11]

The other two references are allusions to the history of anti-Semitism in Canada, particularly related to the Holocaust. The first refers to the MS *St. Louis*, a ship full of some 900 Jewish refugees fleeing pre-Second World War Europe. The ship was turned away from a number of countries including Canada, and the Jews were returned to Europe where many perished in the Holocaust. The second reference is to the more general Canadian policy toward Jewish immigration in the 1930s, made famous in a book by Irving Abella and Harold Troper, *None Is too Many: Canada and the Jews of Europe 1933–1948*.[12] Like the *Komagata Maru* incident both of these referents are often used as symbols for dark parts of Canadian history.

Mr. Trudeau's invocation of these was not only an attempt to illustrate his position on the issue of whether or not it was appropriate to wear a niqab when taking a citizenship oath, it was also an attempt to tie Prime Minister Harper to the virulent racism associated with all three references. There is not space here to argue the specific merits of the link, but Trudeau's technique clearly employs history as a device to impugn both the position and the character of his opponent. He takes three complex and nuanced historical events or policies and uses them simplistically without providing context or specific evidence to support the connections he asserts. To be clear, Mr. Trudeau is not uniquely guilty of this, it is something politicians and other people do all the time. This is one example of what historian Margaret MacMillan calls "the uses and abuses of history." She writes that humans regularly "spin the events of the past to show that we always tend to behave well and our opponents badly or that we are normally right and others wrong."[13]

These two examples demonstrate that engagement with and use of the past occurs regularly across cultures and national boundaries. They illustrate an important wider truth that is central to this book: the past surrounds us all and permeates our everyday lives, often in unrecognized and unexamined ways. It pervades our discourse about museums, historic sites, monuments, other works of art, and commemorative rituals. Public debate about these things, and there is lots of it around the world, is really focused on defining who we are as individuals and communities and who the others are who share the world with us.[14] It goes to the core of our sense of identity and place in the world. The invocation of elements of the past also regularly surfaces as part of our civic and political deliberations. When politicians like President Donald Trump in the United States and pro Brexiters in the UK sling slogans like "make American great again" and "take our country back," they are calling on people to remember better, more glorious times past. In all of these cases the past is invoked not only, not even primarily, to tell us about who we or others were, but also to tell us who we and others are and should be. It is eminently contemporary and relevant. In the words of American novelist William Faulkner, "The past is never dead. It's not even past."[15]

Much of this use of the past to define ourselves and others or score points in civic and political debate is either unconscious or simplistic, often resulting in exclusion, injustice, malicious conflict, and poorly thought out social policies and institutions. The absence of women and Indigenous Peoples from official histories, for example, contributes to their marginalization or outright exclusion from important aspects of civic life and institutions. Kent Monkman's painting *The Daddies* discussed in Chapter 4 was designed to make exactly this point.

The abysmal quality and tone of civic discourse and practice has been the cause of considerable angst in societies around the world. A particularly virulent example is the case of British Labour MP Jo Cox, a passionate campaigner for the remain side during the Brexit referendum campaign in 2016. Ms. Cox was murdered during a rally in her Yorkshire constituency by a man shouting, "Britain first." The killing shook Britain deeply and the raging protagonists on both sides retreated from the campaign trial for 36 hours or so but were soon back at it with every bit as much vitriol. As one reporter for *The Telegraph* put it, "Death threats and images of sexual torment have become part of the job for our MPs."[16] While this level of violence in civic interactions is not common, violent and exclusionary language is. As one French political scientist put it in commenting on the 2016 election in her country:

> I've never been so worried, so stressed out and so shocked. Most unnerving has been the division of the country and the hatred that came out of groups of people who can't discuss anything, can't understand each other, can't talk...It's like they don't even speak the same language.[17]

While the study of history is no panacea for these ills, it does offer the potential to develop the knowledge, skills, and sensibilities to address them in more productive ways. A more complex sense of the past, for example, can help us develop much more nuanced understandings of ourselves and others. The fostering of historical perspective helps students understand that human beings in other contexts operate with different sets of knowledge and assumptions about the world that, while foreign to us, make sense in their milieus. This sense of perspective is relevant not only to understanding others in the past but also in the present. Developing facility with the historical thinking concept of evidence can help students understand the potential and limitations of sources, to make judgements about them, and to use them in constructing points of view about important questions and issues. As is elaborated in some detail below, a deeper sense of historical consciousness, of how people use the past to develop personal and collective identities and situate themselves vis-à-vis others, is a critical element of cross-cultural competency generally and empathy in particular.

It is our contention that history education has never been more necessary or relevant. Its two central missions are to contribute to our growth as human beings and citizens: to help us understand in complex and nuanced ways the many and varied ways to be human; and to use that understanding as a platform for fruitful and vigorous civic engagement. In this book we have shown how attention to the arts can contribute to both those important endeavours in a number of ways that connect to the five scholarly conversations that framed our approach to this book and are discussed in detail in Chapter 2.

Engaging the Arts in History Class Fosters More Complex Understandings of History and the Nature of Truth

In January of 2017 the Canadian Broadcasting Corporation's (CBC) documentary radio programme *Ideas* ran an hour-long show titled "The Truth About Post-Truth." Host Paul Kennedy interviewed three academics asking them to reflect on a number of questions including whether or not the issues with our public discourse were because we live in a "post-truth era" where truth is either impossible to determine or "doesn't matter anymore."[18] CBC was not alone in its interest in how truth is manifest in the contemporary world. Writing separately in the journal *Nature*, University of Texas philosopher Kathleen Higgins, one of the guests on the *Ideas* segment, pointed out that "The Oxford Dictionaries named 'post-truth' as their 2016 Word of the Year."[19]

In their national longitudinal study of emerging adults (18–23 year-olds) in the United States, Christian Smith and his colleagues found that philosophical ideas flowing from postmodernism including "uncertainty, difference, fluidity, ambiguity, multivocality, self-construction, changing identities, particularity, historical finitude, localism, audience reception, perspectivalism, and more" often lost their nuance and complexity when they moved to the more general population. Among study participants these ideas manifested themselves "as a simple-minded ideology presupposing the cultural construction of everything, individual subjectivism, soft ontological antirealism, and absolute moral relativism."[20] All of these contributed to both an inability and an unwillingness to engage in civic discourse designed to wrestle with complex questions about what might constitute the common good and how that might be better enacted through policy and institutional structures.

Higgins acknowledges that philosophers, especially those writing "about epistemic relativism, the view that truth can vary depending on the context," are often blamed for current public ambivalence about the idea of truth.[21] She goes on to argue, however, that

> Scientists and philosophers should be shocked by the idea of post-truth, and they should speak up when scientific findings are ignored by those in power or treated as mere matters of faith. Scientists must keep reminding society of the importance of the social mission of science — to provide the best information possible as the basis for public policy. And they should

> publicly affirm the intellectual virtues that they so effectively model: critical thinking, sustained inquiry and revision of beliefs on the basis of evidence.[22]

While Higgin's article focused on deliberations about public policy related to science, we contend that a well-developed and delivered history education can contribute to the kind of critical thinking, sustained inquiry, and revision of beliefs on the basis of evidence for which she argues. It can do this by fostering more complex ideas about historical truth in particular as well as more general understanding of the nature of truth in human affairs and its relation to evidence and perspective. The study of history demonstrates that while truth is always partial, contextual, and shifting, it is neither endlessly flexible (absolute relativism—everything is true) nor completely elusive (absolute cynicism—nothing is true).

A key aspect of the scholarly debate about the nature of history and historical truth discussed in Chapter 2 and elaborated in a number of other parts of this book, is the recognition of and wrestling with the partial nature of historical truth. It is partial in several ways. First, history includes only selected parts of the past; second, it is limited by the available evidence; and third, it is communicated in forms shaped by people with particular perspectives and purposes, it is never told from an external, neutral standpoint. Comprehensive history education, including encounters with the arts, will engage students with all of these limitations in substantial ways.

A common activity in introducing students to the partial nature of historical truth is to ask them to describe the difference between history and the past. Initially they are often perplexed with the question assuming that history and the past are the same thing. But of course, they are not. The past is everything that has happened, but history only covers a small selection of the past and always from particular perspectives or standpoints. As explored in some detail in several places in this book, a key development in the discipline of history over the past half century or more has been an expansion of the past—or pasts—considered by the discipline. Feminist, labour, and social historians more generally have moved beyond the traditional focus on male political and military leaders and their exploits to cover a broader range of people and topics. While this has not been without controversy as books critical of the shift with titles such as *The Disuniting of America* and *The Killing of History: How*

Literary Critics and Social Theorists Are Murdering Our Past illustrate, the trend continues.[23]

Throughout this book we demonstrate ways in which drawing on the arts can broaden the range of pasts considered by our students. In Chapter 3, for example, we explore, among other things, how period fiction can provide a glimpse into the drawing rooms of Georgian Britain, the lives of women in rural Prince Edward Island, Canada in the early twentieth century, or insight into the lived experience of dustbowl farmers driven off their land and into migrant poverty during the Depression era in the United States. The art of Kent Monkman and other Indigenous artists discussed in Chapters 4 and 6 forcefully inserts other peoples and alternative perspectives into events and processes long regarded as settled parts of the past. In Chapter 5 we argue that critical engagement with local public art installations offers the potential to enhance attention to how even small communities experienced significant world events and processes and foster understanding about how collective memory shapes peoples and places.

Critics of the so-called "new history"[24] and its examination of a wider range of perspectives and peoples, see several related problems: the disparaging of the Western Tradition, which they argue is largely responsible for moral, social, political, and economic progress; giving up on a single, and largely heroic, national narrative in favour of "professing trivia" such as the exploration of "housemaid's knee in Belleville;"[25] and the negative consequences of both of these for social cohesion and national unity. In terms of the latter, one prominent Canadian historian lamented "the privatizing of the mind" flowing from "the sundering of Canadian history" and resulting in the "sundering of Canada."[26] There are echoes of these criticisms in the cries of some participants in contemporary monument controversies to "not allow political correctness to erase our history."[27]

These critiques and the many responses to them are a key element of the scholarly conversation on the nature of history and historical truths explored in several parts of this book, so here we will only say that a significant issue with the claim of the erasure of "our history" is that it was never really "ours" in the full sense. Women, people of African descent in Western countries, Indigenous Peoples in Australia, the United States, and Canada, and working-class people, are just some of the groups that have been marginalized or left out completely from the grand national narratives that have dominated history education. Far from these narratives promoting social cohesion and national unity, they have left people feeling excluded, isolated, and angry. If, as social policy generally and educational policy in particular, advocate in diverse societies around the world, we want to build societies where people understand one another and feel included and engaged, the teaching of diverse elements of and perspectives on the past is essential. This not only helps diverse groups feel included, it fosters cross-cultural competencies as students are required to wrestle with and understand experiences and perspectives quite different from their own. Knowing the "truth" about the world in which we live is only possible if we understand something about the history and contemporary experiences of the diverse range of peoples who populate it. The arts provide an important vehicle for achieving both those ends.

One of the reasons particular groups of people have been left out of historical accounts is the lack of evidence upon which to develop narratives and make claims about them. In 1991 Laurel Thatcher Ulrich won the Pulitzer Prize for a book on US History, *A Midwife's Tale, The Life of Martha Ballard Based on her Diary.* As the title indicates, the book documents the life and work of Martha Ballard, a woman who practised midwifery in southern Maine between 1782 and 1812.[28] It also explores "a larger theme: of how the revolution initiated sweeping social changes that promoted individualism at the expense of the more collective values that had framed Ballard's life."[29]

While Thatcher Ulrich's book was recognized for the story it told, it was also acclaimed for its innovative approach to using historical evidence. A central theme for Thatcher Ulrich is addressing the absence of women from the historical record through deep engagement with new forms of evidence. She points out that "few New England women of [Martha Ballard's] generation left writing in any form," and that which was left was widely considered trivial.[30] Thatcher Ulrich argues that Ballard's diary itself was considered so mundane that "those few historians who have known about the diary have not known quite what to do with it."[31] It was not only male historians who failed to see the potential richness of this source. "Curiously, a feminist history of midwifery published in the 1970s repeated the old dismissal: 'Like many diaries of farm women, it is filled with trivia about domestic chores and pastimes.'"[32]

Thatcher Ulrich, however, recognized the potential of the diary to fill out aspects of the historical record neglected by other sources. In particular, it opened up a fuller consideration of the economic activity that sustained the life and vitality of small communities in the new republic. “A standard merchant’s ledger” for the period, for example, neglects the role of women in the economy altogether. As she points out,

> One might conclude from such a record that Kennebec women had no role in economic life beyond their own households. An intriguing page at the very end of the account book lists flaxseed sold by the Kennebec Agricultural Society, yet there is little evidence in the account book itself of any sort of textile production in the town.

She goes on to highlight the importance of Ballard’s record.

> Martha’s diary tells us what happened to the seed. It not only records when Ephraim Ballard planted the flax, but when she and her daughters weeded and harvested it. It not only identifies the male helpers who turned and broke it, but the many female neighbors who assisted her and her daughters with the combing, spinning, reeling, boiling, spooling, warping, quilling, weaving, bucking, and bleaching that transformed the ripe plant into finished cloth. Martha’s diary fills in the missing work–and trade–of women.[33]

Part of the scholarly conversation about the nature of history and historical truth is shifting ideas about what constitutes historical evidence and how new forms of evidence might be included in filling out the historical record. Thatcher Ulrich’s work with Martha Ballard’s diary is one important example of that conversation, but as we show throughout this book, artistic representations also have potential to open consideration of more diverse aspects of the past. In various parts of this book, for example, we have discussed the potential of public art as a source of knowledge about the past.

In one example of this we write about different sets of murals and one diorama, created almost contemporaneously in the 1920s and 1930s, displayed in four very different public spaces: St. Stephen’s Hall in the Palace of Westminster, London (Chapter 6); The rotunda of the British Columbia Legislature in Victoria, BC (Chapters 4–6); the theatre in Humberside Collegiate School in Toronto, Ontario (Chapter 6); and The American Museum of Natural History in New York City (Chapter 6). In three of the four cases actual events are represented, while in the other (the mural at Humberside Collegiate) historical themes and relationships are illustrated. All deal with themes related to Western domination and colonialism in different parts of the world, and all are designed, in the words of Sir Henry Newbolt, to "go beyond fact, and to symbolize the inner meaning of certain events."[34]

While Newbolt, an advisor on the St. Stephen's Hall murals, and the other creators of these pictures intended them as accounts to be absorbed passively, they offer evidence of the attitudes of those in power in the time they were created. Close interrogation of them as primary sources reveals important aspects of social organization, power relations, and the perspectives of the dominant culture in the 1920s and 1930s in Britain, Canada, and the United States. They allow us to engage more fully with important historical themes such as conquest, colonialism, racism, and power. Their diverse placement illustrates the pervasive nature of similar ideas about the pre-eminence of European "civilization" in the early to middle part of the twentieth century.

As we have argued throughout this book, a key aspect of this and other kinds of evidence from the arts, is its power to impact us viscerally and therefore extend our understandings of the impact particular forms of social organization or discourse might have on different groups of people. Pictorial or textual fictional accounts of the experience of racism and social marginalization can help us deepen our sense of historical perspective both about the attitudes and experiences of those in mainstream society and those on the margins. As we will discuss more fully below, students will also learn to contextualize these forms of evidence with that gathered from other sources to bring new perspectives and ideas to the historical record. It is not so much that the previous historical knowledge—or truths—are wrong, although in some cases they may be, but that they are incomplete. Students should learn from this that truth in history, and other areas, is neither impossible to determine nor unimportant, but it is tentative and should be asserted with a degree of humility that allows for adaptation in the face of new voices being included and new evidence considered.

While there is wide consensus across the community of academic historians that historical truth is partial and contingent in the ways described above, there is also community-wide commitment to the importance of grounding truth claims in rigorous analysis of primary and secondary sources. The available sources for any particular event, era, or set of ideas being studied may be used to support a range of interpretations and perspectives. They also, however, establish parameters that exclude support for some perspectives. Serious engagement with sources will allow for a range of opinion, but not an infinite range.

In their book *The Case for Contention: Teaching Controversial Issues in American Schools*, historian Jonathan Zimmerman and philosopher Emily Robertson take up the point that evidence and argument constrain public consideration of alternative positions on important questions. "There are issues," they argue, "where reasonable arguments can be made on different sides of the question," but there are also more settled questions where "there is one position that is decisively supported by the available arguments." For example, "since historical evidence overwhelmingly supports the claim the Holocaust happened, this question is not controversial."[35] They go on to provide detailed ideas for how considering contested questions, wrestling with evidence, and learning about the nature of expertise can enhance students' abilities to engage in productive civic discourse. History education provides both examples of how others have done this, and opportunities for students to do it themselves.

Engaging the Arts in History Class Fosters Cross Curricular/Disciplinary Connections

The second scholarly conversation taken up in Chapter 2 and illustrated throughout the book is the relationship between history and the arts. In the winter of 2020 award-winning Canadian journalist and novelist, Linden MacIntyre explored this relationship in a public lecture titled "Making (Up) History" which was largely an exploration of his own work as a journalist, popular historian, and novelist. He began by considering the widely held view that "making things up while writing history, is a serious offence, an intellectual crime, a creative sin." The problem with that, he went on, is that "everything I have written, over more than fifty years, journalism or fiction, everything I've read including history is unavoidably, and sometime deliberately, to some extent, made up." That is because "any account of any event that has already happened, even if it was written by someone who was part of the event, will be recorded after the fact and therefore is an act of remembering." How we remember, he continued, is shaped by many factors including missing or conflicting pieces of evidence and the perspectives and biases we bring to the enterprise. Any account of the past is recreation, and "recreation is a creative enterprise."[36]

Macintyre's point here is that historians are at some level artists engaged in creative acts of storytelling, but his lecture also dealt with the flip side of that, artists are often historians seeking to tell complex truths about events from the past. In September 1982 a horrific massacre occurred in the Palestinian refugee camps of Sabra and Shatila in southern Lebanon. As a journalist working in the region MacIntyre was assigned to cover the event and arrived just a day or two after the killings. The situation was so devastating "it demanded to be remembered," but by the time he arrived an "aggressive campaign of deception" was already mobilized. The governments of both Lebanon and Israel, as well as a number of private militias, were all actively involved in covering up evidence and spinning accounts to focus blame away from themselves and onto others. As MacIntyre said, "The attempt to conceal what had happened would permanently obscure the truth of who did what to whom and why." Any reporting of this incident, he went on, would require "judgement calls and conjecture."[37]

As well as he could, MacIntyre covered the situation as a journalist but was left unsatisfied with the result. He felt his, and others', accounts failed to get at the essence of the story, to show this was more than a single event but "a catastrophic human story of what people were capable of doing to other people." He thought this story illustrated a key aspect of the history of the twentieth century, "a century defined by massacre."[38] To explore the impenetrable complexity of the event MacIntyre turned not to history but to fiction, writing the historical novel *The Only Café*.[39] He felt this artistic medium better enabled him to get at "the essence of what happened."[40]

Throughout this book we explore a number of examples of these kinds of blurred boundaries between history and the arts. In Chapter 3, for example, we argue that period novels are important primary sources allowing historians windows into aspects of the past often ignored. In Chapters 4 and 5 we show that visual art and public commemorative art are also important traces that provide evidence of significant aspects of the historical contexts in which they were created. In Chapter 6 we discuss ways to engage students in the detailed and complex work of reading artistic works as sources of information about the past, including the importance of contextualizing those sources with regard to other forms of evidence.

The arts as evidence are valuable for doing history, but they are also important as historical accounts. As we illustrate in Chapter 3, many writers of historical novels draw extensively from primary and secondary sources of evidence and, like Linden MacIntyre, intend their work to communicate important "truths" about the past. They are, in fact, acting as historians. As shown in Chapters 4 and 5, the same is often true of painters and sculptors. In painting his *The Death of General Wolfe* (Chapter 4), for example, Benjamin West intended to shape how viewers of the work thought about Wolfe, the events at Québec in September of 1759, and the burgeoning British Empire more generally. Historian Simon Schama argues the artist was immensely successful in controlling the narrative well into the future. "After West," he writes, "nothing could dispel the odour of sanctity that lay over Wolfe's memory."[41]

Throughout this book, but especially in Chapter 6, we argue that history education should take seriously both the creative nature of historical work and the historical nature of artistic endeavours. Students should be taught to systematically interrogate all historical accounts considering the context in which they were created, the perspectives and purposes of the creators, and the creative techniques they employ to make their arguments and challenge or obscure the accounts of others. Again, this engages students in complex consideration of the nature of truth and how it is communicated.

At one in the same time in an American high school it might be possible for students to be reading the novel *To Kill a Mockingbird* in English class, considering the sculpture *Foot Solider* (Chapter 5) in art class, and studying the civil rights movement in history class while never making connections among the three. One of us has written elsewhere about school subjects as "fortified silos" rather than "interconnected webs."[42] When curriculum is approached like the former, the students in English class might never consider the wider historical and social context of Harper Lee's novel, while in art class where the focus might be on the sculptor's technique, questions about the shaping of his historical narrative might never arise, and in history class students might not be asked to think about how artistic representations, like Lee's novel and Ronald McDowell's sculpture, have shaped their own and others' ideas about race relations in America. It is our contention that student learning would be enhanced if these subjects were treated more like interconnected webs.

Engaging the Arts in History Class Fosters Consideration of the Relationship Between History, Historical Consciousness, and Collective Memory

We opened this chapter discussing the narrowing of school curricula to focus on subjects considered to enhance employability. No single organization has had more impact on this than the Organization of Economic Cooperation and Development (OECD), through its Programme for International Student Assessment (PISA). PISA is an international testing programme that traditionally assesses student achievement in reading, mathematics, and science. The tests are administered in almost 100 countries or regions around the world. The results are reported widely, generate considerable press in many countries, and shape discussions and decisions about educational policy and practice in important ways. One group of scholars writes that "PISA has arguably become the most influential educational assessment today," and goes on to emphasize that the programme was developed "to assist the OECD with its economic mandate and that this rationale informed the assessment's framework and continues to guide its development."[43]

In 2018, in response to perceived growing social and cultural fragmentation and conflict, the PISA programme moved beyond the three traditional subject areas to begin assessing "global competence" which was described as "a multidimensional capacity." According to the OECD, "Globally competent individuals can examine local, global and intercultural issues, understand and appreciate different perspectives and world views, interact successfully and respectfully with others, and take responsible action toward sustainability and collective well-being."[44] While the OECD has not diverted from its economic focus arguing, among other things, that "educating for global competence can boost employability," it seems to us that a broadly humanistic approach to history education would be the most effective way to foster the particular elements of global competence outlined in their description.[45]

At the centre of the OECD's conception of global competence is intercultural perspective taking and the ability to work with others to productively address common issues. Peter Seixas and Tom Morton identify perspective taking as one of the six foundational aspects of historical thinking.[46] Perspective taking is also deeply connected to understandings of historical consciousness and collective memory which are described in some detail in Chapter 2. We know that people, individually and as cultural, ethnic, or national collectivities, narrate themselves temporally in terms of the past, present, and future. We begin Chapter 6 with an illustration of the way this worked itself out in the lives of Rumanians and Hungarians in their disputes over the territory of Transylvania in the 1930s. Each of these groups had a widely shared collective memory of the region extending back two thousand years and those memories shaped how they thought about the proper national location of the territory in their own time and into the future.

Given that situating Transylvania within the nation of Rumania was a contested result of the Treaty of Versailles which sought, among other things, to create a new international order, this is just the kind of global issue the OECD proposes that globally competent citizens should be able to address. It would be impossible for these groups, or others working with them, to "understand and appreciate different perspectives and world views, interact successfully and respectfully with others, and take responsible action toward sustainability and collective well-being" without taking into account the collective memories described above. Those memories, which are part of the collective historical consciousness of the peoples involved, define contemporary positions and constrain possibilities for the resolution of conflicts about the territory. That is not to say accommodations and even a final resolution to the issue are impossible, but they will require hard work including careful attention to, and empathy for, the perspectives shaping the views of interested parties.

Throughout this book we provide examples of how engagement with the arts can foster deeper understandings of the perspectives of people in other times and places. In Chapter 3, for example, we argue that period novels often capture aspects of the spirit, or collective understandings, of particular historical contexts. Lucy Maud Montgomery's novel *Rilla of Ingleside*, for example, provides insight into how rural Canadians responded to the horror of the Great War and its aftermath. The novel's verisimilitude shaped the way succeeding generations remembered the war, an issue that continues to have salience in public discourse in Canada. Chapter 5 focuses on public commemorative art which both reflects collective sensibilities from the time and place in which the works were created but is also designed explicitly to shape shared understandings into the future. That chapter also draws on several examples of public commemorative art of the Great War to demonstrate that collective memory is not static but can shift significantly over time in response to changing contexts. The critical audit of public historical art suggested in Chapter 6 as an activity for students, is one way to begin to build a deeper understanding of the historical consciousness and collective memory of communities and to consider how those exclude some individuals and groups and shape the way we think about possibilities for the future.

In his book *How Propaganda Works*, philosopher Jason Stanley recognizes the ubiquitous and powerful nature of "group identities" which he calls

> the coral reefs of cognition: much of the beauty of the production of human intellect is due to their existence. But certain group identities are democratically problematic: the Teutonic identity constructed by National Socialism is an obvious example. Such identities channel rational and affective streams in specific ways, creating obstacles to self-knowledge, as well as to the free flow of deliberation required in a healthy democracy.[47]

Stanley goes on to develop the concept of "civic rhetoric" as a counter to flawed ideology and demagoguery.[48] Civic rhetoric tries to improve the reasonableness of debate through "appeal to empathy and understanding to lead people to include the perspectives of some citizens whose perspectives had previously been ignored."[49] In other words, those who employ civic rhetoric attempt to help others understand their perspective by demonstrating areas of deep connection between the collective ideologies of both groups. This requires, of course, close attention to the collective consciousnesses of one's opponents. Stanley gives the example of American civil rights advocate W. E. B. DuBois who wrote and spoke using liberal democratic ideals themselves to "draw attention to the fact that cherished ideals among the Whites are also cherished among the Blacks."[50] This kind of "civic rhetoric is an attempt to share the perspective of a group whose perspective has been made invisible thereby preventing democracy; civic rhetoric is the tool required in the service of repairing rupture."[51] It is also a tool, we argue, that would be greatly enhanced by close attention to historical consciousness and collective memory and the arts provide a window into deeper understanding of those.

Engaging the Arts in History Class Fosters the Introduction of Indigenous Perspectives

In 2017 Indigenous carver Charles Joseph had a large totem he had created installed for several months on a main street of the city of Montreal in front of the Montreal Museum of Fine Arts. The totem drew on traditional Kwakwaka'wakw (Kwakiutl) forms but adapted them "to tell a tragic story that shaped Joseph personally," the story of Indian Residential Schools in Canada.[52] Joseph's account flows from his own sense of historical consciousness but also connects to the collective memory of residential school survivors and their descendants about the devastating impact of a policy and process designed to "to kill the Indian in the child."[53]

Joseph's work is just one example of a burgeoning collection of art designed to bring Indigenous perspectives on the past into public spaces. The front lobby of Marshall D'Avray Hall at the University of New Brunswick, the building where one of us works, contains a large sculpture in the form of a Wampum Belt, a traditional Indigenous form of storytelling and commemoration. The sculpture was developed under the auspices of Project of the Heart, "an inquiry based, hands-on, collaborative, inter-generational, artistic journey of seeking truth about the history of Aboriginal people in Canada."[54] It was created by many people across the province of New Brunswick under the direction of the Aboriginal Visual Arts Programme at the New Brunswick College of Craft and Design. Like Joseph's work it seeks "to bring awareness of the atrocities associated with the Residential Schools" from the perspective of survivors.[55]

These are two of the many examples of how Indigenous perspectives on the past are portrayed in artistic forms. In Chapter 2 we discuss five scholarly conversations that frame and inform our work. As we point out there, these conversations do not have hard boundaries between them and often overlap and run together. This is particularly true of the conversations related to historical consciousness and collective memory and Indigenous perspectives. It could be argued that issues around paying attention to Indigenous perspectives in history education are really a subset of the larger category of collective memory. At one level this is true, but we argue history itself mandates particular attention to Indigenous concerns and perspectives. In their work on historical thinking Seixas and Morton identify the ethical dimension of history as one of the six key concepts foundational to the study of history. In delineating the critical attributes of the concept they write, "a fair assessment of the ethical implications of history can inform us of our responsibilities to remember and respond to contributions, sacrifices, and injustices of the past."[56] We contend that the injustices of the past both in terms of the experiences of Indigenous Peoples in Canada and many other parts of the world, and in how their history has been portrayed or ignored in academic and public history, mandate separate and substantial attention to Indigenous perspectives in history education.

The arts provide opportunities to engage with Indigenous perspectives in history education in at least two ways. First, is the critical examination of the representation of Indigenous Peoples in artistic forms across time and contexts. One of us has written about the portrayal of Indigenous Peoples in the illustrations and photographs used in Canadian school history textbooks arguing that "depictions of Aboriginal people of the more distant past can be placed in two categories: spectator and savage warrior. Aboriginal people of the more recent past and present can be placed into five categories: exotic, problem, uniquely spiritual, protestor and invisible."[57] The artworks dealt with in this book provide examples of virtually all of these. The painting, *The Fathers of Confederation* (Chapter 4) is an example of Indigenous People (and a number of other groups including women) as absent from the founding of the Canadian nation-state. The murals in the British Columbia legislature (Chapters 4–6), The American Museum of Natural History (Chapter 6), and Humberside Collegiate School in Toronto (Chapter 6), present Indigenous Peoples as spectators to European action or recipients of settler largesse both in material and spiritual terms. Benjamin Wolfe's *The Death of General Wolfe* (Chapter 4) presents the exotic Indigenous person deep in contemplation about the passing of the great man. Simon Schama points out this was a fiction invented by the painter and in no way reflected the history of the event, where the Indigenous People present fought with the French, or feelings of Wolfe himself who regarded Indigenous People as "irredeemable barbarians, cruel and depraved."[58]

It is important that history education engage students in analysis of the historical images and sculptures of Indigenous Peoples that surround them at historical sites, in and around civic and other public buildings, in their school textbooks, and on the walls of their schools. That analysis should include critical questions such as those outlined in describing the audit of public art described in Chapter 6. One approach can be to ask students to decide what should be done with works of art that are anachronistic and offensive in their portrayal of Indigenous Peoples. That is the question that faced an expert panel considering the murals at the British Columbia Legislature in Canada and the curatorial staff and advisors working with the diorama at the American Museum of Natural History. In the case of the former "the panel considered five options for the murals: maintain the murals as they are, maintain the murals as they are with the addition of other materials, alter the murals, cover the murals, and remove the murals."[59] The Museum of Natural History professionals considered a similar range of options.[60]

In BC the decision was made to remove the murals as the location itself, inside the main hall of the provincial legislative assembly, gave the appearance of attributing official sanction to the images. The museum, on the other hand, opted to historicize the diorama by adding material that would help visitors contextualize and critique the display. In Chapter 6 we discuss the study conducted by Peter Seixas and Penney Clark that clearly demonstrates high school students' ability to engage with these kinds of questions.[61]

Sometimes the critique of traditional and demeaning portrayals itself comes in artistic form. The work of Kent Monkman, particularly his paintings *The Daddies* and *The Scream*, discussed extensively in Chapter 4, are examples of this. Monkman adapts or plays off traditional images and themes to create works that present powerful challenges to culturally dominant themes and ideas.

A second way the arts can help incorporate Indigenous perspectives in history education is through their ability to present those perspectives in compelling ways. The two examples that open this section illustrate the fact that Indigenous Peoples from very different parts of the territory now called Canada are adapting traditional artistic and cultural forms to present accounts of their own experience with the past in that land. Again, Kent Monkman is a leader in this movement. His recent works mounted in the entrance hall to the Metropolitan Museum of Art in New York City (Chapter 6) both challenge traditional ideas about Indigenous history and present new narratives. In both paintings mounted there, Indigenous people are presented as central actors and agents with Europeans pushed to the margins.[62]

Monkman's work and the two examples at the beginning of this section are all new works. It is also important to engage with historical art from Indigenous communities as something other than curios of "a disappearing race."[63] In his reflection on totem poles as Canadian symbols, historian John Lutz argues this important medium for traditional stories and community history has been stripped of its deeper meaning and turned into common tourist trinkets. He points out the irony that the world's largest collection of totem poles is in the Great Hall of the Canadian Museum of History where they "glare with fixed wooden eyes directly at Parliament, where politicians had tried for many years to suppress Indigenous culture while appropriating Indigenous art."[64] Working with Indigenous communities, elders, and educators, history educators should work toward including examples of Indigenous art from the past as both historical sources and accounts.

As we argue in Chapter 2, the scholarly conversation about including Indigenous perspectives in history education is relatively new and highly contested. This makes it difficult terrain for history educators to navigate. That difficulty cannot be an excuse for doing nothing. The record of past distortions of history and the injustices that accompany and flow from those mandates action as reflected in recent reports in Canada and the United Nations Declaration on the Rights of Indigenous Peoples.[65] In moving forward it is essential that Indigenous people be involved as collaborators at every step. In the words of the common saying, "Nothing about us without us."

Engaging the Arts in History Class Fosters the Development of History Education

In 2012 Ken Osborne wrote an article reflecting on his more than fifty years as a history teacher and professor of education. In that piece titled, "A History Teacher Looks Back," Osborne wrote, "I hold great hopes for the current emphasis on teaching students to think historically,"[66] but he also went on to make the point that many of the key elements of the historical thinking movement have been around for a century and have not made a substantial impact on the teaching of history in schools. Commenting on his own efforts to produce a history of the field he wrote:

> My pursuit of the history of history education has been both intriguing and depressing; intriguing in that I discovered a largely forgotten history of debate, argument, and experimentation stretching back to the 1880s; depressing in that it had so little impact on the classroom. I concluded

> that ever since the 1920s we have known what is involved in teaching history well, but we have been unable to translate what we know into classroom reality.[67]

In response to Osborne's absolutely correct assertions that inquiry-oriented history education generally and historical thinking in particular has been around in some form for more than a century and over that time it has had very little impact on actual practice in public education, one of us wrote a piece articulating what is different about contemporary approaches to historical thinking that might make it both longer lasting and more effective.[68] That article identified eight elements of the current historical thinking movement that give reasons for hope that it might move beyond the academy and policy to impact practice:

- There is a pervasive consensus around the world and across various sectors that fostering historical thinking is an important key component of history education;
- There is a substantial and growing evidentiary base about how people think and learn about the past that provides a basis for curriculum development and implementation;
- The core concepts and procedures central to historical thinking are being clearly delineated in ways that are accessible to practitioners;
- High-quality teaching materials that support the inquiry orientation of historical thinking, such as primary source documents, are more widely available than they have ever been;
- Cross-sector scholarly and professional communities including historians, educationists, curators, teachers, and others have been created and are maintained by regional, national, and international organizations;
- Sophisticated and practical ideas for assessing historical thinking are being developed and disseminated;
- Cross-disciplinary approaches to both pre-service and in-service professional education are being theorized, developed, and implemented; and
- Historical thinking is increasingly being given official sanction as central to teaching history by educational jurisdictions around the world.[69]

As we point out in Chapter 2 the model of historical thinking that is dominant in Canada and influential in other parts of the world is that developed under the leadership of Peter Seixas of the University of British Columbia. We have been collaborators with Seixas since the beginning of his work and therefore research and practice in the field are central to our own scholarship and to what we have tried to do in this book. Throughout this book we seek to build on a number of the elements outlined above in order to address Osborne's concern and foster better practice in history education.

We draw on scholarship related to historical thinking and apply it to using the arts in the teaching of history. In a number of places we illustrate how the work on prior conceptions, or cognitive frames, has contributed to knowledge of how learners think about the past as well as how that thinking might be enhanced. The new and exciting work of Lévesque and Croteau (Chapters 2 and 6), for example, is helpful in understanding the cognitive frames of groups of Canadian young people and in thinking about the intersections between historical thinking and historical consciousness/collectivememory[70] We also draw on similar studies from Canada and other parts of the world in this area and show how it connects to using the arts in history teaching.[71]

We have also examined some of the scholarship on students' interactions with commemorative places and, in particular how the sacredness of memorial sites constrains asking and investigating critical historical questions (Chapter 5). Catriona Pennell, for example, investigates the connection between battlefield tours and critical history education, wondering, "can history education and remembrance be blended so easily?"[72] Her work demonstrates that public commemorative sites have the kind of visceral power we argue is characteristic of art, and that power often overwhelms students' experiences at the sites. "The lack of space for critical reflection is in stark contrast to the emphasis placed in tour content on remembrance practices."[73] Throughout this book and elsewhere we have examined this tension between art's ability to communicate compelling and powerful ideas about the past and the danger of having one's critical judgement weakened by that very power.

Our work contributes to the nuanced deliberation of concepts and issues related to historical thinking. In particular, we spend a lot of time discussing the nature of primary source evidence and how artistic forms such as novels (Chapter 3), paintings (Chapters 4 and 5), sculptures, and memorial sites (Chapter 5) can be engaged as evidence. As we write earlier in this chapter the expansion of what is considered evidence has been critical to the evolution of the field of history over the years, it is also critical to the ongoing development of the field of historical thinking. In Chapter 6 we developed some applied ideas about how teachers might help students develop expertise in reading and analyzing artistic works as both primary source evidence and secondary accounts of the past.

Two related concepts in historical thinking also feature prominently in our work: perspective taking and the ethical dimension of history. In regard to the former, we argue throughout the book that artistic forms provide clear windows into the perspectives of other times and peoples. In Chapter 3, for example, we argue that period novels give a rich sense of how people thought about and experienced social and cultural phenomena such as primogeniture, social exclusion, or poverty. We present many examples of how public commemorative art reflects prevailing attitudes and perspectives of particular times and places such as the prevalence of nationalism and Christianity in the memorials created just after the Great War and the almost total absence, even rejection, of those in more contemporary monuments to the same war (Chapter 5).

Throughout the book, we argue that artistic works provide a rich potential source of accessible and engaging teaching materials to foster historical thinking. One of the biggest challenges for teachers seeking to incorporate historical thinking into their work has been locating materials that students find interesting and can use. As we have pointed out in a number of places in this book, historical art permeates our world and is just waiting for creative teachers and students to take it up in critical ways as both primary source evidence and secondary accounts.

While strong and diverse cross-disciplinary communities of historians, curators, educationists, and practitioners have increasingly been a feature of the contemporary historical thinking movement, artists are noticeably absent. As we show in Chapters 2 and 3 as well as above in discussing the works of Linden MacIntyre, writers of historical novels do a lot of public reflecting on the relationship between their genre, their own work in that genre, and history. Other artists such as the sculptor Ronald McDowell (Chapter 5), or the painters Benjamin West (Chapters 1, 4, and 6) and Kent Monkman (Chapters 4 and 6) also explicitly understand their work as presenting historical accounts. It seems to us it is long past time that the artistic community be included in deliberations about history education generally and historical thinking in particular.

One of the strengths of current approaches to historical thinking, especially Seixas's model, is fluidity; the ability and willingness to adapt in the face of new evidence or theorizing. Over the years we have observed the articulation of core historical thinking concepts change in response to empirical work with students and theorizing about the nature of history and historical inquiry. The scholarly conversations exploring the connections between history and memory and academic history and Indigenous perspectives on the past are two examples of this. As demonstrated in Chapter 2 these conversations have had a significant impact on the theory and practice of historical thinking. The models produced by Seixas and Lévesque and Croteau for combining attention to academic history and collective memory in history education are examples of this evolution.[74] This book is also designed to push scholars and practitioners of historical thinking in particular and history education more generally to think about and engage in the field in new ways through more explicit attention to the multilayered possibilities of the arts for teaching history.

Conclusion

As we completed this book in the late winter and early spring of 2020 Canada experienced a significant economic crisis due to weeks long blockades of railway lines and other key transportation links by protesters supporting opposition to a natural gas pipeline by Indigenous groups in British Columbia. India was plagued with deadly demonstrations because of a new citizenship law that was perceived as discriminating against Muslims. In the midst of a violent dispute with the United States the Iranian military mistakenly shot down a Ukrainian commercial airliner, precipitating an international crisis. After years of intense wrangling a divided United Kingdom began its exit from the European Union. The president of Russia pushed lawmakers in that country to make constitutional changes allowing him to sidestep legal term limits to his time in power. All of these countries and more were caught up in a global pandemic brought on by Coronavirus disease (COVID-19).

This is just a sampling of the news stories from around the globe that were capturing the world's attention while we worked on our book. While they were very different, they had some distinct similarities. They all had significant national and international implications, they all impacted people of diverse linguistic and cultural backgrounds, they all were rooted in deliberations about public policy, and they all were infused with aspects of the past. Even the coronavirus, while itself new, was subjected to vigorous historical analysis. Commentators examined how that outbreak was similar to or different from contagions of the past such as the Spanish Influenza of 1918–20 or Sever Acute Respiratory Syndrome (SARS) of the early 2000s. Claims were made in public discourse about the lessons that had been learned and applied from those earlier events or where opportunities to learn lessons had been missed. One article from the website of the World Economic Forum extended the links even further back with a headline proclaiming, "From the Black Death to the coronavirus: What we haven't learned from history."[75] Politicians and public health officials appealed to aspects of that history to justify the positions they were taking and public policy directions they were promoting.

All of the examples above and many others from around the world arose in particular historical contexts. It would be impossible to understand any of them in a complex way without some sense of history, and public discussion of them all included historical claims and counter claims designed to shore up support for particular policy directions both in national affairs and international relations. These are just the kind of global issues the OECD claims require globally competent citizens to address. Our contention is that globally competent citizenship requires comprehensive, inquiry-oriented attention to the past. To engage with others in working for the common good people have to have some sense of the context of the issues they face, including the complicated historical factors that have brought them to the fore. They also have to know something about the others with whom it will be necessary to join forces in order to address the issues, whether those others are next door or across the globe. There is no way to develop a deep, empathetic understanding of others without knowing something about their history and the collective memories that inform their worldviews. To know others and understand the civic contexts we share are the humanizing and civic missions of history education. In this book we have argued that attention to the arts will enhance both aspects of that enterprise.

Notes

1. Adele Perry, "The CHA Asks the Public Service Commission to Change Its Advertisements for Employment," The Canadian Historical Association, 2019, https://cha-shc.ca/english/what-we-do/what-we-do.html/advocacy/the-cha-asks-thepublic-service-commission-to-change-its-advertisements-for-employment.
2. Peter E. Rider, "Museums, Nation and Political History in the Australian National Museum and the Canadian Museum of Civilization," *Museum and Society* 3, no. 1 (2005): 35, https://doi.org/10.29311/mas.v3i1.63.
3. Rider, "Museums," 37.
4. Stuart Macintyre and Anna Clark, *The History Wars*. New edition (Melbourne: Melbourne University Press, 2004), 193. See also, Keith Windschuttle, *The Killing of History: How Literary Critics and Social Theorists Are Murdering Our Past*, Reprint edition (New York: Encounter Books, 2000).
5. Macintyre, and Clark, *The History Wars*.
6. For a full discussion of the latter see, Anna Clark, *History's Children: History Wars in the Classroom* (Sydney: University of New South Wales Press, 2008).
7. Macintyre, and Clark, *The History Wars*, 3.
8. Macintyre, and Clark, 222.
9. Macintyre, and Clark, 222.
10. Aaron Wherry, "For the Record: Justin Trudeau on Liberty and the Niqab—The Text of Justin Trudeau's Controversial Speech," 2015, http://www.macleans.ca/politics/for-the-record-justin-trudeau-on-liberty-and-the-niqab/.
11. Hugh Johnston, "Komagata Maru," The Canadian Encyclopedia, 2016, https://www.thecanadianencyclopedia.ca/en/article/komagata-maru.
12. Irving Abella and Harold Troper, *None Is too Many: Canada and the Jews of Europe 1933–1948* (Toronto, ON: Key Porter Books, 2002).
13. Margaret MacMillan, *The Uses and Abuses of History* (Toronto, ON: Viking, 2008), 103.
14. Many books and articles have been written about the so-called history or monument wars. For a small sampling see, MacIntyre and Clark, *The History Wars*; Clark, *History's Children*; MacMillan, *The Uses and Abuses of History*; Gary B. Nash, Charlotte Crabtree, and Ross Dunn, *History on Trial: Culture Wars and the Teaching of the Past* (New York: Knopf, 1997); Tony Taylor and Robert Guyver, eds. *History Wars and the Classroom: Global Perspectives* (Charlotte, NC: Information Age Publishing, 2012); Edward T. Linenthal and Thomas Engelhardt, eds. *History Wars: The Enola Gay and Other Battles for the American Past* (New York: Metropolitan Books, 1996); Kirk Savage, *Monument Wars: Washington,*

D.C., the National Mall, and the Transformation of the Memorial Landscape, First edition (Berkeley: University of California Press, 2009); Fred Evans, *Public Art and the Fragility of Democracy: An Essay in Political Aesthetics* (New York: Columbia University Press, 2019).

15. William Faulkner, *Requiem for a Nun* (New York: Random House, 1951).
16. Sophy Ridge, "Jo Cox Murder: Death Threats and Sexual Torment Have Become Part of the Job for Our MPs—Enough Is Enough," *The Telegraph*, June 17, 2016, http://www.telegraph.co.uk/women/politics/jo-cox-murder-death-threats-and-sexual-torment-have-become-part/.
17. Nicole Bacharan quoted in, Paul Waldie, "After Nastiest Presidential Campaign in Memory, France Faces Trump Moment," *Globe and Mail*, 2017, https://www.theglobeandmail.com/news/world/after-shocking-campaign-french-face-profound-choice-to-upend-status-quo/article34907627/.
18. Naheed Mustafa, *The Truth About Post-truth* (CBC Ideas, 2017), http://www.cbc.ca/radio/ideas/the-truth-about-post-truth-1.3939958.
19. Kathleen Higgins, "Post-truth: A Guide for the Perplexed," *Nature* 540, no. 7361 (2016): 9, https://doi.org/10.1038/540009a.
20. Christian Smith et al., *Lost in Transition: The Dark Side of Emerging Adulthood* (New York: Oxford University Press, 2011), 15.
21. Higgins, "Post-truth," 9.
22. Higgins, 9.
23. Arthur Schlesinger Jr., *The Disuniting of America* (New York: Norton, 1992); Windschuttle, *The Killing of History.*
24. Gertrude Himmelfarb, "Some Reflections on the New History," *The American Historical Review* 94, no. 3 (1989): 661–70.
25. Jack Granatstein, *Who Killed Canadian History?* (Toronto: HarperCollins, 1998), 73.
26. Michael Bliss, "Privatizing the Mind: The Sundering of Canadian History, the Sundering of Canada," *Journal of Canadian Studies* 26, no. 4 (1991): 5–17. See also, Margaret Conrad, "A Brief Survey of Canadian Historiography," in *New Possibilities for the Past: Shaping History Education in Canada*, ed. Penney Clark (Vancouver, BC: UBC Press, 2011), 33–54.
27. Andrew Sheer, leader of the Official Opposition in the Parliament of Canada, quoted in Matthew A. Sears, "Monuments Aren't Museums, and History Suffers When We Forget That," *MacLeans*, 2018, https://www.macleans.ca/opinion/monuments-arent-museums-and-history-suffers-when-we-forget-that/.
28. Laurel Thatcher Ulrich, *A Midwife's Tale: The Life of Martha Ballard, Based on Her Diary* (New York: Knopf, 1990).
29. Alan Taylor, "Keeping the Story in History," The Pulitzer Prizes, 2020, https://www.pulitzer.org/article/keeping-story-history.
30. Thatcher Ulrich, *A Midwife's Tale*, 9.

31. Thatcher Ulrich, 8.
32. Thatcher Ulrich, 9.
33. Thatcher Ulrich, 29.
34. Henry Newbolt, *The Building of Britain: A Series of Paintings in St. Stephen's Hall, Westminster* (London: Thomas Nelson and Sons, 1927), 4.
35. Jonathan Zimmerman and Emily Robertson, *The Case for Contention: Teaching Controversial Issues in American Schools* (Chicago and London: University of Chicago Press, 2017).
36. Linden MacIntyre, "Making (Up) History," Public Lecture, St. Thomas University: Annual History Lecture, Fredericton, NB, January 23, 2020. See also the audio recording of the lecture at Linden MacIntyre, *Making (Up) History*, Audio Recording (Fredericton, NB: SoundCloud, 2020), https://soundcloud.com/user-437205194/lindenmacintyre.
37. MacIntyre, "Making (Up) History."
38. MacIntyre, "Making (Up) History."
39. Linden MacIntyre, *The Only Café* (Toronto, ON: Vintage Canada, 2018).
40. MacIntyre, "Making (Up) History."
41. Simon Schama, *Dead Certainties, Unwarranted Speculations* (New York: Knopf, 1991), 37.
42. Alan Sears, "Fortified Silos or Interconnected Webs: The Relationship Between History and Other Subjects in the Curriculum," in *Debates in History Teaching*, ed. Ian Davies (London and New York: Routledge, 2010), 272–81.
43. Sam Sellar, David Rutkowski, and Greg Thompson, *The Global Education Race: Taking the Measure of PISA and International Testing* (Edmonton, AB: Brush Education, 2017), 7 and 13, http://search.ebscohost.com/login.aspx?direct=true&scope=site&db=nlebk&db=nlabk&AN=1500013.
44. OECD, "Preparing Our Youth for an Inclusive and Sustainable World The OECD Pisa Global Competence Framework" (Paris: Directorate for Education and Skills, 2018), 4.
45. OECD, "Preparing Our Youth," 5.
46. Peter Seixas and Tom Morton, *The Big Six Historical Thinking Concepts* (Toronto, ON: Nelson Education, 2013).
47. Jason Stanley, *How Propaganda Works* (Princeton, NJ and Oxford: Princeton University Press, 2015), 3–4.
48. Stanley, *How Propaganda Works*, 5.
49. Stanley, 112.
50. Stanley, 117.
51. Stanley, 124.
52. Robert Everett-Green, "Totem of a Painful Legacy Rises on Montreal's Golden Square Mile," *Globe and Mail*, May 5, 2017.

53. Quoted in, Truth and Reconciliation Commission of Canada, *Final Report of the Truth and Reconciliation Comission of Canada, Vol. I: Summary: Honouring the Truth, Reconciling for the Future* (Toronto; James Lorimer, 2015), 369, http://www.trc.ca/websites/trcinstitution/File/2015/Findings/Calls_to_Action_English2.pdf.
54. Project of the Heart, "What Is Project of Heart?" Project of the Heart, n.d., http://projectofheart.ca/what-is-project-of-heart/.
55. Allison Green and Marilyn Ingram, *Trails of Light and Hope: From Project of the Heart* (Fredericton, NB: New Brunswick College of Craft and Design, n.d.), 2.
56. Seixas and Morton, *The Big Six*, 184.
57. Penney Clark, "Representations of Aboriginal People in English Canadian History Textbooks: Toward Reconciliation," in *Teaching the Violent Past: History Education and Reconciliation*, ed. Elizabeth A. Cole (Lanham, MD: Rowman & Littlefield, 2007), 103.
58. Simon Schama, *Dead Certainties, Unwarranted Speculations* (New York: Knopf, 1991), 30.
59. Peter Seixas and Penney Clark, "Murals as Monuments: Students' Ideas About Depictions of Civilization in British Columbia," *American Journal of Education* 110, no. 2 (2004): 148, https://doi.org/10.1086/380573.
60. Ana Fota, "What's Wrong with This Diorama? You Can Read All About It," *The New York Times*, March 21, 2019, sec. Arts, https://www.nytimes.com/2019/03/20/arts/design/natural-history-museum-diorama.html.
61. Seixas and Clark, "Murals as Monuments."
62. Jessica Wong, "'Big, Bold, Audacious' Kent Monkman Artworks 'at Home' at the Met, Says Curator," CBC, December 17, 2019, https://www.cbc.ca/news/entertainment/kent-monkman-met-new-paintings-1.5395216.
63. John Sutton Lutz, "Totem Pole," in *Symbols of Canada*, ed. Michael Dawson, Catherine Gidney, and Donald Wright (Toronto, ON: Between the Lines, 2018), 31–41.
64. Lutz, "Totem Pole," 41.
65. Truth and Reconciliation Commission of Canada, *Honouring the Truth, Reconciling for the Future*, http://www.trc.ca/websites/trcinstitution/File/2015/Findings/Calls_to_Action_English2.pdf.National; Inquiry into Missing and Murdered Indigenous Women and Girls, "Read the National MMIWG Inquiry's Calls for Justice," APTN, 2019, https://aptnnews.ca/2019/06/03/read-the-national-mmiwg-inquirys-calls-for-justice-here/; United Nations, "United Nations Declaration on the Rights of Indigenous Peoples," New York: United Nations, 2008), https://www.un.org/esa/socdev/unpfii/documents/DRIPS_en.pdf.

66. Ken Osborne, "A History Teacher Looks Back," *The Canadian Historical Review* 93, no. 1 (2012): 130.
67. Osborne, "A History Teacher," 132.
68. Alan Sears, "A History Educator Looks Forward," *A Report on the National Meeting of the Historical Thinking Project* (Vancouver: The Historical Thinking Project, January 23, 2014), 13–15.
69. Sears, "A History Educator Looks Forward."
70. Stéphane Lévesque and Jean-Philippe Croteau, *Beyond History for Historical Consciousness: Students, Narrative, and Memory* (Toronto, ON: University of Toronto Press, 2020).
71. Jocelyn Létourneau and Sabrina Moisan, "Young People's Assimilation of a Collective Historical Memory: A Case Study of Quebeckers of French-Canadian Heritage," in *Theorizing Historical Consciousness*, ed. Peter Seixas (Toronto, ON: University of Toronto Press, 2004), 109–28; Jocelyn Létourneau, "Remembering Our Past: An Examination of the Historical Memory of Young Québécois," in To *the Past: History Education, Public Memory, and Citizenship in Canada*, ed. R.W. Sandwell (Toronto, ON: University of Toronto Press, 2006), 71–87; Mario Carretero, Milel Asensio, and Maria Rodríguez-Moneo, ed., *History Education and the Construction of National Identities* (Charlotte, NC: Information Age Publishing, 2012); Alan McCully and Keith C. Barton, "Schools, Students, and Community History in Northern Ireland," in *Contemplating Historical Consciousness: Notes from the Field*, ed. Anna Clark and Carla L. Peck (New York and Oxford: Berghahn Books, 2019), 19–31; Edda Sant et al., "How Do Catalan Students Narrate the History of Catalonia When They Finish Primary Education?" *McGill Journal of Education* 50, no. 2/3 (2015): 341–62.
72. Catriona Pennell, "Taught to Remember? British Youth and First World War Centenary Battlefield Tours," *Cultural Trends* 27, no. 2 (2018): 85, https://doi.org/10.1080/09548963.2018.1453449.
73. Pennell, "Taught to Remember," 92.
74. Peter Seixas, "A History/Memory Matrix for History Education," *Public History Weekly—The International Blogjournal* (blog), 2016, https://public-history-weekly.degruyter.com/4-2016-6/a-historymemory-matrix-for-history-education/; Lévesque and Croteau, *Beyond History.*
75. World Economic Forum, "From the Black Death to Coronavirus: What We Haven't Learned from History," World Economic Forum, 2020, https://www.weforum.org/agenda/2020/03/coronavirus-and-the-black-death-spread-of-misinformation-and-xenophobia-shows-we-haven-t-learned-from-our-past/.

Bibliography

Abella, Irving and Harold Troper. *None Is too Many: Canada and the Jews of Europe 1933–1948*. First edition. Toronto, ON: Key Porter Books, 2002.

Bliss, Michael. "Privatizing the Mind: The Sundering of Canadian History, the Sundering of Canada." *Journal of Canadian Studies* 26, no. 4 (1991): 5–17.

Carretero, Mario, Milel Asensio, and Maria Rodríguez-Moneo, eds. *History Education and the Construction of National Identities*. Charlotte, NC: Information Age Publishing, 2012.

Clark, Anna. *History's Children: History Wars in the Classroom*. Sydney: University of New South Wales Press, 2008.

Clark, Penney. "Representations of Aboriginal People in English Canadian History Textbooks: Toward Reconciliation." In *Teaching the Violent Past: History Education and Reconciliation*, edited by Elizabeth A. Cole, 81–120. Lanham, MD: Rowman & Littlefield, 2007.

Evans, Fred. *Public Art and the Fragility of Democracy: An Essay in Political Aesthetics*. New York: Columbia University Press, 2019.

Everett-Green, Robert. "Totem of a Painful Legacy Rises on Montreal's Golden Square Mile." *Globe and Mail,* Friday, May 5, 2017.

Faulkner, William. *Requiem for a Nun*. New York: Random House, 1951.

Fota, Ana. "What's Wrong with This Diorama? You Can Read All About It." *The New York Times*, March 21, 2019, sec. Arts. https://www.nytimes.com/2019/03/20/arts/design/natural-history-museum-diorama.html.

Green, Allison, and Marilyn Ingram. *Trails of Light and Hope: From Project of the Heart*. Fredericton, NB: New Brunswick College of Craft and Design, n.d.

Higgins, Kathleen. "Post-truth: A Guide for the Perplexed." *Nature* 540, no. 7361 (2016): 9. https://doi.org/10.1038/540009a.

Himmelfarb, Gertrude. "Some Reflections on the New History." *The American Historical Review* 94, no. 3 (1989): 661–70.

Johnston, Hugh. "Komagata Maru." *The Canadian Encyclopedia*, 2016. https://www.thecanadianencyclopedia.ca/en/article/komagata-maru.

Létourneau, Jocelyn. "Remembering Our Past: An Examination of the Historical Memory of Young Québécois." In*To the Past: History Education, Public Memory, and Citizenship in Canada*, edited by R.W. Sandwell, 71–87. Toronto, ON: University of Toronto Press, 2006.

Létourneau, Jocelyn and Sabrina Moisan. "Young People's Assimilation of a Collective Historical Memory: A Case Study of Quebeckers of French-Canadian Heritage." In *Theorizing Historical Consciousness*, edited by Peter Seixas, 109–28. Toronto, ON: University of Toronto Press, 2004.

Lévesque, Stéphane and Jean-Philippe Croteau. *Beyond History for Historical Consciousness: Students, Narrative, and Memory*. Toronto, ON: University of Toronto Press, 2020.

Linenthal, Edward T. and Thomas Engelhardt, eds. *History Wars: The Enola Gay and Other Battles for the American Past*. New York: Metropolitan Books, 1996.

Lutz, John Sutton. "Totem Pole." In *Symbols of Canada*, edited by Michael Dawson, Catherine Gidney, and Donald Wright, 31–41. Toronto, ON: Between the Lines, 2018.

MacIntyre, Linden. "Making (Up) History." Public Lecture presented at the St. Thomas University: Annual History Lecture, Fredericton, NB, January 23, 2020.

MacIntyre, Linden. *Making (Up) History*. Audio Recording. Fredericton, NB: SoundCloud, 2020. https://soundcloud.com/user-437205194/linden macintyre.

MacIntyre, Linden. *The Only Café*. Toronto, ON: Vintage Canada, 2018.

Macintyre, Stuart and Anna Clark. *The History Wars*. New edition. Melbourne: Melbourne University Press, 2004.

MacMillan, Margaret. *The Uses and Abuses of History*. Toronto, ON: Viking, 2008.

McCully, Alan and Keith C. Barton. "Schools, Students, and Community History in Northern Ireland." In *Contemplating Historical Consciousness: Notes from the Field*, edited by Anna Clark and Carla L. Peck, 19–31. New York and Oxford: Berghahn Books, 2019.

Mustafa, Naheed (Producer). *The Truth About Post-truth*. CBC Ideas, 2017. http://www.cbc.ca/radio/ideas/the-truth-about-post-truth-1.3939958.

Nash, Gary B., Charlotte Crabtree, and Ross Dunn. *History on Trial: Culture Wars and the Teaching of the Past*. New York: Knopf, 1997.

National Inquiry into Missing and Murdered Indigenous Women and Girls. "Read the National MMIWG Inquiry's Calls for Justice." APTN, 2019. https://aptnnews.ca/2019/06/03/read-the-national-mmiwg-inquirys-calls-for-justice-here/.

Newbolt, Henry. *The Building of Britain: A Series of Paintings in St. Stephen's Hall, Westminster*. London: Thomas Nelson and Sons, 1927.

OECD. "Preparing Our Youth for an Inclusive and Sustainable World. The OECD Pisa Global Competence Framework." Paris: Directorate for Education and Skills, 2018.

Pennell, Catriona. "Taught to Remember? British Youth and First World War Centenary Battlefield Tours." *Cultural Trends* 27, no. 2 (2018): 83–98. https://doi.org/10.1080/09548963.2018.1453449.

Perry, Adele. "The CHA Asks the Public Service Commission to Change Its Advertisements for Employment." The Canadian Historical Association, 2019. https://cha-shc.ca/english/what-we-do/what-we-do.html/advocacy/the-cha-asks-thepublic-service-commission-to-change-its-advertisements-for-employment.

Project of the Heart. "What Is Project of the Heart?" Project of the Heart, n.d. http://projectofheart.ca/what-is-project-of-heart/.

Rider, Peter E. "Museums, Nation and Political History in the Australian National Museum and the Canadian Museum of Civilization." *Museum and Society* 3, no. 1 (2005): 35–50. https://doi.org/10.29311/mas.v3i1.63.

Ridge, Sophy. "Jo Cox Murder: Death Threats and Sexual Torment Have Become Part of the Job for Our MPs—Enough Is Enough." *The Telegraph*, June 17, 2016. http://www.telegraph.co.uk/women/politics/jo-cox-murder-death-threats-and-sexual-torment-have-become-part/.

Sant, Edda, Neus González-Monfort, Antoni Santisteban Fernández, Joan Pagès Blanch, and Montserrat Oller Freixa. "How Do Catalan Students Narrate the History of Catalonia When They Finish Primary Education?" *McGill Journal of Education* 50, no. 2/3 (2015): 341–62.

Savage, Kirk. *Monument Wars: Washington, D.C., the National Mall, and the Transformation of the Memorial Landscape*. First edition. Berkeley: University of California Press, 2009.

Schama, Simon. *Dead Certainties, Unwarranted Speculations*. New York: Knopf, 1991.

Schlesinger, Arthur, Jr. *The Disuniting of America*. New York: Norton, 1992.

Sears, Alan. "A History Educator Looks Forward." *A Report on the National Meeting of the Historical Thinking Project*, 13–15. Vancouver: The Historical Thinking Project, 2014.

Sears, Alan. "Fortified Silos or Interconnected Webs: The Relationship Between History and Other Subjects in the Curriculum." In *Debates in History Teaching*, edited by Ian Davies, 272–81. London and New York: Routledge, 2010.

Sears, Matthew A. "Monuments Aren't Museums, and History Suffers When We Forget That." *MacLean's*, 2018. https://www.macleans.ca/opinion/monuments-arent-museums-and-history-suffers-when-we-forget-that/.

Seixas, Peter. "A History/Memory Matrix for History Education." *Public History Weekly—The International Blogjournal* (blog), 2016. https://public-history-weekly.degruyter.com/4-2016-6/a historymemory-matrix-for-history-education/.

Seixas, Peter and Penney Clark. "Murals as Monuments: Students' Ideas About Depictions of Civilization in British Columbia." *American Journal of Education* 110, no. 2 (2004): 146–71. https://doi.org/10.1086/380573.

Seixas, Peter, and Tom Morton. *The Big Six Historical Thinking Concepts*. Toronto, ON: Nelson Education, 2013.

Sellar, Sam, David Rutkowski, and Greg Thompson. *The Global Education Race: Taking the Measure of PISA and International Testing*. Edmonton, AB: Brush Education, 2017. http://search.ebscohost.com/login.aspx?direct=true&scope=site&db=nlebk&db=nlabk&AN=1500013.

Smith, Christian, Kari with Christoffersen, Davidson Hilary, and Patricia Snell Herzog. *Lost in Transition: The Dark Side of Emerging Adulthood*. New York: Oxford University Press, 2011.

Stanley, Jason. *How Propaganda Works*. Princeton and Oxford: Princeton University Press, 2015.

Taylor, Alan. "Keeping the Story in History." The Pulitzer Prizes, 2020. https://www.pulitzer.org/article/keeping-story-history.

Truth and Reconciliation Commission of Canada. *Final Report of the Truth and Reconciliation Commission of Canada, Vol. I: Summary: Honouring the Truth, Reconciling for the Future*. Toronto, ON: James Lorimer, 2015.

Ulrich, Laurel Thatcher. *A Midwife's Tale: The Life of Martha Ballard, Based on Her Diary*. New York: Knopf, 1990.

United Nations. "United Nations Declaration on the Rights of Indigenous Peoples." New York: United Nations, 2008. https://www.un.org/esa/socdev/unpfii/documents/DRIPS_en.pdf.

Waldie, Paul. "After Nastiest Presidential Campaign in Memory, France Faces Trump Moment." *Globe and Mail*, 2017. https://www.theglobeandmail.com/news/world/after-shocking-campaign-french-face-profound-choice-to-upend-status-quo/article34907627/.

Wherry, Aaron. "For the Record: Justin Trudeau on Liberty and the Niqab—The Text of Justin Trudeau's Controversial Speech." 2015. http://www.macleans.ca/politics/for-the-record-justin-trudeau-on-liberty-and-the-niqab/.

Windschuttle, Keith. *The Killing of History: How Literary Critics and Social Theorists Are Murdering Our Past*. Reprint edition. New York: Encounter Books, 2000.

Wong, Jessica. "'Big, Bold, Audacious' Kent Monkman Artworks 'at Home' at the Met, Says Curator." CBC, December 17, 2019. https://www.cbc.ca/news/entertainment/kent-monkman-met-new-paintings-1.5395216.

World Economic Forum. "From the Black Death to Coronavirus: What We Haven't Learned from History." World Economic Forum, 2020. https://www.weforum.org/agenda/2020/03/coronavirus-and-the-black-death-spread-of-misinformation-and-xenophobia-shows-we-haven-t-learned-from-our-past/.

Zimmerman, Jonathan and Emily Robertson. *The Case for Contention: Teaching Controversial Issues in American Schools*. Chicago and London: University of Chicago Press, 2017.

Index

P. Clark and A. Sears, *The Arts and the Teaching of History*,
https://doi.org/10.1007/978-3-030-51513-3

J

K

L

M

CPSIA information can be obtained
at www.ICGtesting.com
Printed in the USA
LVHW060919151220
673849LV00039B/65

9 783030 515126